O'REILLY WOULD LIKE TO HEAR FROM YOU.

✔ **KT-370-989**

FROM O'REILLY & ASSOCIATES, INC.

SERVER-SIDE INCLUDES (SSI)

CONFIG – *changes configurable items used in SSI*
```
<!--#config errmsg="value"-->
<!--#config timefmt="value"-->
<!--#config sizefmt="value"-->
```

DAYCNT – *displays daily number of requests for the page*
```
<!--#daycnt-->
<!--#daycnt file="pathname"-->
<!--#daycnt virtual="URLpath"-->
```

ECHO – *inserts value of the named HTTP extra header*
```
<!--#echo var="name"-->
```

EXEC – *inserts output of the CGI program*
```
<!--#exec cgi="vpath"-->
```

FLASTMODE – *displays document's last modified date/time*
```
<!--#flastmode file="pathname"-->
<!--#flastmode virtual="URLpath"-->
```

FSIZE – *displays document's size in bytes*
```
<!--#fsize file="pathname"-->
<!--#fsize virtual="URLpath"-->
```

INCLUDE – *inserts contents of the document*
```
<!--#include file="pathname"-->
<!--#include virtual="URLpath"-->
```

LASTZERO – *displays date/time counters last zeroed*
```
<!--#lastzero-->
<!--#lastzero file="pathname"-->
<!--#lastzero virtual="URLpath"-->
```

NOSSI – *stops SSI processing of document*
```
<!--nossi-->
```

RDAYCNT – *displays daily requests; doesn't increment TOTCNT*
```
<!--#rdaycnt-->
<!--#rdaycnt file="pathname"-->
<!--#rdaycnt virtual="URLpath"-->
```

RTOTCNT – *displays total requests since counters last zeroed; doesn't increment DAYCNT*
```
<!--#rtotcnt-->
<!--#rtotcnt file="pathname"-->
<!--#rtotcnt virtual="URLpath"-->
```

TOTCNT – *displays total requests since counters last zeroed*
```
<!--#totcnt-->
<!--#totcnt file="pathname"-->
<!--#totcnt virtual="URLpath"-->
```

WINDOWS CGI VARIABLES

CGI_SERVERSOFTWARE – *name and version of the server software*

CGI_SERVERADMIN – *email address of the server's administrator*

CGI_VERSION – *CGI version of the server*

CGI_GMTOFFSET – *number of seconds from GMT*

CGI_REQUESTPROTOCOL – *name and revision of the protocol*

CGI_REFERER – *URL that referred to the CGI program*

CGI_FROM – *email address of the user (rarely supplied)*

CGI_REMOTEHOST – *hostname of the browser's host*

CGI_REMOTEADDR – *IP address of the browser's host*
CGI_ACCEPTTYPES – *CGI accept types*

VISIT WEBSITE CENTRAL™ FOR THE LATEST PRODUCT INFORMATION
http://website.ora.com/

O'REILLY™

CGI_NumAcceptTypes – *number of CGI accept types*

CGI_ExecutablePath – *path of the CGI program*

CGI_LogicalPath – *logical path or extra path information*

CGI_PhysicalPath – *physical path*

CGI_RequestMethod – *method used in the request*

CGI_ServerPort – *port number associated with the request*

CGI_ServerName – *server hostname for the request*

CGI_QueryString – *encoded portion of the URL after the ?*

CGI_ContentFile – *full pathname of the file containing attached data*

CGI_ContentType – *content type of requests with attached data*

CGI_ContentLength – *length of the attached data in bytes*

CGI_FormTuples – *name=value pairs supplied in form data*

CGI_NumFormTuples – *number of name= value pairs*

CGI_HugeTuples – *large name=value pairs*

CGI_NumHugeTuples – *number of huge tuples*

CGI_AuthUser – *name of the authorized user*

CGI_AuthPass – *password of the authorized user*

CGI_AuthType – *authorization method*

CGI_AuthRealm – *realm of the authorized user*

CGI_ExtraHeaders – *extra headers supplied by the browser*

CGI_NumExtraHeaders – *number of extra headers*

CGI_OutputFile – *full pathname of the CGI program's response*

CGI_DebugMode – *CGI tracing flag from server*

CGI Utility Routines

ErrorHandler() – *global exception handler*

FieldPresent() – *test for the presence of a named form field*

GetSmallField() – *retrieve the contents of a named form field*

PlusToSpace() – *convert + delimiters to spaces*

Send() – *write a string to the output spool file*

SendNoOp() – *send a complete response causing the browser to do nothing*

Unescape() – *remove URL-escaping from a string, return modified string*

WebDate() – *Return a date/time string (GMT)*

O'REILLY™

101 Morris Street, Sebastopol, CA 95472 • 800-998-9938
707-829-0515 • info@ora.com • http://www.ora.com

THE WEB PUBLISHER FOR EVERYONE

WEBSITE™

FROM O'REILLY & ASSOCIATES, INC.

BUILDING YOUR OWN WEBSITE

EVERYTHING YOU NEED
TO REACH YOUR
AUDIENCE ON THE WEB

BUILDING YOUR OWN WEBSITE

EVERYTHING YOU NEED TO REACH YOUR AUDIENCE ON THE WEB

SUSAN B. PECK & STEPHEN ARRANTS

O'REILLY™

BONN • CAMBRIDGE • PARIS • SEBASTOPOL • TOKYO

BUILDING YOUR OWN WEBSITE

by Susan B. Peck and Stephen Arrants

PRINTING HISTORY

July 1996:　　　　　First Edition

TRADEMARKS

WebSite, WebSite Professional, and WebSite Central are trademarks of O'Reilly & Associates, Inc.

WebView, WebIndex, and WebFind are trademarks of Enterprise Integration Technologies, Inc./Verifone. Microsoft is a registered trademark, and Windows and Windows NT are trademarks of Microsoft Corporation. HotDog is a trademark of Sausage Software. Spyglass is a trademark of Spyglass, Inc. Mosaic is a trademark of the University of Illinois.

All other names are registered trademarks of their respective companies.

SUGGESTIONS AND SUPPORT

Your suggestions for *Building Your Own WebSite* are welcomed. Please email your comments to *website@ora.com*. Technical support questions will not be answered from this email address.

WebSite technical support is available on a per-incident basis or through an annual technical support contract. For per-incident technical support, please call one of the numbers listed below. To set up an annual support contract, contact O'Reilly & Associates Customer Service at (800) 998-9938. WebSite technical support hours are Monday through Friday, 7 AM to 5 PM, Pacific Time. For WebSite questions and answers, related software, and other product information, check out WebSite Central: *http://website.ora.com/* and O'Reilly Software Online (*http://software.ora.com/*)

O'Reilly & Associates, Inc.
101 Morris Street
Sebastopol, CA 95472
Phone: (707) 829-0515　(800) 932-9302
FAX: (707) 829-0104

ISBN: 1-56592-232-8

TABLE OF CONTENTS

BUILDING YOUR WEB

Administering WebSite

WebSite signals the coming of personal network publishing, whether that network is the global Internet or an internal intranet. WebSite brings the power of network publishing to the desktop. And it brings the power of desktop publishing to the network. With WebSite, anyone can become a Web publisher.

What does it mean to be a Web publisher? It means you can distribute your information to other people, regardless of their location or choice of computing platform. You might share information with others in your company, your community, or your family. You can publish information to develop a market for your products or to share assignments with your students. In essence, you are using the Internet as it was meant to be used—as a two-way communications medium. As a Web publisher, you become an information provider yourself and put together your own network of customers and colleagues.

At O'Reilly, we make our living as publishers. We are best known for publishing books that help people solve information problems. With WebSite, you have a platform for solving information problems for yourself and others. WebSite is a publishing tool for the Web. It is more than just a Web server: it is a complete environment for creating, managing, and administering your web. *Building Your Own WebSite* shows you with tutorials, step-by-step instructions, and examples how to use that environment for your own Web publishing.

WebSite is the result of a devoted team effort from people at O'Reilly & Associates and other organizations. Bob Denny and Jay Weber led the software development effort, with the assistance of other developers at Enterprise Integration Technologies (EIT). O'Reilly & Associates provided testing, technical support, marketing, design, and other aspects of the product.

You can learn more about WebSite and the WebSite team at WebSite Central, the web site dedicated to WebSite (*http://website.ora.com*). You can learn more about O'Reilly & Associates by visiting *http://www.ora.com*. We encourage you to check out our Web resources to get ideas for developing your own.

CONTRIBUTORS

Building Your Own WebSite received technical and editorial input from a variety of contributors. The authors wish to thank each one for the time and effort given to make this book a useful tool in the hands of novice and advanced webmasters alike. Specifically, we wish to acknowledge the work of Linda Mui, who helped set the standard for WebSite documentation. Robert B. Denny provided invaluable input and original source material for the CGI programming section, while John Olsen contributed the source material for the chapter on using C++ and MFC to write Windows CGI programs.

In addition to these named contributors, we wish to thank members of the O'Reilly Software team and the many WebSite users who have alerted us to errors, suggested areas for clarification and enhancement, and passed on numerous tips. Such feedback is essential for making O'Reilly books accurate, complete, and high-quality. We look forward to hearing from you, our new readers, as you put into practice the ideas and information included in *Building Your Own WebSite*.

HOW TO USE THIS BOOK

This book is divided into 5 sections, with a total of 18 chapters and 4 appendixes, as described below. We recommend you read the first three chapters before installing WebSite and then use the remaining chapters as necessary to accomplish your specific information publishing tasks.

SECTION 1: GETTING STARTED

Before you can start using WebSite, you need to install the software. You should also take a few minutes to become familiar with the components of WebSite and the concepts underlying the Web.

- Chapter 1, *Why Publish with WebSite?*
- Chapter 2, *Before You Start*
- Chapter 3, *Installing WebSite*

SECTION 2: BUILDING YOUR WEB

In addition to the WebSite server itself, the power of WebSite is in the WebView, HotDog, WebIndex, and Map This! programs. Together, these programs let you create and manage your Web documents easily.

- Chapter 4, *Managing Your Web Using WebView*

- Chapter 5, *HTML Tutorial and Quick Reference*
- Chapter 6, *Indexing and Searching Your Documents*
- Chapter 7, *Working with Image Maps*
- Chapter 8, *Extending HTML with Server-Side Includes*

SECTION 3: ADMINISTERING WEBSITE

You configure the WebSite server through the Server Admin program. Using Server Admin, you can map web document directories, set up virtual servers with multiple IP addresses, and set parameters for automatic directory listings. You can also enforce security on your data and take advantage of the numerous logging features of the WebSite server. You can complete any of these tasks from a remote location if desired.

- Chapter 9, *Mapping*
- Chapter 10, *Virtual Servers and WebSite*
- Chapter 11, *Automatic Directory Listings*
- Chapter 12, *Controlling Access to Your Web*
- Chapter 13, *Logging*
- Chapter 14, *Remote Administration*

SECTION 4: THE COMMON GATEWAY INTERFACE

The WebSite server has three CGI interfaces for processing input from users of your web and returning valuable data, often from other applications. You can create CGI programs in many different languages including Visual Basic, Visual C++, and Perl. Windows CGI lets you pull data from other Windows applications such as databases and spreadsheets.

- Chapter 15, *Introduction to the Common Gateway Interface*
- Chapter 16, *Developing Applications with Windows CGI*
- Chapter 17, *Developing Windows CGI Applications with C++ and MFC*
- Chapter 18, *The Standard and DOS CGI Interfaces*

SECTION 5: APPENDIXES

The four appendixes cover the server demonstration and self-test, the WebSite Registry keys, troubleshooting, and upgrading the HotDog editor.

- Appendix A, *WebSite Server Self-Test*
- Appendix B, *WebSite Registry Keys*

- Appendix C, *Troubleshooting Tips*
- Appendix D, *Upgrading the HotDog HTML Editor*

TYPOGRAPHIC CONVENTIONS

We use the following typographic conventions.

Italic

> is used for new terms where they are first defined, titles of publications, Uniform Resource Locators (URLs), email addresses, filenames, hostnames, and directory names.

`Courier`

> is used in examples to show the output from commands or the contents of files and for names of program variables in text.

`Courier Italic`

> is used to show variables within code examples, as shown here:
>
> The syntax for specifying an image map is:
>
> `<A HREF="/~imagemap/name"> <IMG SRC="imagefile" ISMAP> </A>`
>
> The variables are `name` and `imagefile`.

Angle Brackets < >

> are used to surround the HTML (Hypertext Markup Language) tags used to structure your documents.

GETTING STARTED

You are about to enter a world once reserved for skilled system administrators and network managers—the world of Web servers. This section provides the big picture of the Web and gives you many practical ideas for using WebSite. It also covers the basic information you need to get WebSite up and running. To get a vision for using WebSite, read Chapter 1. Then complete the pre-installation checklist in Chapter 2 before installing WebSite. Use Chapter 3 to install and test WebSite and its many features.

CHAPTER ONE

WHY PUBLISH WITH WEBSITE?

You have information—product literature, technical specs, financial data, customer and employee records, employment opportunities, schedules of events, reports. The information is in a variety of formats—text, graphics, video, audio. People want that information—customers, vendors, colleagues, friends, family.

How do you get this varied information into the hands of the right people (and keep it out of the hands of the wrong people)? Publish it with WebSite, the powerful, fully featured, easy-to-use Web server from O'Reilly & Associates.

With WebSite you can publish your information directly on the Internet and reach the millions of people who use the World Wide Web every day. Or, you can use WebSite to publish on an internal network and share important company information with the people who need it most. You can even use WebSite's virtual server capability to publish in both environments with a public web connected to the Internet and a private web running on your internal LAN.

To administer, build, and manage your web, WebSite comes with a complete set of tools. WebView lets you see and develop your web in a graphical environment. The HotDog Web Editor lets you create HTML files with ease, while MapThis! makes creating clickable image maps a breeze. WebIndex lets you create search indexes for all or any parts of your web. With Server Admin you configure your server through an easy-to-use graphical interface.

This book is dedicated to showing you how WebSite works and how you can use it to meet your information goals. This first chapter sets the stage with ideas for using WebSite, some background on the Web, an overview of the WebSite server and tools, and a look at some of WebSite's key features.

HOW CAN I USE WEBSITE?

Running a Web server is essentially a new way to publish information. Publishing on the Web differs from traditional paper-based publishing by giving you the ability to include multimedia elements, to link information from many locations, to update and distribute information quickly, and to create virtual documents from other sources and applications. Taking these general capabilities as a jumping-off point, let's look at some ways you might want to use WebSite in publishing your own information.

- Whether your business is a global corporation or an independent consultancy, WebSite lets you tell other people on the Internet about your business. Product and service information, competitive analyses, philosophy of business, biographies of key people, employment opportunities, press releases, and pricing data are topics you may want to include. WebSite's powerful Common Gateway Interface (CGI) lets you create forms for interactive contact with visitors to your web. Links to and from other webs bring more traffic to your own web.

- In a department or office, WebSite is an easy way to make data readily available to others on the local area network. For example, you have employee records, accounting information, sales projections, project plans, and customer data that coworkers need to use on a regular basis. You can easily create and maintain web documents for these valuable records. If you have existing databases and spreadsheets of data to share, you can use WebSite's CGI to generate virtual documents with current data from those applications. Instead of making a request directly to the application, the user gives information to the CGI program through a browser. The CGI program makes the request of the application and displays the information in a web document. WebSite's full 32-bit framework for developing CGI programs to execute Windows applications is a powerful tool in building a web. Note, too, that this particular application of WebSite is an internal use and does not require access to the Internet.

- WebSite's virtual server capability lets you host webs for other clients, departments, or individuals. Each web has its own IP address and is completely separate from the other webs, yet all share one copy of WebSite. WebSite's Identity wizard and graphical setup of virtual servers is a new feature of Version 1.1.

- Often, large companies have frequently updated procedural information to share among employees. If you are responsible for updating and distributing this information, you know how difficult it is to keep track of multiple copies. If you receive updates regularly, you know how time-consuming it is to file the new procedures and dispose of the old. Putting procedures (or other frequently updated information) on a WebSite server solves both the updating and distribution problems. Updates are completed once, and when the files are added to the WebSite server the distribution is complete. The files don't even have to be in HTML; simply configure your users' browsers to correctly display or download other file types such as Microsoft Word or WordPerfect. For sensitive information, WebSite lets you restrict access to particular users or groups of users. This solution works well for companies with only one location or with many locations around the world, since the Internet is an existing global network.

- A company with business partners in different buildings, cities, states, or around the world can use WebSite to exchange product designs, specs, reviews, and progress reports. For example, at company headquarters in California, product managers can post designs and specs for a manufacturer in Singapore to review and download. The factory in Singapore can post responses, revised designs (based on capability), and progress reports on their WebSite for the company to review and respond to. Exchanging information on products under development takes full advantage of WebSite's access control restrictions.

- Managers required to write and distribute weekly or monthly status reports will find WebSite a great time saver. They can write the report and make it available on the server. Those who need to read it can retrieve it at their convenience, completely eliminating the copying and distributing steps.

- Setting up a WebSite server can be a great solution for busy educators. You can create a web with links to course descriptions, current assignments, summer reading lists, and class schedules. Your web can also have links to external resources such as libraries or databases that your students need for research. A CGI program for pulling students' grades from your electronic grade book allows your students to always know where they stand in your class. Of course, you want to restrict the CGI program's URL to require user authentication. Including a *mailto* URL on a web page leaves your students no excuse for not communicating with you.

- Clubs, civic organizations, and church groups have information that is valuable to members and non-members alike. WebSite is a perfect vehicle for publishing that information. You can include the history, current events, and biographies of officers and leaders. News about special projects or needs can be set up in a What's New page. Including links to other sites and resources on the Internet helps your members find other useful information. A CGI program can be used for collecting and posting comments from members. If the club members are far apart, you can use your web for electing officers by creating a forms-based ballot requiring user authentication.

- If you just want to have fun, use WebSite as a personal server. Put up a web about your interests and your life philosophy. Include photos, artwork, audio, and video clips. Write a weekly newsletter and post it for your family and close friends. Like-minded (or possibly unlike-minded) readers will gather around your WebSite and create a virtual community. Changing your WebSite often and making it interesting (as is true of interactions in any community) is the key for a successful personal web.

These are just a few ideas; you probably have many more for publishing your information. This list referred to several features of the Internet, the World Wide Web, and WebSite. Read on to learn more about them.

HOW DOES IT WORK?

The Internet, the World Wide Web, WebSite. How do they all fit together? How do users find your information? To answer these questions, take a few minutes to look at the big picture and some basic concepts.

AN OVERVIEW

Figure 1-1 depicts the components of the Internet and particularly the World Wide Web.

In this illustration, you can see that

- The Internet is a network of networks that spans the globe.
- The World Wide Web is a collection of linked information on the Internet.
- Web browsers, such as Spyglass Mosaic or Netscape Navigator, find and display information from the Web.
- Web servers, such as WebSite, house that information and send it to the browser when requested.
- Your information in text, graphic, or multimedia format is the most important piece of this picture. Publishing your information is why you are setting up a Web server.

Figure 1-2 seems quite similar to Figure 1-1. It shows the same Web components but on an internal network, such as a local area network, instead of the Internet— sometimes called an intranet. You can use WebSite in either situation: on the Internet for public, global use; or on an internal network for local, private use.

BASIC CONCEPTS

Whether you plan to run a public or a private WebSite server, you should be familiar with the few basic concepts that make it work. As you use WebSite and explore its capability, these concepts will become clear. This section describes the concepts, gives you a bit of history, and introduces the specifications on which the Web relies.

HYPERTEXT

When Tim Berners-Lee decided to use hypertext technology in developing the World Wide Web, he did away with the typical linear approach to published material. You're familiar with that: you open a book, skim the table of contents, and go to a specific topic. To find similar information in the same book, you may have to check the index (or a cross-reference) and turn there.

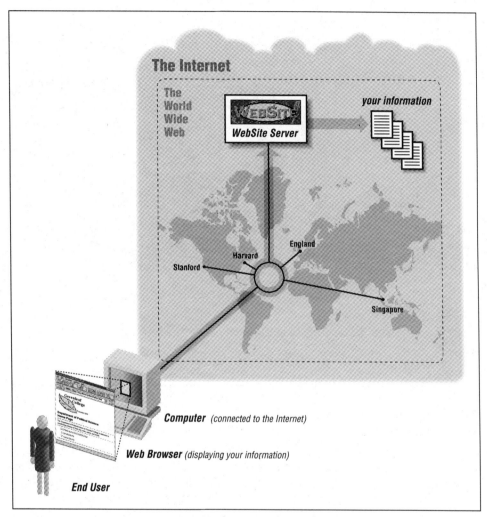

FIGURE 1-1: THE WORLD WIDE WEB

Hypertext, on the other hand, allows for many relations within a document and between documents. Hypertext links in a web document allow the reader to instantly find additional information, which may be text, graphics, video, or audio and may be located half a world away! "Web" is an apt term to picture how hypertext works on the Internet, where links can span computers around the globe. By using hypertext as a navigational system, users can move freely from one document to another, regardless of where the documents are located.

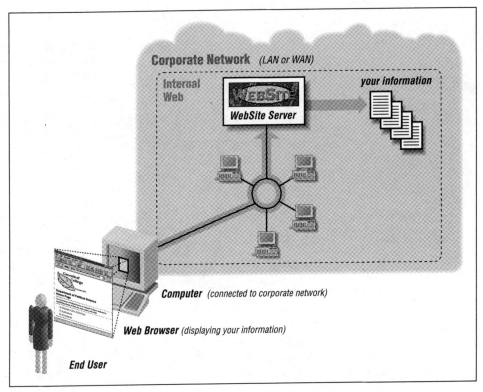

FIGURE 1-2: AN INTERNAL WEB

WEB BROWSERS

The Web is based on client/server architecture. Simply put, a server holds documents that a client requests. On the Web, the client is called a browser. A Web browser takes a user's request (in the form of a URL, explained below), retrieves the document from the proper Web server, interprets the contents, and presents it to the user.

A graphical Web browser, such as Mosaic, can display text and GIF graphics. Web browsers have varying capabilities of manipulating the display of text. We recommend you test your web documents on several browsers to verify their proper appearance.

A Web browser can also be configured to automatically call external viewers, such as Lview, Wham, and MPEGPlay, or other applications to properly display specific types of documents. Web browsers are becoming more sophisticated every day with built-in capabilities. It is important that you keep up on browser improvements so that the documents on your web take full advantage of new features.

WEB SERVERS

The other half of the client/server relationship is the server. On the Web, a server houses documents and returns them to a Web client when requested. As its name implies, a server "serves" up the document to the client. The WebSite server is a fully featured Web server providing support for multiple IP addresses (virtual servers), mapping capabilities, basic user authentication and access control, automatic directory listing, and logging. These topics are discussed in detail in Section 3 of this book.

Web servers not only return text and multimedia documents to browsers, they can also execute special programs that enable them to act as gateways to other applications or information resources. These programs are called Common Gateway Interface (CGI) programs. WebSite supports CGIs for the Windows environment, the standard (POSIX) environment, and the DOS environment.

For example, a WebSite Windows CGI program can execute a request for data from a Microsoft Access database or a calculation from a Lotus 123 spreadsheet and return the results to the browsers in an HTML document. WebSite's full 32-bit support for Windows CGIs makes it unique among Web servers. Windows CGIs for WebSite can be written with a variety of tools including Visual Basic 4, Visual C++, and Delphi. Section 4 of this book provides a detailed discussion of CGIs.

HYPERTEXT MARKUP LANGUAGE (HTML)

Text documents on the Web are ASCII (plain text) files that contain codes of a special tagging language called Hypertext Markup Language (HTML). HTML describes the structure of a document but not its exact formatting. That is, you can identify some text as a top-level heading with a special tag:

```
<H1>Hypertext Markup Language (HTML)</H1>
```

However, how that text looks to the user depends on the browser. The head will certainly stand out, but it doesn't mean it will appear as 18-point Helvetica boldface while the body text is 12-point Times Roman. Working with HTML means adjusting your thinking away from WYSIWYG (what you see is what you get) desktop publishing to deciding what role an element plays in your document. Is it a head? Is it text? Is it a list? In many ways, HTML formatting simplifies the life of an author because if concentrates on content, not format.

The most powerful part of HTML is the ability to embed hypertext links in documents. As you guessed, links have special tags. HTML also includes tags that ask the user for input, either with simple questions or complex forms.

The current version of HTML is version 2.0. It is based on some of the concepts of SGML, the Standard Generalized Markup Language, which is an ISO standard used for marking up documents for both print and online publication. The next version of the HTML specification, HTML 3, will move HTML into full SGML compliance and provide more tags. WebSite supports both HTML 2.0 and HTML 3. Chapter 5, *HTML Tutorial and Quick Reference*, covers HTML in detail, and also covers HotDog, the HTML editor shipped with WebSite.

GLOBAL ADDRESSING: URLs

With documents residing on Web servers around the world, how do Web browsers know where to find a specific document? Every document on the Web has a unique address called a Uniform Resource Locator, or URL. You can think of URLs as a global addressing system that provides several pieces of information to the Web browser.

Let's look at the URL for the list of external viewers at the NCSA at the University of Illinois at Urbana-Champaign:

```
http://www.ncsa.uiuc.edu/SDG/Software/WinMosaic/viewers.html
```

The first part of the URL, *http://*, tells what protocol is used to reach the target server. In this URL the protocol is HTTP, which means this is a Web server. (Yes, you can reach FTP servers and Gopher servers by using URLs with the correct protocol.) The rest of the URL is the path for the document. The server name is first (*www.ncsa.uiuc.edu*), followed by the full URL path of the document *viewers.html*.

The URL path is not necessarily the same as the physical path of the file on the server. The URL path is determined by how the web is mapped on the server. Chapter 9, *Mapping*, covers mapping in detail; the important thing to remember now is that the physical path and the URL path may have absolutely no correlation to each other.

Often URLs don't include filenames. For example, the URL for WebSite Central, the web site dedicated to WebSite information and support is:

```
http://website.ora.com/
```

With this URL, the browser can locate the server and a directory within the server's web, but not a specific document. Which document to return is up to the server. If the server has a default home page or index file defined, and a file by that name exists in the specified URL directory, the server returns that document. If the file doesn't exist, the server returns a directory listing. The server can also be configured to return nothing to protect sensitive information. Automatic directory listing, with its many features, is discussed in Chapter 11, *Automatic Directory Listings*.

HTTP

The "glue" that holds the Web together is the Hypertext Transfer Protocol (HTTP). Web browsers and Web servers use HTTP when requesting and returning documents. In HTTP, every document request from a Web browser to a Web server is a new connection. For example, when a Web browser requests an HTML document from a Web server, the connection is opened, the document is transferred, and the connection is closed.

The current version of HTTP is 1.0 (often written as HTTP/1.0). WebSite meets the HTTP/1.0 specification and includes all the required features. If you're interested, the HTTP/1.0 specification is available through the Tech Center at WebSite Central (*http://website.ora.com/*).

A BRIEF HISTORY OF THE WORLD WIDE WEB

The World Wide Web originated in 1989 at the European Particle Physics Laboratory (CERN) in Geneva, Switzerland. Tim Berners-Lee, an Oxford University graduate who came to CERN with a background in text processing and real-time communications, wanted to create a new kind of information system in which researchers could collaborate and exchange information during the course of a project. He saw the need for physicists to collaborate in real time, and not just on one project, but on many.

Tim used hypertext technology to link together a web of documents that could be traversed in any manner to seek out information. In cooperation with others at CERN, Tim defined an Internet-based architecture using open, public specifications and free, sample implementations for both clients and servers. The team at CERN implemented a line-mode browser, which is the lowest common denominator among browsers and can be used from almost any kind of terminal. Lynx, a browser with a full-screen interface, was later developed at the University of Kansas. Although these browsers supported the hypertext environment, they did not support graphic or multimedia elements.

The widespread appeal of the Web did not come until 1993 with the release of Mosaic, a graphical browser. Marc Andreessen, a student at the University of Illinois at Urbana-Champaign (UIUC), was working part-time at the National Center for Supercomputing Applications (NCSA) at the university. His job was to build tools for scientific visualization. Out of that work came Mosaic, a Web browser with an easy-to-use interface that lets you click on a link to navigate the Web, as well as the ability to display graphics. Extending Mosaic with external viewers added multimedia capability.

The World Wide Web and graphical browsers have made the Internet important beyond the scientific or educational community. Most references you see to the Internet in consumer or business-oriented settings are to the World Wide Web. Generally you'll see a picture of a Web browser showing a home page. The Web has made an exciting contribution to the information age. We will continue to see refinements to Web servers and browsers and a major shift in the information publishing paradigm.

WHAT COMES WITH WEBSITE?

WebSite includes the Web server and a full range of tools to manage the server and develop your web. This section briefly describes those components and also touches on security and performance issues, topics which may be of concern to you.

WEBSITE SERVER AND TOOLS

WebSite Server

The heart of WebSite, the server handles requests from clients (browsers) for documents, whether they be text, graphic, multimedia, or virtual. The WebSite server is a full 32-bit, multithreaded HTTP server that runs under Windows NT or Windows 95. The server takes full advantage of the operating system's Registry and multithreading support. Under NT, the server can run as an application or as a service. Usually the server appears as an icon on your desktop or task bar with the status shown as either idle or busy. Configuring the server is the job of Server Admin.

Server Admin

Server Admin lets you configure the WebSite server to meet the needs of your environment. Although the install program handles the basic configuration, you will probably want to enhance your server by changing some settings. Mapping, identities for virtual servers, automatic directory listings, access control, and logging parameters are set through Server Admin. The General settings in Server Admin are covered in Chapter 3, *Installing WebSite*; the other settings are covered in Section 3 (Chapters 9 to 14).

WebView

WebView helps you build and manage your web by graphically depicting it. WebView shows all hypertext links between and within documents—internal or external, broken or complete. WebView not only lets you see your web from a bird's eye view, it also lets you edit individual files. In WebView you can launch an appropriate editing application based on the file's type, or you can drag a file into the desired application using WebView's drag and drop capability. If you're building a new web, start with WebView. If you are managing an existing web, use WebView to make improvements and fix problems. WebView diagnoses HTML coding problems and lets you see activity reports on any part of your web. WebView works on any web, not just the local one. WebView also includes HTTP proxy support to work behind a firewall. WebView is the subject of Chapter 4, *Managing Your Web Using WebView.*

WebIndex and WebFind

WebIndex and WebFind work together to provide full-text search capability for users of your web. WebIndex appears in the WebSite program group or program list while WebFind is a CGI program. WebIndex lets you create the indexes used in WebFind searches. Before WebFind can work, you must run the WebIndex program and indicate which portion of your Web is to be searchable. You can create multiple indexes with WebIndex and keep them separate or merge them. A variety of preferences allow you to tailor index contents. When users click on a WebFind hypertext link in one of your documents, WebFind first displays a search form for the user to complete and then executes the search. WebIndex and WebFind are covered in Chapter 6, *Indexing and Searching Your Documents.*

HotDog Web Editor

Creating HTML documents with a plain text editor is time-consuming both in the initial input and in later error correcting. The HotDog Web Editor simplifies coding by supplying the tags you specify around the text you enter. Now you can concentrate on what you are saying and not how the tags are typed. Including hypertext links, images, and other multimedia elements is barely more than a button click. The HotDog Web Editor is a product of Sausage Software. Chapter 5, *HTML Tutorial and Quick Reference*, covers HotDog in detail.

Map This!

Clickable image maps—images that have hotspots that send the user to other locations—are a great addition to any web. Many webs use clickable image maps on the home page to help users navigate through the contents of the Web. WebSite Central is a good example of a clickable image map. Point your browser at *http://website.ora.com/* and you will see an image map at work. Map This! lets you create clickable image maps easily, in a graphical environment. Map This! supports both NCSA file-based image maps and client-side image maps. Map This! is the topic of Chapter 7, *Working with Image Maps.*

Spyglass Mosaic

Spyglass Mosaic is supplied with WebSite to give you a fully featured Web graphical browser. Other browsers are available; some are distributed freely over the Internet while others are sold commercially. Since the display of Web documents depends on how the browser interprets HTML, we recommend you view your web using different browsers just to see what others might see. Spyglass Mosaic 2.11 includes support for the HTML 3 specification and many other extensions to HTML.

PERFORMANCE AND SECURITY ISSUES

Before you make your web available to users either on the Internet or on a local area network, you probably have some questions about performance and security. How much load can the server handle? Will it handle requests fast enough in a busy environment? What will cause performance degradation? Will the rest of my files be safe if browsers have access to my web? Can I impose additional security? If you've asked any of these questions, take a few minutes to read this section.

PERFORMANCE

The WebSite server is as robust as any Web server currently in use. Given the same basic hardware setup (network connection, disk capacity, disk speed, CPU type and speed), the WebSite server performs as well as any other NT- or UNIX-based Web server (and, historically, UNIX has been the platform of choice for Internet servers). In an equal hardware environment, WebSite is as fast or faster and can handle an equal load.

In addition, WebSite fully supports symmetric multi-processing. Running on a computer with multiple 486 CPUs, the server can saturate a T1 line. Running the server on a single Pentium with a fast bus would have the same effect. In short, server performance is limited only by the hardware being used. To improve performance, we recommend upgrading your hardware—both the computer system (particularly RAM) and your Internet connection.

For a more detailed discussion of WebSite's performance capability and the results of performance tests, see the Performance White Paper in the Developer's Corner of the Tech Center at WebSite Central.

SECURITY

Security is certainly an issue of concern for server administrators. Unauthorized access to computers and files on the Internet can range from annoying to disastrous depending on the intruder's intent and abilities. Even if your web is on a private network or otherwise protected, you may still have some security concerns.

Although no Internet service is 100% safe, the World Wide Web is safer by design. If you think of the Web as a web, the limited nature of what a user can see or have access to becomes clear. The Web has boundaries, defined by the document links. A Web browser doesn't have the capability to freely browse a server; it can only view documents that are part of the document tree, beginning with the document root. This limitation is controlled by mapping, which is the topic of Chapter 9.

In addition, WebSite provides two standard (basic) methods of access control, which can be applied to the whole Web or any URL in your web:

- Class restrictions, which allow or deny access to the Web (or portions of the Web) based on the Internet address or hostname of the Web browser. Class restrictions are often referred to as IP or hostname filtering.

- User authentication, which allows or denies access to the Web (or portions of the Web) based on a username and password. Usernames and passwords are specific to the server and are not related to usernames and groups established on your system. Making someone a user on your server does not give them an account on your computer.

Perhaps the best advice we can give to deal with security issues is to keep an eye out for any suspicious activity on your server. You should also regularly check WebSite Central for security updates.

NOTE

You may need greater security than the basic security provided with WebSite 1.1. For example, if you want to conduct credit card transactions over the Web, you may want to use encryption-based security. Two protocols provide this enhanced security for Web transactions: SSL (Secure Sockets Layer) and S-HTTP (Secure HTTP). Both of these protocols are available in WebSite Professional. Please contact O'Reilly & Associates Customer Service at 800-998-9938 for information on upgrading to WebSite Professional.

WHAT ARE SOME WEBSITE FEATURES?

As you use WebSite, you'll discover many powerful, easy-to-use features. The following list covers some of those features and should give you some ideas for using WebSite to meet your information publishing needs.

Some of the features you'll see in WebSite Version 1.1 include:

- HotDog Web Editor for easily creating HTML documents

- Full support for multiple virtual servers (multiple home pages, each with its own IP address) through graphical administration and in all the WebSite tools

- Server has a pause feature to allow for maintenance and more elegant shut-downs

- The WebSite server can run as a "service" under Windows 95, allowing the server to run continuously when no one is logged in. Under Windows 95, the server icon can appear in the Tray or on the Task Bar (regardless of whether you run it as a service or an application).

- Server supports the Connection: Keep Alive feature implemented by the Microsoft Internet Explorer and supported by most other browsers, including Spyglass Mosaic (This feature permits browsers to reuse connections for fetching inline graphics and other elements that are referenced in an HTML document. The Keep Alive feature makes transfer of documents more efficient and less time-consuming.)

- A manual switch for Keep Alive is available on the General page of Server Admin. If the server experiences problems with Keep Alive, we recommend you turn off the feature.

- Preferences in WebView including HTTP proxy support for working behind a firewall

- WebView supports incremental display of trees and interrupts the display of a tree at any point; also tests links in virtual documents and automatic directory lists created on the local server

- WebIndex creates multiple indexes, merges indexes, and accepts a variety of preferences for tailoring index contents

- Map This! image map editor works with both NCSA file-based image maps and client side image maps (processed by the browser)

- Server-side includes allow you to splice into an HTML document the contents of another HTML document or the value of a variable, such as the date or time (WebSite includes a special set of page counter server-side includes that indicate how many users have visited your web.)

- Server-side include processing operates on normal CGI output and on documents resulting from local redirects. To enable SSI processing of CGI output, simply use the content type *wwwserver/html-ssi* instead of *text/html* in the CGI program.

- Automatic directory listings can use the HTML 3 table format

- Automatic directory listings can be disabled on a per-URL basis

- Access control can be applied when both user authentication and class restrictions are met or when either are met

- *wsauth* utility lets you manage users and groups from a browser or the command line, including adding users from a flat file database, providing a mechanism for self-registration, and allowing users to change their own passwords via the browser

- You can create separate access logs for virtual servers

- Access logs can be generated in one of three formats. The older NCSA/CERN format includes basic information (and was used in previous versions of WebSite). The combined NCSA/CERN format includes fields for the referring URL and the browser type. The Windows log format lets you import access log data directly to many Windows programs for processing and analysis.

- Remote administration is supported by all the WebSite tools

- A new Windows CGI 32-bit framework with full support for Visual Basic 4.0, Visual C++, and other 32-bit programming tools, such as Borland's Delphi. (The CGI chapters in this book have been significantly reworked to provide more conceptual underpinning. Windows CGI examples are given in Visual Basic 4.0, and a new chapter on using Visual C++ for writing Windows CGIs has been added.)

- Support for server-push CGI applications

- Support for forms-based uploading to the server

CHAPTER TWO

BEFORE YOU START

"Before You Start" chapters are easy to skip. It's tempting to jump right to installing the software. However, we politely request that you *read this chapter before installing WebSite.*

To make completing pre-install requirements less painful, the chapter starts with a checklist of the important items you need. Once you complete the checklist, go to Chapter 3, *Installing WebSite*, and install WebSite.

If you aren't sure about something on the checklist, take some time and read the rest of this chapter. You'll find the basic information you need regarding hardware, software, and connectivity requirements. We also discuss the pros and cons of running WebSite as a desktop application or as a service. Additional resources are listed if you want more detailed information about any of the topics covered.

So sharpen your pencil and complete the checklist, then get ready to unleash the power of WebSite.

WEBSITE INSTALLATION REQUIREMENTS

Before you install WebSite, please complete this checklist. These requirements are explained in the remainder of this chapter.

HARDWARE

- ❑ 80486 or higher microprocessor; Pentium recommended
- ❑ 16 MB RAM for Windows NT; 32 MB recommended
- ❑ 12 MB RAM for Windows 95; 24 MB recommended
- ❑ 10 MB free hard disk space (for program files only)
- ❑ VGA video display adapter; SVGA recommended

- ❏ 3.5" floppy drive
- ❏ Network card or modem (9600 bps minimum; 14.4 or 28.8 kbps recommended)

SOFTWARE

- ❏ Windows NT 3.51 or higher, with Service Pack 4 installed recommended; WebSite runs successfully under all beta versions of Windows NT 4.0

  – OR–
- ❏ Windows 95
- ❏ Web browser

CONNECTIVITY

- ❏ TCP/IP stack installed and running

> **IMPORTANT: YOUR SYSTEM MUST BE RUNNING TCP/IP,**
> **EVEN IF YOU DO NOT PLAN TO ALLOW INTERNET ACCESS.**

- ❏ IP Address:_____.____.____.____
- ❏ Fully Qualified Domain Name (FQDN) for your server
  hostname.domain name: _____
- ❏ Internet email address for WebSite server administrator:

  _____
- ❏ Domain Name System (DNS) server (optional, but highly recommended)
  DNS Server 1:_____.____.____.____   DNS Server 2:_____.____.____.____
- ❏ WebSite server registered with DNS (optional, but highly recommended)

OTHER

- ❏ System Date/Time set to the correct date, time, and time zone
- ❏ Administrator or Backup privileges for installing WebSite as a service (NT only)

ADD-ONS AND APPLICATION DEVELOPMENT TOOLS (OPTIONAL)

- ❏ PolyForm, Web forms construction kit, from O'Reilly & Associates
- ❏ WebBoard, Web conferencing system, from O'Reilly & Associates

❏ Graphics editor/viewer such as LView Pro, Paint Shop Pro, Adobe Photo-shop, or Corel Photo-Paint

❏ Audio editor/player such RealAudio, Sound Recorder, or Gold Wave

❏ Video editor/player such as QuickTime or MPEGPlay

❏ Adobe Acrobat Exchange, Distiller (available in Acrobat Pro), or Amber

❏ Visual Basic development environment; Pro version 4.0 recommended

❏ Visual C++, 2.x

❏ Java Developers Kit (JDK) for Win32 from Sun Microsystems, Inc.

❏ Delphi programming environment from Borland International, Inc.

❏ NT Perl programming language

❏ POSIX Shell and tools from the Windows NT Resource Kit

HARDWARE REQUIREMENTS

One of the major advantages of WebSite is that it runs on readily available, relatively low-cost hardware. Most Web servers on the Internet today run on expensive UNIX-based computers, which are also more complex to maintain. The minimum hardware requirement allows WebSite to run at a level of performance equal to a Web server running on a similarly configured UNIX system. WebSite is a powerful, rugged server, limited only by the hardware on which you choose to run it and connect it to the Internet.

If you expect high volume traffic or plan to run many heavy-duty applications such as database services, you should expand your hardware. Perhaps the single most significant hardware component that affects performance is RAM. WebSite performance increases substantially with increased amounts of RAM.

WebSite also fully supports symmetric multiprocessing (that is, multiple processors in a single computer) to handle processing-intense web applications. You may also want to investigate a high-speed connection to the Internet, such as ISDN or a leased T1 or T3 line.

SOFTWARE REQUIREMENTS

WebSite runs under two operating systems: Windows NT 3.51 (or higher) or Windows 95. Under Windows NT, WebSite can run on either a FAT file system or NTFS. WebSite also runs successfully under all beta versions of Windows NT 4.0 and the new shell that is part of that version.

Note that previous versions of WebSite ran under Windows NT 3.5; WebSite requires version 3.51 of Windows NT. In addition, we recommend you install

Service Pack 4 for Windows NT. This service pack fixed several bugs that can adversely affect WebSite's performance. You can obtain the service pack from the Microsoft Web site.

You must also have a Web browser to take advantage of WebSite's online resources and capabilities. You can install Spyglass Mosaic 2.11 while installing WebSite or use another browser of your choice.

You can upgrade to WebSite from any previous version of WebSite (1.0, 1.1, or any of the interim service releases). You do not need to uninstall an existing copy of WebSite to upgrade. All configuration information and any data files you created with a previous version of WebSite are preserved during the upgrade process.

CONNECTIVITY REQUIREMENTS

Networking and connectivity issues are often at the root of problems you may encounter when starting WebSite. For that reason, *please read this section thoroughly.*

TCP/IP

WebSite requires that your system have a TCP/IP stack installed and running. TCP/IP is the suite of networking protocols that the World Wide Web—in fact, the whole Internet—requires. TCP/IP stands for Transmission Control Protocol/Internet Protocol. You don't need to understand all the nuances of TCP/IP, but you do have to have it running successfully on your computer to use WebSite. TCP/IP capability is built in to both Windows NT and Windows 95 and no additional software is needed.

If you are on a networked system or have an existing Internet connection, you probably don't have to worry about your TCP/IP setup. Check with your network administrator or Internet service provider to make sure you have the items required by WebSite.

If you don't have TCP/IP running, you must set it up before installing WebSite. You can do so through the Network option of the Control Panel. For more information on installing and configuring TCP/IP on your computer, see the operating system's documentation.

NOTE

In any of the following cases, your system *must* be running TCP/IP. You can use your WebSite server in one of three ways: (1) as an internal web server to be reached only by other computers on your internal network—an intranet, (2) as a web server connected to the Internet and reachable by other computers on the Internet, or (3) as a development system for Web applications with no physical connection to the Internet or a network.

IP ADDRESS

An important piece of information you need to know about your TCP/IP setup is the IP address assigned to your server. The IP address is a set of four numbers, one to three digits each, separated by periods (or dots), for example, 204.148.40.6. You will need the IP address for testing the server.

TCP/IP CONNECTION TO AN INTERNAL NETWORK

Using WebSite on an intranet to provide an internal web (such as for a department or departments of a company) requires that the network be running TCP/IP, and that the computer on which you install WebSite has a properly configured connection to that network. If you are on a network, get the IP address for the WebSite server from your network administrator.

TCP/IP CONNECTION TO THE INTERNET

If you want your web to be reachable by other computers on the Internet, you need an Internet connection that puts your computer "on the Internet." There are three primary ways a computer can be connected to the Internet, as shown in Figure 2-1.

Dial-up shell account
  Although inexpensive and readily available, a dial-up shell account will not work for WebSite because it does not support the TCP/IP protocol suite.

NOTE

  Commercial online service providers such as Prodigy, CompuServe, and America Online currently offer some type of Internet access and expect to offer fuller access in the near future. However, these services will not give you the kind of connection necessary to run the WebSite server.

PPP or SLIP Account
  Also, a dial-up account, PPP (Point-to-Point Protocol) and SLIP (Serial Line Internet Protocol) *can* work for WebSite because they support TCP/IP and graphical Web browsers such as Mosaic. A PPP/SLIP account requires a high-speed modem (9600 bits per second minimum; 14.4 or 28.8 kbps are better) to connect your computer to an Internet service provider. Once the connection is established, your computer is actually part of the Internet. If both types of accounts are available, we recommend a PPP account.

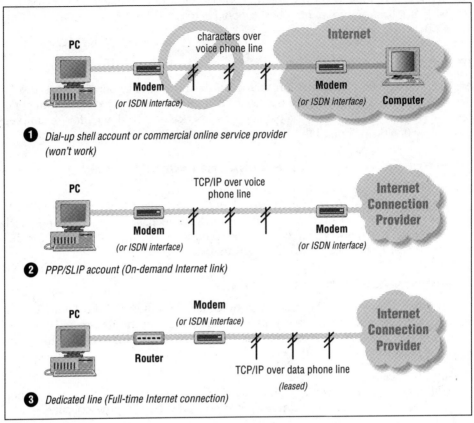

FIGURE 2-1: CONNECTING TO THE INTERNET

Your PPP/SLIP provider will assign an IP address for your computer. The service provider will also assign (or let you choose) a name for your computer, provide DNS name server addresses, and register your computer's name with DNS (see below for more).

If you choose to use a PPP or SLIP connection, you will need software to dial the Internet service provider and establish the proper connection. The Remote Access Service (RAS) under Windows NT or Dial-Up Networking under Windows 95 can handle these tasks.

Most Internet Service Providers (ISPs) charge monthly fees and hourly usage fees. They may also have special packages for businesses requiring 24-hour connections. You should discuss various packages with your Internet service provider before choosing a connection.

Dedicated Line

The most expensive and difficult to set up, a dedicated line (such as a T1 line) gives you a full-time, high-speed connection to the Internet. If you expect a lot of traffic on your WebSite server, you should consider a dedicated line, which requires an additional piece of hardware, a *router*, to handle Internet traffic. If you already have full-time access to the Internet from your computer, you probably have a dedicated line. Check with your network administrator to make sure your computer is configured correctly and that you have the correct IP address.

NOTE

ISDN (Integrated Services Digital Network) is a specialized type of phone line that can be used for both voice and data (at the same time). If ISDN is available from the local phone company, an ISDN line can work for either an on-demand (PPP/SLIP) or full-time (dedicated line) network and achieve speeds as great as some leased-line connections. ISDN connections require a special piece of hardware similar to a modem.

INTERNET EMAIL ADDRESS OF THE WEBSITE ADMINISTRATOR

During installation WebSite requests the Internet email address for the WebSite server administrator. This address includes a name and a domain name. The easy way to spot an Internet email address is to look for the @ separating two names. For example, *website-support@ora.com* is the email address for WebSite technical support.

The email address can be for any location, not necessarily the system on which the WebSite server resides. Also, the email address is for the WebSite administrator, not the system administrator (although it may be the same person and thus the same address). This email address is used in a few WebSite documents, such as search forms.

FULLY QUALIFIED DOMAIN NAME (FQDN)

In addition to a unique numeric address (the IP number), every computer that is on a TCP/IP network (internal or Internet) may also have a unique name, called a domain name. For example, *website.ora.com*, *www.ncsa.uiuc.edu*, and *www.census.gov* are domain names used to identify computers connected to the Internet. You'll notice that these names have multiple pieces separated by periods (or dots, as they are generally called). The first piece in these domain names is the hostname; the rest is the name of the domain in which the host exists.

For WebSite, you need to know the fully qualified domain name for *your* server. A fully qualified domain name (FQDN) includes the full hierarchical name of the computer—that is, the hostname and the name of the domain. An FQDN is written from the most specific address (a hostname) to the least specific address (a top-level domain). Sometimes fully qualified domain names are called fully qualified hostnames (FQHN). The designations mean the same thing, and you may find them used interchangeably in this book and in other WebSite support materials.

So if your server's hostname is *happy* and the domain is *dopey.com*, then your server's FQDN is *happy.dopey.com*. Either your Internet Service Provider or network administrator can provide you with the FQDN for your WebSite server.

DOMAIN NAME SYSTEM (OPTIONAL)

While domain names are easier for people to remember, computers on the Internet use the numeric IP addresses to communicate with each other. Mapping IP addresses to fully qualified domain names is the job of the Domain Name System (DNS). Domain name servers are set up around the Internet to provide IP information when you submit a request using a domain name rather than an IP address.

Having DNS available for your WebSite server makes interactions with the Internet faster. To use DNS, you must configure TCP/IP with addresses for DNS name servers. Again, if you are on a TCP/IP network (internal or Internet), this is probably already configured for you. Ask your Internet Service Provider or network administrator for these addresses.

DNS REGISTRATION OF WEBSITE SERVER (OPTIONAL)

Your Internet service provider or network administrator will know how to register your server's name with DNS. Registering with DNS makes it faster for browsers to find your WebSite server. It has no effect on how well your server performs, but it will affect how fast others can reach the information on your web.

ADD-ONS AND APPLICATION DEVELOPMENT TOOLS

Depending on how you plan to use your web, you may want to install some additional software. Add-on applications let you enhance your web with specialized elements (such as graphics, video, and audio) and functionality (forms processing, conferencing) to your web. Application development tools are essential for writing CGI programs.

The following lists are by no means comprehensive. However, they include some of the most useful tools readily available on the Web as shareware or commercially from a software vendor. Web technology is changing daily and new add-ons, plug-ins, and programming environments will be continually appearing. Look for your favorites the next time we publish this list!

ADD-ON APPLICATIONS FOR WEBSITE

Add-on applications let you add interest and functionality to your web. Full-color images, video, and audio elements require tools to create and preview. Web utilities help you monitor and fine-tune your server's performance and analyze the information you gather from visitors to your web. Adding interactivity to your web, processing form data, and other capabilities require programs beyond those included with WebSite. Here's a list of some of our favorites for completing these objectives; check WebSite Central for others:

- PolyForm, from O'Reilly & Associates, for constructing web forms and processing the submitted data without writing CGI programs
- WebBoard, from O'Reilly & Associates, for adding threaded conferencing to your web
- LView Pro, Paint Shop Pro, Adobe Photoshop, and Corel Photo-Paint for creating, editing, converting, and viewing full-color images
- Real Audio, Sound Recorder, and Gold Wave for creating, editing, and reviewing audio files (requires a sound card)
- QuickTime and MPEGPlay for creating and viewing MPEG movies
- Adobe Acrobat Exchange, Distiller (available in Acrobat Pro), or Amber for creating and viewing PDF files.

APPLICATION DEVELOPMENT TOOLS

To write and execute Common Gateway Interface (CGI) programs on your web, you need a few additional pieces of software. CGI programs allow you to execute operations in other Windows, NT shell, or DOS applications and return the data to the web browser. For example, you may have a Microsoft Access database of customer information, which is updated often and needs to be readily available to your sales people. First, you write a CGI program in Visual Basic or Delphi to execute a query on the database. Then you attach the CGI program to a URL. To run the CGI program, the user simply asks a web browser for that URL. The URL points to the CGI program, which executes the query and returns the answer to the browser. CGI programming is thoroughly covered in Chapters 15 through 18.

Depending on what type of programs you write and use on your web, you may need the following software:

Visual Basic development environment (Visual Basic Professional 4.0 recommended)
Used for writing CGI programs, including ones that execute other Windows applications such as Microsoft Access, WordPerfect, or Lotus 123. The Professional version is recommended, and is required for any serious database work. Visual Basic 4.0 is also recommended because it is a full 32-bit application. You do not need the Visual Basic environment to run Windows CGI programs, such as those included with WebSite or ones you may get from other sources. See Chapter 16, *Developing Applications with Windows CGI,* for more information.

Visual C++ programming language
Used for writing CGI programs in Visual C++. This powerful programming language adds even more capabilities to your web. Visual C++ 2.x is recommended. See Chapter 17, *Developing Windows CGI Applications with C++ and MFC.*

Java Developer's Kit
Used for creating Java applets for your web. Java is a new programming language designed for the Internet. It is small, robust, and architecture neutral. You can download the JDK from Sun Microsystems' web site.

Delphi programming environment
Used for writing CGI programs. Developed by Borland International, Delphi is an object-oriented programming environment available in both 16-bit and 32-bit versions. Delphi allows you to create Windows CGI programs quickly and easily. Creating CGI programs with Delphi follows the same principles as creating CGI programs with any other development environment (such as Visual Basic). See Chapter 16 for more information.

NT Perl programming language
Used to create and execute Perl-based CGI programs. Perl is a high-level programming language that has strong text and file manipulation features and is well suited to most CGI programming tasks. In fact, Perl is often called the "Swiss Army Chainsaw of Programming." Many CGI programs that run on UNIX-based web servers are written in Perl and are readily available on the Internet. An updated version of NT Perl, which also runs under Windows 95 and supports sockets as file handles, is available on WebSite Central. See Chapter 18, *The Standard and DOS CGI Interfaces,* for more information.

POSIX shell and tools from the Windows NT Resource Kit 3.5
Used for running CGI programs in the POSIX subsystem. These scripts have usually been developed for the UNIX Korn shell. Note that supporting tools such as *sed* and *awk* are not included in the Resource Kit, but ports of these tools are available from other sources. See Chapter 18 for more information.

SERVICE OR APPLICATION?

The WebSite server can be run as a system service or as a desktop application, under either Windows NT or Windows 95. There is no difference in performance or operation of the server or related tools. You can change how WebSite is running at any time through the Server Admin application.

The advantage of running WebSite as a service is that it runs when no one is logged onto the computer (a security feature), and it can restart automatically without someone having to log in and launch it (such as after a power failure). Under Windows NT 3.51, you can set up WebSite to display or not display its icon when it runs as a service. Under Windows 95 or Windows NT 4.0, the WebSite server icon appears in the system Tray of the Task bar. To run as a service under Windows NT, WebSite must have administrator privileges.

With WebSite as a desktop application, you can start it manually or have it start automatically whenever you log in (by placing it in your startup group). Although WebSite will not stay running when you log out, you can leave it running and simply lock your screen to prevent unauthorized use. The advantage of running WebSite as an application is that it is easier to stop and start, an advantage when you are initially setting up or administering the server and web.

Unless you are familiar with Windows NT services and the identity issues involved, we recommend you start by using WebSite as a desktop application. You will find it easier to set up initially and can switch it to a service later. If you are already using several other services on your computer and are familiar with how they work, you may prefer to run WebSite as a service from the beginning.

TO LEARN MORE

If you'd like more information about these topics or about other Web and Internet topics in general, we suggest reading the online help and documentation for your operating system. We also recommend the following books published by O'Reilly & Associates (*http://www.ora.com/*):

- *The Whole Internet for Windows 95*, by Ed Krol and Paula Ferguson
- *The Whole Internet User's Guide and Catalog, Second Edition*, by Ed Krol
- *Managing Internet Information Services: World Wide Web, Gopher, FTP, and More*, by Cricket Liu, Jerry Peek, Russ Jones, Bryan Buus, and Adrian Nye
- *Getting Connected: The Internet at 56K and Up*, by Kevin Dowd
- *Networking Personal Computers with TCP/IP*, by Craig Hunt
- *HTML: The Definitive Guide*, by Chuck Musciano and Bill Kennedy

- *Designing for the Web: Getting Started in a New Medium*, by Jennifer Niederst with Edie Freedman
- *CGI Programming on the World Wide Web*, by Shishir Gundavaram
- *Java in a Nutshell: A Desktop Quick Reference for Java Programmers*, by David Flanagan
- *Exploring Java*, by Patrick Niemeyer and Joshua Peck
- *Learning Perl*, by Randal L. Schwartz
- *Programming perl*, by Larry Wall and Randal L. Schwartz
- *Programming Perl 5* (due October 1996), by Larry Wall and Randal L. Schwartz
- *Perl 5 Desktop Reference*, by Johan Vromans
- *Inside the Windows 95 Registry* (due Summer 1996), by Ron Petrusha
- *DNS and BIND*, by Paul Albitz and Cricket Liu

Also, check out the resources and links to other Web sites at O'Reilly Software Online (*http://software.ora.com/*).

CHAPTER THREE

INSTALLING WEBSITE

Before starting installation, you'll need to collect some information about your hardware, software, connectivity, and other options before you can begin to install WebSite. This information is described in Chapter 2, *Before You Start*. With that information and a properly configured system and Internet connection (either dialup or through a network), installing WebSite is a simple job handled by the setup program.

Installing WebSite takes only a few minutes. Following installation, you must test the server. These tests include making sure the server is running and testing the server from both the local computer and a remote computer. Running these tests is important to ensure that the server is installed correctly and operating properly.

During installation, WebSite uses the information you provide as well as information from your Windows 95 or Windows NT system Registry and configuration files to set the basic parameters for the server. This general information is recorded in the General property sheet page of Server Admin. We'll look at this information and show you how to make changes to it.

We'll also show you how to activate the WebSite Administrator's account and how to run WebSite as a service.

This chapter begins with a quick start summary, followed by detailed installation instructions for both a new installation of WebSite 1.1 and an upgrade from WebSite 1.0 for Windows 95 and Windows NT. Next, it walks through the server tests and the general information included in Server Admin. Finally, it tells you how to activate the administrator's account, install WebSite as a service, and where to find help.

QUICK START SUMMARY

Take the following steps to install and test WebSite. These steps are explained fully in the next sections.

1. Complete the WebSite Installation Requirements checklist (see Chapter 2). You may need to ask your network administrator or Internet Service Provider for information about the Connectivity section.

2. If you are upgrading from a previous version of WebSite, make backup copies of the DENNY and EIT Registry keys.

3. If you are running other Windows applications, close them before starting installation.

4. Start the WebSite Setup program on the CD-ROM by double-clicking *setup.exe* in the File Manager or Windows Explorer.

5. Enter your name and company or organization information to personalize your copy of WebSite.

6. Choose the destination directory for the WebSite software.

7. If you have an existing web document structure, provide the full pathname for the existing document root.

8. Choose the server run mode.

9. Enter the Fully Qualified Domain Name for the server.

10. Enter the Administrator's email address.

11. Test the server's operation from the local computer.

12. Test the server's operation from a remote computer.

13. Run the server self-test.

14. Review the General page of Server Admin.

15. Activate the WebSite server administrator account.

INSTALLING THE WEBSITE SOFTWARE

WebSite comes on the CD-ROM inserted in the back of this book. The software includes the WebSite Server and Server Admin software; the WebSite applications Map This! Image Map Editor, WebView, and WebIndex; a copy of the Spyglass Mosaic web browser and the HotDog HTML Editor; and the WebSite self-test and other web documents. These components are installed by the WebSite Setup program.

NOTE

You must have installed TCP/IP as a network protocol in order for WebSite to operate, even if you don't plan to allow Internet access. For more information on installing TCP/IP in Windows NT or Windows 95, see your Windows documentation.

PERFORMING A NEW INSTALLATION

The following procedures will install the WebSite software. Read each installation screen for instructions and information. Some of the steps listed are specific to a Windows NT or Windows 95 installation.

To install WebSite for the first time, complete these steps:

1. Start your computer and log on to Windows NT or Windows 95. If you are installing WebSite under Windows NT, you must be the Administrator or have Administrator privileges.

2. Insert the CD-ROM into your CD-ROM drive.

3. If using Windows NT, display the CD-ROM in the File Manager and double-click on *setup.exe*. If using Windows 95, display the CD-ROM in the Windows Explorer and double-click on *Setup* (or *Setup.exe)*.

4. The WebSite Setup program displays the welcome screen. Click Next to begin installation.

5. In the Registration window, enter your name and company or organization information to personalize your copy of WebSite. Click Next to continue. (See Figure 3-1.)

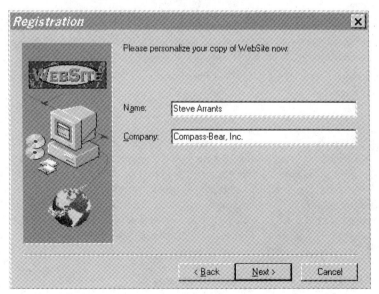

FIGURE 3-1: WEBSITE REGISTRATION SCREEN

6. WebSite asks you to confirm this information. Choose Yes to continue, or No to reenter the information.

7. Choose the installation directory for the WebSite software. The default is \WebSite, but you can install the software in another directory. Click Next to accept the default, or click Browse to choose another directory.

8. Setup asks you to select the components to install. There are three options: Server, Essential Tools, and Samples; Spyglass Enhanced Mosaic Browser; and HotDog Standard HTML Editor. Select the items you want to install. For example, if you already have HotDog Professional installed, you should not install HotDog Standard.

NOTE

If you do not have a browser installed on your system, make sure you install Spyglass Mosaic. You need a browser to perform the WebSite tests and to read the WebSite Resources. If you are using a version of Spyglass Mosaic prior to 2.11, you should upgrade at this time.

You can also change the installation directory if you want. The Select Components dialog box displays the amount of disk space required for installation and the amount of disk space available. To change the installation drive, click on the Disk Space button. Choose Next when you are finished. Setup confirms that you have enough space available.

9. If you *don't* have an existing web on your computer, accept the defaults for the document root and home page in the Existing Web dialog box. (See Figure 3-2.) If you do have an existing web, type the root directory of your web documents and the name of your index document.

10. Choose how you want the WebSite server to run in the Server Run Mode dialog box.

NOTE

If you choose to install WebSite as a service under Windows NT, you should be well-acquainted with the subject of Windows NT identity. By default, a service assumes the identity of the system account (you can change this on the services control panel). WebSite requires this default setup to run properly. If you encounter problems running WebSite check the identity of the server's account and make sure it is the system account. We also recommend you first test WebSite as a desktop application.

If installing under Windows NT, choose one of the following:

– Application (manual start). Installs the WebSite server as an application that you must start each time you log in to Windows NT. This is the default setting.

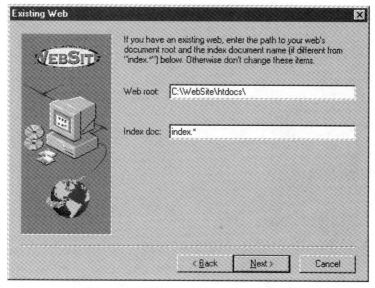

FIGURE 3-2: EXISTING WEB DIALOG BOX

- Application (login start). Installs the WebSite server as an application in the Startup Group, causing it to start automatically when you login to Windows NT.

- Service (invisible). Installs the WebSite server as a service. The WebSite server icon does not appear on the Desktop.

- Service (icon visible). Installs the WebSite server as a service. The WebSite server icon appears on the Desktop, and you can interact with it. If you are installing under NT 4.0, the icon is placed in the Tray. You can later change it to a Task Bar icon, if desired.

If installing under Windows 95 (Figure 3-3), choose one of the following:

- Application (manual start). Installs the WebSite server as an application that you must start each time you log in to Windows 95. The server icon appears in the Tray, but you can later change it to appear on the Task Bar, if desired. This is the default setting.

- Application (login start). Installs the WebSite server as an application in the Startup folder, causing it to start automatically when you log in to Windows 95. The server icon appears in the Tray, but you can later change it to appear on the Task Bar, if desired.

- Service (system start). Installs the WebSite server as a service. The server icon appears in the Tray, but you can later change it to appear on the Task Bar, if desired.

11. Enter the host's fully qualified domain name in the Host's Domain Name dialog box and then click Next (Figure 3-4). The domain name includes the

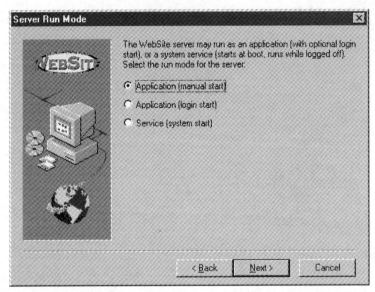

FIGURE 3-3: SERVER RUN MODE DIALOG BOX (WINDOWS 95)

server's specific name and the larger domain name, such as *myserver.mycompany.com.* This is the name used in URLs to reach your WebSite server and is also called the Fully Qualified Domain Name (FQDN). If you don't have an FQDN for your server, use the IP address (for example, 123.333.222.123).

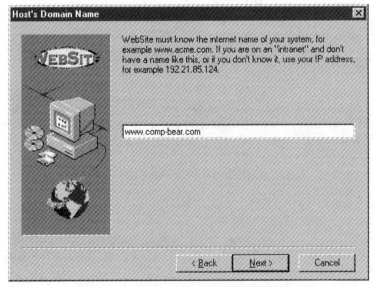

FIGURE 3-4: HOST'S DOMAIN NAME DIALOG BOX

12. Enter an email address that WebSite will use for *mailto:* URLs in the Administrator's Email Address dialog box. This address can be at your site or at another site. For example, your website might be *comp-bear.com* but your email might be received at *tech.comp-bear.com*. Use the address at which email is received, and then click Next.

13. The WebSite Setup program installs the software on your system. The program displays progress indicators and tells you which files are being installed. Setup also adds information to your Windows Registry and builds the program group or Start menu folder.

14. If you are installing under Windows NT and selected Service as the run mode, Setup displays the Service Startup dialog box with instructions for starting the WebSite server as a service (Figure 3-5). See the section "Running WebSite as a Service," later in this chapter, for details. Press Next to continue.

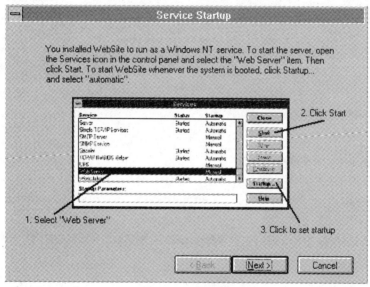

FIGURE 3-5: WINDOWS NT SERVICE STARTUP DIALOG BOX

NOTE

By default, the service identity is System Account. If you are going to make any changes, be sure you are familiar with "identity" under Windows NT.

15. Under Windows NT, Setup next displays information about the Windows NT Performance Monitor (Figure 3-6). The Performance Monitor gives you information about the performance of your system and selected programs and

services. For more information about using the Performance Monitor, see your Windows NT documentation and Chapter 13, *Logging*, in this book.

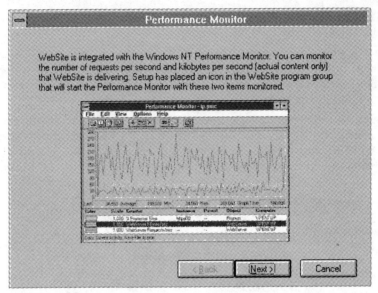

FIGURE 3-6: WINDOWS NT PERFORMANCE MONITOR INFORMATION

16. Setup next displays the WebSite Setup Complete dialog box (Figure 3-7). You can choose to view the README file and/or start WebSite. Click Finish to close the Setup program.

You're now ready to begin testing the installation as described later in this chapter.

UPGRADING FROM A PREVIOUS VERSION OF WEBSITE

If you are upgrading from a previous version of WebSite, you need to perform the following actions:

- Back up the Registry keys HKEY_LOCAL_MACHINE\SOFTWARE\Denny and HKEY_LOCAL_MACHINE\SOFTWARE\EIT. Use the Registry editor (*regedt32.exe* or *regedit.exe*) supplied with Windows NT or Windows 95 to export or save each of these keys and their subtrees. These programs are usually installed in your \Windows directory. Save the keys under a new name.

- If you are upgrading from a previous installation that was installed as a Windows NT service, check the identity under which WebSite is running. If you run as an application, WebSite assumes the identity of the person currently logged on. As a service, it assumes a separate identity, which by default is the system account, configurable by the control panel.

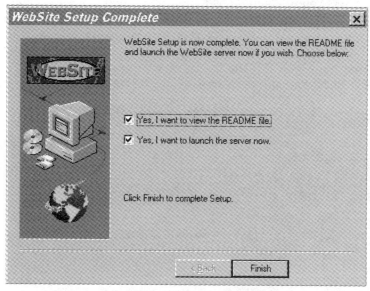

FIGURE 3-7: WEBSITE SETUP IS COMPLETE

- Save a copy of *emosaic.ini* in your Windows directory. Do not overwrite the template copy in the Emosaic directory.

- If you currently have a copy of HotDog, save a copy of the *hotdog.ini* file in the Windows directory, unless you have an unregistered and expired shareware copy.

- Back up your entire WebSite installation, from the server root on down. If something goes wrong with the update installation, you'll be glad you did this!

After you've completed the actions in the above list, perform these steps:

1. Start your computer and log on to Windows NT or Windows 95. If you are installing WebSite under Windows NT, you must be the Administrator or have Administrator privileges.

2. Make sure the WebSite server is not running.

3. Insert the CD-ROM into your CD-ROM drive.

4. If using Windows NT, display the CD-ROM in the File Manager and double-click on *setup.exe*. If using Windows 95, display the CD-ROM in the Windows Explorer and double-click on *Setup* (or *Setup.exe*).

5. The WebSite Setup program displays the welcome screen. Click Next to begin installation.

6. In the Registration window, enter your name and company information to personalize your copy of WebSite and click Next.

7. WebSite asks you to confirm this information. Choose Yes to continue, or No to reenter the information.

8. The Setup program displays the Updating Existing Installation dialog box (Figure 3-8). This dialog box shows the location of the existing WebSite software, and warns you that the format of WebIndex files has changed. You'll need to rebuild your indexes after installing this update.

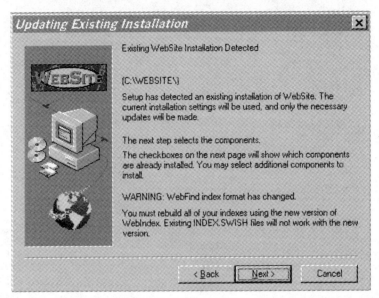

FIGURE 3-8: UPDATING EXISTING INSTALLATION DIALOG BOX

9. Setup asks you to select the components to install. There are three options: Server, Essential Tools, and Samples; Spyglass Enhanced Mosaic Browser; and HotDog Standard HTML Editor. Select the items you want to install. For example, if you already have HotDog Professional installed, you should not install HotDog Standard.

NOTE

If you do not have a browser installed on your system, make sure you install Spyglass Mosaic. You need a browser to perform the Web-Site tests and to read the WebSite Resources. If you have a version of Spyglass Mosaic prior to 2.11, you should upgrade it by selecting this component.

10. The WebSite Setup program installs the selected files on your system. The program displays progress indicators and tells you which files are being installed. Setup also adds information to your Windows Registry.

11. The setup program displays the Windows CGI Update dialog box (Figure 3-9). For more information about CGI programming, see Section 4 of this book.

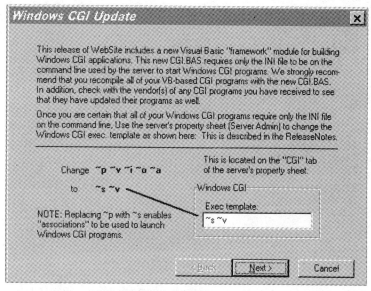

FIGURE 3-9: WINDOWS CGI UPDATE INFORMATION

12. When complete, Setup displays the WebSite Setup Complete dialog box (Figure 3-10). You can view the README file and start WebSite. Click Finish to close the Setup program.

You're now ready to begin testing the installation as described in the next sections.

NOTE

Remember to rebuild your indexes with the new version of WebIndex. For information on using WebIndex, see Chapter 6, *Indexing and Searching Your Documents*.

TESTING THE WEBSITE SERVER

After installing WebSite, you must test the server to verify that it is installed and operating properly. The verification test has four parts:

- Making sure the server starts properly
- Viewing a WebSite document from the local computer
- Viewing a WebSite document from a remote computer

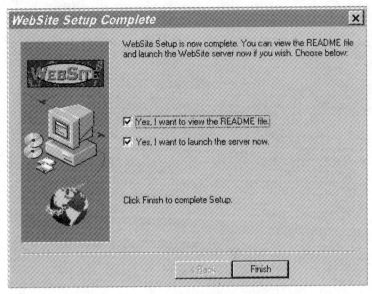

FIGURE 3-10: WEBSITE SETUP IS COMPLETE

- Running the server self-test and demonstration (from the default home page)

IS THE SERVER RUNNING?

When you finish WebSite Setup, the first test is to make sure the WebSite server starts and stays running. If you asked Setup to start WebSite when it finished, the server should be running. Depending on how you chose to run WebSite during setup, the server icon should appear on your screen if the server started with no problems. If you can see the icon on your screen, then the server has passed the first test—it's running. The icon title indicates the server's status as *idle* or *busy*. Note that under Windows 95, the server's icon may be in the Tray portion of the Task bar. To see its status in a pop-up label, move the mouse cursor over the server icon in the Tray.

If the icon doesn't appear and you asked Setup to start the server, then you may have elected to run the server as a service with no desktop icon (under Windows NT only). To check that the server is running, open the Services settings in the Control Panel. Scroll through the list of services until you see Web Server and check the status. If it says "started," the server is running and has passed the first test.

If you didn't ask Setup to start the server, you must do so now. Under Windows 95, click on the WebSite Server item (in the WebSite 1.1 program folder of the Start menu). Under Windows NT, double-click on the WebSite Server icon in the

WebSite 1.1 program group (if you are using Windows NT 4.0 with the new user interface shell, follow the Windows 95 instruction). The server should start and minimize to an icon on the desktop.

If the server does not start, check the server log (in the *logs* directory of WebSite) for possible reasons. The most common is that TCP/IP is not configured properly. Also see Appendix C, *Troubleshooting Tips*.

CAN YOU VIEW A WEBSITE DOCUMENT FROM THE LOCAL COMPUTER?

The easiest way to test if your computer and WebSite are set up correctly is with a Web browser. To test your setup, follow these steps:

1. Make sure your TCP/IP connection is open. If you are on a TCP/IP network or have a dedicated connection to the Internet, this is probably transparent to you. If you are on a standalone computer and get your TCP/IP connectivity with a dial-up SLIP or PPP account, make sure that the connection is working.

2. Make sure your WebSite server is running (as described in the preceding section).

3. With your Web browser, open the following file (use Open or Open Location from the File menu):

   ```
   file:///C:/WebSite/wsdocs/index.html
   ```

   (Use the drive letter and WebSite directory appropriate for your installation.)

4. The browser displays the server's Welcome page file, as shown in Figure 3-11. However, displaying this document does not verify that the server is working because the browser did not find it by contacting the server. (You can view local files in a browser without using the server.)

5. Select the hypertext link *Click Here* in the Important paragraph. The link is for the URL

   ```
   http://localhost/wsdocs/index.html
   ```

   The browser sends out the request for this URL, which is interpreted by the browser and server as the Welcome page document on the local computer. (Note that using *localhost* in a URL won't work when you try to reach your server from another computer.)

   If the server and computer are set up correctly, the server's Welcome page again appears in the browser window, as shown in Figure 3-11. This time, however, the browser contacted the server and the server returned the document. The URL field shows the URL *http://localhost/wsdocs/index.html*.

6. Next, test the server using the IP address. In the URL field of the browser, type in the URL for the server's Welcome page, using the following format:

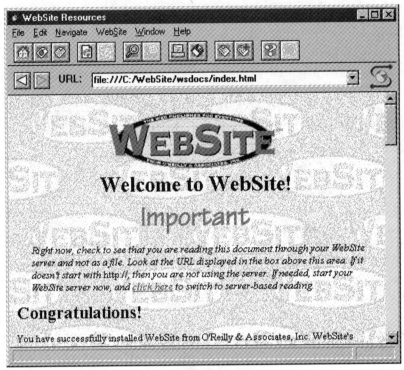

FIGURE 3-11: WEBSITE RESOURCES WELCOME PAGE FILE

```
http://server.IP.address/wsdocs/index.html
```

where *server.IP.address* is the IP address of your server, such as 123.234.29.1. The browser should display the same document as shown in Figure 3-11, except that the URL field displays the URL with the server's IP address.

7. If your server's domain name is registered with DNS, test the server using the domain name. In the URL field of the browser, type in the URL for the server's Welcome page, using the following format:

```
http://your.server.name/wsdocs/index.html
```

where *your.server.name* is the fully qualified domain name (FQDN) of your server, such as *www.comp-bear.com*. The browser should display the document shown in Figure 3-11, except that the URL field displays the URL with the server's name.

CAN YOU VIEW A WEBSITE DOCUMENT FROM ANOTHER COMPUTER?

The next step in testing the server is to view a document on your WebSite server from a different computer, either one on your internal network or one connected to the Internet. This test is essentially the same as the previous one, only from a different location. To complete this test you must have access to another computer that has a working Web browser.

To test the WebSite server from another computer, follow these steps:

1. Make sure your WebSite server is running.

2. From the other computer, launch a Web browser such as Spyglass Mosaic or Netscape Navigator.

3. Specify the URL for your server's Welcome page, using the following format:

   ```
   http://server.IP.address/wsdocs/index.html
   ```

   where *server.IP.address* is the IP address of your server. The browser uses the URL to locate your WebSite server. If everything is set up correctly, you will see the WebSite Welcome page (Figure 3-11).

4. If your server's domain name is registered with DNS, test the server by specifying the URL again, using the following format:

   ```
   http://your.server.name/wsdocs/index.html
   ```

   where *your.server.name* is the fully qualified domain name (FQDN) of your server. If everything is set up correctly, you will see the WebSite Welcome page (Figure 3-11), with the domain name in the URL field.

If you performed this test from a computer on your local network and it does not work, make sure the server is running and then check the TCP/IP configuration of the computer and the network. If you continue to have difficulties, consult your network or system administrator.

If you conducted this test from a computer connected to the Internet and it failed, try again. Sometimes heavy traffic on the Internet can cause connections to time-out. If after several tries you still cannot reach the server, recheck the TCP/IP connections on both computers. Also make sure your server's name is a fully qualified domain name and that it is registered with DNS. If you continue to have difficulties, consult your Internet service provider.

RUNNING THE SERVER SELF-TEST AND DEMONSTRATION

So far you have tested that the server is running, that it can serve documents locally, and that the IP address and/or hostname is resolving correctly. Now it's time to put the server through its paces by running the server self-test. This last test has two primary benefits: first, it tests that the server is configured correctly and that all the features are working; second, it introduces you to the server's many capabilities.

Depending on what you plan to do with your WebSite server, the self-test can provide valuable examples and plentiful ideas. Note that some of the items in the server self-test are quite advanced. Don't worry if you don't understand them at first. The rest of this book is dedicated to explaining WebSite's features and how (and why!) you use them.

NOTE

Since you will want to run the self-test and demonstration more than once (for example, whenever you make major configuration changes to your web or to collect data for troubleshooting problems), we created a checklist that includes all the server's features tested. You can find the checklist in Appendix A; we recommend you photocopy it, date it, and then complete it as you work through the self-test.

To start the WebSite self-test and demonstration, do one of the following:

- In your Web browser, open the URL *http://localhost/wsdocs/32demo/*.
- From the server's Welcome page, click on the link to *Server Self-Test and Demonstration*.

Note the checklist near the beginning of the self-test. If you are not currently able to meet all these requirements (for example, you may not have all the viewers or programming languages installed), we still recommend you complete the self-test. Just note that some features will not work correctly. For example, if your browser is not configured for sound, you will receive an error message when you test the audio link. Such an error is not a server problem, it only indicates that your browser could be configured differently.

Remember to record the server's responses to each item in the self-test on a copy of the checklist from Appendix A. If you encounter too many errors, please read the Frequently Asked Questions, available from the Welcome page.

USING THE SERVER'S CONTROL MENU

Although powerful and fully-featured, the server requires very little attention from you. In fact, it has very few commands available to you directly, since all server configuration is done through the Server Admin application. The server's Control menu lists only three items: Properties, Pause, and Exit. You can display the server's Control menu by maximizing the server's icon or by single-clicking on the minimized server icon with the right mouse button (Windows 95) or the left mouse button (Windows NT).

The three Control menu items include:

Properties

Displays the server's property sheet. You can change the server's configuration on the property sheet (also called the Server Admin application). The server's general properties are covered in the following section of this chapter; the other properties are covered thoroughly in Section 3 of this book.

Pause

Lets you pause the server without exiting it. Pausing the server is useful for quick updates to your web or for server maintenance. When you pause the server, a dialog box pops up in which you can enter a message that users requesting documents from your web will see. (Note that some browsers replace this message with their own error message.) This message lets the user know that the server is only temporarily offline.

If you are running WebSite as a service under Windows NT, the Pause item is not available from the WebSite Control menu. You must use the Services Control Panel or the utility *wsctl*. See "Running WebSite as a Service," later in this chapter.

Exit or Close

Stops the server and closes the application. Once the server exits, users receive no messages when they request documents.

REVIEWING WEBSITE'S GENERAL PROPERTIES

During installation, WebSite puts specific information about your server in the Windows 95 or Windows NT Registry. This configuration information is used by many of the WebSite applications, including Server Admin, which you use to administer the server. We will deal with Server Admin in great detail in Section 3 of this book, but for now, let's take a look at the most general information included there. You may need to make changes to the general setup at some point and this will acquaint you with the particulars. Also, if you choose to change whether WebSite runs as a service or a desktop application under Windows NT, you need to make that change here.

To view the general information, launch Server Admin from the WebSite program list or group. The General page is displayed, as shown in Figure 3-12.

The top of the page provides information about your WebSite server:

Working Directory

Indicates where WebSite is installed. This directory is also called the *server root*. We discuss this concept in detail in Chapter 9, *Mapping*. Do not change this entry unless you move WebSite to a new location.

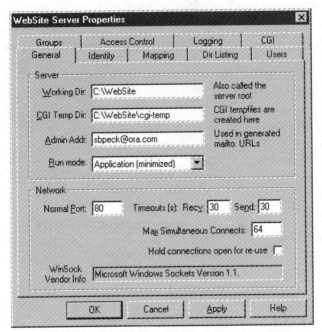

FIGURE 3-12: SERVER ADMIN GENERAL PAGE

CGI Temporary Directory

Indicates the temporary location Common Gateway Interface (CGI) programs use. CGI programs are discussed in detail in Section 4. You can change this directory if necessary by typing in a new one.

Administrator Address

Shows the complete email address of the WebSite server administrator. Notice that the address is the Internet address you entered during setup. You can change the address here by typing in a new one.

Run Mode

Specifies how WebSite will run the next time it is started. If you want to change WebSite's mode from an application to a service, you must first select a new run mode and then restart the server. For running WebSite as a service under NT, see the instructions later in this chapter.

Under Windows 95 there are four run modes:

- Application (minimized), login or manual start with the server icon in the Task Bar

- Application (tray), login or manual start with the server icon in the Tray

- System service (minimized), continuously running with the server icon in the Task Bar

- System service (tray), continuously running with the server icon in the Tray

Under Windows NT 3.51 there are three run modes:

- Application (minimized), login or manual start with the server icon on the Desktop (the default)

- System Service (hidden), continuously running with no server icon

- System Service (minimized), continuously running with the server icon on the Desktop

Under Windows NT 4.0 two additional run modes let you choose to show the server's icon in the Tray for both service and application.

The rest of the page provides information about your WebSite server's network connections:

Normal Port

Tells the server what port number to use. The normal (TCP/IP) port is 80. Unless you know what you are doing, don't change this number.

Timeouts (Receive and Send)

Fairly standard settings. You may need to increase the timeouts if you are on a slow line, or if users complain that your server seems "slow" or "cuts off" documents. Increase the timeouts to 180 seconds for a PPP/SLIP connection.

Maximum Simultaneous Connects

Limits the number of simultaneous connections. You may need to adjust this for your line speed, to guarantee a minimum level of service. For example, if you have a 28.8 line and 10 simultaneous connections, each user sees only a 2800 baud line, which is very slow for Web traffic. In this case, you would want to decrease the number of maximum connects. If you are on a high-speed line (ISDN, T1, or T3) or running on an internal network, the number can be higher.

Hold Connections Open for Re-Use

Specifies whether or not the server should use the Connection: Keep Alive feature. Several browsers support Keep Alive (including Spyglass Mosaic) to make the transfer of documents more efficient and less time-consuming. This feature permits the browser to reuse a connection for fetching inline graphics and other elements that are referenced in an HTML document. If your users experience trouble, you should experiment with switching this feature on and off.

Winsock Vendor Information

Lists the valid Winsock programs detected on your system. WebSite uses Microsoft's Winsock Version 1.1. You cannot change this field.

As you can see, much of the information on this page is rarely changed. However, if you have a problem with the server, technical support may ask you to change some of the values on this screen.

NOTE

When you make a change to Server Admin and close it, a dialog pops up asking if it should update immediately (and terminate any active corrections) or wait until the server is idle to update. Whichever you choose, when the update is made, you'll hear the computer beep, indicating that the server's configuration has been updated. If the server is not running, you will not hear a beep, but the configuration is in effect the next time you start the server.

ACTIVATING THE ADMINISTRATOR ACCOUNT

WebSite comes with a default user account called *Admin*. This account is dormant, meaning it has no password and belongs to no groups. To activate the account you must assign a password and add it to at least one group. The *Admin* account is useful for restricting certain URLs and server functions to a single account and for remotely administering WebSite. (To learn about restricting access to URLs on your web, see Chapter 12, *Controlling Access to Your Web*; for instructions on remote administration, see Chapter 14, *Remote Administration*.)

To activate the administrator account, you must first select a password. Then complete these steps:

1. Launch Server Admin from the WebSite program list or program group and click on the tab for the Users page (Figure 3-13).

2. In the Users field, select the user *Admin* from the pulldown list (as shown) and click on the Password button. The Change Password dialog appears.

3. Since there is no old password, put the cursor in the New Password field and type in the new password. Press TAB and type in the new password again. The password is hidden. Press OK when finished.

4. In the Group Membership section of the Users page, highlight Administrators in the Available Groups list and press Add. The group name moves to the Member Of list. Repeat for the group name Users. (You can accomplish the same task by double-clicking on the group name.) Figure 3-14 shows this section with the group memberships assigned.

5. Press OK to update the server and finish the activation. If the server is running, wait for it to beep before trying to use the new account.

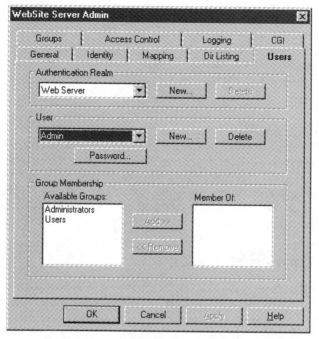

FIGURE 3-13: SERVER ADMIN USERS PAGE

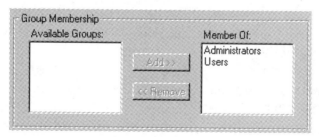

FIGURE 3-14: ADDING USERS TO GROUP

RUNNING WEBSITE AS A SERVICE

You can elect to run WebSite as a service rather than a desktop application under Windows 95 or Windows NT. The advantage of running WebSite as a service is that it runs even when no one is logged on to the computer, a helpful feature if you run your server 24 hours a day and don't want to leave an open account on an unattended computer. In addition, running WebSite as a service allows it to restart automatically when the operating system reboots.

Under Windows 95, the service mode operates in the same fashion as the application mode, except the server runs without anyone being logged in. That is, the Control menu options are available for the server by clicking on the right mouse button. Under Windows NT, however, some of those functions are not available. This section discusses how to set up WebSite as a service and how to start, stop, pause, and continue the service with a simple utility program.

NOTE

If you are installing WebSite as a service on a Windows NT system, you should be well-acquainted with the subject of Windows NT identity. By default, a service assumes the identity of the system account (you can change this on the services control panel). WebSite requires this default setup to run properly. If you encounter problems running WebSite, check the identity of the server's account and make sure it is the system account. We also recommend you first test WebSite as a desktop application.

SETTING UP THE SERVICE

To change WebSite from a desktop application to a system service requires only a few quick steps. All the information the operating system needs is in place—you simply have to shut down the server as an application, make one change in Server Admin, and start it up again as a service as described in these steps:

1. Exit the WebSite server if it is running.

2. Launch Server Admin and make sure the General page is displayed.

3. On the General page, from the Run Mode pulldown list select System Service, with the desired icon option.

4. Close Server Admin.

5. Under Windows 95, start the server from the WebSite Start menu folder. The server is now running as a service.

6. Under Windows NT, you must complete some additional steps. In the Windows NT Control Panel, open Services.

7. Scroll through the listed services until you come to Web Server, as shown in Figure 3-15.

8. Highlight Web Server and press Start. Services starts the WebSite server and, if you elected to run it with a desktop icon, the server icon appears on your screen.

9. If you want WebSite to start automatically whenever the system starts, press Startup on the Services window and complete the necessary information. Refer to the operating system guide for more help in setting up services.

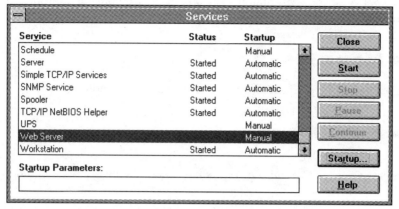

FIGURE 3-15: WINDOWS NT SERVICES WINDOW

NOTE

To return WebSite to a desktop application, simply stop the service, reset the Run Mode in Server Admin, and launch the server as an application.

STARTING, STOPPING, PAUSING, AND CONTINUING THE SERVICE

As described in the previous section, under Windows NT you can start the WebSite service from the Services window of the Control Panel. In addition, a utility program comes with WebSite for Windows NT that lets you start, stop, pause, and continue the server from the command line. The utility is called *wsctrl* and is located in the WebSite Support directory.

You can use *wsctrl* as a quick alternative to the Control Panel or as part of regularly scheduled maintenance activities. If you pause the server with *wsctrl*, the server sends a Service Unavailable message so that users know the server is only temporarily offline (this is the same effect as using the Pause control option when the server is running as a desktop application).

You run *wsctrl* from a Command Prompt (depending on how your path is set up, you may need to use the full pathname of the program or be in the *WebSite\support* directory). *wsctrl* requires one of the following four options:

- *start*—starts the server as a service
- *stop*—stops the server
- *pause*—pauses the server while it is running
- *continue*—restarts the server from a paused state

If you forget these options, simply type *wsctrl* at the command prompt and the program displays usage information.

FOR MORE HELP

Several sources of help are available to WebSite users, including:

- This book, *Building Your Own WebSite*
- WebSite Resources
- WebSite Online Help
- WebSite Central (*http://website.ora.com/*) and O'Reilly Software Online (*http://software.ora.com/*)
- WebSite Technical Support

GETTING THE MOST OUT OF THIS BOOK

Building Your Own WebSite provides comprehensive instructions for installing and using the various applications and tools that make up WebSite. This book takes a task-oriented approach, presenting as much procedural material as possible in a real-life, hands-on manner. The numerous tutorials give you an opportunity to practice the skills you need for building and maintaining a successful web. We encourage you to work through the tutorials and apply the steps to your own specific web.

In addition, we've included scenarios for how your web can be more practical and useful to others. Helpful hints, ideas for using the server, and notes for avoiding difficulties are scattered throughout the book. And don't overlook the appendixes, which include valuable reference and troubleshooting material. For example, if you're having problems with WebSite, first consult Appendix C, *Troubleshooting Tips*.

USING WEBSITE RESOURCES

The WebSite Resources icon in the program group or Start menu folder is the starting point for a wealth of information about WebSite. Various diagnostic tools, examples, reference material, tutorials, and links to other resources are available from WebSite Resources. These online resources are HTML-based and require a browser to view. The server self-test, troubleshooting tips, the latest release notes, Visual Basic examples, and the Windows CGI specification are among the resources you can tap from the Resources home page. We suggest you start with the WebSite Resources when you need information about WebSite that you can't find in this book.

USING ONLINE HELP

Each WebSite application has online help available through either a menu item or a screen button. In addition, you can bring up the help system by pressing F1 in any window.

The WebSite online help gives definitions and specific procedures regarding the current application. As in online help for other Windows-based applications, WebSite help includes hyperlinks to associated topics and topic searching.

CHECKING OUT WEB RESOURCES

You should also regularly consult the Web-based resources for news and information on WebSite and other O'Reilly software products. WebSite Central is a web site dedicated to supporting WebSite by the staff of O'Reilly & Associates. WebSite Central provides product information, answers to frequently and infrequently asked questions (FAQs and IFAQs), troubleshooting help, advice for particular implementations of WebSite, ideas for new uses of WebSite, sample HTML files, helpful utility programs, and opportunities to interact with the technical support staff and other WebSite users. You will find the Tech Center helpful as you expand your web and add features to it. The WebSite-Talk mailing list allows you to ask questions of other WebSite users and to gain from their experience.

Reaching WebSite Central is simple; point your browser at *http://website.ora.com*.

We also recommend you visit O'Reilly's umbrella Web site, O'Reilly Software Online (*http://software.ora.com*). From this page you can learn about other O'Reilly products such as PolyForm and WebBoard as well as general news about O'Reilly's products.

CONTACTING TECHNICAL SUPPORT

If you've thoroughly investigated all the other sources for help and still need assistance, O'Reilly & Associates provides technical support on a per-incident basis or through annual technical support contracts. For per-incident support, call (707) 829-0515 or (800) 932-9302 between 7:00 a.m. and 5:00 p.m. (Pacific Time). For more information or to set up an annual tech support contract, call O'Reilly Customer Service at (800) 998-9938 or send email to *website@ora.com*.

BUILDING YOUR WEB

Once you have WebSite up and running, you'll want to start writing your own Web documents. In this section, you'll learn about the various tools included with WebSite for developing your Web. Chapter 4 describes Web-View, your primary tool for managing and building your Web through its graphical depiction of your Web's documents and their properties as well as its ability to launch the other tools. In Chapter 5 you'll find instructions for creating HTML documents using the HotDog Web Editor. Making your Web searchable is the topic of Chapter 6, which describes the WebSite tools WebIndex and WebFind. Chapter 7 gives you instructions for creating clickable image maps using MapThis! and how you can incorporate image maps into your Web. Finally, Chapter 8 describes server-side includes, bits of code that let you add variable information to your HTML documents such as the date, time, or number of visitors to your Web.

CHAPTER FOUR

MANAGING YOUR WEB USING WEBVIEW

As you build and manage your web, you will find WebView an invaluable tool. If you've ever tried to build—or even imagine—a web, you probably ended up with a white board filled with boxes and lines drawn every which way. Or maybe you resorted to posting yellow sticky notes on your monitor to remind you of links that needed to be completed. WebView replaces those methods with a graphical representation of your entire web. WebView shows all links to all documents—whether they are on the same server or an external one—and what type of document the link is including: HTML, text, graphic, audio, video, or virtual. WebView indicates broken links, which are links to non-existent documents. WebView also provides access control, mapping, diagnostics (for your HTML coding), and activity data about specific documents in your web (including IP addresses or domain names of visitors to your web). WebView also gives you up-to-date activity reports for your whole web.

Not only does WebView show you your web, it also lets you manipulate the objects that make up your web. For example, WebView will launch an appropriate application to edit an HTML or graphics file—or you can use one of WebView's wizards to create a typical HTML home page, what's new page, under construction document, and keyword searches. You can also use WebView to change access control on a URL or to locate specific components of your web. From WebView you can launch the other WebSite applications including Server Admin, Image Map Editor, WebIndex, QuickStats, and a Web browser of your choice.

In a sense, WebView is a *meta-authoring* environment. It lets you author the *whole* web, as well as helping you edit the individual documents that make up the web. In this chapter we first describe WebView's many features and some basics for using WebView. Then, since many people learn best by doing, you may want to work through the tutorial to build a web.

A GRAPHICAL WEB

Representing a multidimensional environment in the two dimensions provided by a typical computer screen is a challenge. WebView relies on a tree metaphor to visually present the relationships between links in a web. The tree structure is probably familiar to you from using the Windows NT File Manager (also available under Windows 95). As in File Manager, you can expand and collapse the tree and open multiple trees at once. You can also view the elements in the tree from different perspectives.

Figure 4-1 shows what WebView displays when you first start it. Of course, the server name (in this example, *sapphire.west.ora.com*) would be the name of your Web server. That is WebView's default.

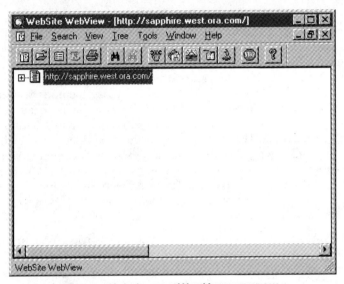

FIGURE 4-1: INITIAL WEBVIEW WINDOW

To the left of the server name is an expansion box with a + in it, indicating it can be expanded, and an icon that looks like a yellow piece of paper. That icon tells you what type of file this is. The yellow paper icon indicates an HTML file. In fact, this file is the home page, or index file, for the server *sapphire.west.ora.com*.

If we expand the first tree branch, more links appear with other file-type icons, as shown in Figure 4-2.

Three more HTML files are linked to this web as shown by the yellow paper icon (and by the *.html* file extension). One of the linked documents has an icon with a desert scene. As you might guess, this is a graphics file (a conclusion confirmed by the *.gif* extension). The icon to the right of the link indicates that it is an *inline* graphic, which the Web browser reads directly into the document displayed rather than requiring an external viewer (an external graphic would not have that icon). The white piece of paper identifies a plain text file (*.txt* extension). The completely blank sheet is an unknown file type (in reality this URL is to a directory). The envelope icon next to the final link indicates an email link, while the

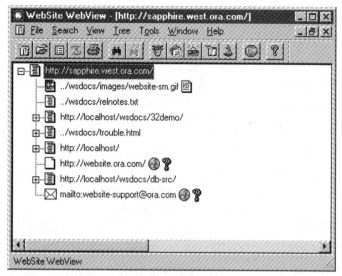

FIGURE 4-2: WEBVIEW TREE EXPANDED

globe says that these last two links are to external webs. The question mark tells us that WebView could not verify the link.

WebView uses icons to identify document types. It also uses icons to identify document and link attributes. Some of the most common and useful attribute icons are

- Virtual link, to a virtual document created by a CGI program
- External link, one outside your server's web
- Broken link, target does not exist

As you can see, the graphical representation includes not only the physical links shown by the tree, but also informative icons, as shown in Table 4-1. You can see all the icons with brief descriptions at any time from the WebView online help.

TIP

If your web has many external links and you don't want WebView to verify them all, you can turn off the Verify External Links feature in WebView Preferences, as described later in this chapter.

THE VALUE OF DIFFERENT VIEWS

WebView can depict your Web in five different ways. The Views menu lists these five choices: hyperlink, filename, label, title, and URL. You may wonder why

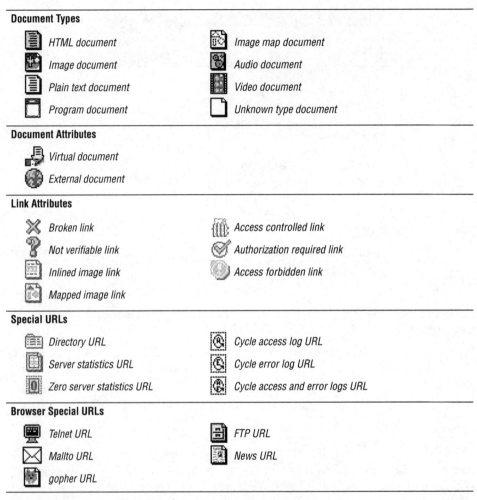

Document Types

HTML document   Image map document

Image document   Audio document

Plain text document   Video document

Program document   Unknown type document

Document Attributes

Virtual document

External document

Link Attributes

Broken link   Access controlled link

Not verifiable link   Authorization required link

Inlined image link   Access forbidden link

Mapped image link

Special URLs

Directory URL   Cycle access log URL

Server statistics URL   Cycle error log URL

Zero server statistics URL   Cycle access and error logs URL

Browser Special URLs

Telnet URL   FTP URL

Mallto URL   News URL

gopher URL

TABLE 4-1: ICONS USED IN WEBVIEW TREES

there are so many possibilities. The following figures and descriptions show the different views and give some uses for each one.

TIP

For examples of using some of the different views, see Step 5 of the Web-View Tutorial.

HYPERLINK VIEW

Figure 4-3 shows a portion of the WebSite server self-test (an expanded version of Figure 4-2) in the hyperlink view. The hyperlink is the partial URL for web links and may be absolute or relative to the current document. The hyperlink view shows you the exact way the link is defined in the document.

FIGURE 4-3: WEBVIEW TREE: HYPERLINK VIEW

The hyperlink view is useful for seeing the relative structure in the current web and how the links are defined in the documents. For example, if you read the *index.html* file for the WebSite server self-test, you see that the first hypertext link is

```
<IMG SRC="../images/website-sm.gif">
```

This is the same as the first hyperlink shown in Figure 4-3. The hyperlink view is a quick way to spot inconsistencies or wrong hypertext links.

FILE NAME VIEW

Figure 4-4 shows the same portion of the server's self-test in the filename view. This view gives the local filename for each document in the web. The pathnames include the disk drive, directory, subdirectory(ies), and filename, if applicable. Note that WebView can't show you the physical location of external or unverifiable links.

As you may have guessed, the filename view is useful for finding the physical location of a document that is part of your web. You will probably use this view in conjunction with the other views for locating specific links you wish to edit or when you encounter questions about mapping (discussed in Chapter 9, *Mapping*).

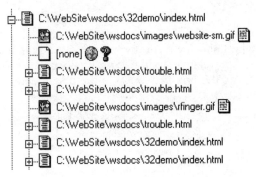

FIGURE 4-4: WEBVIEW TREE: FILENAME VIEW

TITLE VIEW

Figure 4-5 shows the same portion of the server's self-test in the title view. This view gives the title of each document in the web. The title is defined by the HTML tag <TITLE> and is typically used by Web browsers for building hotlists and displaying in the browser window with the document's URL. Not all documents are required to have titles; in fact, only HTML files can have them.

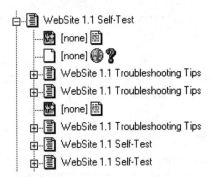

FIGURE 4-5: WEBVIEW TREE: TITLE VIEW

In this example, the title for the server self-test appears in the document as

```
<TITLE>WebSite 1.1 Self-Test</TITLE>
```

WebView looks at each file and pulls out the title text for this view. If no title is found, WebView displays the title [none].

Since document titles are used by browsers, they are often what users recall when they want to revisit your server. You can use the title view to quickly check that your document titles that have clarity and meaning and are used consistently.

LABEL VIEW

Figure 4-6 shows the same portion of the server's self-test in the label view. This view gives the anchor—or label—text that accompanies links in the web. Not all links have labels, only those created with the HTML hyperlink reference anchor tag (<A HREF>) or the image alternate name tag (<img src="" alt=""). For example, the first hyperlink reference in the self-test home page file is

```
<IMG SRC = "/wsdocs/images/website-sm.gif" ALT = "WebSite">
```

WebView pulls the words "Release Notes" from the anchor tag and puts them in the label view. If there is no anchor, WebView displays [none].

FIGURE 4-6: WEBVIEW TREE: LABEL VIEW

The label view is useful for seeing the choices presented to users of your web. You can compare labels in various portions of your web and use consistent references. You can also edit out overuse of vague references, such as "Click here" and add text anchors where none exist, if necessary.

URL VIEW

Figure 4-7 shows the same section of the server's self-test in the URL view. The URL, or Uniform Resource Locator, is the full address for the document on the Internet. The URL view includes the protocol used for reaching a document (*http*), the server name (*sapphire.west.ora.com*), and the URL directory path on the server (with or without filename).

In this example, you may wonder about the server name *localhost* in the first link. The server's name isn't *really* localhost (you already know that this example is running on *sapphire.west.ora.com*). The server name *localhost* is used to identify the current server, regardless of name. It is used in this link to the WebSite server self-test to overlook problems of connectivity. The actual URL for the link (on this computer) is *http://sapphire.west.ora.com/wsdocs/32demo*.

On your computer, the actual server name will be different, of course.

FIGURE 4-7: WEBVIEW TREE: URL VIEW

The URL view is particularly useful for giving you an "absolute" picture of the relationships among documents in a web. It is also helpful for identifying links to other types of Internet servers, such as *ftp*. In a URL to an FTP site, the URL would start with *ftp* rather than *http*. The URL view will also help you diagnose problems with mapping.

Each view for depicting a web tree has value by itself and in conjunction with the other views. As you build and maintain your web, use these varying views to streamline your tasks and make your web consistent.

SEARCHING FOR WEB NODES

As your web grows, you'll find it more difficult to locate links by scrolling through the tree. WebView's search function locates specific links or documents in your web. Each link or document is referred to as a *node,* which you can think of as any branch of the WebView structure. Figure 4-8 shows the first search dialog, Find Node.

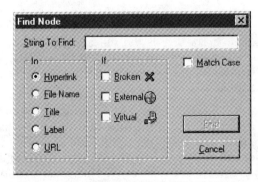

FIGURE 4-8: WEBVIEW FIND NODE DIALOG

You can use the search function to find a string in any one of the five WebView views. To find the next occurrence of a node including *index.html,* type that string in the dialog and select a view in which that string might appear. In this case either Hyperlink, File Name, or URL views would return the right answer, since they all show nodes that might contain the string *index.html.*

Suppose you needed to update the text of certain labels. After selecting Find Node from the Search menu, type in the old text, click on In Label, and press Find. To refine the search to an exact match of capitalization, click Match Case. (To change the text, you have to open and edit the document, as explained in the following section.) To find the next occurrence, select Find Next Node from the Search menu. The two search options are also available on the Toolbar (the binoculars).

You can further refine a search by asking WebView to find a link if it is broken, external, and/or virtual. A broken link is one whose target does not exist. An external link is one outside your server's web. A virtual link points to a virtual document created by a CGI program. You can search for node types with or without including a text string—a handy trick for locating broken links throughout your web. Quickly locating these special links makes managing your web easier.

NOTE

Don't confuse searching for nodes on a web with the WebIndex and WebFind tools. The searching in WebView finds links or nodes in the web. The searching in WebFind finds text strings *within* documents or document titles on the web, and only for documents that have been indexed by WebIndex. WebView searching helps you build and maintain your web, while WebIndex and WebFind help others locate information in your web. For more information about WebIndex and WebFind, see Chapter 6, *Indexing and Searching Your Documents.*

EDITING WEB DOCUMENTS

WebView makes editing your web documents easy. You can open any file on the displayed web with an appropriate editor and make changes. The WebView tree is instantly updated when you close the files.

The editor WebView uses for a document is determined by the application associated with the file type by the operating system. Under Windows NT, associations are made in the File Manager (File menu, Associate). Under Windows 95, associations are made in the Explorer (View menu, Options, File Types). For example, you may want to associate HTML files with an HTML editor or simply with the Notepad, and GIF files with HiJaak Pro or LView.

You can change these associations at any time. For example, if HotDog is not associated with HTML files, you may want to make the association so you can easily use the special edition version included with WebSite (see Chapter 5, *HTML Tutorial and Quick Reference*, for more details). Whenever you decide to change the association for HTML files, make sure you include both the *.html* and *.htm* extensions. To change the association, follow the standard procedures for your operating system.

To open a document and launch an associated editor, complete one of these procedures:

- Highlight the document and double-click.
- Highlight the document and select Open from the File menu.
- Highlight the document and click on the Open icon in the toolbar.
- Highlight the document and type Ctrl-O.
- Highlight the document, press the right mouse button, and select Open from the pop-up menu.
- Highlight the document and press RETURN.

WebView also supports drag and drop of files into open applications. The advantage of using drag and drop to edit files is that a new copy of the application is not launched every time you want to edit a file; simply drag a new file into the same application window at any time. Other methods of editing files cause a new application window to be started each time.

To use drag and drop, highlight the document, hold down the mouse button, drag the document to an open application, and release the mouse button. *The target application must be enabled to accept dropped documents.* For example, Notepad accepts dropped HTML or text documents, and Lview accepts dropped GIF documents. You can tell if an application supports drag and drop if the cursor changes from a "no" cursor (circle with a diagonal line) to a blank paper with a + in it.

If you select a broken text link to edit, WebView asks you if you want to use the associated editor or a WebView wizard to create the file. Read on to learn about WebView's wizards.

TIP

For examples of editing documents, see Step 2 of the WebView Tutorial.

BUILDING DOCUMENTS WITH WIZARDS

When you want to create an HTML document, you can use either an HTML editor such as WebSite's HotDog editor, a text editor such as Notepad, or one of

WebView's wizards. The wizards create common types of HTML files as part of your web. You can use the file created by the wizard exclusively or you can edit it further. Some of the wizards let you enter your own text and all of them let you select links to include in the document. The wizards make adding documents to your web quick and easy, with no need for manual HTML coding.

This section describes the four WebView wizards:

- Find Form wizard for creating search forms for your web
- Home Page wizard for creating home pages
- Under Construction wizard for creating placeholder pages while you build portions of your web
- What's New wizard for creating and maintaining pages that tell users what is new on your web

TIP

Always preview new documents you create for your web with one or more Web browsers. Different browsers display documents differently.

USING WIZARDS TO CREATE NEW DOCUMENTS

In WebView, a typical way to create a new document is to create a broken link and then resolve it. You can create broken links by opening a new web for a non-existent URL (described later in this chapter) or by inserting a hyperlink reference (HREF) to a nonexistent document in an existing document. The broken link appears in the WebView window as a link with a red X.

When you try to open the broken link, WebView displays a dialog box asking you to choose an editor or a wizard to create a new document. To use one of the wizards, click on the Create a New Document Using a Wizard selection and then select one of the wizards from the list, as shown in Figure 4-9.

If you know you want to use a wizard on an existing or broken document link (not a directory), you can bypass the New Document dialog box and display the list of available wizards directly in one of three ways:

- Highlight the document link and select Wizards from the Tools menu.
- Highlight the document link and click on the wizard icon in the toolbar.
- Highlight the document link, click on the right mouse button, and select Wizards from the pop-up menu.

Each wizard has its own dialog for entering information and choosing links to include, as described in the following sections.

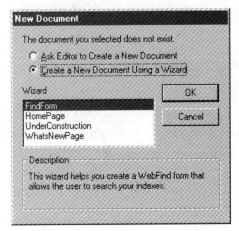

FIGURE 4-9: NEW DOCUMENT DIALOG BOX

FIND FORM WIZARD

The Find Form wizard creates search forms for your web. You can allow users to perform keyword searches on any portion of your web that has been indexed using WebSite's WebIndex application. The Find Form wizard (Figure 4-10) lets you enter a new title and heading, add header text, and select options to be included in the search form. For a full discussion of indexing and searching your web, including using the Find Form wizard, see Chapter 6.

HOME PAGE WIZARD

The home page is the entry point to your web (or a new area on your web). The Home Page wizard (Figure 4-11) asks for information about your company or organization, lets you include a graphic and links, and even lets you choose a flashy or conservative style. Fill in the blanks, make your selections, press Finish, and you have a custom home page.

TIP

For an example of using the Home Page wizard, see Step 1 of the Web-View Tutorial, later in this chapter.

UNDER CONSTRUCTION WIZARD

The Under Construction wizard (Figure 4-12) creates a simple document that tells the user that this particular part of the web is not ready for viewing. This wizard is handy when you are creating or updating portions of your web. You can later remove this document and put the normal web structure in place. You can also

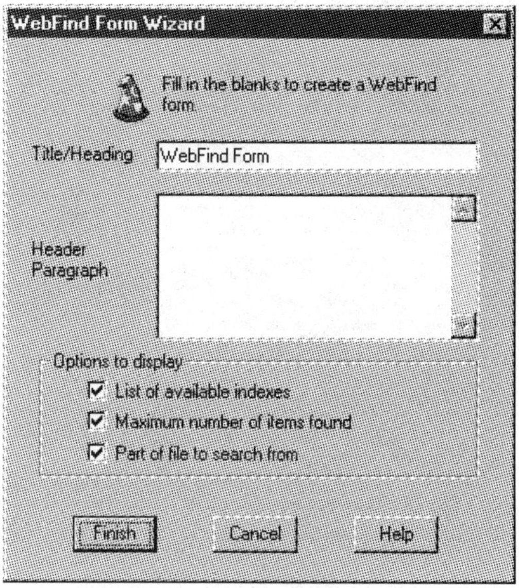

FIGURE 4-10: FIND FORM WIZARD

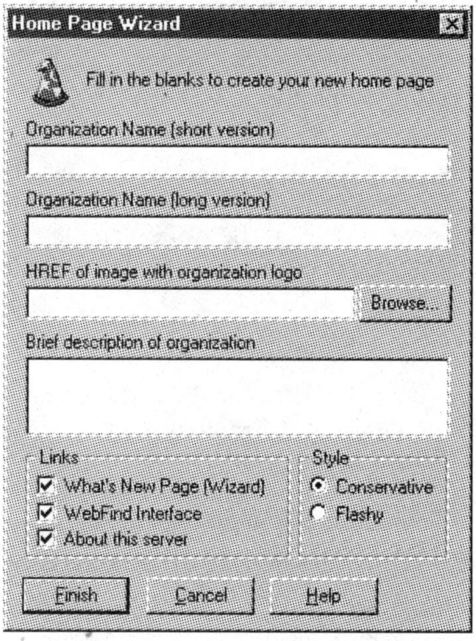

FIGURE 4-11: HOME PAGE WIZARD

use the under construction document as the target for a redirected URL while the actual URL is being worked on. See Chapter 9 for a discussion of redirect mapping.

FIGURE 4-12: UNDER CONSTRUCTION WIZARD

WHAT'S NEW WIZARD

The What's New wizard lets you create and maintain a "what's new" page. This common web page lets you regularly add new information about your web, your company, or anything you like to a standard dated format. Since the Web by definition is always changing, it is important to let users know what is new on your web.

Unlike the other wizards, the What's New wizard also lets you easily add items to an existing what's new document (the other wizards always create a new document, overwriting any previous one of the same name). You can also change or delete what's new items by using the wizard. Figure 4-13 shows the What's New wizard dialog.

To use the What's New wizard, follow these general procedures:

- To add a new item, enter its name in the What's New item field. You must include a hyperlink reference for the item, even if it's to a non-existent file (another way to create a broken link and continue to build your web). If desired, enter a brief description and press Add. The date is automatically inserted for the new item. The new item appears in the list box at the top.

- To add another item, select New Item and repeat the process above.

- To change an existing item, select it from the list box and make the desired edits. Press Change to save the changes.

- To delete an existing item, select it from the list box and press Delete.

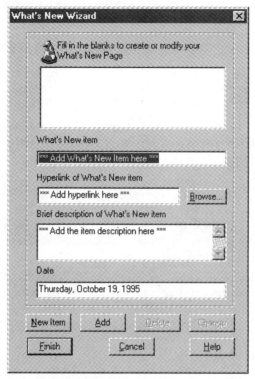

FIGURE 4-13: WHAT'S NEW WIZARD

When you are finished with the wizard, press Finish to save the document. You can later reopen the document with the same wizard and add, change, or delete items.

PREVIEWING WEB DOCUMENTS

As you create and update documents, you'll want to see how they look and work with a Web browser. WebView features browser preview for viewing documents and testing links. The default browser is Enhanced Mosaic, which is included in the WebSite package.

NOTE

You can easily change the default browser and how the browser works. See the section on setting WebView preferences later in this chapter.

To preview a document in a browser, complete one of these procedures:

- Highlight the document and select Browser Preview from the File menu.
- Highlight the document and click on the Browser icon in the toolbar.
- Highlight the document and type Ctrl-B.
- Highlight the document, press the right mouse button, and select Browser Preview from the pop-up menu.

You can also preview a document by dragging it into an open Web browser that supports drag and drop. Depending on how you select and drag the document, the browser treats it differently—either as a local file or as a true URL. These two methods are as follows:

- Display as local file: highlight the document, hold down the left mouse button, drag the document to an open browser, and release the mouse button. The browser displays the document as a local file. This view is useful for seeing the document's appearance, but the relative hypertext links will probably not work as expected.
- Display as URL: highlight the document, hold down the SHIFT key *and* the left mouse button, drag the document to an open browser, and release the mouse button. The browser displays the document as a URL. The browser treats this as any other URL request and retrieves the document. All links work as coded (obviously, they may be wrong; that's one reason you are using browser preview).

TIP

For examples of using browser preview, see Steps 1 and 6 of the Web-View Tutorial.

EXAMINING AND CHANGING DOCUMENT PROPERTIES

Managing your web isn't restricted to structure and document contents. It also means being able to examine and change certain properties of the individual documents in the web. WebView lets you display information about each document in your web in one of four ways:

- Highlight the document and select Properties from the File menu.
- Highlight the document and click on the Properties icon in the toolbar.
- Highlight the document, press the right mouse button, and select Properties from the pop-up menu.
- Highlight the document and press ALT+ENTER.

For HTML documents, WebView shows four properties: general, access control, diagnostics, and activity. For all other document types, only general, access control, and activity properties are available. The following sections describe these properties.

GENERAL

Figure 4-14 shows the General page for the WebSite server's server self-test. This is an informational page and allows no editing.

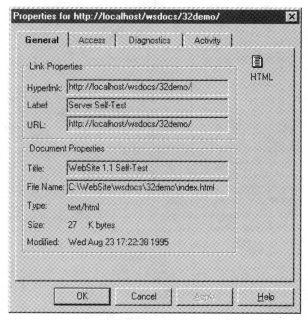

FIGURE 4-14: GENERAL PAGE

The General page is divided into two sections: Link Properties and Document Properties. You'll recognize much of the information about these properties from WebView's different views.

This page also includes the document's content type (for this document it is *text/ html*), its size, and the date last modified. Content types are covered in detail in Chapter 9, *Mapping*. The icons shown with a document in a WebView tree display also appear on this page.

ACCESS CONTROL

Figure 4-15 shows the Access property page for the WebSite server's default home page.

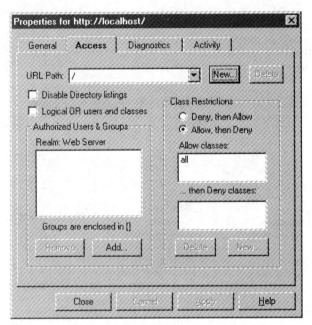

FIGURE 4-15: ACCESS PROPERTY PAGE

This page shows the current access control setting for all URL paths of which this document is a member. All web documents are in the URL root directory, which is indicated by the "/" (since this example uses the server's default home page, the URL is the document root). Other URL paths for the document are listed in the pulldown URL Path field, if access is restricted at any point.

When access to a URL path is limited, the Access page lists authorized users and groups; otherwise this box is blank (as in the example above). The Class Restrictions field shows if and how access is restricted by allowing and/or denying predefined classes of users. Class restrictions invoke IP address and hostname filtering—allowing or denying users access to all or part of the Web based on the IP address or hostname from which they are contacting the server. In the example shown in Figure 4-15 *all* classes of users are allowed. In short, this URL has no access restrictions. You can change the access control of a URL path by making changes on this page.

TIP

For an example of applying access control to a URL path through Web-View, see Step 4 of the WebView Tutorial.

This page is the same as the Access Control page of Server Admin, except it is focused on the specific document. You can change the access control on this page for any URL path of which this document is a member. Note that access can be limited only by URL directory, *not by specific document*.

Access control is a powerful tool for securing your web. Please read Chapter 12, *Controlling Access to Your Web*, before restricting access to your web.

DIAGNOSTICS

Figure 4-16 shows the Diagnostics page for the WebSite server's default home page. As we noted earlier, diagnostics are available for HTML files only. This page is informational and allows no editing.

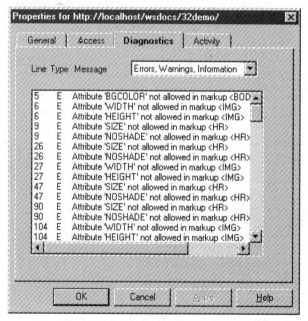

FIGURE 4-16: DIAGNOSTICS PAGE

WebView generates these diagnostics by comparing the document's HTML coding to an HTML parser (or interpreter). The default parser is the HTML 2.0 DTD (document type definition), which includes elements supported by all major graphical Web browsers. In general, Web browsers are forgiving of coding inconsistencies.

However, you should check the diagnostics and correct any errors that appear. You can find the error location using the line number to the left of the message.

TYPES OF MESSAGES

Diagnostic messages are divided into three classes, which indicate their level of severity and what action you might want to take:

- Error messages mean that the coding is not up to the standard. Documents may not display correctly. You should fix errors or at least view the documents in a variety of browsers to make sure the error does not affect the display.

- Warning messages mean that the coding is not completely up to the standard but should not affect the display of the document.

- Information messages mean that the coding is within the acceptable range allowed by the specification.

TIP

For a brief explanation of any diagnostic message, highlight the message and double-click. The explanation will help you determine how to fix a coding error.

AVAILABLE PARSERS

The default parser used for comparing your documents is HTML 2.0. In the Preferences for WebView, you can select a different HTML parser. Each one allows more tags and produces fewer error messages; however, each one also assumes users reach your web with a browser that can properly interpret advanced tags. The different parsers, in order of increasing sophistication, are as follows:

HTML 2.0 with Netscape extensions
Allows all HTML 2 tags as well as tags (such as <center>) supported by the Netscape browser.

HTML 3.0
Still undergoing review, this new standard allows more sophisticated tags than HTML 2. Several of the Netscape extensions are included in HTML 3.

HTML 3.0 with Netscape extensions
The most advanced parser allows HTML 3 tags and additional Netscape tags.

For instructions on selecting a different HTML parser, see the section on setting WebView preferences later in this chapter.

TIP

Remember that if you select an advanced parser, you will not see error messages that may gravely affect how users view your web's contents.

ACTIVITY

Figure 4-17 shows the Activity page for *sapphire.west.ora.com*'s home page. The Activity report gives a quick summary of traffic for a specific document in your web, rather than all the documents in your web. From the Activity page you can also get reports on domains visiting the page and logging information per request, as described below.

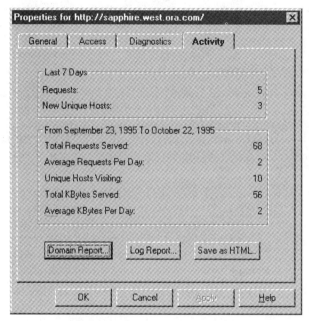

FIGURE 4-17: ACTIVITY PAGE

ACTIVITY SUMMARY

The Activity page is divided into two sections. The top section gives a simple report of activity for the last week, or the number of days specified in WebView Activity Preferences (see "Setting WebView Preferences," below). It shows the total number of times the page has been requested and the number of unique hosts visiting that page for the first time. The second section gives summary and analysis information for the page since the access log was last cycled (cycling the logs is covered in Chapter 13, *Logging*).

The information in the summary is helpful for monitoring the traffic on specific portions of your web. For example, if you have set up a web for your marketing department, you can check the activity for that particular web and report the findings to the department manager.

You can also save the activity information as an HTML formatted file. You can then include a link to the summary file in your web, or use it as input to other data analysis tools. For a similar activity summary for the entire web, use Quick-Stats, which is explained later in this chapter.

DOMAIN REPORT

The Activity page includes two buttons for getting more detailed information from the log data. When you press the Domain Report button, WebView analyzes the log entries and generates a list showing the number of requests and the type of domain the requests came from. Domains are shown as numerical (IP address with no domain name), *com*, *net*, *org*, *edu*, or foreign (usually a two-letter domain identifying the country of origin).

Unless you have DNS Reverse Lookup set for your server (done through the Logging page of Server Admin and described in Chapter 13, *Logging*), the domain report includes only one entry—all requests are from numerical domains, or IP addresses. To show domain names, you can turn on DNS Reverse Lookup for the server (see Chapter 13), which is not recommended since it slows traffic on your server.

An easier way to see domain names is to set the DNS lookup option in the WebView Activity Preferences, described in the "Setting WebView Preferences" section of this chapter. When you set this option, WebView takes the log data, contacts the DNS server for your system, and generates a list showing requests by domain, all without slowing traffic on your server. You can also set how many levels or parts of the domain name are shown, from one to four.

Figure 4-18 shows a Domain Report with DNS lookup set for two levels of the domain name. Note that numerical entries remain. These indicate requests from domains that were not currently available to DNS.

You can save this report as an HTML file, also. Domain report information is especially useful on a busy web for tracking the types of users requesting information. For example, if you are running an international trading venture, you want to see lots of foreign domains coming to your web. On the other hand, if you are a librarian providing research assistance to academicians, you can track the number of requests from *edu* domains.

If you are running WebSite on an internal server, you may want to set the domain levels to four and track requests from specific users or departments to make sure your internal web is being fully used. See the section "Setting WebView Preferences" for instructions.

LOG REPORT

Pressing the Log Report button causes WebView to generate a report listing all requests for the page, as shown in Figure 4-19. The report takes data from the

FIGURE 4-18: DOMAIN REPORT

server's access log and for each request shows the IP address, the date and time of the request, and the status of the request. The status is the HTTP response code the server sends to the browser. The 200 code means the server successfully returned the document to the browser. The 401 code means the server required authentication before returning the document. The log report is sorted in date order, most recent requests first.

FIGURE 4-19: LOG REPORT

You can save the Log Report as an HTML file and use it for more detailed tracking of activity on a page.

NOTE

If DNS lookup is turned on in the WebView Activity Preferences, the IP address in the Log Report is replaced by the full domain name of the requesting browser, if available. If you choose Sort by Domain for the Log Report sort order, the domain name is shown in reverse order (for example, *com.ora.west.sapphire*), so it is easier to see the types of domains visiting a page.

PRINTING THE WEBVIEW WINDOW

In WebSite 1.1, you can print the WebView tree as it appears in the WebView window. The printed version recreates what is in the current window (the active window if you have multiple webs open) including links and icons. You can also preview the web before printing it.

To print the contents of the active window:

- Select Print from the File menu and complete the print dialog
- Click on the Print icon on the toolbar and complete the print dialog

To preview the print job, select Print Preview from the File menu.

SETTING WEBVIEW PREFERENCES

We've alluded to several preferences you can change that affect how WebView works. For example, you can select another browser for Browser Preview, change the parser used for HTML diagnostics, or have WebView look up domain names for activity reports. Setting these preferences and many others is accomplished through the WebView Preferences property sheet. To display the property sheet, select Preferences from the File menu. The property sheet has five pages, which are described in the following sections.

GENERAL

The General Preferences page (Figure 4-20) lets you change some basic information about how WebView works.

HOME

Determines where WebView "wakes up" when it starts. By default, WebView displays the server's root, or home page, document. You can change this location

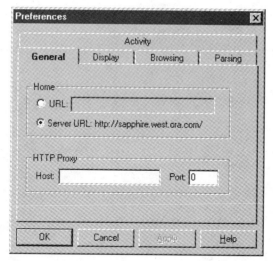

FIGURE 4-20: WEBVIEW GENERAL PREFERENCES PAGE

to any URL. Select the URL button and enter a full URL in the field. Remember that the URL *must* contain the protocol, the server name, URL path, and (optional) the document, for example, *http://sapphire.west.ora.com/products/index.html*. Changing the Home preference is useful if you have a particular portion of the web you are building or closely monitoring.

HTTP PROXY

Allows WebView to verify external documents or view external webs from behind a firewall. You enter the hostname of the proxy server and the port on which WebView should query the proxy. Setting a proxy server in WebView is similar to setting one in a Web browser. If you are unsure about your need for an HTTP proxy, consult your system or network administrator.

DISPLAY

The Display Preferences page (Figure 4-21) lets you change what information WebView verifies and then displays. By default, when you expand a link, WebView tries to verify all external links and displays all inlined images. You can change these display options and two others on this page.

VERIFY EXTERNAL LINKS

If your web contains external links, this preference causes WebView to contact the external servers and verify the links. You may want to turn this verification off if you have many external links and a slow connection or you are simply testing

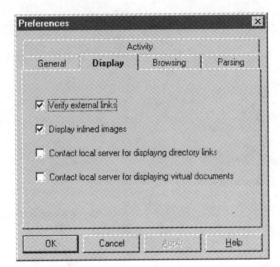

FIGURE 4-21: WEBVIEW DISPLAY PREFERENCES PAGE

your internal links. You should also turn this off if you know your DNS connection is not working.

DISPLAY INLINED IMAGES

Causes WebView to display links to inlined images. Since every graphic element in a document (whether it is your masthead or a single fancy bullet) is called through a hyperlink reference (HREF), the graphical picture of your web may be cluttered with links to inlined images. If your web has a lot of images, you may want to turn off this preference. Note that if you make this change while displaying a web, it affects only future expansions, not the links already expanded.

CONTACT LOCAL SERVER FOR DISPLAYING DIRECTORY LINKS

Normally, when WebView detects a link to a directory with no home page, it simply displays the link with the directory icon and does not look for links within the directory. However, that directory may contain documents that are made available to users as an automatic directory listing (discussed in Chapter 11, *Automatic Directory Listings*). The directory may have header, footer, and description files that contain links. If your web has such directories, you can have WebView verify the links and display them by selecting this preference. Note that WebView verifies directory links only on the local server and the server must be running.

CONTACT LOCAL SERVER FOR DISPLAYING VIRTUAL DOCUMENTS

When WebView detects a link to a virtual document (such as those created by CGI programs), it simply displays the link with the document type (for example, the program icon) and the virtual document icon. It does not try to verify the document by creating it and verifying any resulting links. If your web contains virtual documents, you can select this preference and force WebView to test them and any resulting links. Note that WebView verifies virtual documents only on the local server and the server must be running.

BROWSING

The Browsing Preferences page (Figure 4-22) lets you change the default browser used for Browser Preview. You can also set whether the browser launches a new copy, a new window, or uses the existing open browser window to display a document.

FIGURE 4-22: WEBVIEW BROWSING PREFERENCES PAGE

BROWSER

Shows the path for the browser program used by WebView. The default is Spyglass Mosaic 2.1, which comes with WebSite. To change the browser, type in a new path and program filename. To ensure the path is correct, press the Browse button and find the browser program on your system.

OPEN IN

Determines how the browser will open a document when you select Browser Preview. There are three options:

- Active Window tells WebView to open documents in the same browser window as a previous document. This method prevents multiple copies of the browser from launching when you preview documents.

- New Window tells WebView to open documents in the same copy of the browser, but to open a new window for the document. This method allows you to see multiple documents at the same time in the browser while still launching only one copy of the browser.

- New Instance tells WebView to open a new copy of the browser each time you select browser preview. This method was the only method available in the first version of WebSite.

SERVICE NAME

Is required for opening a document in the active window or a new window of the browser. When you select a browser, WebView attempts to provide the correct service name. Unless you are using a little known browser, the service name provided by WebView should be adequate. If you experience problems with browser preview, check with your browser vendor for the correct service name and enter it in this field.

PARSING

The Parsing Preferences page (Figure 4-23) lets you select a specific parser for diagnosing tagging problems in HTML documents. Each of the four parsers listed in the page allows different tags than the others, as described below. Select the parser that will best test your HTML pages for the type of browser used by most of your audience. Please see the "Diagnostics" section earlier in this chapter for the effect of each parser.

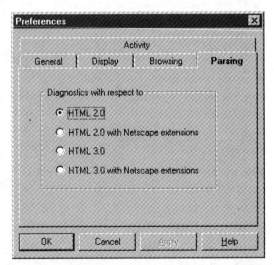

FIGURE 4-23: WEBVIEW PARSING PREFERENCES PAGE

HTML 2.0

Causes WebView to use the HTML 2.0 standard for determining which tags are allowed and not allowed in documents. The most conservative parser, selecting this one produces the most error messages.

HTML 2.0 with Netscape Extensions

Causes WebView to use the HTML 2.0 standard *and* allows Netscape-specific tags (such as <center>). This parser catches many errors but does not flag commonly used Netscape tags as errors.

HTML 3.0

Causes WebView to use the HTML 3.0 specification. Although this specification is still in committee, it is the *de facto* standard and contains many more tags than HTML 2.0.

HTML 3.0 with Netscape Extensions

Causes WebView to use the HTML 3.0 specification *and* allows Netscape specific tags. This parser is the least sensitive to incorrect or incorrectly used tags.

ACTIVITY

The Activity Preferences page (Figure 4-24) lets you set how WebView reports activity on specific pages of your web. The preferences you set on this page affect the results shown on the Activity property page and the domain and log reports. See the "Activity" section earlier in this chapter for more information on how these preferences affect what WebView reports.

FIGURE 4-24: WEBVIEW ACTIVITY PREFERENCES PAGE

GENERAL

- Sets the number of days used by WebView to create the domain and log reports. The default is seven days.
- Sets DNS lookup for IP addresses in the log, which are then used in the domain and log reports. If you select DNS lookup, you must have access to a DNS server. The default is off.

LOG REPORT

Sets the sort mode used in log reports. You can have WebView sort the log by date or by domain name. Since the log report includes every request for the document, changing the sort order gives you a different picture of the activity on that document.

DOMAIN REPORT

Sets the number of levels included in the domain name in the domain report. A fully qualified domain name can have at most four levels, starting with the most specific (the hostname) and ending with the most general (the domain). If you want to know only the domain types (*com*, *net*, *edu*, *org*, and foreign), set this value to 1. If you want more detailed information, increase the number, up to 4. For example, if a domain name is *myserver.westcoast.books.com*, and the value is 1, only *.com* shows in the domain report. When the value is 4, the whole name is shown. Increasing the number does not slow the DNS lookup, but may make it harder to analyze the data in the domain report.

DISPLAYING A NEW OR EXISTING WEB

When WebView starts, it displays the web for your server's home page. To display a different web, whether it is on your server or another, you simply open a new tree using a URL other than the one for your server's root. Opening a tree with an existing URL displays the web for that location. Opening a tree with a non-existent URL (one on your local system) creates a broken link, which is the first step in creating new documents.

You can open a new tree, that is, one with a URL different from the current tree shown, in one of three ways:

- Select New Tree from the File menu.
- Click on the New Tree icon on the toolbar.
- Press CTRL-N.

Each of these methods displays a dialog box in which you enter the URL for the home page or root of the new web (Figure 4-25).

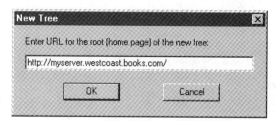

FIGURE 4-25: NEW TREE DIALOG BOX

As you select a new URL, keep these guidelines and thoughts in mind:

- The URL must include at least the protocol and a server name, for example, *http://myserver.westcoast.books.com/*.

- The URL can also contain a path, for example, *http://myserver.west-coast.books.com/new-web*. A URL that contains only a server name and path *must* include the trailing / (slash). If it doesn't, WebView might interpret the URL as a file rather than a directory and treat it differently (go ahead, try it and see the difference between using directory paths that exist and ones that don't exist).

- The URL can also contain a file or document name, for example, *http://myserver.westcoast.books.com/.new-web/index.html*.

- If the URL path or document does not exist, WebView marks the resulting link with a red X, the symbol for a broken link. You can create an HTML document for the link (even if it is a directory) by using one of the wizards. If the directory doesn't exist, WebView creates it for you.

- If you enter a URL that you believe exists but WebView doesn't locate, check to make sure you typed it correctly and included all required slashes. Also, view the resulting link in WebView as a filename and compare it to the actual files on your disk with the File Manager or Explorer.

VIEWING MULTIPLE WEBS SIMULTANEOUSLY

Sometimes you may want to compare your web to another web or compare sections within the same web. You may also want to see and manage several webs (or portions of your web) at once. WebView allows you to accomplish these tasks by displaying several webs simultaneously.

You display a second (or third or fourth) web, the same way you display a new web: from the File menu select New Tree or press the New Tree icon on the toolbar. Type in the URL and press OK. The new web appears in a new window.

Use the options in the Window menu to tile or cascade the windows. Figure 4-26 shows multiple webs tiled in one window.

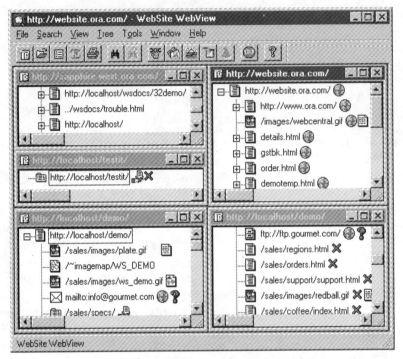

FIGURE 4-26: MULTIPLE WEBVIEW TREES

To view the same tree in multiple windows, select New Window from the Window menu. WebView replicates the current tree in a new window, adding a number to the URL in the title bar so you can keep multiple copies straight.

LAUNCHING OTHER WEBSITE APPLICATIONS

As the "Command Central" for building and maintaining a web, WebView lets you launch other WebSite applications needed for completing specific tasks. We have already discussed how to launch the Web browser. The following WebSite applications are available from the WebView Tools menu or as icons on the toolbar:

- Server Admin (covered in Chapters 9 to 14)
- WebIndex (covered in Chapter 6, *Indexing and Searching Your Documents*)
- Image Map Editor (covered in Chapter 7, *Working with Image Maps*)

TIP

If you are unsure of an icon on the toolbar, put the cursor on it and a pop-up label appears with the icon's name or action.

CHECKING ACTIVITY FOR YOUR WEB

In addition to checking the activity for a specific document in your web, you can get a quick report on the overall activity for your web. The QuickStats tool provides a summary report based on current information in the server's access log. The summary shows general activity for the last seven days and detailed activity and analysis since your log was last cycled. See Chapter 13, *Logging*, for an in-depth discussion of the access log and instructions on how to cycle the server's logs.

You can run QuickStats either from the Tools menu or by clicking on the Quick-Stats icon in the toolbar. When you do, the program scans the access log and presents a window with summary statistics, as shown in Figure 4-27.

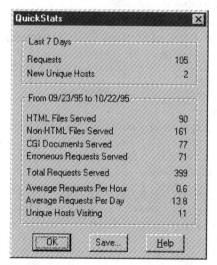

FIGURE 4-27: QUICKSTATS SUMMARY REPORT

The QuickStats report is divided into two sections. The top section gives a broad report of server activity for the previous seven days. (Of course, if you have cycled your access log more recently, this section reports only those number of days). The report includes the total number of requests made of the server and the number of unique hosts whose first request occurred during the last seven (or fewer) days.

The second section provides more detail and a bit of analysis for the entire time the log has been open, not just the previous seven days. The first detailed piece of information is the specific dates covered by the access log. These dates change when the access log is cycled. Let's take a closer look at the other detailed items:

HTML Files Served

Gives the total number of HTML files returned by your server. These are HTML documents residing on your server and not those reached by external links in your web.

Non-HTML Files Served

Refers to all other files returned by your server. These files include GIF, audio, video, text, and unknown file types (such as Microsoft Word or Word-Perfect documents). The files are resident on your server and not external files.

CGI Documents Served

Gives the total number of virtual documents created by CGI (Common Gateway Interface) programs and served from your web. For example, documents created by WebFind searches are virtual documents. For more information on CGI, see Section 4 of this book.

Erroneous Requests Served

Refers to documents the server was unable to return for any number of reasons. The browser displayed an error message to the user in these cases.

Total Requests Served

Is simply the sum of the previous four items.

Average Requests Per Hour

Shows how many requests are coming into your server on an hourly basis, while **Average Requests Per Day** shows the number of requests to your server on a daily basis. Obviously, these are total requests averaged over the number of hours and days since your log was cycled.

Unique Hosts Visiting

Gives the total number of unique hosts that have requested documents from your web since the log was cycled. In this example, 11 unique hosts have visited the web since the log was cycled, but only two new ones in the last seven days.

You can save this useful information. When you press the Save button, WebView displays a standard Save File dialog box. Accept the default name and location or change them. WebView creates an HTML-coded file you can keep as a link on your web or use for other reporting purposes.

As activity on your web grows, you will find QuickStats useful for tracking general log information. You can quickly find out how many requests have been made to your server and by how many different hosts. If you save the data over time, you can spot trends and provide information to others using your web. For more information on logging and analyzing log data, see Chapter 13, *Logging*.

WEBVIEW AND VIRTUAL SERVERS

If your WebSite server is set up to run multiple virtual servers (that is, multiple identities), WebView will help you manage all the webs associated with the virtual servers. In fact, WebView incorporates advanced features to assist in building, managing, and monitoring multiple webs on virtual servers. These features are covered in Chapter 10, *Virtual Servers and WebSite*.

WEBVIEW TUTORIAL: BUILDING A WEB

For this tutorial, we use one of the scenarios suggested in Chapter 1, *Why Publish with WebSite?* :

> A WebSite server can be a great solution for busy educators. You can create a web with links to course descriptions, current assignments, summer reading lists, and class schedules. Your web can also have links to external resources such as libraries or databases that your students need for research. You can also write a CGI program for pulling students' exam grades from your electronic grade book. Of course, you want to restrict the URL path containing this CGI program request to require user authentication. Including a *mailto* URL on the web page leaves your students no excuse for not communicating with you.

To personalize this example, let's say that the instructor, Dr. Montgomery, teaches several courses in political science and government at a small local college. About 150 students, ranging from freshman to seniors, are enrolled in Dr. Montgomery's four courses:

- Introduction to Political Science (PS-101), two sections meeting three times a week

- National Government (PS-201), two sections meeting two times a week

- State and Local Government (PS-202), one section meeting two times a week

- Current Events and Political Movements (PS-405), one section meeting one time a week in a double period

Dr. Montgomery became familiar with the Internet during some recent post-graduate work and wants to prepare her students for the coming information-driven world of politics and society. Upon learning about WebSite, she decides to set up a web containing information about courses, assignments, and links to external resources on the Internet. A computer science student who is taking one of her classes offers to write the CGI program for her students to get their grades from her electronic grade book.

Students can visit her web using their own computers or using computers scattered around the campus. The campus is wired with a TCP/IP-based network and Web browsers are readily available. Within the next year or two, matriculating students will be required to have their own computers.

Dr. Montgomery builds her web using WebView. Let's work along with her.

STEP 1: CREATE A WEB DIRECTORY AND HOME PAGE

To start her new web, Dr. Montgomery opens WebView and selects New Tree from the File menu. The New Tree dialog appears, showing the URL for the server's document root. She adds the name of the directory she plans to use as the root of her web, *polisci,* and the name for the home page, *index.html,* to the URL (see Figure 4-28). If the directory doesn't exist, WebView will create it.

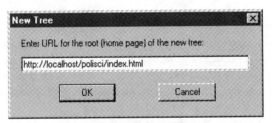

FIGURE 4-28: NEW TREE DIALOG

NOTE

When you create a new tree in WebView, your server's name will appear in the place of *localhost.* We use *localhost* here for simplicity and consistency, but we do not recommend you use it when building your own web because external users may not be able to properly resolve all links.

WebView starts a new tree with the URL *http://localhost/polisci/index.html.* The node appears with an HTML document icon and a broken link icon, as shown in Figure 4-29.

To create a home page for the web, Dr. Montgomery can use either the home page wizard or a text editor. She decides to concentrate on content rather than coding, so she selects WebView's home page wizard by highlighting the new node and clicking on the wizard's hat in the toolbar. Figure 4-11 shows the blank wizard. Figure 4-30 shows the wizard with Dr. Montgomery's input.

Note that she includes a reference (HREF) to the school's logo, a GIF file called *GLC_LOGO.GIF.* To work correctly, the inline image file must be located in the document web *or* be specified with a full URL (that means, the file has to exist

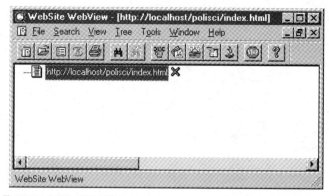

FIGURE 4-29: NEW TREE WITH BROKEN LINK FOR HOME PAGE

somewhere as part of a web). This concept is explained more fully in the document mapping section of Chapter 9, *Mapping*. For now, use the Browse button to find the directories and files that exist in the document web.

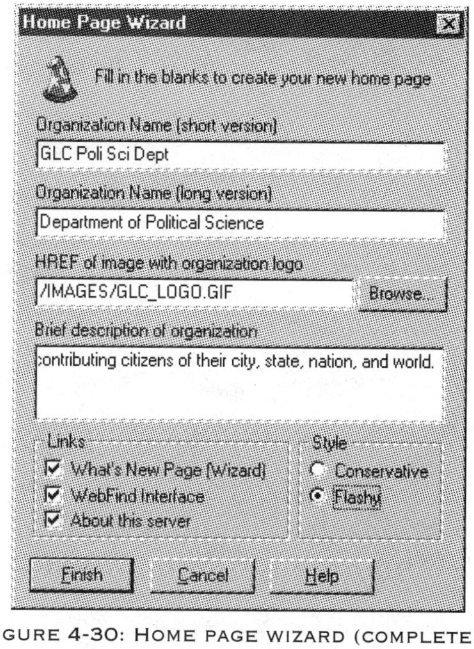

FIGURE 4-30: HOME PAGE WIZARD (COMPLETED)

To see what the home page looks like, Dr. Montgomery highlights the home page node and selects Browser Preview from the File menu. Figure 4-31 shows her home page in Enhanced Mosaic.

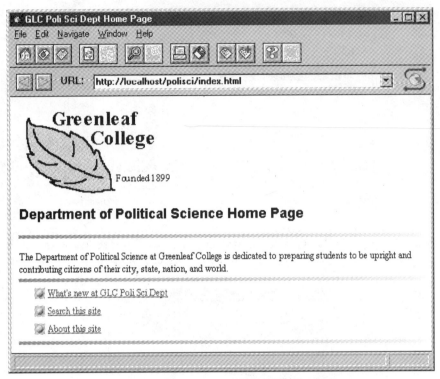

FIGURE 4-31: HOME PAGE MADE BY WEBVIEW WIZARD

STEP 2: EDIT HOME PAGE AND ADD MORE LINKS

Dr. Montgomery likes the way the wizard started the home page, but she wants to change some of the default wording and add some other links. To accomplish both tasks, she must manually edit the *index.html* file that the wizard created. She opens the file by double-clicking on the web's root URL. (The details of HTML coding are covered in Chapter 5, *HTML Tutorial and Quick Reference*.)

To add external links, Dr. Montgomery has to know the URLs of the targets to put in the HREF tag. To add internal links (within the current web), she can use URLs for existing files or non-existent ones. URLs that don't exist are shown as broken links and indicate what portions of the web still need to be created. On the home page, she makes the following changes to links:

- She adds a link for a "Course Descriptions and Policies" page.

- She changes the text of the "What's New" link to "Course Assignments for State and Local Government." She has decided to limit electronic assignment-giving to her smallest sophomore-level class as a test.

- She adds a link for a "Resource Center," which links to a page of URLs for various government agencies and research libraries. Students are expected to use these resources for projects.

- She adds a link called "Find out your grade." The URL of this link is to a page that will require user authentication before students can request the CGI. The page is in a separate directory so that she can add access control to that URL directory.

- She adds a link to the campus-wide events calendar.

- She adds a *mailto* URL so students can send mail to her directly from this page.

- She moves the "Search this Site" and "About this Site" links to less prominent locations on the page.

After making these changes to the home page file and saving it, the WebView window is immediately updated. Figure 4-32 shows the new web with the broken links Dr. Montgomery must resolve.

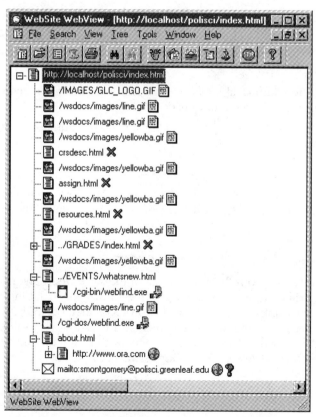

FIGURE 4-32: WEBVIEW WITH BROKEN LINKS

STEP 3: RESOLVE BROKEN LINKS

With the basic structure and links in her web set, Dr. Montgomery begins to resolve the broken links. As in Step 2, she can edit the HTML files by highlighting them and double-clicking to bring up an editor.

ADDING HTML CODES AND HYPERTEXT LINKS

The first broken link is to the course descriptions, *crsdesc.html*. This information exists in other places, so she is able to use that and just add a few HTML codes. To follow good hypertext form, she adds some links to other parts of the web to aid in navigation:

- A link back to the home page
- A link from the course description for State and Local Government to the assignment page for the course
- A link to the college's course catalog, which is maintained on the Records Office web

The second broken link is to the assignments for State and Local Government, *assign.html*. Again, she starts with an existing file, copies it, and makes some appropriate changes. In addition to listing assignments with due dates, she adds two other links:

- A link to the campus library's electronic card catalog to help students find material for an assignment of outside reading
- A link to the Resource Center page from the assignment listing for a large research project

NOTE

Depending on what editor you use with HTML files, your process may vary somewhat; however, the basic principles for adding links remain the same.

CREATING A PAGE WITH EXTERNAL LINKS

The third broken link from the home page is the Resource Center, *resource.html*. The only thing different about this page is the format for including external links. HREFs of external links must include the protocol method and a full URL path. Including the protocol method (such as *http*) is a handy device since it allows you to include links with different protocols such as FTP (for downloading files) and Gopher (for reaching databases with Gopher menus).

Dr. Montgomery creates a page with the following links (their URLs are shown, too):

- White House Home Page (*http://www.whitehouse.gov/*)
- House of Representatives (*http://www.house.gov/*)
- Library of Congress (*http://www.loc.gov/*; gateway to other government servers)
- Department of Treasury (includes Secret Service, IRS, Customs, ATF, and more; *http://www.ustreas.gov/*)
- Postal Service (*http://www.usps.gov/*)
- Campus Library Electronic Card Catalog (*http://lib.greenleaf.edu/cgi-bin/catsearch.exe*)

CREATING A PAGE REQUIRING ACCESS CONTROL

Dr. Montgomery wants to restrict access to her electronic grade book. Since access control is implemented on a directory basis (not a file or document basis) *and* she doesn't want to restrict access to her entire web, she must create a new directory and a document in the directory with a link to the CGI program. As shown in Figure 4-32, the URL for this page is */GRADES/index.html*.

She selects that file to edit and creates a small page with a link to */cgi-win/grades.exe*. CGI programs are typically kept in another portion of the web (see Chapter 9, *Mapping*, for more details on mapping your web). In Step 4, she will add the user authentication access control to the URL.

When these links in the home page are resolved (and new ones added), the web has grown considerably, as shown in Figure 4-33. The only remaining broken link is the CGI program that will allow students to check their most recent test and quiz grades, which is not quite ready yet. When it is, the web will be complete.

STEP 4: ADD ACCESS CONTROL

Dr. Montgomery wants each student checking for grades to verify his or her identity to the server. This type of access control is called user authentication and requires that each authorized user have a username and password. To set up user authentication, Dr. Montgomery must complete these steps:

1. Highlight the URL (*/GRADES/index.html*) and display the Access Control property sheet page. (See Figure 4-15 and the accompanying section for ways to display this page.)

2. Press the New button for the URL Path. A dialog showing the selected URL appears (Figure 4-34). For this web, the default realm is fine. Press OK to accept. The new path appears in the URL Path field.

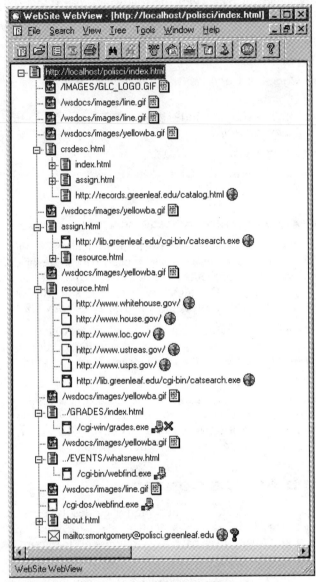

FIGURE 4-33: WEB WITH MOST BROKEN LINKS RESOLVED

3. To put users and/or groups on the authorization list, press the Add button below this field. The list of all available users and groups is displayed (Figure 4-35). The students in the State and Local Government class are already members of the group PS-202 and each member has a password. (See

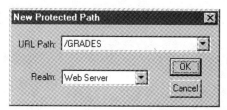

FIGURE 4-34: ACCESS CONTROL NEW PATH DIALOG

Chapter 12, *Controlling Access to Your Web*, for instructions on setting up users and groups.)

FIGURE 4-35: AVAILABLE USERS AND GROUPS LIST FOR ACCESS CONTROL

4. To add users and groups, highlight the entry and press Add. Repeat for each entry. Dr. Montgomery adds herself, the group PS-202, and the server administrator (Admin) just as a precaution. Figure 4-36 shows the completed page.

NOTE

Class restrictions refer to IP address and hostname filtering. See Chapter 12, *Controlling Access to Your Web*, for instructions on adding this type of access control.

5. Press Close to update the server.

6. To test the authentication, launch the browser on the URL. If everything is entered correctly, the browser displays a user authentication form requesting the user's name and password before displaying the page (Figure 4-37). A correct username and password returns the page with the link to the CGI program.

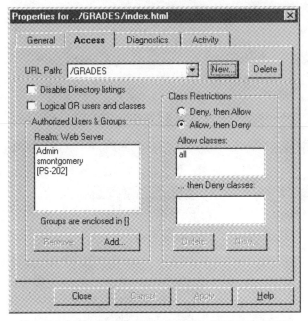

FIGURE 4-36: COMPLETED ACCESS CONTROL PAGE

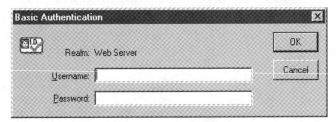

FIGURE 4-37: USER AUTHENTICATION FORM

STEP 5: CHECK OTHER VIEWS

The hard part is over; now comes the final polishing and testing. The first way to check completeness and consistency of the web is to look at it using the title and label views.

The title view lets Dr. Montgomery see that all the HTML documents have clear, descriptive titles. The title of an HTML document appears at the top of a user's Web browser and is what is captured in the browser's hotlist. Thus the title should clearly state what the user will find at this location.

The label view shows the text associated with links. Not all links have labels; many graphics files don't have labels. However, most links to text and external documents should have labels. Labels should be clear and consistent to help the user in navigating the web. In short, labels are what the user sees.

STEP 6: TEST WITH WEB BROWSER

The final test is to look at the web with a Web browser. Of course, Dr. Montgomery has been checking all along (a wise practice), but the final test means starting with the home page and following every link. The browser test lets her see what the pages look like and how they fit together. It also lets her test how and if the links work. Again, some adjustments are necessary for clarity, but all the links work correctly as entered.

Another wise practice is to test the web with several different Web browsers, to see where errors may occur and how pages appear to users.

WHAT NEXT?

This is one example of building a web using WebView. We hope it has given you ideas for your own web. The other tools that you need to build and manage your web and your server are the topics of the rest of the chapters in this section.

CHAPTER FIVE

HTML Tutorial and Quick Reference

This chapter presents an introduction to and tutorial in HTML authoring, using the HotDog Web Editor from Sausage Software provided with WebSite. HTML, Hyper-Text Markup Language, is the language of documents on the World Wide Web.

If you're new to creating web (HTML) documents, you may want to use the exercises in each section. These exercises cover the following topics:

- The basic document: titles, headers, and paragraphs
- Character formatting: inline text
- Block formatting
- Lists: ordered lists, unordered lists, and definition lists
- Links and URLs: anchors and images
- Forms

The exercises don't cover each topic exhaustively, but combined with the additional information given in the "HTML Quick Reference" at the end of this chapter, you should be able to master the topics.

The first exercise may be used as a "quick start" that shows you how to create an HTML file with the HotDog editor. When you've finished that section, you can continue on to the other sections or, if you feel comfortable using or experimenting with HTML, you can skip over the rest of the exercises and refer to the "HTML Quick Reference" when you need to find out something about HTML.

What Is HTML?

HyperText Markup Language is a way of adding various attributes to plain text files that are published on the World Wide Web. HTML lets you mix graphics with text, change the appearance of text, and create hypertext documents that interact with the user.

HTML is based around the concept of tags. A tag looks like this: <B>. Most HTML functions have an opening and closing tag, and the tag applies to all text in between. For example, <B> is the tag for "bold." Any text between a <B> tag and a </B> tag will be displayed in bold type when the document is viewed by the appropriate browser. So <B>hello world</B> would be displayed as **hello world**. When writing HTML, remember that it isn't "WYSIWYG"—What You See Is What You Get. You need to view your document in a browser to see how the tags format your text.

You can use any word processor or application that saves data as plain text to write an HTML file (such as Notepad). We've included the HotDog Standard software to help you create HTML files.

The HTML language has a number of different specifications. Most browsers today support the HTML 2 specification. HTML 3 is the next generation of the HTML language.

One of the key strengths of HTML is that a document conforming to the HTML standard can be understood no matter what sort of software or computer the reader has. For example, the same page can be interpreted by someone using Netscape in Windows, someone using Lynx on UNIX, or even a blind person using special software.

There is much debate on the Internet about what constitutes "good" HTML. The original intention of HTML was to create a universal way of storing and viewing information. The subscribers to this theory see HTML as a content-based language—what's in the document is much more important than how it looks.

New features added to HTML, especially those supported by the Netscape browser, allow authors to create fancy graphical effects. This has led to a whole new class of HTML artists, for whom creating aesthetically pleasing pages is the main concern. Unfortunately, if you're using a text-based browser or one that doesn't support some of the special tricks involved in these pages, they won't display properly—or at all.

The first group maintains that standards are there to be followed, and deviations from the standards simply to make pages look pretty are unacceptable. The second group believes that the only way standards will advance is if they're broken, sort of like George Bernard Shaw's idea that "all progress depends on the unreasonable man."

It is worth noting that the best HTML authors manage to create attractive and innovative Web sites that display well on all browsers. This obviously takes more work; it's up to you to decide if you're prepared to put this effort in for the benefit of all Internet users.

THE HOTDOG EDITOR

The HotDog Web Editor helps you design HTML pages for the World Wide Web. Browsers like Netscape and Mosaic read the HTML files and display them on the screen. The difference between an HTML document and a word processing document is that the same HTML document can be read on many different computer platforms, for example, PC, Macintosh, and UNIX. The browser interprets the HTML tags and displays the pages accordingly.

HotDog supports both HTML 2.0 and HTML 3. You can use HotDog to write "standard" HTML, or to implement Netscape and HTML 3 extensions.

HotDog offers many ways of making HTML documents easier to create. If you are an experienced HTML author, you can type all the formatting tags directly, or select them from menus and pop-up lists. If you are new to HTML, HotDog has screens to let you insert images, formatting, and hypertext links into your document without having to learn the HTML language.

Hot Dog includes the following features:

- Support for both Netscape Extensions to HTML and proposed HTML 3 elements
- Dialogs let you perform complex tasks like creating forms and tables in a few seconds
- Time-saving features such as finding duplicate links and converting DOS files for use on UNIX systems
- Numerous options you can configure to change how HotDog behaves
- Auto-memory of hypertext links, so you don't need to keep typing long URLs
- Drag and drop for inserting links, images, and text files from the File Manager, Windows Explorer, or the internal HotDog File Manager
- Support for editing your CGI programs as well as HTML files
- Options for automatically saving your work, and creating backup files whenever work is saved
- Advanced options such as translating extended characters into HTML codes while you're typing
- Publishing features automatically replace text at Preview. For example, you can abbreviate references to your home page as {homes}, and HotDog inserts your home page's full URL.
- Context-sensitive help. Press F1 from any screen to get help for each part of the screen.

See the online help for more information on other HotDog features.

NOTE

The version of HotDog Standard that comes with WebSite is a 16-bit program. That means it is limited to short filenames (the standard DOS 8.3 filename format, for example, *yourfile.txt*). When creating HTML files with HotDog, you should use the extension *.htm*, rather than *.html*. Web browsers and servers (including WebSite) are generally configured to recognize either file extension. The other limitation of the standard version of HotDog is that your HTML files can be no larger than 32K bytes.

As of publication time, the 32-bit version of HotDog Standard was in final testing. You can upgrade to the final version for free by contacting Sausage Software directly (*http://www.sausage.com/*). If you prefer, you can purchase the Professional version of HotDog, which supports larger file sizes, includes a spell checker, templates, a real-time output viewer, and many other useful features. HotDog Professional is available as a 16-bit or 32-bit program. See Appendix D for more information.

HTML Basics

HTML has three conventions: tags, attributes, and URLs.

Tags

The tag is the most basic element in an HTML document. Tags are usually bracketed by the "less than" and "greater than" symbols—< and >. Tags affect the way text and graphics are displayed, and they can direct the browser to perform an action, like moving to another location within the document or the World Wide Web. End tags look like start tags with a slash mark preceding the tag name. For example, <H1> is a start tag. All text typed after this tag has the Heading 1 attributes. </H1> is the corresponding end tag. It tells the browser that Heading 1 attributes are to be "turned off" after the tag. Below is an example of tags:

```
<TITLE>The Science Fiction Home Page</TITLE>
<H1> Top Ten SF Novels this Month</H1>
```

Some tags work without end tags. Usually these tags tell the browser to insert an image or other information. For example,

```
<IMG SRC="file:///c|/home/images/roadmap.gif">
```

loads the GIF file "roadmap.gif."

Some tags can be added together to merge certain text attributes. For example, you can have both bold and italic, and bold-italic text in the same sentence, as in the following example:

```
The <B>best</B> source of alternate history information and
        discussion is the newsgroup <B><I>alt.history.what-if.</
        I></B>
```

which produces the following:

The **best** source of alternate history information and discussion is the newsgroup ***alt.history.what-if***.

ATTRIBUTES

With some tags, you need to use attributes to define exactly how the action will work. These attributes vary from tag to tag. The syntax for using attributes is:

```
<TAG ATTRIBUTE="VALUE">
```

URLS

Attributes are often used to specify files as links. To specify a file, use the document's URL (Uniform Resource Locator) as the value. For example,

```
<IMG SRC="file:///c|/home/images/roadmap.gif">
```

The IMG (image) tag takes the attribute SRC (source) to tell the browser what file to display.

CREATING AN HTML DOCUMENT

To create an HTML document, you need to enter text and format it, and you need to create links to other documents. First, let's create a simple HTML document. We'll create a simple personal home page.

A BASIC DOCUMENT

Start HotDog. You will see the default editing template, as shown in Figure 5-1.

The text in the document window contains the minimum information needed for a legal HTML document. Each HTML document must have a doctype description. The tags <HTML> and </HTML> surround all the data in your HTML document. <TITLE></TITLE> contains the text displayed in the browser's title bar. The sequence <HEAD></HEAD> contains information about the document. The <BODY></BODY> tags surround all displayable information in your document.

The first step we recommend is saving your work. This will put the filename on the document bar at the end of the screen, and make it easier for HotDog's autosave feature to recover files. Choose Save from the File Menu, or click the button on the Elements Bar. Enter a name for the file.

All HTML documents must have a title. You can type this directly into your document, where it says type_Document_Title_here, or you can specify it from the Format Document dialog box. To give your document a title, choose Document from the Format Menu. Enter the title in the box provided. The document title will appear in the caption bar of most browsers when your document is viewed; it will not otherwise be visible to users. You can enter any text you like for the document title.

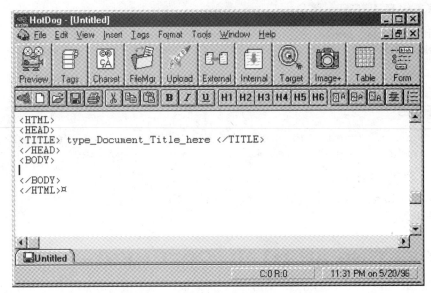

FIGURE 5-1: NEW DOCUMENT IN HOTDOG

The content of your document must come after the <BODY> tag. Everything before the <BODY> tag is information that describes your document to Web Browser and Server software. To enter information in your document that is visible to the user, position the cursor between the <BODY> opening tag and the </BODY> closing tag.

It often pays to give your document a heading that will be visible to the user. In most cases, this will be the same as or similar to the document title. To create a heading for your document, just type the text you want for the heading. Then highlight it with the mouse, and click one of the buttons on the Elements Bar marked H1 through H6. H1 is the largest size heading, which you would normally use at the start of a document. H6 is very small. Click the H1 button now.

Type the text: Who Am I? into your document and highlight the text. This time, instead of using the H1 button, use the next size down. Click the H2 button.

Now we need to enter some information into the document. Two paragraphs about who you are and what you do is probably enough. To create a Paragraph, click the button on the Elements Bar. This will insert a <P> tag. Next type the paragraph. To add a new paragraph, you must insert another <P> tag. HTML ignores carriage returns, tabs, and extra spaces in formatting.

At this stage, you should have a document containing two headings and two paragraphs of text. Now is probably a good time to take a look at how this will actually be displayed on the World Wide Web.

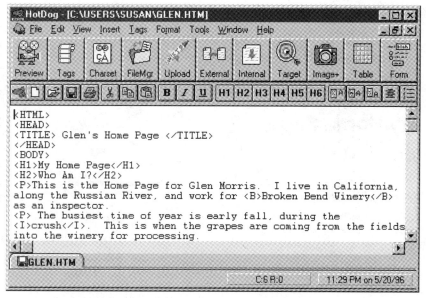

FIGURE 5-2: A DOCUMENT WITH TEXT AND HTML CODES

To preview your work, click the Preview button on the Button Bar or choose Preview Document from the File Menu. If this is the first time you've used HotDog, you will need to tell it where to find your browser. If you don't have a browser, you will need to choose one. Select the browser from the file dialog, then click OK. HotDog will start your browser and display a copy of your document, which will look similar to the document in Figure 5-3. Notice the difference in size between the H1 and H2 text.

To return to your document, just minimize your browser. HotDog will interact with it, so you don't have to start a new copy of your browser every time.

By now, you should have a document containing two paragraphs of text. Let's provide a visual clue to the user to separate these two paragraphs even further. Position the cursor before the <P> tag that starts the heading for the second paragraph. Choose Horizontal Line from the Insert Menu, or click the button on the Elements Bar. This will insert an <HR> tag at the cursor position.

Preview your document again. There should be a recessed horizontal line dividing the two paragraphs (Figure 5-4).

Save your work again. You have created a basic HTML document

In this first lesson, you learned how to enter and format text into an HTML document. You added headings, paragraph text, and a divider line. In the next lesson, you'll learn how to use text formatting.

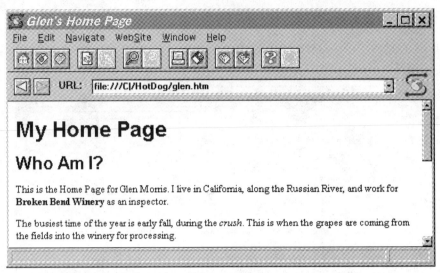

FIGURE 5-3: THE SAME HTML DOCUMENT IN A BROWSER

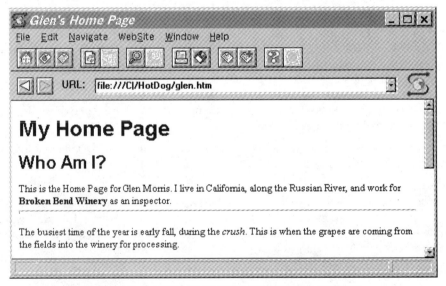

FIGURE 5-4: HOME PAGE WITH HORIZONTAL DIVIDER

FORMATTING TEXT

This section is about formatting text. In an HTML document, you add emphasis to a piece of text by surrounding it with formatting tags. You can change the font, make it bold, italic, change its layout, etc. Formatting attributes include:

- <EM>...</EM> for emphasis
- <STRONG>...</<STRONG> for strong emphasis
- <B>...</B> for bold text
- <I>...</I> for italic text
- <U>...</U> for underlined text

Note that there are two kinds of text formatting attribute tags in HTML. Physical styles (bold, italic, and underline) specify the exact look of the text. Logical styles (emphasis, strong emphasis) format on the basis of the author's intentions.

Generally, you should use logical rather than physical styles. Every browser understands the logical styles and displays them in a relative, rather than absolute way. That is, while different browsers might display <EM> or <STRONG> text differently, they will display <EM> text as louder than plain text, and <STRONG> text as louder than <EM> text.

Try not to underline text. It can confuse the user into thinking the text is a hypertext link, which are often underlined.

PREFORMATTED TEXT

There are times when you want to control the exact way text displays. Use the <PRE> and </PRE> tags. Preformatted text always appears in a monospaced font such as Courier, and, unlike other HTML text, carriage returns and extra spaces can be used in the display. A good use for preformatted text is in a table, such as:

```
<PRE>
River's Cup WinnersYear
Rustlers Cove      1992
Rainbow's Castle   1993
Titanic Too        1994
Korbel Krushers    1995
</PRE>
```

You can use most other tags, including hypertext links, within preformatted text.

ADDRESS FORMAT

The <ADDRESS> and </ADDRESS> tags were designed for contact information at the bottom of a page. You can use them for other reasons, such as for a date apart from the rest of the page, etc. Text appears in italics.

SPECIAL CHARACTERS

Sometimes you will need to use special characters that have special meaning to the HTML interpreter, such as the <, >, &, and ". You need to use special key combinations called escape sequences to represent these characters in HTML documents. They are:

Use this text	to display this character
&lt;	<
&gt;	>
&amp;	&
&quot;	"

NOTE

Escape sequences are case-sensitive, unlike other HTML tags.

You use escape sequences to display non-ASCII characters, such as an "o" with an umlaut (ö). For a complete listing of these, see the online Help for the HotDog Web Editor.

LISTS

You can insert four different types of lists.

Ordered (or Numbered) List

1. Riesling
2. Chardonnay
3. Sirrah

Unordered (or Bulleted) List

- Riesling
- Chardonnay
- Sirrah

Plain List

Riesling

Chardonnay

Sirrah

Definition List

Riesling: sweeter grapes

Chardonnay: most grown grapes

Sirrah: unusual grapes

Let's create a list of your hobbies and interests. To do this, open the document you saved in the previous exercise. After the last paragraph, type the text "Hobbies and Interests" into your document and highlight the text. Click the H2 button.

Type each item on a separate line. You don't need to add the <P> ... </P> tags. Highlight the entire list, and click on the Bulleted List icon in the toolbar. HotDog inserts formatting tags.

Preview your new list. It should look something like Figure 5-5.

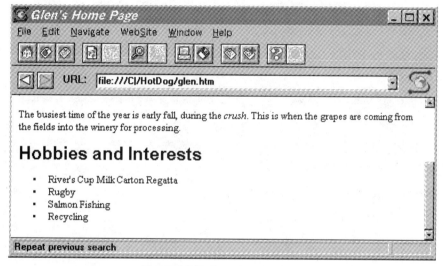

FIGURE 5-5: A BULLETED LIST

To create a numbered or unnumbered list, follow the same instructions, but choose the appropriate icon in the toolbar. The icons in the toolbar will create basic lists. If you want more control over the appearance of your lists, use the Lists command from the Insert menu. For example, you can add a heading to your list, use an image or icon as a bullet, change the spacing between items, etc. For more information on this command, see the online Help.

Definition lists, or glossaries, are structured so that each item is a term followed by its definition. Let's create a definition list for the list of hobbies and interests

1. Open your document if it isn't already open, and delete the list under "Hobbies and Interests."

2. Position the cursor after the </H2> end tag, and choose the Definition List icon in the toolbar. HotDog inserts the tags for a definition list as shown below:

   <DL>

```
<LH></LH>
</DL>
```

3. Move the cursor before the </DL> end tag, and choose "Definition Item of the Lists" command from the Tag menu. Notice that HotDog has added a new tag set and text:

```
<DL>
<LH></LH>
<DT>term<DD>description</DL>
```

4. Highlight the word term and type a hobby, then highlight the word description and type some descriptive text about the hobby. Do the same for the rest of the items in the list.

When you preview your document, your browser displays the items, similar to those shown in Figure 5-6.

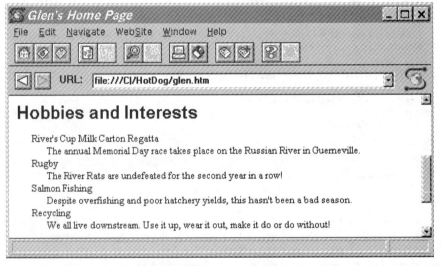

FIGURE 5-6: A DEFINITION LIST

You can change the character formatting of the term and definition. For example, you can make the term bold or italic.

ADDING LINKS AND URLS

HTML documents often have links to other documents, which can be located anywhere on the WWW. These links are provided by URLs (Uniform Resource Locators), which name the location and filename of a document, and the method used to access it.

There are three types of URLs: absolute, relative, and local. Absolute URLs completely describe how to get to a file or location on the Internet. Relative URLs and local URLs both specify a file on the same server as the document they appear in.

ABSOLUTE URLS

Absolute URLs can be used to reference any resource on the Internet. Although you can use absolute URLs for local files, it's better to use relative URLs for local resources.

The full syntax for an absolute URL is:

```
access_method://hostname[:port]/directory/filename
```

The access method can be *http, gopher, ftp,* or *telnet.* Each of these protocols has its own default port assigned to it, but since default ports are only a convention you may occasionally have to specify a port. Generally, HTTP servers run on port 80, Gopher servers use port 70, Telnet servers use port 23, and FTP servers use port 21. If you see a hostname followed by a colon and number, it's because the server is using a non-standard port. For example, the MIT SIPB Web server is accessed as *http://www.mit.edu:8001/.*

The hostname is the DNS hostname. If your name server is having trouble parsing the hostname, you can substitute an IP address.

Here are some examples of absolute URLs:

- *http://gnn.com/*
- *http://192.190.21.10/*
- *http://www.whitehouse.gov/White_House/Family/other/spcks.au*
- *gopher://gopher.ora.com/*
- *ftp://microsoft.com/win95/pub/qanda.doc*

The trailing slash at the end of some URLs indicates that the target URL is a directory, not a filename.

Some Web browsers support other access methods. They are:

Access method	Used for	Example
news	reading news	news:alt.history.what-if
mailto	sending email	*mailto*:support@sausage.com

RELATIVE URLS

Relative URLs assume that you want to access a document from the sever you're currently on, using the same access method (e.g., HTTP). For a relative URL, you specify the pathname to the target URL using its position relative to the current URL. For example, to point to another file in the same directory:

```
<A HREF="rugby.htm">Rugby Rules</A>
```

You might also reference a file in a parallel directory tree. For example, to point to a file in the */wineries* directory:

```
<A HREF="../wineries/merlots.htm">Merlots</A>
```

Remember to use front slashes (/) instead of back slashes in the HTML directive.

NOTE

A server never actually sees a relative URL. When the user selects a relative URL, the browser translates it into an absolute URL before parsing. It appends the relative URL to the trunk of the current URL. This means that you can't use relative URLs in all situations, such as with image maps, since the URL for the image map uses the special syntax */~imagemap/.*

Using relative URLs lets you write your documents without concerning yourself with the final placement of those documents. As long as the file directory structure remains static (i.e., all the files in the directory stay together), relative URLs will work. You might also easily "mirror" your documents onto another server without having to make any changes to the files.

URLs can also be written in reference to the document root of the server, simply by using an initial front slash (/) in the pathname. For example:

```
<A HREF="/index.htm">Back to the home page!</A>
```

This lesson will take you through creating several different types of Hypertext Link in your document.

Hypertext links make your documents interactive. When the user clicks on the link, something happens—the user is taken to another HTML document, another part of the same document, etc. This tutorial will show you how to create links that:

- Take the user to another document
- Take the user to another point within this document
- Let the user download a file
- Let the user send mail to you
- Take the user to a Usenet newsgroup

LINKING TO ANOTHER DOCUMENT

Often, you want to have links in your document to documents on other parts of the Internet. You can add these links to your pages with a few simple steps.

1. Start HotDog and open a document. You can use the document you created in the previous lessons. The first link we'll create is to an HTML document somewhere else on the Internet. The document we'll use is the Sausage Software home page at *http://www.sausage.com*.

2. To create a link to a document on another system, choose Jump To A Document On Another System from the Insert Menu, or click the External button in the Button Bar. You will be taken to the Build External Hypertext Link dialog. Enter the document information here:

   - Resource type is http

   - Host Address is *www.sausage.com*

   - Leave the other fields blank.

   As you typed the above information, you saw the contents of the URL box change. This is the full URL address for the hypertext link. When you choose OK, this URL will be added to the drop-down list for future reference.

3. Move down to the Description box. This lets you specify the text that the user will click on to follow the link. Type Sausage Software's home page here. Now choose OK. HotDog will insert something like

   ```
   <A HREF="http://www.sausage.com">Sausage Software's home page</
   A> into your document.
   ```

4. Preview the document. If you're connected to the Internet, when you click the text "Sausage Software's home page" your browser will take you to this page.

LINKING WITHIN A DOCUMENT

Sometimes you want to give the user the opportunity to quickly move through a document. For example, you might have a list of products. The user can click on a product and immediately move further on in the document to view a description. This type of link is a little more complicated, because you must create a destination for the link as well as the link itself.

1. To create a destination target for a hypertext link, position the cursor at the point you want users to jump to, then click the Target button in the Button Bar, or choose Hypertext Target from the Insert Menu.

2. You will be asked to enter a name for this link. This should be something that makes sense if you want to refer to the link from another document. Type the name, for example, "test target," and press Enter.

3. Move to the place where you want the users to click on to go to the destination target.

4. Click the Internal button in the Button Bar, or choose Jump Within This Document from the Insert Menu. You will see a list of all links in the current document. Click on the "test target" link to highlight it.

5. Type the text you want the user to click on in the Description box, then press Enter or click the OK button. HotDog should insert something like this:

```
<A HREF="#test target">Go to the test target</A>.
```

Preview the file to see the link.

CREATING A LINK TO DOWNLOAD A FILE

Now, let's create a link that lets the user download a file. In this example, we'll create a link to download the latest version of the HotDog Web Editor.

1. Position the cursor at the point where you want to insert the link, then choose Launch an Internet Service from the Insert Menu, or click the Internet button on the Button Bar. You will see a list of common Internet services.

2. Click the FTP button. You will be taken to the Build External Hypertext Link dialog. Enter the document information here:

   - Resource Type is FTP
   - Host Name is *sausage.clever.net*
   - Path is *pub/sausage*
   - File Name is *hdgsetup.exe*

3. Enter the description for the link, then press Enter. HotDog will insert something like this:

```
<A HREF="ftp://sausage.clever.net/pub/sausage/
hdgsetup.exe">Download the HotDog Web Editor</A>.
```

4. Preview the link

CREATING A MAILTO: LINK

Sometimes you want the user to send you email. You might want the user to request more information about a product, give her reactions to your web page, or provide other information to you. To create an email link:

1. Position the cursor at the point where you want to insert the link, then choose Launch an Internet Service from the Insert Menu, or click the Internet button on the Button Bar.

2. Click the Mail button.

3. Enter your email address and the link description in the boxes provided, then click OK. HotDog will insert something like this:

```
<A HREF="mailto:sales@sausage.com">Sausage Software</A>.
```

When the user chooses this link, she can then send email to the address listed. You don't have to use your address for the *mailto:* link. Any valid email address is accepted.

CREATING A LINK TO A NEWSGROUP

Creating a link to a newsgroup is almost exactly the same as creating an email link. To create a link to a Usenet newsgroup:

1. Position the cursor at the point where you want to insert the link, then choose Launch an Internet Service from the Insert Menu, or click the Internet button on the Button Bar.

2. Click the News button.

3. Enter the name of the newsgroup and the link description in the boxes provided, then click OK.

HotDog will insert something like this:

```
<A HREF="news:alt.elvis.sighting">Find out if anyone's seen the
         King!</A>
```

CREATING A LINK TO A DOCUMENT ON YOUR WEB SITE

The final type of link we'll create is to a document on your web site. Save the current document, then open a new one by choosing New from the File Menu. To create a hypertext link to another document on your Web site:

1. Choose Jump to a document in this system from the Insert Menu. You will see a standard Windows file dialog.

2. Find the test document that you've just saved and click OK. HotDog will insert something like this:

   ```
   <A HREF="test.htm"></A>.
   ```

3. Type the description of the link between the = and the </A>.

Note that this link uses a relative reference *"test.htm"*, rather than an absolute reference, *HREF="http:/www.sausage.com/pub/sausage/test.htm"*. This link will always jump to *test.htm*, no matter what web site it's stored on (provided, of course, that a file called *test.htm* exists in the same directory).

ADDING GRAPHICS

You can include two types of graphics in your documents. Inline images are those that appear within the page. External images can be viewed with external viewers that aren't a part of your browser. Most browsers support the JPEG and GIF graphic formats. If you use other formats, your users may not be able to view them unless they have the proper external viewer.

When adding graphics, keep two things in mind. Some users may not use a graphical browser. Other users may not have a fast enough modem or connection, or network traffic might slow down image loading. Remember that your text should be self-sufficient. Consider adding an alternate path from the top-level home page for these situations. For example,

```
<A HREF="charindx.htm">Click here if your viewer doesn't support
        graphics.</A>
```

INLINE IMAGES

The <IMG> tag inserts an inline graphic. This tag always requires a source attribute (SRC), which defines the URL of the file to insert. The URL can point to a file on any computer on the Internet, although it is probably safer to maintain inline graphic files locally, in case the other computer is inaccessible.

You can include two other attributes in the tag:

ALIGN
> Specifies how the graphics and/or text should align. The values are TOP, MIDDLE, and BOTTOM. They tell the browser to align nearby text with the top, middle, or bottom of the graphic.

ALT
> Defines some alternate text to display in case the browser cannot display graphics. This is important for users of non-graphical browsers such as Lynx.

Suppose you want to insert a photo of yourself and have some text line up with the bottom of the image. For users without graphical browsers, we'll display the line "[Photo of me]." Here is the tag:

```
<IMG SRC="mypic.gif" ALIGN=BOTTOM ALT="[Photo of me]">
```

Images appear with square outlines. It is possible to create images with translucent outlines, so that the background color of the document shows through. For information on creating and using translucent backgrounds, refer to the URL *http://melmac.corp.harris.com/transparent_images.html*.

You should always consider the browser limitations for web visitors. Some display only a certain number of colors. Mosaic for X Window Systems only allocates 50 colors for itself. Some Microsoft Windows users have a limit of 16 colors. If a browser tries to display more than the allotted number of colors, the results are unpredictable.

EXTERNAL IMAGES AND MULTIMEDIA

External images are images that appear to be part of a document, but are shown in a separate viewer. To include an external image in your document, enter the URL as you would for an external document. For example,

```
Click <A HREF="rugby.gif"> here</A> to see a picture of a rugby
        game.
```

An external image can be almost any format, as long as the browser recognizes it and knows which viewer to use for it.

External images are an easy way of inserting images in your document without having to convert it to GIF or XWD format. It is also a good way to point to an image on the Internet, since you point to a URL, and not a local file.

When the user requests an external image, the file is transferred to her local disk (usually to the TEMP directory). After the file is transferred, the browser starts the external viewer. The file is removed after exiting the viewer.

You can also use sound, animation, and other multimedia files if the user has an application that can translate the file. Some examples include WAV sound files, ANI and MOV animation files, etc.

CONTENT TYPES

How does a browser know what external viewer to use? When the user requests an external link, the server tries to determine the content type or MIME type of the file and sends that information to the browser. On WebSite, the server determines the content type from the file's extension. For example, *.gif* is a GIF file, *.wav* is a sound file, etc.

When the browser receives the content type, it determines how to display or play back that file to the user. Some content types, such as *text/html* or *text/plain* are read directly by the browser. For other types, the user must configure viewers for each type. Generally, when a file type isn't recognized, the browser asks the user to assign a viewer to the file type.

For more information on content types, see Chapter 9, *Mapping*.

USING GRAPHICS AS ANCHORS

A graphic can also be used as a hypertext link. For example,

```
<A HREF="regatta.htm"><IMG SRC="boats.gif" ALT="For a list of past
        winners of the River's Cup Milk Carton Regatta, click
        here."></A>
```

displays a picture of a boat. Clicking on the image displays the file *regatta.htm*.

Anchored graphics are used for providing custom buttons and navigation aids. For example, you might have users click on a picture of a product in a catalog in order to get a description of the item.

NOTE

Always provide an alternate anchor for users of character-based browsers.

Another use for graphic anchors is thumbnails. A thumbnail is a smaller version of an image. This way, users can see what they will be downloading. For example,

```
<A HREF="big_boat.gif"><IMG SRC="boat.gif"></A>
```

IMAGE MAPS

Clickable image maps let you designate specific areas of an image as the "hot spots" for action. For example, you could have a map of a city, with points of interest designated as the jumping off points to more information. When the user clicks on a designated area, she can zero in on that area.

In WebSite, use the Image Map Editor to create these images. For detailed information on image maps, see Chapter 7, *Working with Image Maps*.

Let's use HotDog to add images to a document. This lesson assumes that you have some .GIF or .JPG files in your system to use for images.

The first type of picture we'll create is called an In-Line Image. This is a picture that displays inside your document, but doesn't do anything. If the reader clicks on it, nothing will happen.

1. Start HotDog and open a new document.

2. Position the cursor at the point where you want to insert the image, then choose Image from the Insert Menu or click the Image button on the Button Bar. You will see the Insert Image dialog. If you want to use an image that you already have in your system, click the folder button and choose the file. If you want to link to an image on another system, click the hand button. This will let you create a hypertext link to the image.

3. Leave the Document To Launch field box blank, and click OK. HotDog will insert something like this:

   ```
   <IMG SRC="hr_brass.gif">
   ```

4. Preview your document to see the effects of this.

Now let's create an image that's also a hypertext link.

1. Position the cursor at the point where you want to insert the image, then choose Image from the Insert Menu or click the Image button on the Button Bar. You will see the Insert Image dialog. If you want to use an image that you already have in your system, click the folder button and choose the file. If you want to link to an image on another system, click the hand button. This will let you create a hypertext link to the image.

2. In the Document To Launch box, choose the document the user will be taken to when they follow the link. As with the image, this can be a file on the current system or an external link. If you've completed the Adding Hypertext Links tutorial, click the drop-down arrow at the right of this box. Some of the links you created in that tutorial will be listed.

3. When you enter something in the Document To Launch box, another box will appear for you to describe the link. If you fill this in, the image will have some text next to it, which the reader can also click on to follow the link. If you leave it blank, then only the image will be displayed.

4. When you choose OK, HotDog will insert something like this:

```
<A HREF="hotdog.htm"><IMG SRC="hotdog.gif"> Sausage Software</A>.
```

FORMS

A form in an HTML document lets the user enter some information and then call a program, located on a web server, that processes the information.

Suppose that as part of your home page you want to ask users for their opinions on its design. Or suppose you want to get their names and addresses so you can send them information about a product or service. HTML provides a special construct called a form. You can use forms to get information from users of your site. The data you receive is processed by programs run on your server. The technical term for this mechanism to run programs is the Common Gateway Interface, or CGI. See Chapters 15 through 18 of this book for information on writing your own CGI programs.

NOTE

For easy forms creation and processing of forms data (including email and database population), we recommend you use PolyForm from O'Reilly & Associates. Download a 60-day evaluation copy of PolyForm from O'Reilly Software Online (*http://software.ora.com/download/*).

DESIGNING FORMS

Before you start creating a form, spend some time planning and designing it. While forms are a very powerful tool, a poor design can adversely affect the way users see your site. Bad form design can make the difference between getting good information from users and no information at all. Here are a few simple rules for form design.

- Plan it out on paper. Take the time to sketch out how the form will look onscreen. The form should be balanced. That is, all elements such as text boxes, buttons, etc. should align. There should be a natural flow from one element to another. Don't make the user decide where to go next on the page—make the flow logical.

- Always tell the user *why* you are asking for information. Some users get suspicious when a form asks for more than an email address and a comment. Are you going to add the user to a mailing list? Will you be selling or exchanging information about the user? Will you be contacting the user in the future? Let the user know exactly what is going to happen when he submits the form.

- Give the user a way out. Always include a Reset button so that the user can clear information if he decides not to send you the information. Also, include a link to the appropriate page, such as the Home page and background information on the form.

- Help the user. Give instructions for the form on the form. Some users are new to computers and the Windows interface. If most of your target audience are novices, you may need to explain simple procedures such as using a selection box, filling out a multiple line text box, etc.

- Work closely with your CGI programmer. If you don't do the programming yourself, explain your design and what you expect to use the form for to the CGI programmer. Often, she can suggest a more efficient way of using the feature of a browser.

- Keep it simple! Avoid creating a form that is more than two pages or screens. The more questions you ask, the fewer users will complete and submit the form.

- Test, test, test. Always test your form before putting it on your server. Test with at least two different graphical browsers and one text-based browser, such as Lynx. Create sample data to test your CGI program. Test the response of the form with different modem speeds.

WRITING FORMS IN HTML

Forms are written in HTML with the expectation that the browser will properly parse the users' response and then send that response back to the Web server.

The form shown in Figure 5-7 is written with the following code:

```
<HTML><HEAD><TITLE>WebSite Guest Book</TITLE></HEAD>
<BODY><H1>WebSite Guest Book</H1>
Feel free to <A HREF="mailto:" & CGI_ServerAdmin & "">send me
        email</A>
<HR>
Thank you for taking the time to sign my guest book.
<FORM ACTION="/cgi-win/guestbk.exe" METHOD="POST">
<PRE>
Your name: <INPUT SIZE=25 NAME="name">
E-mail address: <INPUT SIZE=25 NAME="email">
Your system: <SELECT NAME="system">
    <OPTION SELECTED>Unix type
    <OPTION>Windows 3.x
    <OPTION>Windows NT
    <OPTION>Windows 95
    <OPTION>OS/2
```

```
    <OPTION>Macintosh
    <OPTION>Other
</SELECT>
Comment:           <INPUT SIZE=40 NAME="comments">
</PRE>
To register, press this button: <INPUT TYPE="submit"
VALUE="Sign Guest Book">
<HR>
</FORM></BODY></HTML>
```

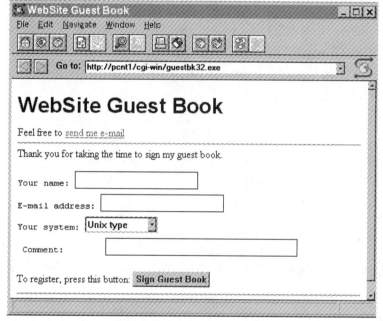

FIGURE 5-7: A SAMPLE FORM

You should already be familiar with many of the HTML codes such as <HTML>, <HEAD>, <TITLE>, <BODY>, <H1>, <A>, <PRE>, and <HR>. The other codes are all specific to defining forms.

INITIALIZING THE FORM

A form is started using the HTML <FORM> tag and closed with the </FORM> tag. Within a form, any HTML code is legal, with the exception that you cannot embed one form inside another.

The guest book form shown in Figure 5-7 is initiated with the following lines:

```
<FORM ACTION="/cgi-win/guestbk32.exe" METHOD="POST">
```

The <FORM> tag has two attributes that you need to pay special attention to:

ACTION
> The action to take when the form is completed (i.e., the name of the CGI program). The default is the current URL.

METHOD
> The method used to transfer data to the CGI program. The available methods are GET and POST (GET is the default, but POST is recommended).

WARNING

We strongly recommend that you use the POST method to transfer data. If you are using any 16-bit applications to process the CGI (Visual Basic 3, Visual Basic 4 (16-bit) or the current version of DELPHI), there is a limit to the length of the command line that can be passed. If the command line passes this limit, it is truncated, and your program will fail.

The program that the form sends its data to is */cgi-win/guestbk32.exe*, using the Windows CGI. The method is defined as POST.

SIMPLE TEXT INPUT, CHECKBOXES, AND SUBMISSIONS

The INPUT tag supplies an input field to the user. For example, the line prompting for the user's name in Figure 5-7 reads:

```
Your name: <INPUT SIZE=25 NAME="name">
```

The string "Your name:" is the prompt printed before the input field. The <INPUT> tag contains the SIZE attribute to set the size of the input field to 25 units, and the NAME attribute to define the name of the variable that the user's response is stored in. The attributes supported by the <INPUT> tag are:

TYPE
> The type of input, described below.

NAME
> The variable name for the value returned in the input field.

VALUE
> The default value that is placed in the variable.

CHECKED
> Whether a checkbox or radio button should be checked initially.

SIZE
> The size of text and password input fields. The default is 20.

MAXLENGTH
>The maximum number of characters accepted as input for text and password fields.

No "type" of input field is specified in the example above, so it uses the default type, TEXT. An equivalent INPUT tag might read:

```
Your name: <INPUT TYPE="TEXT" SIZE=25 NAME="name">
```

In addition to regular text, there are several other input types that you can specify using the TYPE attribute.

TEXT INPUT

TYPE=TEXT

A text entry field (the default). Figure 5-8 displays a sample text input field.

FIGURE 5-8: TEXT INPUT FIELD

Additional attributes you can specify for TEXT input types are:

NAME
>You must specify a NAME attribute for text input, specifying the name of the parameter with which to associate the user's input. For example, if you specify NAME="first_name" and the user enters "John," the CGI program is passed the string "first_name=John".

VALUE
>An initial value to place in the text input box. For example:

```
<INPUT TYPE=TEXT NAME="username" VALUE="anonymous">
```

SIZE
>An alternate size for the input box.

MAXLENGTH
>The maximum number of characters accepted as input. By default, there is no limit.

PASSWORD INPUT

TYPE=PASSWORD

A text entry field in which the input is echoed back as asterisks (useful when prompting for passwords). Figure 5-9 displays a sample password input field.

Additional attributes you can specify for PASSWORD input types are:

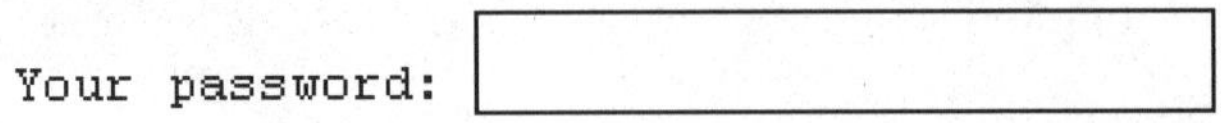

Your password:

FIGURE 5-9: PASSWORD INPUT FIELD

NAME

You must specify a NAME attribute for text input, specifying the name of the parameter with which to associate the user's input. For example, if you specify `NAME="password"` and the user enters `"notobvious,"` the CGI program is passed the string `"password=notobvious"`.

VALUE

An initial value to place in the text input box (i.e., a default password).

SIZE

An alternate size for the input box.

MAXLENGTH

The maximum number of characters accepted as input. By default, there is no limit.

CHECKBOXES

TYPE=CHECKBOX

A single toggle button, generally a small box that can be checked on or off. The value returned into the NAME variable is "on" if the box is checked; no value is returned if the box is left unchecked. Figure 5-10 displays a sample checkbox input field.

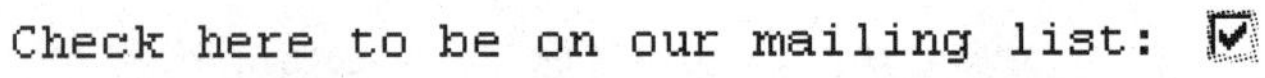

Check here to be on our mailing list: ☑

FIGURE 5-10: CHECKBOX INPUT FIELD

Additional attributes you can specify for CHECKBOX input types are:

NAME

You must specify a NAME attribute for checkboxes, specifying the name of the parameter with which to associate the user's input. For example, if you specify `NAME="send_catalog"` and the user checks the box, the CGI program is passed the string `"send_catalog=on"`.

VALUE

The string returned if the checkbox is checked (instead of "on"). For example:

```
<INPUT TYPE=CHECKBOX NAME="send_catalog" VALUE="yes">
```

CHECKED

Whether the box should be checked initially or not. For example:

```
<INPUT TYPE=CHECKBOX NAME="send_catalog" VALUE="yes" CHECKED>
```

In writing forms, beware that some older Web browsers may not recognize check-boxes, and instead treat them like text input.

RADIO BUTTONS

TYPE=RADIO

A single toggle button similar to a checkbox, but meant to be combined with other radio buttons. When multiple radio buttons each use the same NAME variable, only one can be selected at a time. Additional attributes you can specify for RADIO input types are:

NAME
> You must specify a NAME attribute for radio buttons, specifying the name of the parameter with which to associate the user's input. The NAME attribute must be identical for each radio button.

VALUE
> The string returned if the checkbox is checked (instead of "on"). In order for radio buttons to be useful, you must specify a different VALUE for each button.

CHECKED
> Whether the box should be checked initially or not. You can only have one box checked initially.

For example:

```
What is your annual household income?
      Under $15,000   <INPUT TYPE="RADIO" NAME="income"   VALUE="0-
         15">
   $15,000 to $24,999   <INPUT TYPE="RADIO" NAME="income" VALUE="15-
         25">
   $25,000 to $39,999   <INPUT TYPE="RADIO" NAME="income" VALUE="25-
         40">
   $40,000 to $59,999   <INPUT TYPE="RADIO" NAME="income" VALUE="40-
         60">
      Over $60,000   <INPUT TYPE="RADIO" NAME="income"
         VALUE="60+">
 None of our business   <INPUT TYPE="RADIO" NAME="income"
          VALUE="NOYB" CHECKED>
```

The resulting output might appear as in Figure 5-11.

In writing forms, beware that some older Web browsers may not recognize radio buttons, and instead treat them like text input.

SUBMIT BUTTONS

TYPE=SUBMIT

```
What is your annual household income?
                Under $15,000   ○
        $15,000 to $24,999       ○
        $25,000 to $39,999       ○
        $40,000 to $59,999       ○
                Over $60,000     ○
      None of our business       ◉
```

FIGURE 5-11: RADIO BUTTONS

A button that, when pressed, causes the form to be sent to the target URL speci-fied on the <FORM> tag. Figure 5-12 shows a typical Submit button.

An additional attribute you can specify with SUBMIT buttons is:

VALUE
> The string to display. Without a specified VALUE, you use the default value of the browser (e.g., "Submit" or "Submit Form").

FIGURE 5-12: SUBMIT BUTTON

IMAGE SUBMISSIONS

TYPE=IMAGE

Similar to SUBMIT, only instead of displaying a "Submit" button it displays an image. Additional attributes you can specify with IMAGE buttons are:

SRC
> The actual URL of the target image is specified using the SRC attribute to <INPUT>. You must specify an SRC attribute with every IMAGE type. For example, if you have a cute GIF icon for people to click on to submit their form, called GO.gif:
>
> ```
> <INPUT TYPE=IMAGE SRC="/images/GO.gif">
> ```

ALIGN
> The alignment of the image. This attribute takes the same values of an ALIGN attribute to the <IMG> tag: TOP, MIDDLE, and BOTTOM.

NAME
> The name to assign the image submission.

You can use an image submission like an image map. In addition to submitting the form, the coordinates of the pointer's position on the image are transmitted to the browser in the form x=mm and y=nn, or name.x=mm and name.y=nn if a name was assigned with the NAME attribute. A CGI program might use this to behave differently depending on where on the image the user clicks. For example, the image might be a series of buttons, and the program might know which coordinates correspond to which buttons and behave differently accordingly.

RESET BUTTONS

TYPE=RESET

A button that, when pressed, causes all fields in the form to be set to their default values.

An additional attribute you can specify with RESET buttons is:

VALUE
> The string to display. Without a specified VALUE, you use the default value of the browser (e.g., "Reset" or "Clear").

FIGURE 5-13: RESET BUTTON

HIDDEN

TYPE=HIDDEN

No button or text area is shown. Instead, a "hidden" input field just gives you a way to send any additional parameter to the CGI program, invisible to the user. For example, if you wanted to turn on a flag for the CGI program from the form itself:

```
<INPUT TYPE=HIDDEN NAME="debug" VALUE="on">
```

In writing forms, beware that some older Web browsers may not recognize the hidden input type, and will instead treat it like text input.

The attributes to specify with HIDDEN input types are:

NAME
> The name of the parameter.

VALUE
> The value to assign the parameter.

CGI programs can use hidden fields to transfer information from one program to another. For example, suppose a user types her name in one form, and the CGI program then hands her a second, follow-up form. The second form can retain the user's name in a hidden field so the user doesn't have to supply it again.

SELECTION BOXES

A <SELECT> tag allows the user to select from a menu of choices. It is similar to a radio box selection, but slightly more elegant, more flexible, and easier to code.

<SELECT> starts a menu selection, and </SELECT> ends one. Between the two delimiters, only <OPTION> tags are allowed, each followed by short strings to be included as menu items. This is the code for asking the user to specify what sort of system she uses. The output is shown in Figures 5-14 and 5-15.

```
Your system: <SELECT NAME="system">
    <OPTION SELECTED>Unix type
    <OPTION>Windows 3.x
    <OPTION>Windows NT
    <OPTION>Windows 95
    <OPTION>OS/2
    <OPTION>Macintosh
    <OPTION>Other
 </SELECT>
```

When you first open the form, you'll see it as:

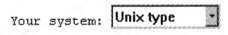

FIGURE 5-14: SELECTION BOX

To see the full menu, press the mouse button on the down-arrow button.

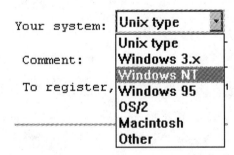

FIGURE 5-15: A FULL SELECTION BOX MENU

The attributes to SELECT are:

NAME
   The variable name for the value selected. This attribute must be included in all SELECT tags.

SIZE

Determines how many items will be visible at a time. The default is 1.

MULTIPLE

Allows multiple selections. When you specify a multiple selection, the appearance of the selection box changes to display multiple items at once, depending on the browser. For example, the selection box may appear as a scrollable list.

The <OPTION> tag accepts two attributes:

SELECTED

Select this option as default. If the MULTIPLE attribute has been specified to the SELECT tag, then multiple options can be specified as selected.

VALUE

The value to return if the option is selected. By default, the value returned is the option text.

MULTIPLE-LINE TEXT INPUT

Occasionally, you might want to allow the user to write more than one line of input, for example, when asking for comments. For that, use the <TEXTAREA> tag.

<TEXTAREA> gives you an entry field with the requested number of rows and columns and a scrollbar. There is no limit to the amount of text you can enter into a text area. The only caveat is that if you think users may supply long blocks of text, you should be sure to use the POST method with your form.

Since you may want to provide default text, the <TEXTAREA> tag requires both opening and closing tags. For example:

```
Please tell us what you think of us.
<TEXTAREA NAME="comments" ROWS=5 COLS=40>(No comment.)</TEXTAREA>
```

The resulting text box is shown in Figure 5-16.

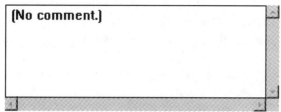

FIGURE 5-16: A TEXTAREA FIELD

In many (if not most) cases, you will choose not to supply any default text, so the ending tag will come immediately after the opening tag.

The attributes to the <TEXTAREA> tag are:

NAME
> The variable name given to the contents of the text area
> (Note that all newlines are retained.)

ROWS
> The number of rows of the text entry field

COLS
> The number of columns of the text entry field

USING HOTDOG TO CREATE FORMS

You can create a form with any text editor, or you can use the HotDog software provided with WebSite. HotDog comes with a set of menus and dialog boxes to help you create forms.

To create a form, click on the Form button or choose Form Element from the Insert menu. HotDog displays the dialog box shown in Figure 5-17.

You will be asked to choose what sort of form element you want to create. Choose a form element in the Form Item area, and then enter its properties in the Properties area. The specific properties you can modify depend on what type of element you want to insert. If this is the first form element in your document, when you choose OK you will be taken to the Create Form screen (Figure 5-18).

NOTE

> The Forms screen remains visible when you press OK. This is so that you can create a form with multiple elements without having to reload the screen each time.

The Create Form screen specifies attributes for the entire form. These are:

Method
> This may be either GET or POST. This depends on what you want to do with the form, and the setup of your server. We recommend that you use the POST method.

URL to Send Data to (Action)
> The ACTION attribute is the URL that will process the form data. Generally, this will be a CGI program, but can be any valid Internet resource. For example, you could use *mailto:sales@ora.com* as your Action URL.

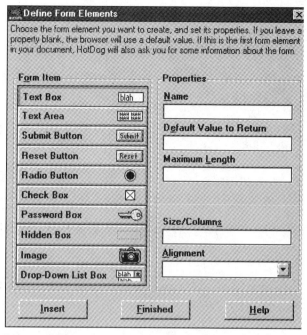

FIGURE 5-17: THE DEFINE FORM ELEMENTS DIALOG BOX

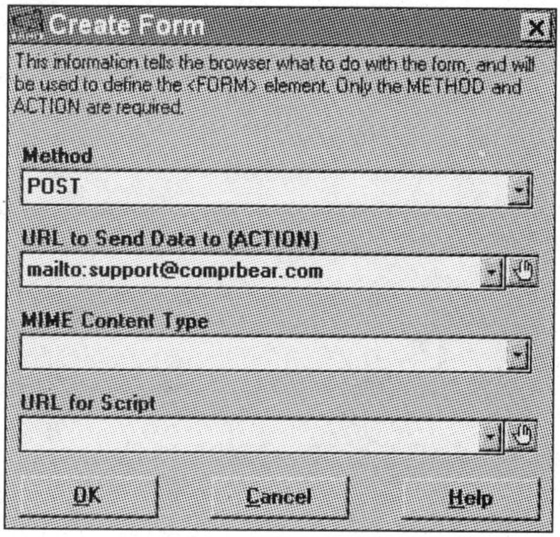

FIGURE 5-18: THE CREATE FORM DIALOG BOX

MIME Content Type

Specifies the MIME encoding for the form. This will vary depending on what the form does and how it works. The MIME Content Type is not required.

URL for Script (HTML 3)
This lets you specify the URL for scripts that will be downloaded to the user's machine and processed locally.

When you are finished creating your form, you can preview it with your browser.

TESTING FORMS

If you've written a form and would like to test the values it generates independent of the CGI program meant to process it, you can test the form easily by following these steps:

- Change the form's ACTION attribute to call the URL */cgi-win/cgitest.exe/Form*.
- Make sure the form is using the METHOD=POST attribute.

For example, suppose you have the following form in a document:

```
<form method=GET action="/cgi-bin/webfind.exe">
Type your keywords here:<input name=keywords size=50>
<p>
<input type=submit value="Find Documents">
<input type=reset value="Clear">
</form>
```

If you want to ensure that the "keyword" parameter is properly receiving the correct input, you can change the first line as follows:

```
<form method=POST action="/cgi-win/cgitest.exe/Form">
```

Now load the document in your browser (or reload, if it was already loaded), and enter data into the fields. When you press the submit button, your form is sent to the special *cgitest.exe* program written for the Windows CGI. (It doesn't matter if your form was meant to run with a Standard CGI program, you can still test it with the Windows CGI.) You'll receive a report listing each parameter and the values entered on the form.

You can use this feature for testing forms. For example, it can help in situations when you may not be sure if the reason your program isn't working is because of an error in the form or because of the CGI program being called.

HTML QUICK REFERENCE

Following is a quick reference to HTML tags. For complete information on HTML tags and examples, please see the online Help for the HotDog Web Editor.

DOCUMENT STRUCTURE ELEMENTS

These elements are required within an HTML document.

- <HTML> ... </HTML>
- <HEAD> ... </HEAD>
- <BODY> ... </BODY>

In order to identify a document as HTML, each HTML document should start with the prologue:

```
<!DOCTYPE HTML PUBLIC "-//IETF//DTD HTML//EN//2.0">.
```

<HTML> ... </HTML>

This element identifies the document as containing HTML elements. It should immediately follow the prologue_document identifier and serves to surround all of the remaining text, including all other elements. That is, the document should be constructed thus :

```
<!DOCTYPE HTML PUBLIC "-//IETF//DTD HTML//EN//2.0">
<HTML>
Here is all the rest of the document, including any elements.
</HTML>
```

The HTML element is not visible upon HTML user agent rendering and can contain only the <HEAD> and <BODY> elements.

<HEAD> ... </HEAD>

The head of an HTML document is an unordered collection of information about the document. It requires the Title element between <HEAD> and </HEAD> elements thus:

```
<HEAD>
<TITLE> Introduction to HTML </TITLE>
</HEAD>
```

The <HEAD> and </HEAD> elements do not directly affect the look of the document when rendered.

<TITLE> ... </TITLE>

Every HTML document must have a Title element. The title should identify the contents of the document in a global context, and may be used in history lists and as a label for the windows displaying the document. Unlike headings, titles are not typically rendered in the text of a document itself.

The Title element must occur within the head of the document and may not contain anchors, paragraph elements, or highlighting. Only one title is allowed in a document.

NOTE

The length of a title is not limited, however, long titles may be truncated in some applications. To minimize the possibility, titles should be fewer than 64 characters. Also keep in mind that a short title, such as "Introduction" may be meaningless out of context. An example of a meaningful title might be 'Introduction to HTML elements.'

This is the only element that is required within the Head element. The other elements described are optional and can be implemented when appropriate

```
<HEAD>
<TITLE> Introduction to HTML </TITLE>
</HEAD>
```

<BODY> ... </BODY>

The body of an HTML document contains all the text and images that make up the page, together with all the HTML elements that provide the control/formatting of the page. The format is:

```
<BODY>
The document included here
</BODY>
```

The <BODY> and </BODY> elements do not directly affect the look of the document when rendered, although they are required in order for the document to conform to the specification standard.

<BASE...>

The Base element allows the URL of the document itself to be recorded in situations in which the document may be read out of context. URLs within the document may be in a "partial" form relative to this base address.

Where the base address is not specified, the HTML browser uses the URL it used to access the document to resolve any relative URLs.

The Base element has one attribute, HREF, which identifies the URL.

<ISINDEX...>

The ISINDEX element tells the HTML user agent that the document is an index document. As well as reading it, the reader may use a keyword search.

The document can be queried with a keyword search by adding a question mark to the end of the document address, followed by a list of keywords separated by plus signs.

NOTE

The ISINDEX element is usually generated automatically by a server. If added manually to an HTML document, the HTML user agent assumes that the server can handle a search on the document. To use the ISINDEX element, the server must have a search engine that supports this element.

<LINK...>

The Link element indicates a relationship between the document and some other object. A document may have any number of Link elements.

The Link element is empty (does not have a closing element), but takes the same attributes as the Anchor element.

Typical uses are to indicate authorship, related indexes and glossaries, older or more recent versions, etc. Links can indicate a static tree structure in which the document was authored by pointing to a "parent" and "next" and "previous" document, for example.

Servers may also allow links to be added by those who do not have the right to alter the body of a document.

<NEXTID...>

The NEXTID element is a parameter read and generated by text editing software to create unique identifiers.

```
<NEXTID N=Z127>
```

When modifying a document, existing anchor identifiers should not be reused, as these identifiers may be referenced by other documents. Human writers of HTML usually use mnemonic alphabetic identifiers. HTML user agents may ignore the NEXTID element. Support for the NEXTID element does not impact HTML user agents in any way.

BLOCK FORMATTING ELEMENTS

Block formatting elements are used for the formatting of whole blocks of text within an HTML document, rather than single characters. They should all (if present) be within the body of the document.

The essential block formatting elements are:

- <ADDRESS> ... </ADDRESS>—Format an address section

- <H1> ... </H1>—Format six levels of heading
- <HR>—Render a hard line on the page
-
—Force a line break
- <P>... </P>—Specify what text constitutes a paragraph
- <PRE> ... </PRE>—Use text already formatted
- <BLOCKQUOTE> ... </BLOCKQUOTE>—Quote text from another source

<ADDRESS> ... </ADDRESS>

The Address element specifies such information as address, signature, and authorship, often at the top or bottom of a document.

Typically, an Address is rendered in an italic typeface and may be indented. The Address element implies a paragraph break before and after.

<H1> ... </H1> HEADINGS

HTML defines six levels of heading. A Heading element implies all the font changes, paragraph breaks before and after, and whitespace necessary to render the heading.

The highest level of heading is <H1>, followed by <H2> ... <H6>.

<HR>

A Horizontal Rule element is a divider between sections of text such as a full-width horizontal rule or equivalent graphic.

The Line Break element specifies that a new line must be started at the given point. A new line indents the same as that of line-wrapped text.

<P> ... </P>

The Paragraph element indicates a paragraph. The exact indentation, leading, etc. of a paragraph is not defined and may be a function of other elements, style sheets, etc.

Typically, paragraphs are surrounded by a vertical space of one line or half a line. This is typically not the case within the Address element and is never the case within the Preformatted Text element. With some HTML user agents, the first line in a paragraph is indented.

<PRE> ... </PRE>

The Preformatted Text element presents blocks of text in fixed-width font and so is suitable for text that has been formatted on screen.

The <PRE> element may be used with the optional WIDTH attribute, which is a Level 1 feature. The WIDTH attribute specifies the maximum number of characters for a line and allows the HTML user agent to select a suitable font and indentation. If the WIDTH attribute is not present, a width of 80 characters is assumed. Where the WIDTH attribute is supported, widths of 40, 80, and 132 characters should be presented optimally, with other widths being rounded up.

Within preformatted text:

- Line breaks within the text are rendered as a move to the beginning of the next line.

- The <P> element should not be used. If found, it should be rendered as a move to the beginning of the next line.

- Anchor elements and character highlighting elements may be used.

- Elements that define paragraph formatting (headings, address, etc.) must not be used.

- The horizontal tab character (encoded in US-ASCII and ISO-8859-1 as decimal 9) must be interpreted as the smallest positive non-zero number of spaces that will leave the number of characters so far on the line as a multiple of 8. Its use is not recommended, however.

NOTE

References to the "beginning of a new line" do not imply that the renderer is forbidden from using a constant left indent for rendering preformatted text. The left indent may be constrained by the width required.

<BLOCKQUOTE> ... </BLOCKQUOTE>

The BLOCKQUOTE element is used to contain text quoted from another source.

A typical rendering might be a slight extra left and right indent, and/or italic font. The BLOCKQUOTE element causes a paragraph break, and typically provides space above and below the quote.

Single-font rendition may reflect the quotation style of Internet mail by putting a vertical line of graphic characters, such as the greater than symbol (>), in the left margin.

<A...> ... </A> ANCHOR

An Anchor element is a marked text that is the start and/or destination of a hypertext link. Anchor elements are defined by the <A> element. The <A> element accepts several attributes, but either the NAME or HREF attribute is required.

LIST ELEMENTS

HTML supports several types of lists, all of which may be nested. If used they should be present in the body of an HTML document.

- <DL>... </DL>—Definition list.
- <DIR> ... </DIR>—Directory list
- <MENU> ... </MENU>—Menu list
- <OL> ... </OL>—Ordered list
- <UL> ... </UL>—Unordered list

<DL> ... </DL>

A definition list is a list of terms and corresponding definitions. Definition lists are typically formatted with the term flush-left and the definition, formatted paragraph style, indented after the term.

The opening list element must be <DL> and must be immediately followed by the first definition term (<DT>).

If the <DT> term does not fit in the <DT> column (one third of the display area), it may be extended across the page with the definition <DD> section moved to the next line, or it may be wrapped onto successive lines of the left-hand column.

Single occurrences of a <DT> element without a subsequent <DD> element are allowed, and have the same significance as if the <DD> element had been present with no text.

The definition list type can take the COMPACT attribute, which suggests that a compact rendering be used, because the list items are small and/or the entire list is large.

Unless you provide the COMPACT attribute, the HTML user agent may leave white space between successive <DT>, <DD> pairs. The COMPACT attribute may also reduce the width of the left-hand (<DT>) column.

If using the COMPACT attribute, the opening list element must be <DL COMPACT>, which must be immediately followed by the first <DT> element:

<DIR> ... </DIR>

A Directory List element is used to present a list of items containing up to 20 characters each. Items in a directory list may be arranged in columns, typically 24 characters wide. If the HTML user agent can optimize the column width as a function of the widths of individual elements, so much the better.

A directory list must begin with the <DIR> element, which is immediately followed by a <LI> (list item) element.

<MENU> ... </MENU>

A menu list is a list of items with typically one line per item. The menu list style is more compact than the style of an unordered list.

A menu list must begin with a <MENU> element, which is immediately followed by a <LI> (list item) element.

<OL> ... </OL>

The Ordered List element is used to present a numbered list of items, sorted by sequence or order of importance.

An ordered list must begin with the <OL> element, which is immediately followed by a <LI> (list item) element.

The Ordered List element can take the COMPACT attribute, which suggests that a compact rendering be used.

<UL> ... </UL>

The Unordered List element is used to present a list of items that is typically separated by whitespace and/or marked by bullets.

An unordered list must begin with the <UL> element, which is immediately followed by a <LI> (list item) element.

The Unordered List element can take the COMPACT attribute, which suggests that a compact rendering be used.

INFORMATION TYPE AND CHARACTER FORMATTING ELEMENTS

The following information type and character formatting elements are supported in the HTML 2.0 specification

- <CITE> ... </CITE>—Citation
- <CODE> ... </CODE>—An example of Code

- <EM> ... </EM>—Emphasis
- <KBD> ... </KBD>—User typed text
- <SAMP> ... </SAMP>—A sequence of literal characters
- <STRONG> ... </STRONG>—Strong typographic emphasis
- <VAR> ... </VAR>—Indicates a variable name

NOTE

Different information type elements may be rendered in the same way. For example, STRONG formatting may display the same as BOLD formatting.

Character formatting elements include:

- <B>... </B>—Boldface type
- <I>... </I>—Italics
- <TT>... </TT>—TypeType (or Teletype)

Character-level elements are used to specify either the logical meaning or the physical appearance of marked text without causing a paragraph break. Like most other elements, character-level elements include both opening and closing elements. Only the characters between the elements are affected:

```
This is <EM>emphasized</EM> text.
```

Character-level elements are interpreted from left to right as they appear in the flow of text. Level 1 HTML user agents must render highlighted text distinctly from plain text. Additionally, <EM> content must be rendered as distinct from <STRONG> content, and <B> content must rendered as distinct from <I> content.

Character-level elements may be nested within the content of other character-level elements; however, HTML user agents are not required to render nested character-level elements distinctly from non-nested elements:

```
plain <B>bold <I>italic</I></B>
may be rendered the same as

plain <B>bold </B><I>italic</I>
```

<CITE> ... </CITE>

The Citation element specifies a citation; typically rendered as italic.

<CODE> ... </CODE>

The Code element indicates an example of code; typically rendered as monospaced. Do not confuse with the Preformatted Text element.

<EM> ... </EM>

The Emphasis element indicates typographic emphasis, typically rendered as italic.

<KBD> ... </KBD>

The Keyboard element indicates text typed by a user; typically rendered as mono-spaced. It might commonly be used in an instruction manual.

<SAMP> ... </SAMP>

The Sample element indicates a sequence of literal characters; typically rendered as monospaced.

<STRONG> ... </STRONG>

The Strong element indicates strong typographic emphasis, typically rendered in bold.

<VAR> ... </VAR>

The Variable element indicates a variable name; typically rendered as italic.

<B> ... </B>

The Bold element specifies that the text should be rendered in boldface, where available. Otherwise, alternative mapping is allowed.

<I> ... </I>

The Italic element specifies that the text should be rendered in italic font, where available. Otherwise, alternative mapping is allowed.

<TT> ... </TT>

The Teletype element specifies that the text should be rendered in fixed-width typewriter font.

<IMG...> IN-LINE IMAGES

The Image element is used to incorporate in-line graphics (typically icons or small graphics) into an HTML document. This element cannot be used for embedding other HTML text.

The Image element, which is empty (no closing element), has these attributes:

ALIGN
     The ALIGN attribute accepts the values TOP, MIDDLE, or BOTTOM, which

specifies if the following line of text is aligned with the top, middle, or bottom of the graphic.

ALT

Optional text as an alternative to the graphic for rendering in non-graphical environments. Alternate text should be provided whenever the graphic is not rendered. Alternate text is mandatory for Level 0 documents.

ISMAP

The ISMAP (is map) attribute identifies an image as an image map. Image maps are graphics in which certain regions are mapped to URLs. By clicking on different regions, different resources can be accessed from the same graphic.

SRC

The value of the SRC attribute is the URL of the document to be embedded; only images can be embedded, not HTML text. Its syntax is the same as that of the HREF attribute of the <A> element. SRC is mandatory. Image elements are allowed within anchors.

FORMS

The inclusion of the Form elements, allowing user input/feedback on HTML documents, was the major difference between the HTML specification 2.0 and its predecessors.

They are created by placing input fields within paragraphs, preformatted/literal text and lists. This gives considerable flexibility in designing the layout of forms.

The following elements are used to create forms:

- <FORM> ... </FORM>—A form within a document
- <INPUT...> ... </INPUT>—One input field
- <OPTION...>—One option within a Select element.
- <SELECT...> ... </SELECT>—A selection from a finite set of options
- <TEXTAREA...> ... </TEXTAREA>—A multi-line input field

Each variable field is defined by an INPUT, TEXTAREA, or OPTION element and must have a NAME attribute to identify its value in the data returned when the form is submitted.

Many platforms have existing conventions for forms, for example, using Tab and Shift keys to move the keyboard focus forwards and backwards between fields, and using the Enter key to submit the form. Generally, the SUBMIT and RESET buttons are specified explicitly with special purpose fields. The SUBMIT button is often used to email the form or send its contents to the server as specified by the ACTION attribute, while RESET resets the fields to their initial values. When the form consists of a single text field, it may be appropriate to leave such buttons out and rely on the Enter key.

The Input element is used for a large variety of types of input fields. To let users enter more than one line of text, use the TEXTAREA element.

<FORM> ... </FORM>

The Form element is used to delimit a data input form. There can be several forms in a single document, but the Form element can't be nested.

The ACTION attribute is a URL specifying the location to which the contents of the form is submitted to elicit a response. If the ACTION attribute is missing, the URL of the document itself is assumed.

<INPUT...> ... </INPUT>

The Input element represents a field whose contents may be edited by the user. Here are the attributes of the Input element:

ALIGN
> Vertical alignment of the image. For use only with TYPE=IMAGE in HTML level 2. The possible values are exactly the same as for the ALIGN attribute of the image element.

CHECKED
> Indicates that a checkbox or radio button is selected. Unselected checkboxes and radio buttons do not return name/value pairs when the form is submitted.

MAXLENGTH
> Indicates the maximum number of characters that can be entered into a text field. This can be greater than specified by the SIZE attribute, in which case the field will scroll appropriately. The default number of characters is unlimited.

NAME
> Symbolic name used when transferring the form's contents. The NAME attribute is required for most input types and is normally used to provide a unique identifier for a field, or for a logically related group of fields.

SIZE
> Specifies the size or precision of the field according to its type. For example, to specify a field with a visible width of 24 characters: INPUT TYPE=text SIZE="24".

SRC
> A URL or URN specifying an image. For use only with TYPE=IMAGE in HTML Level 2.

TYPE
> Defines the type of data the field accepts. Defaults to free text.

VALUE
> The initial displayed value of the field, if it displays a textual or numerical value; or the value to be returned when the field is selected, if it displays a Boolean value. This attribute is required for radio buttons.

<OPTION...>

The Option element can only occur within a Select element. It represents one choice, and can take these attributes:

DISABLED
> Proposed, may not yet be part of the Standard.

SELECTED
> Indicates that this option is initially selected.

VALUE
> When present, indicates the value to be returned if this option is chosen. The returned value defaults to the contents of the Option element.

The contents of the Option element is presented to the user to represent the option. It is used as a returned value if the VALUE attribute is not present.

<SELECT...> ... </SELECT>

The Select element allows the user to chose one of a set of alternatives described by textual labels. Every alternative is represented by the Option element. Attributes are:

ERROR
> Proposed, may not yet be part of the Standard.

MULTIPLE
> The MULTIPLE attribute is needed when users are allowed to make several selections, e.g., <SELECT MULTIPLE>.

NAME
> Specifies the name that will be submitted as a name/value pair.

SIZE
> Specifies the number of visible items. If this is greater than one, then the resulting form control will be a list.

The Select element is typically rendered as a pull-down or pop-up list

If no option is initially marked as selected, then the first item listed is selected.

<TEXTAREA...> ... </TEXTAREA>

The Textarea element lets users enter more than one line of text.

The text up to the End element (`</TEXTAREA>`) is used to initialize the field's value. This End element is always required even if the field is initially blank. When submitting a form, lines in a Textarea should be terminated using CR/LF.

In a typical rendering, the ROWS and COLS attributes determine the visible dimension of the field in characters. The field is rendered in a fixed-width font. HTML user agents should allow text to extend beyond these limits by scrolling as needed.

The WRAP attribute changes word wrap. The default is OFF. Other values can be VIRTUAL, displays wordwraps with no breaks where the line is wrapped or PHYSICAL, which displays text with line breaks.

<!-- COMMENTS -->

To include comments in an HTML document that will be ignored by the HTML user agent, surround them with <!-- and -->. After the comment delimiter, all text up to the next occurrence of --> is ignored. Hence comments cannot be nested. White space is allowed between the closing -- and >, but not between the opening <! and --.

CHAPTER SIX

INDEXING AND SEARCHING YOUR DOCUMENTS

Suppose you have a large collection of documents on your Web server. How can you make it easy for users to find the documents they want without having to navigate a series of hyperlinks? A convenient way to sort through large amounts of information is through free-text keyword searches.

You could enable keyword searching by allowing users to search files directly. However, if every search request required opening and searching multiple files, the searches might take a very long time. Instead, keyword searches in WebSite have been streamlined by separating the process into two parts: the WebSite administrator creates a keyword index for specific files, and users search the *index* rather than the files. This process makes searches more efficient; since all keywords are already indexed, the user doesn't have to wait while each file is opened and searched.

WebSite accomplishes this two-part process with the tools WebIndex and WebFind. WebIndex is the WebSite administrator's tool for creating one or more keyword indexes of all or part of the web. With WebIndex you can set preferences for what types of files should be indexed by content or only by name. You can also specify a list of commonly-used words to ignore or give the program general parameters to determine its own list of commonly used words to ignore. If you have a very large web to index (such as an ongoing archive of articles or policies), you can create multiple indexes and merge them into one large one.

Users will find searching your web easy with WebFind, a forms-based CGI program that lets them enter single or multiple search strings and other parameters. The WebFind search generates an HTML page with each match listed as a hyperlink. You can use the standard WebFind form or create your own form using the FindForm wizard, available through WebView.

This chapter first describes how to create and maintain indexes with WebIndex. Next it shows you how WebFind works and how to create your own custom search forms with the FindForm wizard. Finally, it discusses using WebIndex and WebFind from the command line, which is useful for generating indexes during low-usage hours using the scheduler service under Windows NT or a System Agent under Windows 95 (available from the Windows 95 Plus! Package).

If you are running virtual servers under WebSite, see Chapter 10, *Virtual Servers and WebSite*, for specific tips on using WebIndex and WebFind in an environment with multiple identities.

NOTE

If you are upgrading from WebSite 1.0, you will find many new and exciting features in WebIndex and WebFind. However, you must regenerate the index you created under WebSite 1.0, an easy process since WebIndex remembers which URLs you previously included in an index.

WHY INDEX?

Adding search capability to your web gives your users a powerful way to find and use the information on your server. Instead of wading through multiple layers of hyperlinks and (maybe!) finding the appropriate document, users can simply request a specific piece of information and let WebSite do the work. Using WebIndex also saves you the time and effort of setting up and maintaining such a hyperlink hierarchy.

To determine if creating an index and adding searching to your web is practical (it *is* easy), here are a couple of examples. These situations also highlight the new capabilities of WebIndex and provide ideas for improving your web's current search capability if you are upgrading from WebSite 1.0.

SITUATION

You have set up WebSite for a history magazine, which has archives of articles for the past 15 years. The magazine is published six times a year with a special semi-annual issue dedicated to California history. You'd like to make the archives available to your subscribers, editors, and other qualified researchers.

SOLUTION

For a full keyword index of the contents, you must *first* convert the articles to HTML or ASCII (and save the ASCII files with a standard extension, such as *.txt*). Next, to streamline searches, organize the articles from the main publication by year. Finally, create an index for each year. For example, all articles published in 1994 would be in an index called *1994 Articles*. To allow specialized searches of the California issues, keep those articles in a separate location and create a California history index called *California*. You can also create a master index by merging the smaller indexes (each year and the California index) into one. Users can select which index to use from the custom search form you create using the FindForm wizard.

SITUATION

You are running WebSite internally at your company and want to make human resources policies and forms available to all employees. You don't want to convert the files, which exist as Word for Windows files, to text or HTML. In fact, one goal of making these native files available on your internal web is to enable users to download and integrate them into other documents. The files are named either by policy number or a two-letter topic code. Employees may or may not be familiar with the naming scheme.

SOLUTION

WebIndex allows you to index filenames as well as contents, preventing the need for costly and (in this case) unnecessary conversions. Simply tell WebIndex to index only the filenames for files with the *.doc* extension. These documents can be located anywhere in your web's URL space; that means you can maintain your current physical organization of policy documents but include them all in the search results. (Of course, you can also create multiple indexes if that makes sense for the information.) Since filenames based on policy numbers or two-letter codes may not be obvious to users, you can add a descriptive list to the search form you create with the FindForm wizard to assist users in finding the right document. When a user selects a found document, the browser can either display it or download it. Make sure your users' browsers are configured to handle *.doc* files for viewing or downloading, as desired.

PREPARING AN INDEX: OVERVIEW

To prepare a searchable index of all or part of your document web, you will complete the following general steps:

1. Determine what documents are to be included in the index. You may find it easiest to place the documents in the same directory or in multiple directories that make sense to you. The directory or directories you choose must be part of the overall document web, or URL space.

   By default, the document web begins in the directory *C:\WebSite\htdocs*. Thus, you can create one or more subdirectories in *htdocs* to store documents to be indexed. To index documents that reside in directories outside *htdocs*, you must add those locations to your web's document mapping, a topic that is covered in Chapter 9, *Mapping*.

   Note that WebIndex refers to directories by their URL directory names rather than by their physical location. For example, the default URL directory name for *C:\WebSite\htdocs* is */*. The subdirectory *C:\WebSite\htdocs\myindex* would be the URL directory */myindex*.

2. Use WebIndex to select the URL directory or directories to be indexed and create the index. WebIndex allows you to create multiple indexes, which can exist as separate indexes and/or be merged into larger ones. You can also set a variety of preferences to fine-tune the indexing process, such as specifying which types of files are to be indexed and what commonly used words should be ignored. This step is covered in the section "Working with WebIndex," later in this chapter.

3. Test the index by searching with WebFind, a CGI program that displays an HTML form to the browser and then executes the search of the specified index. WebFind generates an HTML document listing the items matching the search criteria. Each item is a hyperlink to its target document. The default URL for WebFind is *http://localhost/cgi-shl/webfind.exe*. This step is covered in the section "Searching the Index with WebFind," later in this chapter.

4. Create a hyperlink in your document web to point to a search form for your indexes. You can point directly to the WebFind program or you can create a custom form using the FindForm wizard, available through WebView. You can also create your own form using an HTML editor (such as HotDog) or simply add a few lines of code to an existing document to execute a search. This step is covered in the section "Adding Searches to Your Web," later in this chapter.

NOTE

Whenever you change existing documents or add new ones to an indexed URL space, you must run WebIndex again to update the index.

WORKING WITH WEBINDEX

You can start WebIndex in one of the following ways:

- From the WebSite sub-menu of the Start Menu or the WebSite program group in the Program Manager
- From the WebView Tools menu or toolbar

When it starts, WebIndex first scans your web's URL hierarchy (or space) and then displays the first page of the WebIndex application, as shown in Figure 6-1.

The Create Index page of WebIndex shows two list boxes. The list box on the left shows the URL directories that were not included in the *last* index you created, even if it was created under an earlier version of WebSite. The list box on the right shows the URL directories included in this last index. If you have never used WebIndex to create an index, the list box on the right will be empty, as shown in Figure 6-1.

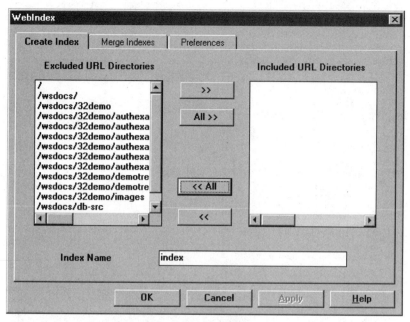

FIGURE 6-1: WEBINDEX CREATE INDEX PAGE

CREATING A NAMED INDEX

The Create Index page of WebIndex (Figure 6-1) shows the name of the last index created in the Index Name field. If this is the first index you are creating (or you have just upgraded from WebSite 1.0, which allowed only one index), the default name appears, *index*.

Let's use the history magazine example and create two named indexes: *1994 Articles* and *California*. For this example, assume that the files have been converted to HTML or ASCII. To create the indexes, launch WebIndex and complete the following steps:

1. Place the HTML or ASCII files in appropriate directories. All the 1994 articles are in a directory called *C:\WebSite\htdocs\1994*. The articles from the California supplements are divided into three directories, each containing articles for five years, called *C:\WebSite\htdocs\California.1*, *C:\WebSite\htdocs\California.2*, and *C:\WebSite\htdocs\California.3*. The corresponding URL directories for these physical directories are */1994*, */California.1*, */California.2*, and */California.3*.

2. Scroll through the list of excluded URL directories to find the URL */1994*.

3. Highlight the URL */1994* and press the >> button (or simply double-click on the URL). The URL directory name moves to the included URL directory list.

4. In the Index Name field, type in *1994 Articles*. Note that spaces are allowed in the index name since the index is a standard Windows NT or Windows 95 file. Figure 6-2 shows the WebIndex window for steps 3 and 4.

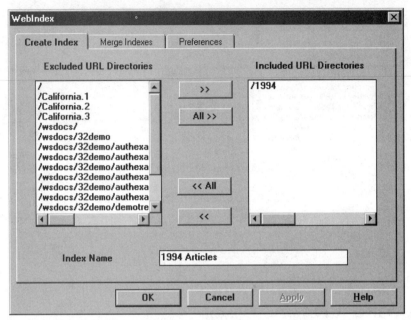

FIGURE 6-2: CREATING A NAMED INDEX WITH WEBINDEX

5. Press OK. WebIndex builds the index, displaying a message box showing the name of each document in the included URL directory. The process takes varying lengths of time depending on how many or how big the files are. Note that you can cancel the index process at any time by pressing Abort on the message box. WebIndex exits when it completes the index.

6. To create the California index, start WebIndex again.

7. Scroll through the excluded list to find the three URLs */California.1, /California.2*, and */California.3*.

8. Highlight the three California URLs. Since they are next to each other in the list, you can drag the cursor over them to highlight all three or hold down the shift key and select them as a range. Press the >> button to move the URLs to the included list.

9. Highlight the URL */1994* in the included list (left there from our previous index) and press the << button (or double-click) to move it to the excluded URL list.

10. In the Index Name field, type in *California*.

11. Press OK.

You have now created two indexes: *1994 Articles* and *California*. The indexes are stored in the directory *C:\WebSite\index* with the extension *.swish*. You need this information for deleting index files or if you run the index or search programs from the command line. Technical support may also ask you to view this directory if you have problems using WebIndex.

If you are not sure of the names of existing indexes, check the list on the Merge Index page before selecting a new name.

MERGING INDEXES

WebIndex makes it easy to create a merged, or combined, index from two or more existing indexes. A merged index can be a master index of all the indexes for your web or it can be a combination of any two or more indexes. You can have several merged indexes for different parts of your web. Merged indexes provide a way to manage your indexes both from an administrative and a user perspective. You may consider merging indexes for any of the following reasons:

- You have several indexes organized by date or topic, which are useful for specialized searches. However, a single master index would help users who want to search across the existing indexes.

- You have documents that are new on a regular basis (such as a magazine or newsletter that is published monthly). You want to maintain a combined index of all previous documents (such as previous magazine articles) and create a new index for each new set of documents (such as the current month's magazine). When the new documents are ready to be published, you create a new index for those documents and merge the previous index into the combined index.

- You have a very large document web to index, which changes often. Creating a single index is not practical because of the time and system resources needed to generate and update it. Instead you can create several smaller indexes for different parts of your web (or at different times) and then merge them into a larger index.

To continue the example from the previous section, let's create a master index for all 1994 articles and all California articles. To do so, merge the two indexes *1994 Articles* and *California* by completing the following steps:

1. Launch WebIndex and click on the Merge Indexes tab (see Figure 6-3). The existing indexes are listed.

2. Highlight the indexes to be included in the merged index by clicking on each one. To deselect an index, click on it again.

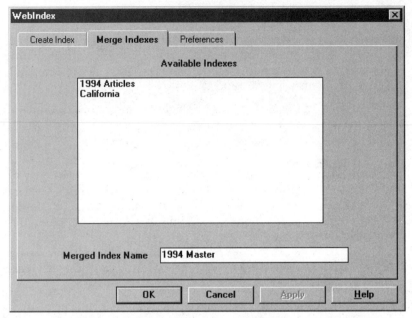

FIGURE 6-3: MERGING INDEXES WITH WEBINDEX

3. In the Merged Index Name field, type in the new index name. This example uses the name *1994 Master*.

4. Press OK. A dialog box tells you that WebIndex is merging the indexes. The application exits when the merged index is completed.

The merged index is stored in the directory *C:\WebSite\htdocs\index*, with the extension *.swish*. In this example, the merged index file is named *1994 Master.swish*.

SETTING WEBINDEX PREFERENCES

You can fine tune the index generated by WebIndex by setting preferences. You can tell WebIndex to index only certain types of files, to index only the names (not the contents) of certain types of files, ignore a standard or a custom list of words, and even generate its own list of common words to ignore based on a specified number of occurrences.

You can modify the preferences each time you create an index or use the same preferences. WebIndex remembers the last preferences you used and reloads them the next time you run the program. If you will be running the program from the command line, you can use preferences saved in a configuration file.

AN OVERVIEW OF WEBINDEX PREFERENCES

Figure 6-4 shows the default WebIndex Preferences page. Let's take a quick look at the preferences in general before completing an example using them.

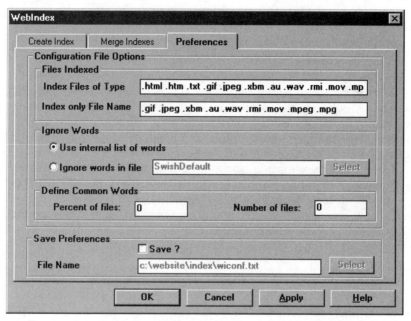

FIGURE 6-4: WEBINDEX PREFERENCES PAGE (DEFAULT SETTINGS)

- **Index Files of Type** lets you limit what kinds of files WebIndex will include while generating an index. Only files with extensions shown in this field are part of the final index. If one of the default file types doesn't suit your needs, highlight it and delete it. To add another file type, insert the cursor in the field after an existing type, and enter a new extension. Be sure to leave a space between extensions and include the period (dot) at the beginning of the extension.

- **Index only File Name** lets you limit some or all index entries to just the names—not the contents—of the files indexed. The values in this field are a subset of those in the preceding field; to index filenames, you must include the file type in the Index Files of Type field as well as in the Index only File Name field. For example, only HTML or ASCII files can be indexed for full-text keyword searches, but you still want to make other types of files—such as audio or graphics—available to users of your web. The best way to do this is to include non-text files in the index by their filenames only. When users request a search, WebFind returns any keyword (content) matches *and* any filename matches for the search string.

- **Use Internal List of (Ignored) Words** tells WebIndex to exclude common words from the final index using its built-in list of words. This is the default setting, and for most uses, this list is sufficient.

- **Ignore Words in File** lets you specify an alternate list of words to ignore. This file must be a text (ASCII) file with each word to be ignored separated by a space. Type the name of the file in the field provided or choose a file using the Select button. The default list of ignored words, SwishDefault, is shown in the field unless you have entered a filename. You *cannot* edit this list.

- **Define Common Words** tells WebIndex how to identify commonly used words to be ignored during indexing. The first field states a percentage of files to be indexed; the default is 80 percent. The second field states a minimum number of files that must be indexed before the percentage is valid; the default is 256 files. For example, if WebIndex finds a certain word, say "book," in 80 percent of the files to be indexed and there are at least 256 files, then it does not include book in the final index. You can raise or lower these figures depending on the size of the index and the depth of indexing desired. If you have large files or a large number of files to be indexed, you may want to lower the percentage and number of files to make the indexing, and searching, more efficient. These common words are ignored in addition to those on the default list or a list you specify.

- **Save Preferences** lets you choose whether or not the configuration you set up should be saved in a file and what that file should be named. Saving the configuration to a file is useful only if you plan to run WebIndex from the command line (the command is *index.exe*) or use the Windows 95 System Agent or the Windows NT scheduler service to generate indexes. If you do, you can use a saved configuration file in the command. For more information on using the *index* command, see the section called "Indexing Your Web from the Command Line" at the end of the chapter. To save the current configuration to a file, check the Save box and then accept the default filename or enter a new one. Note that you cannot recall this configuration file to use with WebIndex, WebSite's graphical indexing program.

AN EXAMPLE OF USING WEBINDEX PREFERENCES

You'll recall from the beginning of this chapter the WebSite administrator who wanted to make human resources documents available to employees over an internal web running WebSite. All the files were Word for Windows files with the extension *.doc*. Creating an index or multiple indexes for these files requires setting WebIndex preferences and then completing the steps for creating an index described earlier in this chapter.

Figure 6-5 shows the Files Indexed section of the Preferences page for this situation. Note that the extension *.doc* is in both of the fields. The first field tells WebIndex to include *.doc* files in the search (rather than ignoring them completely), while the second field tells the program to include only the filename for each *.doc* file in the index. To put these changes into effect, press Apply before returning to the Create Index page.

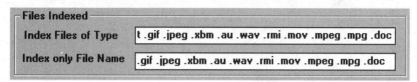

FIGURE 6-5: SETTING FILE PREFERENCES IN WEBINDEX

You'll notice that none of the default file types was deleted for this example. You need to delete them only if files of these types exist in the directories to be indexed for this specific index *and* you don't want them (or their contents) included in the index. For this example, the directories contained only *.doc* files. Unless you want to exclude specific file types, we recommend leaving the default types and adding other types to these fields.

UPDATING AN INDEX

What if you add new documents to the indexed portion of your web or change a document that was already indexed? What if you want to add another URL directory to an existing index, for example, the California articles for the current year?

When in doubt, you should regenerate an index to keep it current. Keeping your indexes current requires tracking when indexes were made and what URL directories they included. When a change occurs, you simply rerun the index for the URL directories that made up the original index and any new ones you wish to add (or previous ones you wish to exclude). Use the same name for the updated index. Note that you must keep track of which portions of your web are in a specific index, WebIndex only tracks the last index created.

Whenever you update an index, it is immediately ready for users to search; no further updates are needed.

SEARCHING THE INDEX WITH WEBFIND

Before you make a new index part of your web, you'll want to test it with a few searches. The easiest way to do so is to use WebFind. WebFind is a CGI program that generates a form for search requests, searches the specified index, and returns the URLs of all matching files in HTML format.

To see how WebFind works, use your web browser and point to the URL *http:// localhost/cgi-shl/webfind.exe*. Figure 6-6 shows the default form generated by WebFind. (For more information on creating HTML forms, see Chapter 5, *HTML*

Tutorial and Quick Reference. For more information on processing forms, see Section 4, *The Common Gateway Interface.*)

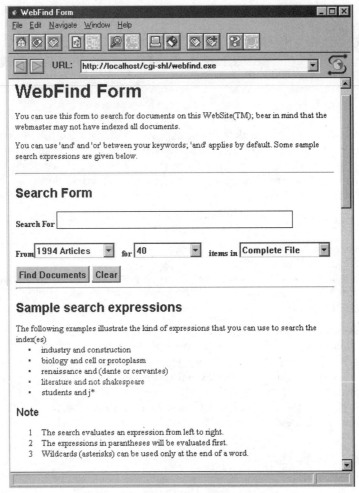

FIGURE 6-6: WEBFIND FORM

AN OVERVIEW OF THE WEBFIND FORM

The WebFind form shows all possible ways to search for an indexed entry, including the various search expression combinations and other options. However, the easiest way to search is to enter a word and press Find Documents. WebFind looks for documents that match the search string. You can choose not to show the other options (such as what index to use or how many matched items to display) when you create your own forms using the FindForm wizard or with an HTML editor. The search expression combinations are always available.

NOTE

To give your users an overview of the many ways to search for a document, you can use all or part of this section as a guide. You may even want to create a document for your web including these instructions.

The WebFind search form lets you specify several things about your search:

- **Search Expression.** The search expression field accepts one or more words and the following parameters in any logical combination:
    - *and*—finds instances of two or more words in a document (for example, industry *and* construction). Note that if you enter multiple words and no conjunction, WebFind assumes you mean *and*.
    - *or*—finds instances of one of two words in a document (for example, biology *or* zoology; biology *and* cell *or* protoplasm)
    - *parentheses*—finds instances of the expression in parentheses first and then the rest of the expression in a document (for example, renaissance *and* (dante *or* cervantes) searches for dante or cervantes first and then renaissance)
    - *not*—finds instances of one or more words and not another word in a document (for example, literature *not* shakespeare)
    - ***—finds instances matching any form of the word (for example, students and j*). *Note that you can use a wildcard asterisk only at the end of a word.*
- **What Index to Use.** This pulldown list lets you select any of the available indexes to complete the search. The indexes are listed in alphabetical order.
- **How Many Instances.** This pulldown list lets you select the maximum number of instances of the search expression WebFind should return.
- **What Part of File.** This pulldown list lets you select which portion of an HTML file WebFind should search for the expression. Limiting where WebFind searches speeds up the search and returns fewer (but more focused) instances.

AN EXAMPLE OF USING THE WEBFIND FORM

To see some of WebFind's search capability in action, let's search the index of articles about California for information regarding the Gold Rush and the miners of 1849. To give the widest search we use *or* in the search string. Then we select California from the pulldown list of indexes (Figure 6-7).

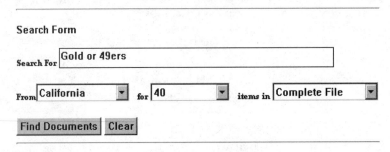

Search Form

Search For Gold or 49ers

From California ▼ **for** 40 ▼ **items in** Complete File ▼

Find Documents   Clear

FIGURE 6-7: SEARCHING FOR TWO KEYWORDS FROM A SPECIFIC INDEX

Press Find Documents and WebFind returns a list of all documents that contain the words Gold or 49ers. (See Figure 6-8.) Each entry in the list is a hyperlink to a document that matched the search string. WebFind lists either the contents of the document's title (HTML files only) or the filename. The icon to the left of the link tells you the file type (in this case they are all HTML files).

You'll notice that the listing contains documents that refer to football! Those must be articles about the San Francisco 49ers football team. To eliminate those documents from a future search, limit the search string by adding *not* to the expression, *Gold or 49ers not Football*.

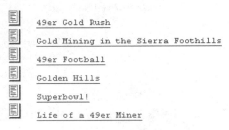

WebFind Results

Keywords = '**Gold or 49ers**'

Results generated at Thu Oct 12 13:48:03 1995 GMT

Document Title

49er Gold Rush

Gold Mining in the Sierra Foothills

49er Football

Golden Hills

Superbowl!

Life of a 49er Miner

FIGURE 6-8: WEBFIND RESULTS

NOTE

The format of WebFind results pages is built into the program. If you want to change the format, you must edit the WebFind source code and recompile the executable. You can obtain the source code and instructions for modifying the results format from WebSite Central (*http://web-site.ora.com/*). Make sure you keep a copy of the original *webfind.exe* program.

ADDING SEARCHES TO YOUR WEB

Once you have created and tested an index, the next step is to add search capability to your web. There are three ways to do this, as described in this section:

- Create a link from a document in your web to a non-existent search form. Then use the FindForm wizard in WebView to create the search form. The resulting file is in HTML, which you can edit to further tailor the form to meet your web's needs.

- Create a link from a document in your web to the WebFind CGI program. When a user clicks on this link, the server returns the default WebFind form. (See Figure 6-6.)

- Add the appropriate HTML coding, explanatory text, and search action to an existing HTML document to create an "in document" search form.

CREATING YOUR OWN FORM USING THE FINDFORM WIZARD

Creating your own form allows you to include both text and form components that meet the needs of your web. For example, you may want to provide more detailed instructions to users in the beginning paragraph. The WebSite administrator creating an index for human resources policies needs to add an explanation of the codes used to identify certain types of policies. He can do this easily using the FindForm wizard.

Your web may have only one index so there is no need to show the pulldown list for indexes. You may also not want to allow users to limit the number of matches the search finds. If your index has no HTML or text files in it, then searching specific parts of a document makes no sense. The FindForm wizard lets you easily create search forms that include or don't include any of these three options.

The FindForm wizard is available from the WebView toolbar or Tools menu. We assume you are familiar with WebView and the other wizards. If necessary, refer to Chapter 4, *Managing Your Web Using WebView*, for more instructions on working with WebView.

To create a custom search form, follow these steps:

1. In WebView, display the tree in which you want to place the search form.

2. Edit an existing HTML document to add a hyperlink to the new search form. *The link should be to a non-existing HTML file.* For example, the link might look like:

```
<A HREF="search.html">Search</a>
```

for Human Resources policy documents.

The new link should appear in the tree as a broken link.

3. Highlight the broken link and select the wizard's hat from the toolbar or Wizards from the Tools menu. You can also double-click on the link and select the wizard option from the dialog box.

4. Choose the FindForm wizard and press OK. The WebFind Form Wizard dialog box appears as shown in Figure 6-9.

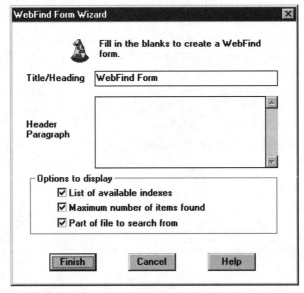

FIGURE 6-9: WEBFIND FORM WIZARD

5. Complete the dialog box by typing in text for the opening paragraph and selecting which options (the three pulldown list boxes) you wish to include. If you select all three, the form looks similar to that generated by WebFind. Figure 6-10 shows the wizard with a header paragraph and only some options selected. Notice that you can include HTML tags in the header paragraph.

NOTE

If your web has multiple indexes, you *must* include the first option, List of available indexes. This option includes the pulldown list of indexes in the search form, allowing your users to select the appropriate index for their search.

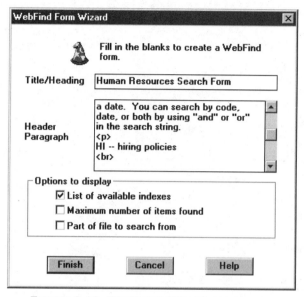

FIGURE 6-10: FINDFORM WIZARD COMPLETED

6. Press Finish to create the document. In the WebView window, the broken link icon for this link is removed.

7. View the search form and test it by launching a browser on the form's link. Figure 6-11 shows the search form created by the FindForm wizard.

You can create as many search forms as necessary for your web using the Find-Form wizard. Follow the procedure outlined above for each search form.

If your web needs a more complex search form than that created by the Find-Form wizard, you can edit the resulting file and add more text or other HTML elements (such as links to other locations). Editing text and adding other HTML elements are topics covered in Chapter 5, *HTML Tutorial and Quick Reference.*

USING WEBFIND FOR SEARCHES

The second method of adding search capability to your web is to add a hyperlink for the WebFind CGI program to any existing HTML document. When a user

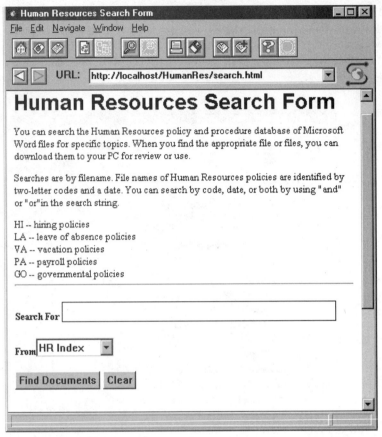

FIGURE 6-11: FORM CREATED BY THE FINDFORM WIZARD

clicks on that link, the server displays the form generated by WebFind. (See Figure 6-6.)

Creating a hyperlink to WebFind is just like adding any other hyperlink to an HTML document but using the URL for WebFind instead of the URL for an HTML document. The URL that you use in an HREF for WebFind is */cgi-shl/webfind.exe*. For example

```
<A HREF="/cgi-shl/webfind.exe">Search this site</a>
```

for articles about California history.

Make sure you have the path to the WebFind program correct and enclose the URL in quotation marks.

ADDING SEARCH FORM CODING
TO AN HTML DOCUMENT

The third way to add search capability to your web is to insert the HTML codes for a form in another HTML document. The advantage of doing so eliminates one link a user must navigate and one document the browser must retrieve, a true advantage if your server has a slow connection. For example, the WebSite administrator creating the human resources indexes might prefer to put the search ability on the human resources department's main page rather than a link to the form created by the FindForm wizard.

The easiest way to add the HTML codes for searching to a document is to first create the form with the components you want with the FindForm wizard. Open the resulting file and copy the lines you need. *Make sure you get all the codes and text between the <form> and </form> tags.* Next, open the file to which you wish to add the search text. Paste the copied lines to the appropriate place in the file. Edit the file as necessary to make it read correctly. The coding should look something like this:

```
<html>
<title>History Journal Home Page</title>
<h1>Welcome to the History Journals Web Site</h1>
<p>
You can search our archives of all articles or those specifically
          about California.
<p>
<form method=GET action="/cgi-shl/webfind.exe">
<p>
<b>Search For</b>
<input name=keywords size=50>
</p>
<p>
<b>From</b><select name="indexname">
<!--To add a new index (whose filename is 'new index.swish')
   --add the following line below
   --  <option>new index
   --Note: Do not insert spaces between the keyword '<option>'
   --          and the name of the index
   -->
<option>California
<option>1994 Articles
</select>
<p>
<input type=submit value="Find Documents"><input type=reset
          value="Clear"></p>
</form>
<p>
<hr>
  . . .
```

View the resulting document in a browser. The revised document should look something like the document shown in Figure 6-12.

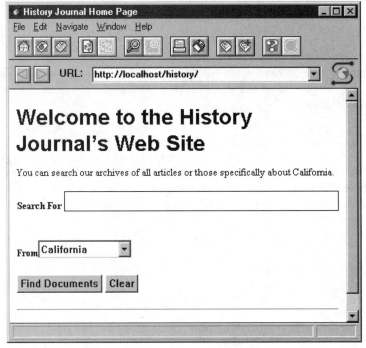

FIGURE 6-12: DOCUMENT WITH SEARCH CAPABILITY

For more information about writing forms from scratch and adding other elements, see Chapter 5, *HTML Tutorial and Quick Reference*.

INDEXING YOUR WEB FROM THE COMMAND LINE

You may find it useful to generate indexes (and search them) from the command line. For example, if you have a large web to index and a very busy site, you can use the Windows NT scheduler service or set up a Windows 95 System Agent (available in the Windows 95 Plus! Package) to generate indexes at a scheduled time during low-usage hours.

Please consult your operating system documentation for the basic steps in setting up scheduling. The command for running WebIndex and WebFind at the command line (which is the format used by both the scheduling service and the System Agent facility) is *index*. The usage and options are as follows:

```
index [-i dir file ... ] [-c file] [-f file] [-l] [-v (num)]
index -w word1 word2 ... [-f file1 file2 ...] [-m num] [-t str]
index -M index1 index2 ... outputfile
index -D file
index -V
        -i : create an index from the specified files
        -w : search for words "word1 word2 ..."
        -t : tags to search in - specify as a string
             "HBthec" - in head, body, title, header,
             emphasized, or comments
        -f : index file to create or search from [index.swish]
        -c : configuration file to use for indexing
        -v : verbosity level (0 to 3) [0]
        -l : follow symbolic links when indexing
        -m : the maximum number of results to return [40]
        -M : merges index files
        -D : decodes an index file
        -V : prints the current version
```

The WebSite *index* command is based on *SWISH*, which stands for Simple Web Indexing System for Humans, created by Kevin Hughes from EIT. For more detailed instructions on using *index* (or *swish*) from the command line, see the documentation at *http://www.eit.com/software/swish/*. More information about using *index* and WebSite, as well as a link to the *SWISH* documentation, is available at WebSite Central (*http://website.ora.com/*).

CHAPTER SEVEN

WORKING WITH IMAGE MAPS

Suppose you want visitors to your web to show you what neighborhood they live in by clicking in a map of their town. Or you want users to select a region of the country to get the latest weather forecast. Or you have a photograph of your prize-winning Boxers, and you want people to be able to click on a dog's image to learn what ribbons she won.

Clickable image maps are one way to add interest to a web page. For example, a campus might have a map of all the buildings, and when you click on one you see a full-color photograph. A pizza parlor might have a map of your city, and when you click on your location it can tell you whether you're in their delivery range. In addition, many sites use clickable maps just for aesthetics; for example, using clickable map images, a series of anchored inline images can be unified into a single integrated graphic.

Clickable image maps work by mapping a set of coordinates in an image to a particular URL. WebSite includes the image map editor Map This!, a graphical editor for easily creating image maps. MapThis! supports both NCSA image maps with file-based configuration information (also called server-side image maps) and client-side image maps, which rely on the browser to interpret the locations. This chapter describes how to use Map This!, with a tutorial on creating a clickable image map and how to integrate image maps into your web documents.

NOTE

WebSite 1.0 supported only Registry-based image maps; all configuration information was stored in the Registry. Although this approach had advantages, a major disadvantage was the inability to use file-based image maps from other sources or to export image maps to other locations. If you have any remaining Registry-based image maps, we recommend that you recreate them as NCSA or client-side image maps using Map This!, as described in this chapter.

GETTING STARTED

The best way to learn Map This! is just to use it. Many readers would be best served by skipping to the tutorial later in this chapter. However, first we thought we'd give you a tour of Map This!.

Initially, Map This! comes up with an empty background, shown in Figure 7-1.

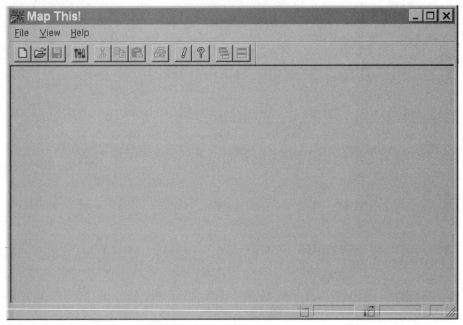

FIGURE 7-1: INITIAL MAP THIS! WINDOW

Map This! includes a series of pull-down menus and a toolbar. Here's a brief synopsis of what these features do:

FILE MENU

Item	Description	Keyboard Shortcut
New	Creates a new image map	CTRL+N
Open File	Opens an existing image map	CTRL+O
Close	Closes the current image map	
Save	Saves the current image map	CTRL+S
Save As	Saves the current image map under a different name	
Preferences	Displays the Preferences dialog box, which you use to set and change Map This! features	
Print	Prints the image map	CTRL+P
Print Preview	Previews the image map	
Print Setup	Displays the Print Setup dialog box, which you use to set printing options	
Recent File	Displays a list of the most recently opened files	
Exit	Exits Map This!	

EDIT MENU

Item	Description	Keyboard Shortcut
Undo	Undoes the last edit	CTRL+Z
Cut	Cuts the current selection from the image map and places it on the Clipboard	CTRL+X
Copy	Copies the current selection from the image map and places it on the Clipboard	CTRL+C
Paste	Pastes the contents of the Clipboard into the image map	CTRL+V
Delete	Deletes the current selection from the image map	
Edit Map Info	Displays the Edit Info about this Mapfile dialog box, which you use to change information about the map file	

VIEW MENU

Item	Description
Toolbar	Toggles the view of the toolbar
Status Bar	Toggles the view of the status bar
Area List	Toggles display of the Area List dialog box

MAPPING MENU

Item	Description
Rectangle	Creates a new hotspot in the shape of a rectangle
Circle	Creates a new hotspot in the shape of a circle
Ellipse	Creates a new hotspot in the shape of an ellipse
Point	Creates a new hotspot in the shape of a point
Polygon	Creates a new hotspot in the shape of a polygon, with as many sides as you like
Arrow	Displays the Select Arrow tool
Zoom In	Zooms in on the image
Zoom Out	Zooms out of the image
Delete	Deletes the currently selected hotspot area, but not the image underneath
Area Info	Displays information for the current hotspot, which you can edit

GOODIES MENU

Item	Description
Grid	Toggles the display of a grid over the image map
Grid Settings	Displays the Grid Settings dialog box, which you use to change grid properties
Create Guides	Displays the Create Guides dialog box, which you use to quickly create predefined rectangles covering the image

WINDOW MENU

Item	Description
Cascade	Overlaps open windows
Tile	Tiles open windows
Arrange Icons	Lines up window icons at the bottom of the Map This! window
Window List	Displays a list of the currently open windows

HELP MENU

Item	Description
Contents	Lists the Help topics available
About Map This!	Displays the version number, copyright information, and authorship of Map This!

WORKING WITH MAP THIS!

Your first steps in using Map This! are to plan out what you're using the image map for, choose the image, and then figure out how the image map should work.

If you just want to try out Map This!, grab any GIF image you can find. If you have a real goal in mind, don't do anything until you've spent some time planning and thinking it through.

CHOOSING AND CONVERTING THE IMAGE

The hardest part of creating the image map may be getting the background image. If you're lucky, you might find a suitable picture already in electronic form. Or, you might have a digital scanner to scan a photograph or a map. If you want truly professional results, you might even hire a graphics designer to help you create the image.

Map This! accepts files in GIF format only. If your image is in another format, you'll have to convert it before you can use it.

PLANNING THE HOTSPOTS

Clickable image maps work by defining *hotspots* in the document. Each hotspot is designated by a shape drawn onto the image and by the URL to connect to when a user clicks in the corresponding region of the image. Once you have your image, consider what parts of the image would make reasonable hotspots and what they should do. In other words, what do you want your users to click, and what should happen when they click there?

For example, a real estate agency might want to set up a web site containing a map of the city. Using a map for a background image makes the most sense, since the location is often the first determining factor for people buying a house. What to do next, however, requires some thought. What happens when you click in a particular neighborhood? Do you see a street map of the area, highlighting all the properties currently on the market? Instead of another map, do you see a listing of all those properties, including the asking prices, square footage, etc.? Or maybe the best thing would be to bring up a page full of photographs of each property, and let the user select which of the houses she'd like more information on.

Take the time to consider your audience before you define your hotspots. Imagine what kind of information the user might be looking for, and how that information would be presented best. Would someone looking for a new home be more interested in seeing pictures of the properties next, or would they want to see a set of price ranges for that neighborhood?

In addition to the localized hotspots, each image map can have a default URL, or *background URL*. The background URL is the URL that is connected to when the user clicks on an area of the image external to any of the hotspots.

NOTE

Remember that some users may not have a graphical browser. Give them an alternative to the image map, such as a plain text page.

STARTING MAP THIS!

Once you've selected the image, select a directory to store it in. For example, you might store it with the rest of the images used by your Web document, such as *C:\WebSite\images*. Copy or move the image file to that directory. Then start Map This!, in one of two ways:

- From WebView, choose Map This! from the Tools menu.
- From the Program Manager, or the Start menu.

LOADING AN IMAGE AND CREATING A NEW IMAGE MAP

To start working on a new image map, load the target image into the editor. There are two ways to load a target image:

- From the File menu, choose New.
- Click on the New Image button in the toolbar.

Map This! displays a dialog box, which you use to select the GIF file. After you choose your file, Map This! loads the image and displays it.

You can start defining your hotspots right away. However, it's a good idea to enter some information about the image. To do this, choose Edit Map Info from the Edit menu. Map This! displays the Info about this Mapfile dialog box, as shown in Figure 7-2.

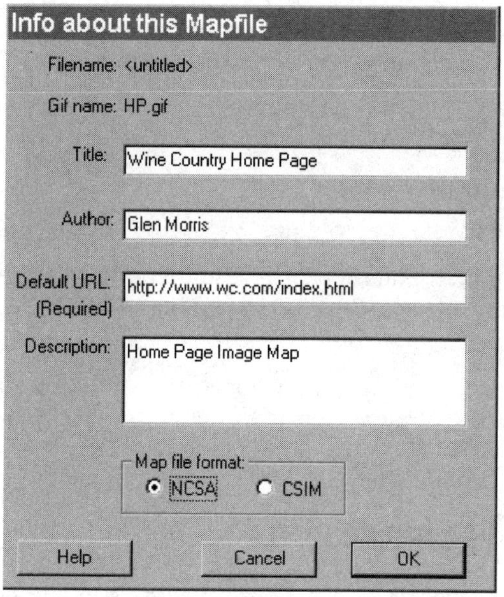

FIGURE 7-2: INFORMATION ABOUT THIS MAPFILE

Enter a title and author. These aren't required, but can help organize your mapfiles. A default URL is required. This is the background URL, the URL that is selected when the user clicks outside any of the hotspots. *This URL, as all image map URLs, should be absolute, not relative.* The URL can be partial (that is, it may not include the protocol and server name), but it should not begin with .., which indicates a relative location. You can also enter a description of the mapfile.

The final item you choose is the format of the image map. You have two choices:

NCSA

Also called a file-based or server-side image map, the NCSA format is the most common. The configuration information is stored in a file and the filename is used in an HREF in your document. WebSite processes requests for locations on the image using its built-in imagemapper. WebSite recognizes NCSA image maps by the *.map* filename extension.

CSIM

Stands for Client-Side Image Map. The configuration information for a client-side image map is stored in a specific HTML file. The coordinates and corresponding URLs for hotspots on the image are HTML tags, which the browser processes. Note that these tags are extensions to HTML and not supported by all browsers. If you have a browser that supports client-side image maps, moving the mouse over an area gives the URL of the hotspot instead of the coordinates.

The NCSA/CSIM formats are complementary to each other and are not used as a replacement for each other, since not all browsers support CSIM.

At this point, it's a good idea to save the map file. There are two ways to save the map file:

- From the File menu, choose Save.
- Click on the Save icon in the toolbar.

In the Save As dialog box, enter a filename and choose the file type. For a file in NCSA format, save the file as *filename.map*. For a file in CSIM format, save the file as *filename.htm* or *filename.html*. Choose OK to save the file.

That's it! You've created and saved an image map file. Of course, there are no hotspots in the file yet. The next step is to define the hotspots and connect them to the proper URLs.

DEFINING HOTSPOTS

Once you have a figure in Map This!, you can start assigning hotspots. In drawing a hotspot, think of it as an outline for the area in which you want users to click.

SELECTING THE HOTSPOT TYPE

To select a shape, you can either use a toolbar button or the Mapping menu. The supported shapes are:

- Rectangle. The position at which you initially press down the mouse button becomes one corner of the rectangle, and the position at which you release the mouse button is the opposite corner of the rectangle. Rectangles are fairly easy to work with.
- Circle. These are also fairly easy to work with. The position at which you initially press down the mouse button is one side of the circle, and the posi-

tion at which you release the mouse button is at the opposite side of the circle.

- Ellipse. These take some practice, and can be confusing, since the position at which you initially press down the mouse button will not be part of the ellipse. Think of it as drawing a rectangle that contains an ellipse, with the resulting ellipse being the largest ellipse that can fit within that rectangle.

- Point. A single point in the image.

- Polygon. These are the most flexible of shapes, since they can have any number of sides. They work slightly differently, however, since you don't have to keep the mouse button pressed. The starting point of the polygon should be one of the corners of the desired shape. Click once, and then move the cursor to the position of an adjacent corner of the desired shape; a line is drawn from the first position to the second position. When you click again, the first line is held in place, and you can draw another line from there. Connecting the line back at its origination point completes the hotspot.

Figure out which shape best lends itself to the object in which you want users to click. A star is an irregular shape, so that's best represented by a polygon. And circular arrows, for example, are best represented by a circle or ellipse.

DRAWING A RECTANGULAR HOTSPOT

Let's start with the buttons at the bottom of the image. Select the shape (a rectangle) and place the pointer at the corner of the first button. Hold down the left mouse button and drag it to make it conform to the shape you want, as shown in Figure 7-3. While dragging, the cursor becomes a rectangle with an arrow, and you'll see an outline with the corners highlighted. Don't worry if you don't get it perfect the first time, since you can easily move and adjust the hotspot afterwards.

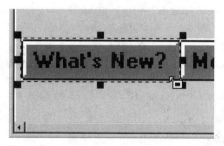

FIGURE 7-3: A RECTANGULAR HOTSPOT

DRAWING A CIRCULAR OR ELLIPTICAL HOTSPOT

When you're through with rectangles, try drawing circular and elliptical hotspots. Ellipses are a little harder to work with. Rather than thinking of it as drawing an

ellipse, it's best to visualize drawing a rectangle that completely encompa
shape.

Select Circle or Ellipse from the Mapping menu or from the toolbar, and
place the pointer at the corner of the imaginary rectangle. For example,
Figure 7-4, we place the pointer above and to the left of the circular arrows, a
then hold down the left mouse button while we drag down and to the right.

FIGURE 7-4: DRAWING AN ELLIPSE

DRAWING A POINT

Drawing a point as a hotspot is very simple. Select Point from the Mapping menu
or from the toolbar. Just place the cursor over the desired area, and click.

DRAWING A POLYGON

Once you've drawn all the rectangles, circles, ellipses, and points on the page, it's
time to outline the star image. For this shape, as for all irregular shapes, a
polygon is best suited.

Select Polygon from the Mapping menu or from the toolbar. Then place the
pointer at one of the corners of the shape and click once. You don't have to hold
down the left mouse button when drawing a polygon.

Now move the mouse pointer to the next corner and click on that corner. A line
is drawn between the two points and remains in place, while a second line
starting from the original starting point continues to follow your pointer.

Continue on to all the corners. You should be outlining the shape. At the last
corner, click the mouse button and the polygon is complete. Figure 7-5 shows a
polygon.

As with the other shapes, you can always adjust a polygon after it is drawn. Just
select the polygon and then move the pointer to one of the corners until the
pointer changes to a small box with crosshairs. Hold down the left mouse button
and drag as desired.

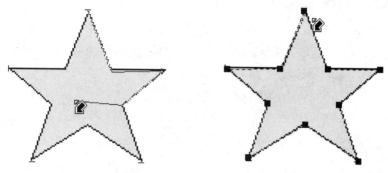

FIGURE 7-5: DRAWING A POLYGON

CONNECTING A HOTSPOT TO A URL

After you've drawn a hotspot, you need to connect it to the proper URL. To connect a hotspot, move the pointer into the hotspot, and double-click the left mouse button. The Area Settings dialog box is displayed, as shown in Figure 7-6. Enter the URL to activate when the user clicks in this hotspot. The URL must be absolute, not relative. That is, it must start with a / or with a protocol (*http://*). A URL that starts with .. is relative and cannot be parsed correctly. *Don't use relative URLs in image maps.* You can also enter a comment about this area, such as a brief description. If you want to delete this hotspot, choose the Delete button. To move it higher or lower in the area list, choose the Up or Down button.

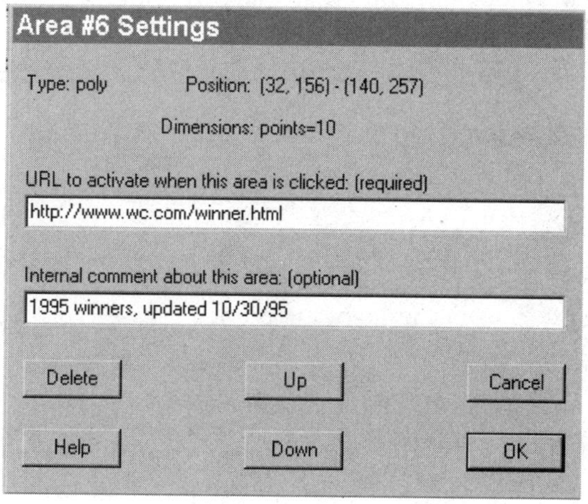

FIGURE 7-6: AREA SETTINGS DIALOG BOX

EDITING HOTSPOTS

Once a hotspot is created, you can make changes to it.

- You can move a hotspot to anywhere else on the background image.
- You can adjust the shape of the hotspot.
- You can edit the target URL or description.
- You can cut, copy, paste, or delete hotspots.

SELECTING A HOTSPOT

To move or edit a hotspot, you first need to make sure it's selected. If you just created the hotspot, it might already be selected. If not, you need to select the hotspot before you can move or edit it. To select a hotspot, move the mouse pointer into the hotspot area. The cursor changes to the "size all" cursor, which resembles a weather vane.

MOVING A HOTSPOT

To move a hotspot, move the cursor into the hotspot. The cursor changes to the "size all" cursor. Press and hold down the left mouse button within the hotspot and drag it to a new location.

ADJUSTING THE SHAPE OF A HOTSPOT

To change the shape of a hotspot, you must first select it. Place the cursor on one of the handles of the hotspot. The cursor changes into a two-way arrow. Press and hold down the left mouse button and move the hotspot handles in either direction. For polygons, the cursor changes into a crosshairs cursor.

CHANGING THE TARGET URL

Once you have selected a hotspot, there are four ways to bring up the Area Settings dialog box to change the URL:

- Press the right mouse button and choose Edit Area Info.
- Select Edit Area Info from the Mapping menu.
- Double-click on the hotspot.
- Select the Edit Area Info button in the toolbar.

Map This! displays the Area Settings dialog box, allowing you to edit the target URL and description.

DELETING A HOTSPOT

Once you've selected a hotspot, you can delete it in four ways:

- Press the right mouse button and choose Delete Area.
- Select Delete from the Mapping menu.
- Select Delete from the Edit menu.
- Select the Delete button in the toolbar.

COPYING THE HOTSPOT ONTO THE CLIPBOARD

Once you've selected a hotspot, you can copy it onto the Clipboard. You may want to do this if you want to duplicate the hotspot on another background image. You can copy a hotspot in four ways:

- Press CTRL+C.
- Press the right mouse button and choose Copy.
- Select Copy from the Edit menu.
- Select the Copy button in the toolbar.

CUTTING THE HOTSPOT INTO THE CLIPBOARD

You can also cut a hotspot into the Clipboard—for example, if you want to move the hotspot to another background image, maintaining both the properties and shape of the hotspot. You can cut a hotspot in four ways:

- Press CTRL+X.
- Press the right mouse button and choose Cut.
- Select Cut from the Edit menu.
- Select the Cut button in the toolbar.

PASTING A HOTSPOT FROM THE CLIPBOARD

Once you have a hotspot in the Clipboard, you can paste it into another image map in four ways:

- Press CTRL+V.
- Press the right mouse button and choose Paste.
- Select Paste from the Edit menu.
- Select the Paste button in the toolbar.

USING GRIDS

You can use the grid feature to help you place a hotspot with precision. To use the grid feature:

- Select Grid from the Goodies menu.
- Select the Grid button in the toolbar.

To set grid properties, use the Grid Settings dialog box (Figure 7-7).

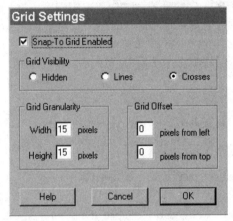

FIGURE 7-7: GRID SETTINGS DIALOG BOX

If you choose Snap-To Grid, your hotspot will move from one point on the grid to another, but not between. You can also set the type of grid visibility—hidden, lines, or crosses—as well as the granularity, or space between grid points, and the grid offset.

USING GUIDES

Guides are predefined hot spots covering the background image. They are defined by their position relative to each other, and a standard size. For example, if you have a row of navigation buttons, you can quickly create the hotspots covering them with the Guide command. To use Guides, choose Create Guides from the Goodies menu. This command displays the Create Guides dialog box (Figure 7-8).

Enter the width and height of the hotspot, then enter the number of pixels to start the grid from the left and from the top of the screen. If you want the guides offset from each other, enter values for the horizontal and vertical offsets. Then enter the number of guides across and down—think of these as rows and columns in a

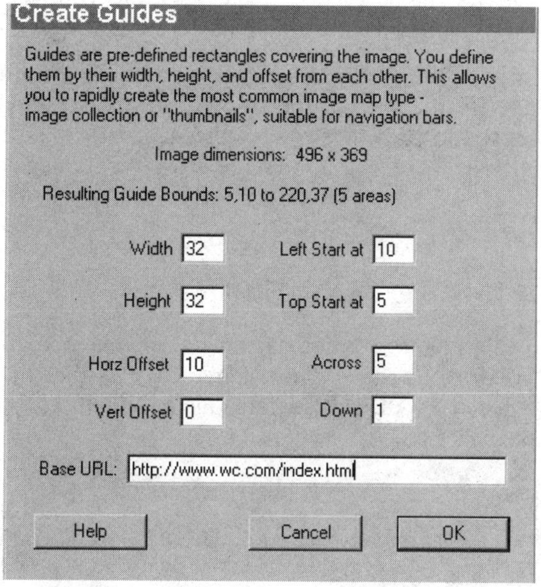

FIGURE 7-8: CREATE GUIDES DIALOG BOX

spreadsheet. Click OK, and Map This! create the guides for you. You can edit each guide.

USING THE IMAGE MAP IN THE DOCUMENT

Once you've defined some hotspots, you'll want to see how it works in a browser. The procedure is slightly different for NCSA and CSIM formats.

NCSA FORMAT

For an NCSA file-based image map, simply add the following lines to the HTML document that is to include the image map:

```
<A HREF=pathname of image file>
<IMG SRC="URL" ALT="descriptive text" ISMAP>
</A>
```

For example:

```
<A HREF=/wsdocs/32demo/self-test.map>
<IMG SRC="/wsdocs/32demo/images/imapdemo.gif" ALT="demo image map"
       ISMAP>
</A>
```

The first line includes the name of the image map file with the .*map* extension. This name tells the server to process the link as an image map.

The second line reads in the background image as an inline image, which must be in GIF format. Specify the URL of the background image file. The ALT parameter includes text shown to browsers that can't display images. The special qualifier *ISMAP* tells the server that the inline image is an image map.

The last line ends the anchor.

CLIENT-SIDE IMAGE MAP FORMAT

As noted earlier in this chapter, when you save an image map in CSIM format, you save it to an HTML file. The coordinates and URLs that make up the image map are stored as special HTML tags, extensions to HTML 2.0. The HTML coding should look something like this:

```
<BODY>
<MAP NAME="test">
<!-- #$-:Image Map file created by Map THIS! -->
<!-- #$-:Map THIS! free image map editor by Todd C. Wilson -->
<!-- #$-:Please do not edit lines starting with "#$" -->
<!-- #$VERSION:1.20 -->
<!-- #$DESCRIPTION:test -->
<!-- #$AUTHOR:sbp -->
<!-- #$DATE:Wed May 15 11:56:14 1996 -->
<!-- #$PATH:C:\WebSite\HTDOCS\ -->
<!-- #$GIF:test.gif -->
<AREA SHAPE=CIRCLE COORDS="108,39,87" HREF=/wsdocs/32demo/
            index.html ALT="test">
<AREA SHAPE=default HREF=http://sapphire.west.ora.com>
</MAP>
</BODY>
```

Note that the HTML code for the image map is placed between the special HTML tags <MAP> and </MAP>. This sample has only one hotspot as defined by the <AREA> tag. It is a circle that points to the home page of the server self-test. The second <AREA> tag is for the default or background URL.

To use the client-side image map in a document, you can either build the rest of the HTML page around the image map, paste the contents of the CSIM HTML file into another HTML document, or include a link to the image map file from another document. If you build the page around the image map, make sure that the rest of the HTML codes and text of the page are inside the <BODY> tags. See Chapter 5, *HTML Tutorial and Quick Reference*, for more instructions on HTML coding.

Whether you build the document around the image map, paste the image map into another document, or include it as a link, you must add a line to call the image map in the same document where the <MAP> tags reside. The syntax for calling a client-side image map is

```
<IMG SRC="path to image (.gif or .jpg) file" USEMAP="#map name"
     ALT="descriptive text">
```

For example:

```
<IMG SRC="maptest.htm" USEMAP="#test" ALT="demo image map">
```

You'll recognize this as a standard <IMG> tag with the special parameter USEMAP, which points to a named anchor in the document. The named anchor is the name of the image map, which is the value of <MAP NAME=> parameter. In this example, the map name is *test*. Note that as with all named anchors, you must precede the name with a # .

The ALT parameter provides a text message for users whose browsers don't support client-side image maps. You can add other parameters to the image tag, such as borders and alignment. As always, we recommend you test the image map before putting up on your web.

CHAPTER EIGHT

EXTENDING HTML WITH SERVER-SIDE INCLUDES

This chapter discusses using server-side includes to enhance HTML pages. You can add special HTML markup codes that instruct the server to insert text from various sources. The server inserts the "included" text at the time the document is sent to the browser, so the included text may vary.

WHAT ARE SERVER-SIDE INCLUDES?

WebSite can insert, or include, text from various sources within an HTML document, replacing special HTML markup with the text. Normally, the *browser* inserts things such as inline graphics into the displayed document, replacing the HTML markup. With server-side includes, it is the *server* that does the insertion.

You've probably connected to a web page that tells you what number visitor you are, or how many times a page has been requested. The WebFind Form included with WebSite uses a date/time server side include. Figure 8-1 shows an example of server-side includes used in a web page.

FIGURE 8-1: AN EXAMPLE OF SERVER-SIDE INCLUDES

The code for this example is:

```
<HTML>
<HEAD>
<TITLE> Wine Country Tour Page </TITLE>
</HEAD>
<H1>Welcome to Wine Country!<IMG SRC="leaf.gif"></H1>
<BODY>
<P>The time is <!--#echo var="DATE_GMT"--> Greenwich Mean Time, and
          you are visitor <!--#totcnt-->.</P>
</BODY>
</HTML>
```

The highlighted markup is HTML comments, within which are the commands that the WebSite server recognizes. In the example, the server replaces the markup with the current date and time (GMT) and the total number of visitors to the page. All included directives must be enclosed in an HTML comment. The quotes are optional unless the argument contains spaces. It's a good idea to get into the habit of quoting all server-side include arguments, just as you do in other HTML tags.

ACTIVATING SERVER-SIDE INCLUDES

Normally, the server simply sends a document to the browser without looking at it. In order to process server-side includes, the server must scan through the HTML document, looking for the HTML comment sequence. The extra processing needed to handle server-side includes can reduce the server's performance significantly. Therefore, WebSite does not perform server-side include processing on normal HTML documents.

When you create an HTML document containing server-side includes, you must give it a filename ending in *.html-ssi*. When the WebSite server sees that the document's filename ends in *.html-ssi*, it will perform the extra processing on the document. Otherwise, the server-side include directives will appear literally in the HTML and will be invisible on the browser (since they are HTML "comments"). In all other respects, a document containing server-side include directives is a normal HTML document.

TIP

You can also tell the WebSite server to recognize other file extensions for server-side include processing. For example, you may have SSI files that end in *.shtml*. Or, you may want all your *.html* files to be processed for SSI. Activate this processing by adding or changing content type mapping for *wwwserver/html-ssi*. See Chapter 9, *Mapping*, for instructions. You can also redirect your *index.html* file to be processed for SSI through redirect mapping, as described in Chapter 9.

CREATING A PAGE COUNTER

One of the most popular things for webmasters to do is put a "page counter" on their home page. WebSite's server-side include engine supports a unique page counter feature that makes it easy to create a dynamic display of page access counts. You can display the number of accesses for the current day, or the number of accesses since a specific date and time.

CREATING A DAILY COUNTER

To include a daily counter on your home page:

1. Rename your home page so its file extension is *.html-ssi*, for example, *index.html-ssi*.

2. Add the following to your home page's HTML text:

   You are visitor number <!--#daycnt--> today.

That's all there is to it! The next time your home page is accessed, WebSite will replace the directive with "1," since it will be the first access for the day. Thereafter, the count will increment for each access. The first time the page is accessed after midnight local time, the count will reset to 1. To remember the count, WebSite creates a file called, in this example, *index.html-ssi.ctr* within your home page's directory. It uses this to keep track of the access count even if the server is stopped and started.

CREATING A TOTAL COUNTER

To include a total counter on your page:

1. Rename your home page so its file extension is *.html-ssi*, for example, *index.html-ssi*.

2. Add the following to your home page's HTML text:

   You are visitor number <!--#totcnt--> since <!--#lastzero-->.

The next time your home page is accessed, WebSite will replace the directives with "1" and the current date and time. Thereafter, the count will increment for each access, and the date/time will remain the same. To remember the count and creation time, WebSite creates a file called, in this example, *index.html-ssi.ctr* within your home page's directory. It uses this to keep track of the access count even if the server is stopped and started. To reset the counter, simply delete the page's counter file. If you want to reset the counter once a week, you can schedule a script to delete the file and have it run at midnight every Sunday. Use any "batch" scheduler for this purpose, such as the Windows 95 Plus! System Agent or the Windows NT WinAT program.

NOTE

If you want to show both a daily and total counter on a page, make sure that one of the SSI directives is the "r" version. For example, you can put <!--#daycnt--> and <!--#rtotcnt--> on a page or <!--#rdaycnt--> and <!--#totcnt--> on a page. The rdaycnt and rtotcnt prevent the counter file from being incremented twice when someone visits your page.

DIRECTIVE REFERENCE

The remainder of the chapter contains a reference list of each server-side include directive that WebSite supports. There is no official standard for server-side includes. The WebSite developers followed the designs of several other popular servers, using the commands and syntax supported by those servers. In WebSite, we've added some new directives at the request of users.

config

SYNTAX

```
<!--#config item="value"-->
```

DESCRIPTION

This tag permits you to change some configurable items in WebSite's server-side include engine. This directive may be used multiple times within a document, and changes affect substitutions following the configuration change. Since this directive causes no substitution, the text is left in the output HTML document so you can see what directives are in effect throughout the document.

Items supported are:

TABLE 8-1: CONFIGURABLE ITEMS

Item Name	Description
errmsg	The string that will result from a failed server-side include operation. The default is **SSI ERROR**
timefmt	The formatting string used to generate date/time strings within WebSite's server-side includes. All SSIs that produce date/time strings are affected. The formatting string is that used by the standard C Runtime Library *strftime( )* function. The default is *%#c*, which produces a "long date" format according to the locale setting in effect for the system.
sizefmt	The formatting used to represent file sizes when using the flastmod directive. The formatting string is that used by the standard C Runtime Library *printf( )* function for integers. The default is *%d*, which prints the size in decimal radix.

EXAMPLE

```
<!--#config timefmt="%#c" use long date/time -->
<!--#echo var="DATE_LOCAL"--><BR>
<!--#config timefmt="%c" now use short date/time -->
<!--#echo var="DATE_LOCAL"-->
```

would produce (US English locale)

Sunday, October 29, 1995 16:43:42
10/29/95 16:43:12

FORMATTING CODES FOR TIMEFMT

The *timefmt* format argument consists of one or more codes; as in *printf*, the formatting codes are preceded by a percent sign (%). Characters that do not begin with % are copied unchanged to the string. The current locale settings affect the output formatting of *timefmt*. The formatting codes for *timefmt* are listed below:

TABLE 8-2: TIMEFMT FORMAT CODES

Format	Description
%a	Abbreviated weekday name
%A	Full weekday name
%b	Abbreviated month name
%B	Full month name
%c	Date and time representation appropriate for locale
%d	Day of month as decimal number (01 - 31)
%H	Hour in 24-hour format (00 - 23)
%I	Hour in 12-hour format (01 - 12)
%j	Day of year as decimal number (001 - 366)
%m	Month as decimal number (01 - 12)
%M	Minute as decimal number (00 - 59)
%p	Current locale's A.M./P.M. indicator for 12-hour clock
%S	Second as decimal number (00 - 59)
%U	Week of year as decimal number, with Sunday as first day of week (00 - 51)
%w	Weekday as decimal number (0 - 6; Sunday is 0)
%W	Week of year as decimal number, with Monday as first day of week (00 - 51)
%x	Date representation for current locale
%X	Time representation for current locale
%y	Year without century, as decimal number (00 - 99)
%Y	Year with century, as decimal number
%z,%Z	Time zone name or abbreviation; no characters if time zone is unknown
%%	Percent sign

As in the *printf* function, the # flag may prefix any timefmt formatting code. In that case, the meaning of the format code is changed as follows:

TABLE 8-3: # FLAG MODIFICATIONS

# Modified Format Code	Meaning
%#a, %#A, %#b, %#B, %#p, %#X, %#z, %#Z, %#%	# flag is ignored.
%#c	Long date and time representation, appropriate for current locale. For example: "Tuesday, March 16, 1993, 12:41:29."
%#x	Long date representation, appropriate to current locale. For example: "Tuesday, March 16, 1993."
%#d, %#H, %#I, %#j, %#m, %#M, %#S, %#U, %#w, %#W, %#y, %#Y	Remove leading zeros (if any).

FORMATTING CODES FOR SIZEFMT

The formatting codes for sizefmt are a subset of those supported by the C Runtime Library *printf()* function. *Use only those formatting codes that apply to integers.* Using other formatting codes will result in an exception being generated in the server-side include engine, which will force the server to disable the server-side include engine until it is restarted.

The syntax and variety of formatting codes are very large; therefore, they will not be repeated in this book. For information on *printf( )*-style formatting codes, consult any C language manual.

daycnt

SYNTAX

```
<!--#daycnt-->
<!--#daycnt file="pathname"-->
<!--#daycnt virtual="URLpath"-->
```

DESCRIPTION

This tag is replaced by the number of requests (the hit count) for the page. The counter is persistent, so server restarts will not affect its value. Separate counters are kept for each document that contains this directive. By default, the counter for a page is kept in a file whose name is the same as the document itself, with *.ctr* appended (e.g., *index.html-ssi.ctr*).

To change the default counter file and specify a counter file with a different name, use the optional *file* or *virtual* parameters. The *file* parameter lets you specify a full path and name for the page's counter file. For example, you may want to use a counter file with an 8.3 name (necessary in a Novell environment) or locate the counter on another computer in the network. The *virtual* parameter lets you specify a URL path to the counter.

You can also use the *file* and *virtual* counters to specify different counters for daycnt and totcnt, to prevent double incrementing.

EXAMPLE

```
You are visitor number <!--#daycnt--> today.
```

echo

Syntax

```
<!--#echo var="name"-->
```

Description

This tag causes the value of a variable or HTTP extra header to be inserted. The names of the variables were taken from the Standard CGI specification (CGI/1.1) for consistency. Variable names are not case-sensitive. If the variable name is not one of the specific ones listed below, WebSite looks in the request's HTTP extra headers for a header whose name is the same as the given variable name. In this case, the value (string following the colon) of the extra header is returned. If no variable or extra header matches the variable name given, the configured server-side include error message is substituted. (See the *config* directive.) WebSite supports the variables shown in Table 8-4.

Table 8-4: Echo Variables

Variable Name	Description
ACCEPT_LANGUAGE	Comma-separated list of the human languages accepted by the browser/user
AUTH_NAME	The name of the realm to which the authenticated user belongs; blank if no authentication was needed
AUTH_TYPE	The method used to authenticate the remote user; always "Basic" in this version
DATE_GMT	The current date and time, GMT
DATE_LOCAL	The current date and time, local
DOCUMENT_NAME	The physical path and filename of the current document
DOCUMENT_URI	The URL path and name of the current document; this does not include the scheme, host, or port
FROM	The name of the browser user; this is defined in the HTTP protocol. However, it is not supported by most browsers due to privacy concerns
HTTP_ACCEPT	Comma-separated list of MIME content types accepted by the browser
HTTP_COOKIE	Netscape-specific persistent state extension to HTTP; see the online documentation at Netscape's site
HTTP_USER_AGENT	The name of the browser software
LAST_MODIFIED	The date and time the current document was last modified

TABLE 8-4: ECHO VARIABLES (CONTINUED)

Variable Name	Description
PRAGMA	Special HTTP header generated by some browsers; typically Pragma: NoCache
QUERY_STRING	The raw text following a ? in the request URL; see the CGI chapters for more information on query strings
QUERY_STRING_ UNESCAPED	The query string with the HTTP "escaping" removed
REFERER	The URL of the document containing the link to the current document; note that some browsers do not implement this reliably, and some not at all
REMOTE_ADDR	The IP address of the browser's system
REMOTE_HOST	The Internet domain host name of the browser's system; note that this will be blank unless WebSite's DNS Reverse Lookup option is enabled (not recommended)
REMOTE_USER	The authenticated user name of the browser's user; undefined if access to the current document did not require authentication
REQUEST_METHOD	The HTTP method used in the current request; always GET in this version.
SERVER_NAME	The internet domain name of the local server; if WebSite is running in the multi-homed mode, this name indicates the identity on which the current request was received
SERVER_PORT	The TCP port number on which the current request was received; normally 80 for normal connections, and 443 for SSL connections
SERVER_PROTOCOL	The version of HTTP supported by the server; always HTTP/1.0 in this version
SERVER_SOFTWARE	The name and version of the local server program; for WebSite this is WebSite 1.1.

EXAMPLE

```
...
<BODY>
<H1>A Title</H1>
<EM>Last Modified: <!--#echo var="LAST_MODIFIED"--></EM>
...
```

exec

SYNTAX

```
<!--#exec cgi="vpath"-->
```

DESCRIPTION

Replace with the output of a CGI program. The *vpath* parameter is the URL to the CGI program. Do not include the scheme (*http://*), the hostname, or the port number in the URL. The URL must be absolute; it must start with a "/".

EXAMPLE

```
...
The average response time for customer service calls
is currently
<!--#exec cgi="/cgi-win/db_get_rsptime.exe"-->.
```

flastmod

SYNTAX

```
<!--#flastmod file="pathname"-->
<!--#flastmod virtual="URLpath"-->
```

DESCRIPTION

Replace with the date/time last modified for the indicated document. For the *file* parameter, the argument is the physical path and filename of the document *relative to the current document's directory*. For the *virtual* parameter, the argument is the URL of the document. In the latter case, WebSite's URL-to-file mapping engine is used to locate the document (See Chapter 9, *Mapping*). The URL must not include the scheme, hostname, or port, and must be absolute, beginning with "/". If the document does not exist, or is inaccessible, the tag is replaced with the configured server-side include error message. (See the *config* directive.)

EXAMPLE

```
The <!--#flastmod virtual="/gen/news.html"--> edition of
the <A HREF="/gen/news.html">Company Newsletter</A> is
now online.
```

fsize

SYNTAX

```
<!--#fsize file="pathname"-->
<!--#fsize virtual="URLpath"-->
```

DESCRIPTION

Replace with the size in bytes of the indicated document. For the *file* parameter, the argument is the physical path and filename of the document *relative to the current document's directory*. For the *virtual* parameter, the argument is the URL of the document. In the latter case, WebSite's URL-to-file mapping engine is used to locate the document (See Chapter 9, *Mapping*). The URL must not include the scheme, hostname, or port, and must be absolute, beginning with "/". If the document does not exist, or is inaccessible, the tag is replaced with the configured server-side include error message. (See the *config* directive.)

EXAMPLE

```
You can download the MS Word format of the
<A HREF="/docs/manual.doc">manual</A>
(<!--#fsize virtual="/docs/manual.doc"--> bytes).
```

include

SYNTAX

```
<!--#include file="pathname"-->
<!--#include virtual="URLpath"-->
```

DESCRIPTION

Replace the tag with the contents of a document. For the *file* parameter, the argument is the physical path and filename of the document *relative to the current document's directory*. For the *virtual* parameter, the argument is the URL of the document. In the latter case, WebSite's URL-to-file mapping engine is used to locate the document (Chapter 9, *Mapping*). The URL must not include the scheme, hostname, or port, and must be absolute, beginning with "/". If the document does not exist, or is inaccessible, the tag is replaced with the configured server-side include error message. (See the *config* directive.)

If you include plain text, the results may not be what you expect. To be certain of the results, enclose the include directive in <PRE></PRE> tags. This will preserve the formatting of the plain text. Normally, you will use this to include HTML text.

WARNING

Include only HTML or plain text documents. Do not attempt to use this feature to insert pictures or other multimedia data.

EXAMPLE

```
The latest mainframe-generated financial summary is
shown below:
<PRE>
<!--#include file="MFRPT\FINSUM.TXT"-->
</PRE>
```

The document FINSUM.TXT must be located in a subdirectory named MFRPT under the directory containing the current document.

lastzero

SYNTAX

```
<!--#lastzero-->
<!--#lastzero file="pathname"-->
<!--#lastzero virtual="URLpath"-->
```

DESCRIPTION

Replace with the date and time (local) when the page counters were last set to zero, or zeroed. To zero a page counter, simply delete the counter file. The next time the page is accessed, the server-side include engine will create a new one with the current date/time. Separate counters are kept for each document that contains this directive. By default, the counter for a page is kept in a file whose name is the same as the document itself, with *.ctr* appended (e.g., *index.html-ssi.ctr*).

To change the default counter file and specify a counter file with a different name, use the optional *file* or *virtual* parameters. The *file* parameter lets you specify a full path and name for the page's counter file. For example, you may want to use a counter file with an 8.3 name (necessary in a Novell environment) or locate the counter on another computer in the network. The *virtual* parameter lets you specify a URL path to the counter.

EXAMPLE

```
You are visitor number <!--#totcnt--> since
<!--#lastzero-->.
```

nossi

SYNTAX

`<!--#nossi-->`

DESCRIPTION

This tag causes the server to immediately stop all SSI processing of the page. You can place this at any point in the file. For example, if you have all your documents processed through SSI but only some of them contain SSI tags, place this directive at the top of the file. As soon as the server encounters this tag, it sends the document to the browser with no further processing. If you have a long document but the SSI tags appear only at the beginning, you can insert this tag after the other SSI tags to cause the server to stop SSI processing and serve the document.

EXAMPLE

```
Welcome!  You are visitor <!--#daycnt--> today.
<!--#nossi-->.
```

rdaycnt

SYNTAX

```
<!--#rdaycnt-->
<!--#rdaycnt file="pathname"-->
<!--#rdaycnt virtual="URLpath"-->
```

DESCRIPTION

This tag is replaced by the number of requests (the hit count) for the page on the specific day without incrementing the counter file. The purpose of this tag is to allow you to have both a daily count and a total count (*totcnt*) appear on the same page without double incrementing the counter. The counter is persistent, so server restarts will not affect its value.

By default, the counter used for this page is the same as the document itself, with *.ctr* appended (for example, *index.html-ssi.ctr*). To change the default counter file and specify a counter file with a different name, use the optional *file* and *virtual* parameters. The *file* parameter lets you specify a full path and name for the page's counter file. For example, you may want to use a counter file with an 8.3 name (necessary in a Novell environment) or locate the counter file on another computer in the network. The *virtual* parameter lets you specify a URL path to the counter.

EXAMPLE

```
You are visitor <!--#rdaycnt--> to this page today and
visitor <!--#totcnt--> since <!--#lastzero-->.
```

rtotcnt

SYNTAX

```
<!--#rtotcnt-->
<!--#rtotcnt file="pathname"-->
<!--#rtotcnt virtual="URLpath"-->
```

DESCRIPTION

This tag is replaced by the total number of requests for the page since the counters were last set to zero without incrementing the counter file. The purpose of this tag is to allow you to have both a daily count (*daycnt*) and a total count appear on the same page without double incrementing the counter. The counter is persistent, so server restarts will not affect its value.

By default, the counter used for this page is the same as the document itself, with *.ctr* appended (for example, *index.html-ssi.ctr*). To change the default counter file and specify a counter file with a different name, use the optional *file* and *virtual* parameters. The *file* parameter lets you specify a full path and name for the page's counter file. For example, you may want to use a counter file with an 8.3 name (necessary in a Novell environment) or locate the counter file on another computer in the network. The *virtual* parameter lets you specify a URL path to the counter.

EXAMPLE

```
You are visitor <!--#daycnt--> to this page today and
visitor <!--#rtotcnt--> since <!--#lastzero-->.
```

totcnt

SYNTAX

```
<!--#totcnt-->
<!--#totcnt file-"pathname"-->
<!--#totcnt virtual="URLpath"-->
```

DESCRIPTION

Replace with the total number of times the page has been accessed since the counters were last set to zero, or zeroed. To zero a page counter, simply delete the counter file. The next time the page is accessed, the server-side include engine will create a new one with the current access count. Separate counters are kept for each document that contains this directive. By default, the counter for a page is kept in a file whose name is the same as the document itself, with *.ctr* appended (e.g., *index.html-ssi.ctr*).

To change the default counter file and specify a counter file with a different name, use the optional *file* or *virtual* parameters. The *file* parameter lets you specify a full path and name for the page's counter file. For example, you may want to use a counter file with an 8.3 name (necessary in a Novell environment) or locate the counter on another computer in the network. The *virtual* parameter lets you specify a URL path to the counter.

EXAMPLE

```
You are visitor number <!--#totcnt--> since
<!--#lastzero-->.
```

ADMINISTERING WEBSITE

As you find your Web growing, changing, and needing to be more complex or flexible, you will want to adjust WebSite's default configuration. Server Admin is WebSite's tool for making these changes to the server's mapping, its identity (or identities), automatic directory listing, access control, and logging capabilities. Server Admin's graphical interface lets you make these changes easily and quickly—from changing the format of automatic directory listings to HTML 3 tables to adding multiple identities to run virtual servers under WebSite. You can update the server while it is running and see the effect of your changes immediately. Server Admin allows you to concentrate on your Web's content, not its operation. Chapter 9 through Chapter 13 cover the tasks for which you use Server Admin, while Chapter 14 walks you through the steps to remotely administer WebSite.

CHAPTER NINE

MAPPING

If you've wondered how the server knows to display your home page for the URL *http://localhost/*, then you're ready to delve into the subject of mapping. You can think of mapping as a behind-the-scenes direction finder for your web. When a browser requests a URL, the WebSite server first compares the URL to several web server mapping tables to see how that URL should be translated on your web. For example, a URL may be mapped to a physical location on your computer or one halfway around the world or it may be mapped to a CGI program that creates a virtual document.

The WebSite server supports three types of mapping:

- URL Mapping, including

  - Document mapping, which maps a logical URL to a physical location on your system

  - Redirection mapping, which maps one URL to another URL, often on another server and generally used only temporarily

  - Executable or CGI mapping, which maps URLs for CGI programs to the location of the specific type of CGI program (Standard, Windows, or DOS) and tells the server to execute rather than display the CGI program.

- Content type mapping, which maps the type of document (as defined by the file extension) to a standard MIME (Multipurpose Internet Mail Extensions) protocol type, used by the web browser to correctly display the document

- Directory icon mapping, which maps icon images used in automatic directory listings to specific content (or MIME) types

The WebSite default mapping is probably sufficient for your web, especially in its early stages. As your web grows and becomes more sophisticated, mapping will become an important tool for making your web flexible and extending its capabilities. If you plan to run virtual servers, mapping is an extremely important concept. Chapter 10, *Virtual Servers and WebSite*, covers this topic in detail but relies on the basic information in this chapter.

This chapter discusses each type of mapping in detail as well as some general concepts about mapping. Common examples for using each type of mapping are included to provide ideas for your own web. The chapter begins with the general procedures for changing your web's mapping using WebSite's Server Admin application.

NOTE

Many of the problems encountered by WebSite users are the result of incorrect mapping. If you must change the mapping for your server, please read the appropriate sections of this chapter first and follow the instructions. You should always test any mapping changes you make.

MAPPING IN SERVER ADMIN

Before we talk about the specific types of mapping and when you would want to use them, let's look first at the Mapping page in Server Admin.

DISPLAYING THE MAPPING PAGE

To work with the Mapping page, you must first:

1. Launch the Server Admin application from the WebSite program or start group, from WebView, or from the server's Control menu (Properties option).
2. Click on the Mapping tab to display the Mapping page (Figure 9-1).

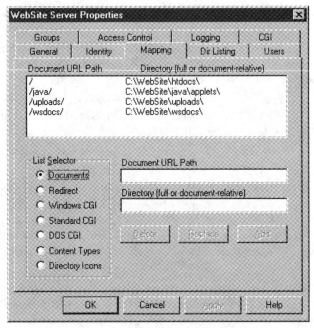

FIGURE 9-1: MAPPING PAGE IN WEBSITE SERVER ADMIN

The top section of the page shows the current mapping in two columns, which change according to the mapping type being displayed. The mapping shown in Figure 9-1 is the WebSite default (note that your drive specification may be different). *C:\WebSite\htdocs* is the default document root of the server (which you may have changed during installation). *C:\WebSite\wsdocs* is the location of documents shipped with WebSite, such as the server self-test and release notes. Because this location is "owned" by the server, you may want to add access control to it at some point. (See Chapter 12, *Controlling Access to Your Web*.)

ADDING, CHANGING, AND DELETING MAPPING VALUES

You can add, change, or delete mapping values using the two edit boxes and Delete, Replace, and Add buttons in the lower right of the page. Follow these steps to add a value:

1. Put the cursor in the first of the two edit boxes and type in the value to be mapped. Press TAB to move the cursor to the second edit box. Type in the value to which you are mapping.

2. Press Add.

Follow these steps to change a value:

1. Highlight the mapping to be changed in the list. The values appear in the two edit boxes.

2. Edit the values in the second box only (if you change the value in the first box, you are actually creating a *new* value to be mapped).

3. Press Replace.

Follow these steps to delete a value:

1. Highlight the mapping to be deleted in the list. The values appear in the two edit boxes.

2. Press Delete.

After you have made all the changes to the mapping type, press Apply. You may select another mapping type to modify or update the WebSite server by pressing Close.

NOTE

Changes made on any Server Admin page are not in effect until you close the application. After exiting Server Admin, a dialog appears asking whether you want to update the server immediately or wait until the server is idle (has no active connections). If the server is not running, the updates are in effect the next time you start the server.

SELECTING OTHER MAPPING TYPES

In the List Selector box of the Mapping page, you will see the other types of mapping available for the server. To view the values for another mapping type, click on the radio button in front of the type. For each type, the mapping values change, as listed in Table 9-1.

TABLE 9-1: MAPPING TYPES IN WEBSITE

Mapping Type	Value Being Mapped	Mapped Value
Documents	Document URL Path	Directory path (full path or relative to the document root path; except for the URL path /, which is mapped to a full path or one relative to the server root)
Redirect	Original URL	Redirected URL
Windows CGI	Win CGI URL Path	Directory path (full path or relative to the document root path)
Standard CGI	Standard CGI URL Path	Directory path (full path or relative to the document root path)
DOS CGI	DOS CGI URL Path	Directory path (full path or relative to the document root path)
Content Types	File Extension (class)	MIME Content Type
Directory Icons	MIME Content Type	Icon File for Directory Listing

The following sections explain the various types, paths, and relationships among them all as well as how you would use them.

DOCUMENT MAPPING

The first type of URL mapping, Document mapping, lets you assign logical pieces of your web (as defined by URLs) to physical locations on your computer, or any other computer on your network. This capability means that the actual files that make up your web can be in a variety of locations, but all are reachable from a single URL hierarchy. The URL hierarchy includes the protocol, hostname, server document root, and any directory and/or filenames added to that URL. For example, in the URL *http://localhost/new_web/index.html*, *http://* is the protocol, *localhost* is the hostname, / is the server's document root, *new_web/* is a directory path, and *index.html* is the filename.

Document mapping can be challenging so we *highly recommend* you read this section before making changes to your server's document mapping. Incorrectly

WEBSITE MAPPING RULES IN A NUTSHELL

WebSite uses mapping to decide whether to return the contents of a file to the browser or to execute the file as a CGI program. If a file falls under document mapping, the server sends it to the browser. If a file falls under CGI mapping, the server tries to execute it.

Definitions

- The *server root* is the directory into which the WebSite server executable and other components are installed.

- A *UNC path* is a directory pathname for a shared directory (a *share*) on another computer connected to the LAN. UNC paths start with \\ instead of a drive letter. UNC stands for Uniform (or Universal) Naming Convention.

- A *relative path* is a pathname that does not start with a path delimiter (\ for directories, / for URLs).

Rules

- URLs for documents and the three types of CGI programs are mapped separately and must be mapped to separate directories. A CGI-mapped directory must not fall within either the document-mapped directory tree or the tree mapped for another CGI type.

- The top of the document URL hierarchy (/, the *document root*) may be mapped to any physical directory or UNC path. If the physical pathname is relative, then it is relative to the *server root* directory.

- Any other document URL path may be mapped to any physical directory or UNC path as long as the physical path does not fall within a CGI-mapped tree. If the physical pathname is relative, then it is relative to the *document root*.

- Any CGI URL path may be mapped to any physical directory or UNC path as long as the physical path does not fall within a document-mapped tree. If the physical pathname is relative, then it is relative to the *server root*.

- Overlapped mappings are permitted; however, if the server must create a URL for a document that is mapped more than once, the results are undefined. This issue affects only URL fixup and directory listings. We recommend that only advanced users employ overlapped mapping.

Note that advanced applications may use special content-type mapping to tell the server to execute files that are document-mapped. These rules do not cover that case. See "wwwserver: A Special WebSite Content Type" for information.

mapped URLs result in an improperly functioning web and errors returned to users, rather than documents.

This section first describes the default document mapping for WebSite. Next it describes a simple mapping change, mapping URLs to other locations on your local system. The third example describes mapping URLs across a network. The ultimate mapping—setting up virtual servers—is touched on briefly. (The next chapter is completely dedicated to the topic.)

DEFAULT DOCUMENT MAPPING

Figure 9-2 shows the default document mapping for WebSite on the Server Admin Mapping page. The default mapping includes the URL paths for the document root (indicated by a /), the Java applet directory (*/java/*), the access controlled forms uploading directory (*/uploads/*), and for the documents shipped with WebSite (*/wsdocs/*). These URL paths are mapped to directories on the same system on which WebSite is running.

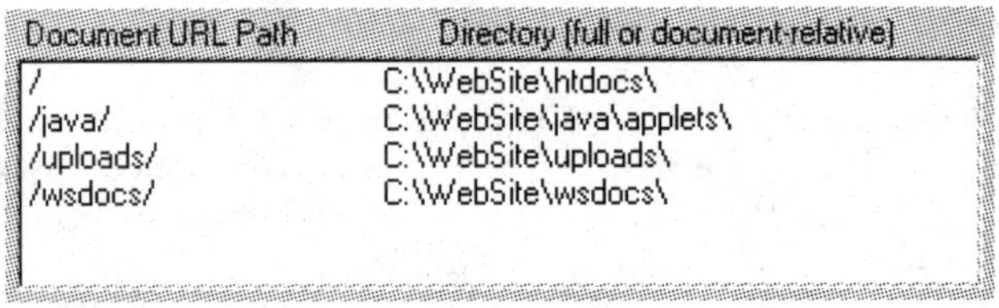

Document URL Path	Directory (full or document-relative)
/	C:\WebSite\htdocs\
/java/	C:\WebSite\java\applets\
/uploads/	C:\WebSite\uploads\
/wsdocs/	C:\WebSite\wsdocs\

FIGURE 9-2: DEFAULT DOCUMENT MAPPING

In this figure, the directory paths are shown as *full* paths. That means they include the drive specification and the full pathname to the mapped location. With this mapping in mind, you can see that the URL *http://localhost/* returns the default home page (that is, the index file) from the directory *C:\WebSite\htdocs*. The URL *http://localhost/wsdocs/* returns the index file from the directory *C:\WebSite\wsdocs*.

You are probably wondering where the URL hierarchy starts. The *document root* (/) is off the *server root*. The default server root is *C:\WebSite*. So the default document root is *C:\WebSite\htdocs*. You may have changed the server and/or the document root during installation. You can find the server root on the General page of Server Admin (in the Working Directory field).

Server Admin lets you enter pathnames either as full or relative. However, unless you fully understand relative pathnames, we recommend you use full pathnames. (See the sidebar, "Relative to What.")

Whether you enter paths as full or relative, the document mapping tells the server where to find pieces of your web. You can now answer the question raised in the introduction: How does the server know where to find its home page? It looks for the document root and returns the default home page (*index.html*). In the WebSite default, the URL *http://localhost/* returns the document *C:\Web-Site\htdocs\index.html*.

CHANGING DOCUMENT MAPPING

The default document mapping may be fine for many WebSite servers. However, as your web grows, you'll find that changing and adding to the document mapping is a powerful tool in building a robust and usable web. For example, you may face one of these situations:

- Your company wants to make its product lines available on the Web, but you don't want to keep all the documents under the server's document root (*htdocs*). You can make those documents part of your web by creating URLs and then mapping them to the directory paths of the documents.

- You are providing space on your web server for other departments and individuals you work with and want to keep their webs separated. They want to maintain their own documents on their local computers, which are part of the network running WebSite. You can create URLs for each person and department and then map the URLs accordingly using UNC pathnames.

- You need to move your web, but you don't want to change the URL(s). Simply change the mapping of the physical directory paths to the new location but leave the URL paths the same.

The examples in this section show you how to change document mappings for the first two scenarios. These examples show the principles you need to master to succeed at mapping. As you become comfortable with mapping, you'll find other reasons to change document mapping.

DOCUMENT MAPPING ON THE SERVER COMPUTER

The Good Food company installed WebSite to advertise its products on the World Wide Web. Its product lines include fine coffees, exotic teas, a full range of spices, and specialty cookbooks. The various product groups have developed

RELATIVE TO WHAT?

Once you get the hang of relative pathnames, you may find they make your web management more efficient and flexible. The easiest way to understand relative paths is with a tree diagram, such as the NT File Manager provides. The callouts in this figure give the path (usually relative) and the URL (if appropriate).

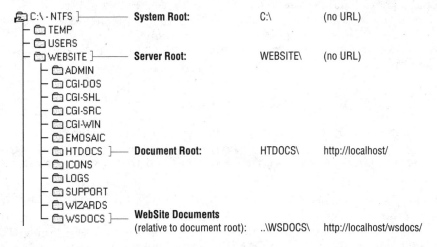

C:\ - NTFS	System Root:	C:\	(no URL)
TEMP			
USERS			
WEBSITE	Server Root:	WEBSITE\	(no URL)
ADMIN			
CGI-DOS			
CGI-SHL			
CGI-SRC			
CGI-WIN			
EMOSAIC			
HTDOCS	Document Root:	HTDOCS\	http://localhost/
ICONS			
LOGS			
SUPPORT			
WIZARDS			
WSDOCS	WebSite Documents (relative to document root):	..\WSDOCS\	http://localhost/wsdocs/

To build a full pathname from a relative pathname, you have to look at all the names in the tree and put them together. For example, to build the full pathname for the server root, we would add WebSite to the path of the directory immediately above it: C:\WebSite. The full pathname of the document root would be *htdocs* plus WebSite\ plus C:\ or *C:\WebSite\htdocs*.

The building process changes when a path is relative to a directory other than the system root, as with *wsdocs*. This directory is relative to the document root, or *htdocs*. To find *wsdocs* from this directory, think of climbing a tree. First you must go *up htdocs* and then *over* to *wsdocs*. The symbol for going up one level is .. (two dots). Thus, ..*wsdocs*\ means go up one level from the current document root *htdocs*, to reach *C:\WebSite*, and then over to *wsdocs*.

To take the example a step further, what would be the relative path (from the document root) of a subdirectory in *wsdocs* called *32demo*? To get to *32demo* from *htdocs*, we must go up one tree and descend *two* subdirectory trees. So the relative path is ..*wsdocs**32demo*.

Most of the paths in WebSite are relative to the document root. However, some paths (such as those for CGI programs) are relative to the server root. As the title of this sidebar says, the important thing to know is "relative to what?"

documents (HTML, graphics, and forms) for each product line. The files are all residing on the D:\ drive of the computer on which WebSite is running.

You must incorporate these documents into the Good Food company's web without moving them to C:\WebSite\htdocs. You can accomplish this by mapping the URLs for each product line's web to its physical location on the system.

You must first find out if URL paths have been assigned to each new piece of the Web. Note that the URL path does not include the protocol or hostname, only the path, starting with the root (/). If a URL path does not exist for each new part of the Web, consult the manager responsible for an appropriate name. Remember that visitors to your web may often get there by guessing at the URL!

Because correct mapping is essential to users receiving the right document when they visit your web site, a bit of up-front planning is necessary. Completing a planning chart is the next important step. Figure 9-3 shows a planning chart with the necessary information for this example.

Document Mapping Changes for http://goodfood.com/	
Document Root is C:\Website\htdocs	
URL	**Full Directory Path**
Full URL: http://goodfood.com/coffee/ URL Path: /coffee/	D:\BEVERAGES\COFFEE\
Full URL: http://goodfood.com/tea/ URL Path: /tea/	D:\BEVERAGES\TEA\
Full URL: http://goodfood.com/spices/ URL Path: /spices/	D:\SPICES\
Full URL: http://goodfood.com/cookbooks/ URL Path: /cookbooks/	D:\COOKBOOKS\
Full URL: URL Path:	
Note: Be sure to add the trailing slash (/, \) on all URLs and directory paths when adding or changing entries in document mapping.	

FIGURE 9-3: DOCUMENT MAPPING PLANNING CHART

Each product line's full URL is given as well as the URL path (used on the Mapping page) and the full directory path. Note that the directories are on the D:\ drive. Completing the table correctly is the hard part.

To make the mapping changes, follow these steps:

1. Launch Server Admin and select the Mapping page. Make sure the List Selector is on Documents.

2. Place the cursor in the Document URL Path field and type in the first URL path from Figure 9-3, */coffee/*. Don't forget the trailing /.

3. Press TAB to move to the Directory field and type in the full directory path for the URL, *D:\Beverages\Coffee*. Don't forget the trailing\.

4. Press Add.

5. Repeat steps 2 through 4 for the other entries in Figure 9-3. Figure 9-4 shows the completed information with full pathnames for the new URLs.

6. Press Close to update the server.

7. Test the new mapping by pointing a Web browser at the new URL. If the physical directory exists, the server will return an index file, an automatic directory listing, or a forbidden message (i.e., listing disabled).

Document URL Root	Directory (full or server-relative)
/	C:\WebSite\htdocs\
/coffee/	D:\Beverages\Coffee\
/cookbooks/	D:\Cookbooks\
/spices/	D:\Spices\
/tea/	D:\Beverages\Tea\
/wsdocs/	C:\WebSite\wsdocs\

FIGURE 9-4: ADDING ENTRIES TO DOCUMENT MAPPING

DOCUMENT MAPPING ON THE NETWORK

If you are using WebSite on a company network, individuals on the network will want to create their own personal home pages (and links to other documents on their computers). Other departments will also want to set up webs that they manage, but are available throughout the company. Document mapping across the network allows you to incorporate these variously located webs into the WebSite server. Let's look at two specific examples:

• Adding the Marketing Department's web to the company web

• Adding your own home page to the company web in a URL path you are establishing for employee home pages (We're assuming that you are the WebSite server administrator.)

First, you need to find out where those webs reside. The Marketing Department has several computers on the network, and has been building their web on the computer named *whizbang* in a directory with the full pathname C:\MKTGWEB. Your web resides on the same computer as the WebSite server but in your home directory, C:\ADMIN\SAM\SWEB. The WebSite server's fully qualified domain name is *goodbooks.com*.

Specifying the paths (and making sure they work) for the marketing web, requires two operating system/networking conditions:

- The network must be up and running.
- The directory C:\MKTGWEB of *whizbang* must be shared by *whizbang*, making it available on the network to other computers and the identity under which WebSite is running. The shared name of the directory for this example is MARKETWEB.

NOTE

There are other methods of making a remote directory available to the server. For example, you can share the entire drive on which MKTGWEB resides. Or, you can mount the share to a local drive letter. The recommended method for WebSite is to use UNC pathnames.

Since these are both networking items, we'll assume they are correct for this example. For more information or instructions, please consult your operating system manual and your network administrator.

Since pictures often help to put complex setups into perspective, you should diagram the mapping you plan to undertake. Figure 9-5 shows the particulars of this example.

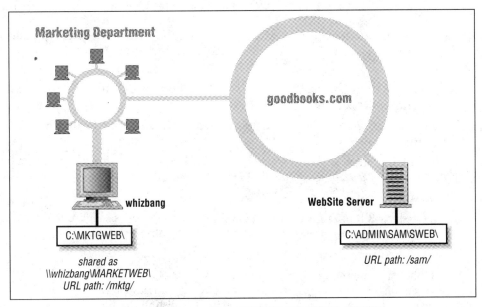

FIGURE 9-5: DOCUMENT MAPPING PLANNING SKETCH

The next planning step is to fill out a planning chart showing the full URL, the URL path, and the full directory path for each new mapping assignment. Figure 9-6 shows the planning chart for this example. Note that if you plan to add other personal home pages to the web, you may want to establish a convention for naming them.

Document Mapping Changes for http://goodbooks.com/	
Document Root is C:\Website\htdocs	
URL	**Full Directory Path**
Full URL: http://goodbooks.com/mktg/ URL Path: /mktg/	\\whizbang\MARKETWEB\
Full URL: http://goodbooks.com/sam/ URL Path: /sam/	C:\ADMIN\SAM\SWEB
Full URL: URL Path:	

Note: Be sure to add the trailing slash (/, \) on all URLs and directory paths when adding or changing entries in document mapping.

FIGURE 9-6: DOCUMENT MAPPING PLANNING CHART

Once you've figured out the new mapping, adding the URLs and directory paths to Server Admin is quite easy. To make the additions from Figure 9-6, follow these steps:

1. Launch Server Admin and select the Mapping page. Make sure the List Selector is on Documents.

2. Place the cursor in the Document URL Path field and type in the first URL path from Table 9-6, /mktg/.

3. Press TAB to move to the Directory field and type in the full directory path for the URL, \\whizbang\MARKETWEB\.

4. Press Add.

5. Repeat steps 2 through 4 for the second entry in Figure 9-6. Figure 9-7 shows the completed information with full pathnames for the new URLs.

6. Press Close to update the server.

7. Test the new mapping by pointing a Web browser at the new URL. If the physical directory exists, the server will return an index file, an automatic directory listing, or a forbidden message (that is, listing disabled).

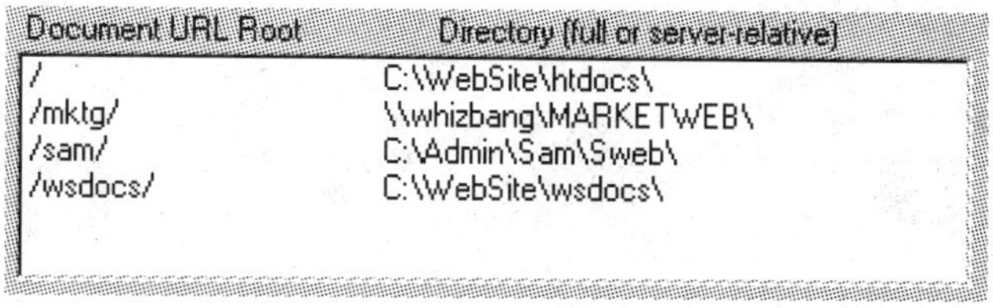

Document URL Root	Directory (full or server-relative)
/	C:\WebSite\htdocs\
/mktg/	\\whizbang\MARKETWEB\
/sam/	C:\Admin\Sam\Sweb\
/wsdocs/	C:\WebSite\wsdocs\

FIGURE 9-7: ADDING ENTRIES TO DOCUMENT MAPPING

DOCUMENT MAPPING FOR VIRTUAL SERVERS

Perhaps the ultimate mapping comes when you set up virtual servers—completely separate web sites with separate IP addresses running under one copy of WebSite. When you set up virtual servers, you first map each IP address to a URL prefix, or nickname. The URL prefix becomes the server root for that IP address and all document and CGI mapping must include the URL prefix.

Chapter 10, *Virtual Servers and WebSite*, covers virtual servers in detail, including the mapping issues. If you plan to set up virtual servers, please see that chapter, but also be ready to refer to this section for basics on document mapping.

TESTING YOUR MAPPING CHANGES

Before you open up your newly mapped documents to the public, you should test them to make sure the mapping is correct. There are two methods you can use to test the document mapping:

- Using a browser that displays full error information (such as Spyglass Mosaic 2.11, which ships with WebSite), point at the newly mapped URL. If the mapping is correct, the browser displays what you expect (a document or a directory listing). If the mapping is incorrect, the browser displays the physical path of the URL as the server is interpreting it. If the physical path is not what you expect, check the mapping and determine where you went wrong. Continue to test until the mapping is correct.

- Using WebView, open a new tree for the newly mapped URL. If the mapping is correct, WebView displays what you expect (an HTML file, a broken link, or a directory link). Switch to the filename view to confirm that the URL is mapped to the appropriate location. If what you expect to see displayed is incorrect or the filename view doesn't match your intended location, check the mapping and correct it. Continue to test until the mapping is correct.

These simple tests will save you and your users a lot of time and aggravation. We cannot recommend strongly enough that you thoroughly test your mappings.

REDIRECT MAPPING

WebSite lets you temporarily assign a URL on your web to another URL—usually a URL on another server—through redirect mapping. When the server receives a request for a redirected URL, it automatically sends the browser to the new URL. The redirection is transparent to the user.

DEFAULT

WebSite includes no default redirected URLs. If you redirect URLs, you map the original URL to the redirected URL. The original URL must be a URL path for your server. The redirected URL can be either a full URL or a relative URL if it is on your local computer. The redirected URL *must be* a full URL (including protocol and/or hostname and path) if it is on another computer. If the TCP/IP port is other than 80 for the target system, include that in the redirected URL as well.

EXAMPLES OF REDIRECTING URLS

Redirect mapping is best used for temporary situations. Here are some times you might find redirect mapping useful for your web:

- A portion of your web is undergoing heavy revision, and you don't want users to see it "under construction." You can redirect the URL for that portion of the web to a document explaining the current situation. If you do so, include an expected "Grand Reopening" date for your web and a teaser to encourage users to come back to the new web; otherwise, people may never visit it again.

NOTE

The Under Construction wizard, available in WebView, quickly creates a page to alert users of changes being made to your web.

- If your web is mirrored on other servers in various locations, you can redirect the URL for one server to the URL for another server. You may want to do this when you are revamping the web or when a network problem for a mirrored site is slowing response time.

- If you use server-side includes on your home page and want users to reach it either by asking for *index.html-ssi* or *index.html*, redirect the URL for *index.html* to the URL for *index.html-ssi*.

To implement redirect mapping, follow the steps described in "Adding, Changing, and Deleting Mapping Values," earlier in this chapter.

CGI MAPPING

WebSite mapping includes three types of CGI (Common Gateway Interface) mapping for the three types of CGI programs WebSite supports. These types are Windows CGI, Standard CGI, and DOS CGI.

CGI mapping accomplishes two things:

- It identifies a URL as a program, and thus the response to the browser will be to execute a program rather than return a document.
- It specifies what type of CGI program is in the URL and where those programs are located on the web.

The three types of CGI programs and their uses are fully discussed in Section 4 of this book, including suggestions for when you might change the mapping values. Here we briefly describe the default values and their relationship to the WebSite server.

DEFAULT

In general, the default CGI mapping in WebSite should be sufficient for your web. Figures 9-8, 9-9, and 9-10 show the default mapping for each type of CGI interface.

Win CGI URL Path	Directory (full or server-relative)
/cgi-win/	C:\WebSite\cgi-win\

FIGURE 9-8: DEFAULT WINDOWS CGI MAPPING

The important thing to know about CGI mappings is that they are *relative to the server root* not to the document root. That is, they are relative to *C:\WebSite* and not to *C:\WebSite\htdocs*. Thus, the URL path */cgi-win/* maps to the physical directory *C:\WebSite\cgi-win*.

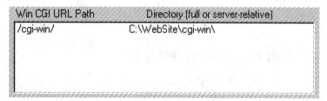

Standard CGI URL Path	Directory (full or server-relative)
/auth/	C:\WebSite\cgi-shl-prot\
/cgi-bin/	C:\WebSite\cgi-shl\
/cgi-shl/	C:\WebSite\cgi-shl\

FIGURE 9-9: DEFAULT STANDARD CGI MAPPING

If you change CGI mappings, you must map them so they *do not* fall into a document area. For example, if you move your web to another location and want to move the CGI programs as well, don't create CGI directories underneath the new document root directory. Instead, create them at the *same level* as the document root (or in another location altogether) and map them accordingly. We highly recommend you write out all proposed mapping changes on a planning chart before proceeding to change the mapping.

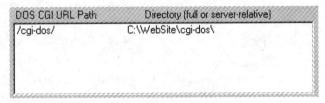

DOS CGI URL Path	Directory (full or server-relative)
/cgi-dos/	C:\WebSite\cgi-dos\

FIGURE 9-10: DEFAULT DOS CGI MAPPING

To edit the CGI mapping tables, follow the steps described in "Adding, Changing, and Deleting Mapping Values," earlier in this chapter.

NOTE

If you change the CGI mappings, make sure you test the new locations and that the programs work correctly before opening them up to the public. See the section earlier in this chapter called "Testing Your Mapping Changes" for testing methods.

CONTENT TYPE MAPPING

One of the HTTP standards for a Web server is that it include a content type with every document returned to a browser. A Web browser must be able to identify the content type and display the document appropriately for the type. For example, if a browser requests an HTML document, the server not only returns the document but also includes the content type in the header information. The browser reads the header information first, knows that it can display an HTML document without an external viewer, and then does so.

If the content type requires an external viewer (such as WHAM for an audio file), the browser tries to launch the appropriate viewer. Content types can also be defined for applications (such as Microsoft Word or Adobe Acrobat), in which case the browser would launch the appropriate application.

These content types are also called MIME types. The standard format of a MIME content type includes a main type and subtype, separated by a slash (/). The MIME content type for HTML is *text/html*.

In mapping content types, you assign a particular class of document to a particular content type. Because the file extension is the most common and consistent way of identifying particular classes of documents, WebSite uses file extensions for mapping to content types. For example, an HTML file has the extension *.html* or *.htm*, which is by default mapped to the content type *text/html*. When the server returns a document with the extension *.html*, it sends the *text/html* content type in the header, and the browser knows how to display it.

A large number of content types exist, including *audio/basic*, *image/gif*, and *video/mpeg*. In addition to the standard content types, you can create new content types as necessary. This section discusses how to use existing MIME types and how to create new ones for a wide variety of document types. It also covers a special application of content types in preparing the server to create automatic directory listings by mapping content types to the icons used in the listing.

NOTE

Content types known to the server must also be defined in the user's Web browser to correctly display documents. Several Web browsers refer to this task as setting up Helpers.

DEFAULT

WebSite includes nearly 50 predefined content types. Figure 9-11 shows part of the list with the file extension in the left column and the content type (in the form *type/subtype*) in the right column.

Note that the file extensions may be any number of characters since WebSite runs under Windows NT or Windows 95, which support long filenames. However, since many legacy documents exist from the MS-DOS and Windows environment, several default WebSite content types are defined for both short and long file extensions. For example:

```
.htm     text/html
.html    text/html
.mpe     video/mpeg
.mpeg    video/mpeg
.mpg     video/mpeg
```

WebSite includes five standard content types (with multiple subtypes) and one custom content type:

text	For ASCII text documents such as HTML files
image	For full-color images to be displayed apart from the document (that is, not as inline graphics) such as JPEG files
video	For video clips such as MPEG files
audio	For audio clips such as WAVE files

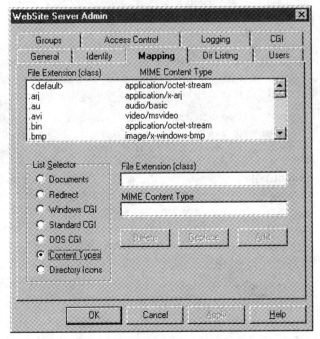

FIGURE 9-11: CONTENT TYPES

application   For specific applications such as Microsoft Word for Windows (defined by .*doc*)

wwwserver   For specific use on the WebSite server

In Figure 9-11, you'll notice that the content type for the file extension .*arj* is written as *application/x-arj*. Beginning the subtype with *x-* is the accepted format convention for user-defined content types. This format prevents confusion between standard content types and user-defined ones. For lists of accepted content types, see WebSite Central or check out *ftp://venera.isi.edu/in-notes/iana/assignments/media-types*.

WWWSERVER: A SPECIAL WEBSITE CONTENT TYPE

The WebSite developers created a special content type called *wwwserver*, which causes the server to handle documents in a special way. Six subtypes for *wwwserver* are defined and included with the server. Three of these identify CGI programs and three handle other special cases requiring processing by the server.

WWWSERVER CONTENT TYPES FOR CGI

The three CGI *wwwserver* content types included in WebSite are

- *wwwserver/shellcgi* (mapped to *.cgi* and *.scgi* extensions)
- *wwwserver/doscgi* (mapped to *.dcgi* extensions)
- *wwwserver/wincgi* (mapped to *.wcgi* extensions)

This content type allows CGI executable files to reside in the regular document tree instead of in the CGI program directories. For example, when the server recognizes a file with the content type *wwwserver/wincgi*, instead of displaying the contents of the file, it attempts to execute it using the Windows CGI interface. In practical terms this means you can have CGI executables in a directory and not have to worry about users nabbing the contents of the program. (It also gives you more flexibility on placing CGI programs in your web.)

A specific example of using the *wwwserver* content type for CGI files would be to map *.pl* (Perl) files to the content type *wwwserver/shellcgi*. When a user points a browser at any *.pl* document, the server executes the document rather than serving up the contents.

WWWSERVER CONTENT TYPE FOR REDIRECTION

The *wwwserver/redirection* content type is mapped to the file extension *.url*. This content type lets you create documents that contain a URL, which the server uses for redirection. When the server encounters a *.url* document, it opens the file, reads the target URL, and sends the new URL to the browser.

If you are running WebSite under Windows 95, you may be familiar with Internet Shortcuts (part of the Windows 95 Plus! package). Internet Shortcuts use the *.url* extension and fit seamlessly into the WebSite redirection scheme. You can include an Internet Shortcut in a directory listing and when a user clicks on it, the server redirects the browser to the new URL. See Chapter 11, *Automatic Directory Listings*, for more information.

WWWSERVER CONTENT TYPE FOR IMAGE MAPS

The *wwwserver/imagemap* content type is mapped to the file extension *.map*. This content type allows you to include NCSA-format imagemaps in your web. When the server detects the *.map* extension, it treats the document as a clickable image map and processes it appropriately.

The WebSite server self-test includes an example of using the *wwwserver/ imagemap* content type with a *.map* file. For more information, see Chapter 7, *Working with Image Maps*.

WWWSERVER CONTENT TYPE FOR SERVER-SIDE INCLUDES

The *wwwserver/html-ssi* content type is mapped to the file extension *.html-ssi*. This content type allows you to incorporate HTML files that contain server side includes into your web. Server-side includes are directives that cause the server to insert pieces of information such as the date or the contents of a counter. The server recognizes these files by the *.html-ssi* extension. For more information, see Chapter 8, *Extending HTML with Server-Side Includes*.

You may want to define other extensions as *wwwserver/html-ssi*. For example, to run all your files through SSI processing, change the content types *.html* and *.htm* to *wwwserver/html-ssi*. If your SSI files use the extension *.shtml,* add that extension to content type mapping and map it to *wwwserver/html-ssi*.

ADDING A NEW CONTENT TYPE

Let's say you have a large library of existing procedures and customer support documents that were created in WordPerfect. You want to make them available to users of your web, but you don't want to convert them to HTML. Adding a content type for WordPerfect allows you to publish these documents through WebSite. Users request a WordPerfect document via a URL, and the browser launches WordPerfect when the document is returned. Of course, the browser must be configured correctly as well.

Before you add a new content type, you must

- Make sure that the class of files uses consistent filename extensions (and that you know what they are). These extensions must not conflict with extensions used by other content types known to your server (or users' browsers). In our WordPerfect example, assume that documents were created with the extensions *.wpf* or *.wp*. Note that *.doc* is already used by Microsoft Word.

- Decide what you are going to call the content type. Since this is an application, the main type is *application*. For this example, the subtype will be *wordperfect*. Since we are creating this content type and don't know what the standard is, we will use the *x-* convention. The new type is *application/x-wordperfect*.

- To add the new content type, follow these steps:

    1. Launch Server Admin and select the Mapping tab. Make sure the List Selector is on Content Types.

    2. Place the cursor in the File Extension (class) field and type in the first file extension *.wpf*

    3. Press TAB to move to the MIME Content Type field and type in the new content type, *application/x-wordperfect*

    4. Press Add.

    5. Repeat steps 2 through 4 for the second file extension *.wp*. Figure 9-12 shows the new content type.

File Extension (class)	MIME Content Type
.wav	audio/wav
.wcgi	wwwserver/wincgi
.wp	application/x-wordperfect
.wpf	application/x-wordperfect
.xls	application/msexcel
.zip	application/zip

FIGURE 9-12: ADDING NEW CONTENT TYPES

6. Press Close to update the server. Don't forget that you must let users know the new content type *application/x-wordperfect* so they can update their browsers.

You can use the same procedure for adding other content types (such as Adobe Acrobat or FrameMaker), as well as for changing or deleting existing types.

DIRECTORY ICON MAPPING

A special use of content types is to map them to icons used in automatic directory listings. Chapter 11, *Automatic Directory Listings*, covers automatic directory lists in detail, so this section touches only briefly on the mechanics of mapping directory icons, an important step in preparing for automatic directory listings.

Table 9-2 shows the default values for directory icon mapping. There are eight content types that have predefined icons. Some of those content types include subtypes while others don't. An asterisk (*) indicates that all subtypes for those main types are included, unless a specific subtype already has a directory icon mapping. Remember that the content types are defined already on the Content Type screen. For example, the content type for an Adobe Acrobat file, *application/pdf*, which is mapped to the extension *.pdf*, on the Directory Icon mapping screen is mapped to the icon *pdf.gif*.

When the server creates an automatic directory listing, it looks at the content type, then looks at the Server Admin table, and includes the appropriate icon for the type of file. Figure 9-13 shows a portion of an automatic directory listing with icons.

The icons listed before the filenames are determined by the content type of the file. For example, the file *note.gif* has a content type *image/gif*. The server looks at the directory icons mapping table for that content type and sees that the icon file to be used is *image.gif*. The two text files (*rubout.txt* and *sample.html*) have content types *text/** so the server displays the *text.gif* icon.

You can add, change, or delete directory icons. Let's say you want to use the WordPerfect logo icon for WordPerfect files. Before you change the mapping, you must do the following two things:

Icon	Content Type	Icon File (\WebSite\icons)	Description
	application/*	binary.gif	Any undefined application file
	application/msaccess	access.gif	Microsoft Access file
	application/msexcel	excel.gif	Microsoft Excel file
	application/mspowerpoint	ppt.gif	Microsoft Powerpoint file
	application/msword	word.gif	Microsoft Word file
	application/mswrite	rtf.gif	Microsoft Write file
	application/pdf	pdf.gif	Adobe Acrobat file
	application/x-java-class	applet.gif	Java Applet file
	application/x-ms-shortcut	shortcut.gif	Windows 95 shortcut file (.lnk)
	application/x-visio-drawing	visio.gif	Visio file
	application/zip	zip.gif	Zipped file
	audio/*	sound.gif	Audio file
	image/*	image.gif	Image file
	image/x-windows-bmp	bmp.gif	Windows Bitmap file
	text/*	text.gif	Text file
	text/html	html.gif	HTML file
	text/rtf	rtf.gif	Rich Text Format file
	video/*	movie.gif	Video file
	wwwserver/redirection	inet.gif	Internet Shortcut file

TABLE 9-2: ICONS FOR AUTOMATIC DIRECTORY LISTING

- Create the icon file (as a GIF file) and place it in the icons directory (\WebSite\icons\). For this example, we'll call the file wordpfct.gif. For transparent icons such as those used by WebSite, create the GIF file as GIF89a image. (You can use LView Pro to save an image in this format.)

- Identify the content type. For this example, we'll use the type we entered above, application/x-wordperfect.

To add a directory icon mapping, follow these steps:

1. Launch Server Admin and select the Mapping page. Make sure the List Selector is on Directory Icons.

2. Place the cursor in the MIME Content Type field and type in the new content type, application/x-wordperfect.

	Name	Last modified	Size	Description
⬆	Parent Directory	25-Oct-95 11:39	-	
	CH09.ZIP	23-Sep-95 23:12	59K	*application/zip*
	basic.html	20-Feb-95 18:19	<1K	Sample Hypertext Document
	basic.txt	29-Apr-94 14:28	<1K	*text/plain*
	ch04new.doc	19-Oct-95 06:38	53K	*application/msword*
	ch04new.rtf	19-Oct-95 06:38	53K	*application/rtf*
	cover.gif	17-Oct-95 11:35	<1K	*image/gif*
	tutor.au	15-May-94 02:06	10K	*audio/basic*
	website.url	23-Sep-95 23:12	59K	Internet Shortcut

FIGURE 9-13: ICONS IN AUTOMATIC DIRECTORY LIST

3. Press TAB to move to the Icon File for Directory Listings field and type in the new filename, *wordpfct.gif*.

4. Press Add. Figure 9-14 shows the added directory icon.

MIME Content Type	Icon File for Directory Listings
application/x-wordperfect	wordpfct.gif
application/zip	zip.gif
audio/*	sound.gif
image/*	image.gif
text/*	text.gif
text/html	html.gif

FIGURE 9-14: ADDING A DIRECTORY ICON MAPPING

5. Press Close to update the server.

In Chapter 11, *Automatic Directory Listings*, we will see how the server uses the directory icons (or doesn't use them, as you may choose).

VIRTUAL SERVERS AND WEBSITE

Once you have successfully set up your WebSite server, you can consider setting up multiple webs on different IP addresses using only one running copy of WebSite. Each web is completely separate and reached by its own IP address. In effect, these separate webs are servers, what we call *virtual servers* because they share one single WebSite server program. Running virtual servers is also sometimes called multi-homing or multiple identities.

Having multiple virtual servers on a single WebSite server has several benefits. Perhaps the most common is to provide separate webs with separate addresses to several different companies, organizations, or individuals. In essence, WebSite lets you become a Web hosting service. Someone looking at the home page for one of your clients uses that client's domain name in the URL, which gives the impression that they are directly connected to the Internet and maintaining their own web.

A variation on this scenario is to set up virtual servers for several departments within a company. Each department has its own domain name and web, but they are all running on the same copy of WebSite. One server administrator can manage the virtual servers from a single location using one set of tools, or you can distribute all or part of the web management to each department. In fact, you will probably want each department to take responsibility for the content if not the administration of its web.

WebSite supports an extremely flexible virtual server environment. Webs can partially overlap, sharing documents and/or CGI programs. Or, webs can be totally separate, with strict access controls applied to maintain security and privacy. Webs (or portions of webs) can be distributed across computers on a local area network or maintained on a single system. This chapter describes how to set up and test virtual servers, how to add access control, and how to use the other WebSite tools with virtual servers. It also gives you several ideas for using virtual servers.

The key to successfully setting up and managing virtual servers is a thorough understanding of your system's networking setup and WebSite's mapping capability. Information regarding your system's networking is beyond the scope of this book. Information regarding mapping in WebSite is covered in Chapter 9,

Mapping, of this book. If you have questions about mapping, read Chapter 9 before proceeding. Without this background, you will experience problems with virtual servers.

HOW DO VIRTUAL SERVERS WORK?

WebSite's virtual servers feature takes advantage of the ability to support multiple IP addresses built into Windows NT and Windows 95. Windows NT supports multiple IP addresses using a single or multiple adapters. Windows 95 supports multiple IP addresses only with multiple adapters—one IP address per adapter. For example, you might have a Windows 95 configuration that included multiple Ethernet cards or an Ethernet card and a modem for PPP/SLIP dialup and have one IP address assigned to each adapter.

NOTE

WebSite can support an unlimited number of IP addresses. However, the operating system does not. Under Windows NT, you can enter up to five IP addresses per adapter through the Control Panel (TCP/IP advanced network configuration). It is also possible to add more IP addresses directly to the system Registry. WebSite users report that up to 256 IP addresses can be used safely under Windows NT 3.51. Note that system performance and consistency may be affected with such a large number of IP addresses. Most important, Microsoft does not support more than five IP addresses per adapter or adding IP addresses directly to the Registry. See Appendix C, *Troubleshooting Tips,* for more details.

To understand how virtual servers work, let's first look at how a server with a single identity works. First, a user requests a specific URL through a browser. The browser locates the server by using its IP address. (If the URL contained a domain name rather than an IP address, the browser found the IP address through DNS.) The browser strips the IP address from the request and sends only the path portion of the URL to the server. The server responds with the appropriate document from its web. For a system with only one identity, this model works fine— all URL paths are for the single server's web.

In a setup with multiple virtual servers, however, there has to be a way to identify which IP address (and therefore which virtual server) the browser's request is intended for. For example, if the browser is looking for the URL *http://good-food.com/coffee/* and the IP address is 123.234.57.47, the browser locates the system with the IP address 123.234.57.47, and asks the WebSite server for */coffee/*. Assuming WebSite has multiple virtual servers running, how does it know which virtual server houses this URL?

The answer lies in the nickname, or URL prefix, you assign to each virtual server's IP address. When a request arrives, WebSite detects the IP address and prefixes the URL path with the nickname. For example, if the IP address 123.234.57.47 has the URL prefix *food*, then the URL path becomes */food/coffee/*. Every request for that IP address is prefixed with */food/*. Requests for other IP addresses are prefixed with their own nicknames. The URL prefix is used only by the server; it is never returned to the browser or displayed to the user.

Assigning URL prefixes to IP addresses is at the heart of making virtual servers work. Each virtual server has its own URL prefix, which must be used for all document and CGI mapping as well as setting access control. The next sections of this chapter explain how to assign URL prefixes and how to set up mapping.

IDEAS FOR USING VIRTUAL SERVERS

The introduction mentioned two common uses of virtual servers: hosting webs for client companies or individuals, and hosting webs for departments within your organization. Here are two other scenarios for using virtual servers:

- Run a public web and an internal web as two virtual servers. The public web can contain information about your company or organization that you want the general public to have access to. The internal web, running across a LAN, can contain information pertinent to colleagues. You can have the two webs share or not share documents and CGI programs as desired.

- Use a virtual server as a test or development web. Assign this server to IP address 127.0.0.1 (localhost) so no one can accidentally have access to it. When the web is ready to be public, simply switch the URL prefix for another IP address to the one you used for the test web and the new web is public.

From these ideas, you can develop other uses that meet the needs of your environment and users.

SETTING UP VIRTUAL SERVERS

WebSite provides a graphical interface for setting up virtual servers, on the Identities page of Server Admin. You can set up virtual servers in one of two ways, depending on your operating system:

- **The Wizard Way**, using the Identity wizard from the Identities page. The wizard gathers information by asking questions and then automates the setup. We recommend using the Identity wizard exclusively unless you have an extremely specialized setup and thoroughly understand mapping and networking issues.

- **The Manual Way**, entering a URL prefix for each IP address on the Identities page, as well as hostnames. You must then complete document and CGI mapping for each URL prefix on the Mapping page of Server Admin. You must also make sure that all directories exist for each new mapping. If you change or delete virtual servers, you will use the manual method.

Regardless of which method you choose, you must complete the steps covered in the next section before setting up the virtual servers in WebSite. After you set up the virtual servers, you must test them. Instructions for testing your servers are also included in this section.

PREPARING FOR VIRTUAL SERVERS

Before you can use the virtual server capability of WebSite, you must obtain IP addresses (and fully qualified domain names), configure your computer to recognize the IP addresses, and then test their accuracy. To do so, complete the following steps:

1. Obtain an IP address and register the fully qualified domain name with DNS for each virtual server you plan to set up. Consult your Internet service provider or network administrator for help on obtaining IP addresses and domain names.

2. Create a planning chart showing the IP address and domain name for each virtual server. Figure 10-1 shows a completed sample chart you may want to use to track your virtual servers. Note that *localhost* (IP address 127.0.0.1) will always be one of your servers.

IP Address	Domain Name (optional)	URL Prefix	Shared CGIs?	Private CGIs?	Physical Location (full path)	Separate Access Log
127.0.0.1	localhost	/local	Yes	No	C:\Website\htdocs\	No
123.234.157.24	webs.provider.com	/webs	Yes	Yes	D:\webs\	webs.log
123.234.157.25	admin.provider.com	/corpweb	No	Yes	\\admin\corpweb\	No
123.234.156.211	www.food.com	/food	Yes	Yes	D:\clients\food\	food.log
123.234.156.151	www.used.books.com	/books	Yes	Yes	D:\clients\books\	books.log

FIGURE 10-1: VIRTUAL SERVERS INFORMATION PLANNING CHART

3. To each virtual server assign a nickname, that is, a URL prefix. This name should be a short, descriptive word; for example, *local* for *localhost*. You may find it convenient to use the first part (the hostname) of each server's fully qualified domain name as the URL prefix. Remember that only you and the

server see this name; users on the Web never do. Add the URL prefix to the chart.

4. For each virtual server, determine if it will share CGI programs with other servers, use private CGI programs, or both. If you are unsure, select both. Note your choice on the chart.

5. To each virtual server assign a subdirectory on your system. The subdirectories do not have to be in the WebSite directory; in fact, it is better to locate them outside the WebSite directory. Keep the names short and mnemonic for each server. If you plan to locate a virtual server on another computer on the LAN, we recommend you use the UNC pathname. The Identity wizard will create subdirectories on the local system for you; however, it will not create UNC paths. We recommend that you create all remote directories and verify UNC paths before using the wizard. If you set up identities manually, you must create all the subdirectories, regardless of location. Add the subdirectory names to the chart.

6. For each virtual server, determine which access log file it will use: a special one or the main access log. Having more than one access log lets you track Web activity for a particular virtual server (or servers) independent of other virtual servers. For example, all your internal virtual servers could share one log while the external virtual servers could share another or each have their own. A virtual server can use an existing log, a new log, or the main access log. Whichever access log you choose to use, each request entered in the log is identified with the server's name. For more information on WebSite's logging capabilities, see Chapter 13, *Logging*. If a virtual server will use a log file other than the main access log, you must assign it a name, such as *local.log* for *localhost*. Note the names of any separate log files on rt.

7. Configure your operating system to answer on each of the IP addresses in the list. Under Windows NT you will find this setup under Control Panel, Network, TCP/IP Protocol, Configure, Advanced. Enter each IP address in the list. If you have multiple network adapters, be sure to select the correct adapter for each IP address. Under Windows 95, set up each adapter with the appropriate IP address. If you have questions about adding IP addresses or network adapters, consult your network administrator or the operating system's documentation.

8. Test the IP addresses and domain names with the *ping* utility. Go to another computer on the network and execute *ping* for each hostname in your list. The hostname should resolve to the proper IP address and each address should be active. The syntax for *ping* is: ping *hostname*.

If one or more of the tests do not work, do not proceed with setting up virtual servers until you solve the problem.

Once you have created a planning chart with information for each server and you have active and properly resolving connections, you are ready to set up the virtual servers. To continue the virtual server setup, choose one of the methods in the following sections and follow the steps.

USING THE IDENTITY WIZARD

You create virtual servers on the Identity page of Server Admin. To start, open Server Admin and click on the Identity tab. The Identity page appears with the current settings displayed, as shown in Figure 10-2. Unless you have previously set up multiple identities, the page displays the server name you supplied during installation and setup.

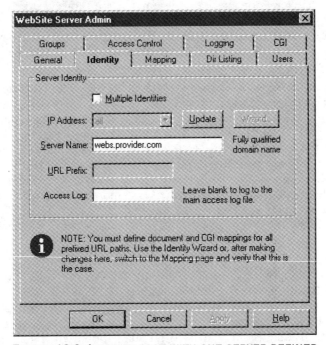

FIGURE 10-2: IDENTITY PAGE WITH ONE SERVER DEFINED

Using the planning chart you created in the previous section, you can quickly step through the Identity wizard and have your virtual servers set up in no time. To use the wizard, follow these steps:

1. On the Identities page of Server Admin, check the Multiple Identities box. An alert box pops up to tell you that IP addresses have been added to the server's configuration and that you must take action. Press OK and the page changes to show all the IP addresses on the system in the pulldown list box. By default the first IP address will always be 127.0.0.1 for *localhost*. (See

Figure 10-3.) Although you must configure *localhost*, we will use one of the other IP addresses for our example.

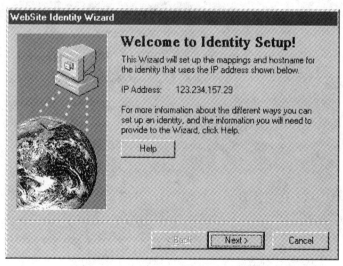

FIGURE 1O-3: IDENTITY PAGE WITH MULTIPLE IDENTITIES

2. From the pulldown list, select the first IP address after 127.0.0.1. (Don't forget to configure that address later with a URL prefix and mappings.) For this example, we'll use the IP address 123.234.157.29. *Don't make any entries in the other fields on this screen; they are reserved for manual configuration.*

3. Press the Wizard button. The first wizard screen appears, as shown in Figure 10-4. This page shows the IP address and gives a summary of the wizard's activity.

FIGURE 1O-4: IDENTITY WIZARD

4. Press Next to continue to the Domain Name screen. Enter the fully qualified domain name for the selected IP address. If you misplaced the form listing the domain name and are connected to the Internet, press the DNS button to have the wizard look up the name. If you do not have a domain name, use the IP address until you resolve the naming issue. The domain name for the address in this example is *webs.provider.com*.

5. Press Next to continue to the URL Prefix screen. Enter the nickname—the URL Prefix—for the IP address. Note that you can use only letters and numbers in the name, no spaces or other special characters. For this example, the URL prefix is *webs*.

6. Press Next to continue to the CGI Program Sharing screen. Check the type of CGI programs the virtual server will use: private, shared, or both. For this example, the server will use both types.

7. Press Next to continue to the Identity Root Directory screen. Enter the full pathname (including the drive specification) for the directory to be used for the virtual server's documents and CGI programs. The directory can be on a local disk or a network share. If you choose a remote location, use the UNC pathname (for example, *admin**corpweb*\\). If the directory exists, you can drag the location from the File Manager or Explorer to the pathname field. Otherwise, type in the full pathname. If the directory is on the local system and does not exist, the wizard creates it. For remote systems, use an existing path. For this example, the pathname is *C:\webs* as shown in Figure 10-5.

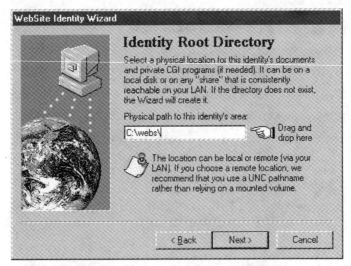

FIGURE 10-5: IDENTITY WIZARD, IDENTITY ROOT DIRECTORY SCREEN

8. Press Next to continue to the Logging Options screen. If the identity is to have a separate log, check the box and type in the new name. Otherwise, do

not do anything on this screen. For this example, the separate log is *webs.log*. Note that if you want the extension *.log* on the file, you must include it; the wizard does not automatically add the extension.

9. Press Next to continue to the Ready for Setup screen. You can review the entries in the previous screens by pressing Back.

10. When you are ready to finish the setup, press Next. The wizard executes the setup and displays a final page.

11. To see what the wizard set up for the virtual server, press View Report. The report tells you the following items. (See Figure 10-6.):

   – *Directories created by the wizard*. These include the document root and CGI directories (if private CGIs were selected) for the server.

   – *URL to directory mappings*. These include the server root URL mapping and CGI mappings (both private and shared) as well as the hostname and URL assignments to the IP address. Note that the private CGI directories are in the virtual server's working directory and use the normal URL (for example, *cgi-src*). The shared directories are in the WebSite directory and have the expression *shr-* added to the URL (for example, *shr-cgi-src*).

   – *Identity assignments*. These include the assigned hostname, URL prefix, and access log file.

   – *Notes*. Useful information that will help you keep your virtual server straight.

   This report is saved as a text file in the virtual server's root directory. The file is named *idwizard-report.txt*. We recommend you print the report for each server and save it for reference.

12. Repeat these steps for each IP address in the pulldown list. Don't forget to configure *localhost*, the first entry in the list. (Note that you cannot change the hostname for *localhost*, but you can configure all other items.) When you are finished, close Server Admin to update the server and then test the setup as described in the next section.

TESTING THE VIRTUAL SERVERS

Now comes the moment of truth. If you have set up your virtual servers correctly and completely, the tests should be quick and painless. If not, the test results give you some hints about the source of the problem. We assume you already tested the connections and IP address/hostname resolution as described earlier in this chapter.

```
Identity setup for webs.provider.com [123.234.157.29] performed
at Wed Nov 01 07:03:39 1995


STEP 1: DIRECTORY CREATION
--------------------------

Created directory C:\webs
Created directory C:\webs\htdocs
Created directory C:\webs\cgi-src
Created directory C:\webs\cgi-dos
Created directory C:\webs\cgi-shl
Created directory C:\webs\cgi-win

STEP 2: URL TO DIRECTORY MAPPING
--------------------------------

Mapped URL http://webs.provider.com/
   to C:\webs\htdocs
Mapped URL http://webs.provider.com/cgi-dos/
   to C:\webs\cgi-dos
Mapped URL http://webs.provider.com/cgi-shl/
   to C:\webs\cgi-shl
Mapped URL http://webs.provider.com/cgi-bin/
   to C:\webs\cgi-shl
Mapped URL http://webs.provider.com/auth/
   to C:\webs\cgi-shl-prot
Mapped URL http://webs.provider.com/cgi-win/
   to C:\webs\cgi-win
Mapped URL http://webs.provider.com/shr-cgi-dos/
   to C:\WebSite\cgi-dos
Mapped URL http://webs.provider.com/shr-cgi-shl/
   to C:\WebSite\cgi-shl
Mapped URL http://webs.provider.com/shr-auth/
   to C:\WebSite\cgi-shl-prot
Mapped URL http://webs.provider.com/shr-cgi-bin/
   to C:\WebSite\cgi-shl
Mapped URL http://webs.provider.com/shr-cgi-win/
   to C:\WebSite\cgi-win

STEP 3: IDENTITY ASSIGNMENTS
----------------------------

Assigned host name webs.provider.com to IP address 123.234.157.29
Assigned URL Prefix webs to IP address 123.234.157.29
Accesses will be logged in webs.log

NOTES
=====

* The URL for webs.provider.com's home page is http://webs.provider.com/

* The "normal" CGI URL paths (e.g. "/cgi-win/") have been mappedto
  the private CGI directories. For example:
        http://webs.provider.com/cgi-win/abcd.exe
  will cause the server to look for abcd.exe in
        C:\webs\cgi-win\

* The shared CGI directories are reachable via newly created URLpaths
  as listed above. For example, the shared cgi-win directory
        C:\WebSite\cgi-win\
  is mapped to the URL
        http://webs.provider.com/shr-cgi-win/
```

FIGURE 10-6: IDENTITY WIZARD SETUP REPORT

NOTE

Before testing your virtual servers, make sure you have created all the virtual server's working, document, and CGI directories. We recommend testing before adding any other documents to the virtual servers' webs.

WITH A BROWSER

Use a browser that displays full error message text (such as Spyglass Mosaic 2.1) for these tests, which tell you if the server names and IP addresses are correct and if the mapping for each server is correct. Follow these steps to complete the first test:

1. Create a subdirectory in each virtual server's document directory called *test*. Put nothing in the directory. For example, *C:\webs\webdocs\test*.

2. Ask your browser to fetch the URL for each *test* directory, without the trailing slash (/). For example, *http://webs/test*. You should see the trailing slash appear at the end of the URL and an empty directory listing of */test/*. If not, the server name for the identity is wrong.

   To fix this problem, make sure you have the correct server name and then fix it on the Identities page of Server Admin. Select the appropriate IP address from the pulldown list, enter the correct server name, and press Update. Close Server Admin and try this test again.

3. Ask your browser to fetch a non-existent URL for each virtual server. For example, *http://webs/bad* (a directory that does not exist). WebSite will return an error message showing the URL *and* the physical path for the URL. Check the pathname against the one you assigned to the server. If the path appears to be correct, go to step 4. If the path is not correct, fix the mapping assignments on the Mapping page of Server Admin. Note that an error message is the correct response to this test—you are looking for the correct URL to physical location mapping in the error message.

4. Repeat step 3 for each type of CGI, both shared and private. For example, for the URL *http://webs/cgi-win*. WebSite will return an error and a pathname as in step 3. Check the pathname to make sure it is correct. If not, fix the mapping. Also, make sure the proper directories exist if you are using private CGI programs. When the pathnames are correct, continue testing with WebView.

WITH WEBVIEW

The final test is to start WebView. If the mapping is correct and document root directories exist for each virtual server, WebView will start as usual and display a window for each virtual server. If the mapping is incomplete or the document root directories do not exist, WebView will display an error message and not start.

When WebView starts successfully and displays a window for each virtual server, switch to the File Name view to verify that the servers are mapped to the correct locations. If the server name or the mapping is incorrect, the WebView tree will not display as expected.

USING MANUAL SETUP

If you choose to set up virtual servers without the wizard or need to change or delete an existing identity, you must follow the procedures for manual setup, described in this section. Remember that you must do two things:

- Assign domain names and URL prefixes to each IP address on the Identity page of Server Admin, *and*
- Set up the document and CGI mappings on the Mapping page of Server Admin.

Follow your summary chart as you work through the steps below. When you finish, make sure you test each server using the instructions given later in the section "Testing the Virtual Servers."

To start, open Server Admin and click on the Identity tab. The Identity page appears with the current settings displayed, as shown in Figure 10-7. Unless you have previously set up multiple identities, the page displays the server name you supplied during installation and setup.

ASSIGNING DOMAIN NAMES AND URL PREFIXES

1. On the Identities page of Server Admin, check the Multiple Identities box. An alert box pops up to tell you that IP addresses have been added to the server's configuration and that you must take action. Press OK and the page changes to show all the IP addresses on the system in the pulldown list box. By default the first IP address will always be 127.0.0.1 for *localhost* (Figure 10-8). Although you must configure *localhost* at some point, we will use one of the other IP addresses for our example.

2. From the pulldown list, select an IP address other than 127.0.0.1. (Don't forget to configure that address later by adding a URL prefix and appropriate mappings.) For this example, we'll use the IP address 123.234.157.29. The server's fully qualified domain name (supplied during installation) appears in the Server Name field.

3. If the server name shown is the correct one for the IP address, go to step 4. If it is not the correct name, enter the correct fully qualified domain name. Refer to the summary chart for IP address and hostname pairings. If you don't have a fully qualified domain name, enter the IP address in this field. For this example, the server name is *webs.provider.com*.

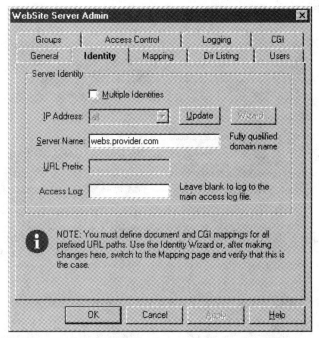

FIGURE 10-7: IDENTITY PAGE WITH ONE SERVER DEFINED

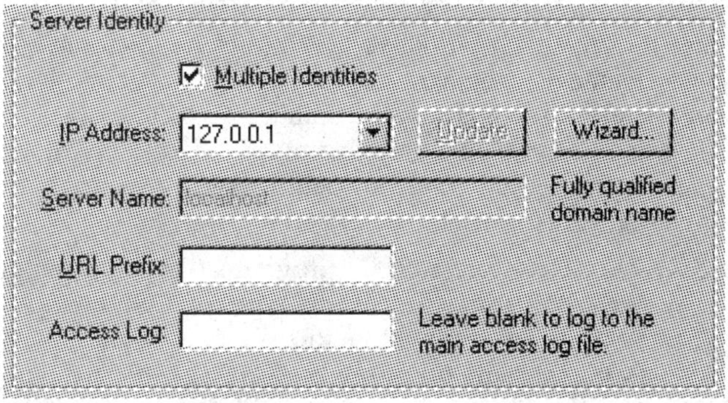

FIGURE 10-8: IDENTITY PAGE WITH MULTIPLE IDENTITES

4. In the URL Prefix field, enter the nickname for the IP address. *You must start the URL prefix with a / .* For this example, the URL prefix is */webs.*

5. If this virtual server will have its own log file, enter the name in the Access Log field. Use the full filename, including *.log*, if desired. For this example, the access log file is *webs.log.* Figure 10-9 shows a correctly completed Identity page.

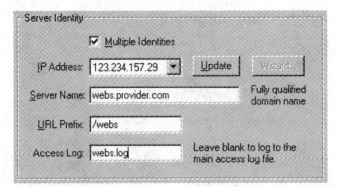

FIGURE 10-9: IDENTITY PAGE COMPLETED FOR MULTIPLE IDENTITIES

6. Press Update.

7. Repeat steps 2 through 6 for each IP address in the list, including 127.0.0.1. (Note that you cannot change the server name of this address, *localhost*.) When you are finished press Apply.

MAPPING THE DOCUMENT ROOT AND CGI DIRECTORIES

If you are not familiar with mapping, please read the sections about Document and CGI mapping in Chapter 9, *Mapping*, before completing this task. If your virtual servers do not function properly, the likely cause is improper mapping. Use the following principles as you complete the mapping for virtual servers.

- The document root for each virtual server should be a subdirectory within the directory you selected for the virtual server (refer to your planning chart for that directory name). We recommend calling the directory *htdocs*, but you may name it whatever you like (for example, *C:\webs\webdocs*). This directory is mapped to the virtual server's document root, which is the URL prefix with a trailing slash (for example, */webs/*).

- If the virtual server will use private CGI programs (that is, programs only available to this server), you must map each type of CGI (Windows, standard, DOS) to specific subdirectories within the server's working directory. These subdirectories should be named *cgi-dos, cgi-shl, cgi-shl-prot,* and *cgi-win* (for example, *C:\webs\cgi-dos, C:\webs\cgi-shl, C:\webs\cgi-shl-prot,* and *C:\webs\cgi-win*).

- If the virtual server will only use shared CGI programs (that is, programs used by other servers that are in the default WebSite server working directory), you must map each type of CGI for the server to the CGI subdirectories of WebSite (for example, *C:\WebSite\cgi-dos, C:\WebSite\cgi-shl, C:\WebSite\cgi-shl-prot,* and *C:\WebSite\cgi-win*).

- If the virtual server will share CGI programs and use private ones, you must map each type of CGI to subdirectories in the virtual server's directory *and* to the shared directories in WebSite. However, for the shared CGIs to work correctly, you must assign them a different URL path (for example */shr-cgi-dos/* and so forth).

TIPS FOR SETTING UP VIRTUAL SERVERS

Use full (not relative) directory pathnames when mapping virtual server URLs.

Use UNC names when adding remote directories to virtual server mappings.

Make sure the directories you map exist. You may create them either before or after mapping.

Make sure conflicting directories don't exist. For example, if you plan to share CGI programs and not use any private ones, *do not* create CGI subdirectories in the virtual server's directory. They can conflict with the directories by the same name in the WebSite directory.

If you plan to develop CGI programs for individual servers, you may want to create a *cgi-src* directory under each server's working directory.

Working through an example will bring these principles into focus. You may also want to add the subdirectories and URLs to your planning chart before beginning. Refer to Chapter 9, *Mapping*, for specific instructions on working with the Mapping page.

1. On the Mapping page of Server Admin, display the Document mappings.

2. Add the document root URL path and the directory pathname for each virtual server. Figure 10-10 shows the virtual server document root URL */webs/* mapped to the physical directory *C:\webs\webdocs*.

Document URL Root	Directory (full or server-relative)
/	C:\WebSite\htdocs\
/webs/	C:\webs\webdocs\
/wsdocs/	C:\WebSite\wsdocs\

FIGURE 10-10: DOCUMENT MAPPING FOR A VIRTUAL SERVER

3. Press Apply when you are finished.

4. On the Mappings page, display the Windows CGI mappings.

5. If you plan to use private CGI programs, add the private Windows CGI URL path and the directory path for each virtual server (if appropriate). For example, map */webs/cgi-win/* to the physical directory *C:\webs\cgi-win*.

6. If you plan to use shared and private CGI programs, add the shared Windows CGI URL path and the directory path for each virtual server (if appropriate). For example, map */webs/shr-cgi-win/* to the physical directory *C:\WebSite\cgi-win*. Figure 10-11 shows the mapping for steps 5 and 6.

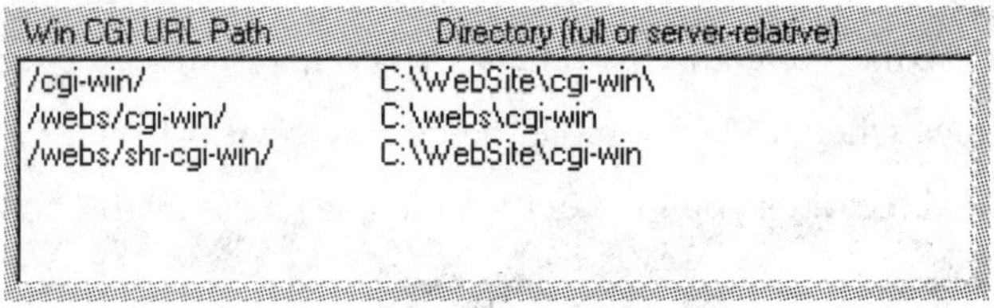

Win CGI URL Path	Directory (full or server-relative)
/cgi-win/	C:\WebSite\cgi-win\
/webs/cgi-win/	C:\webs\cgi-win
/webs/shr-cgi-win/	C:\WebSite\cgi-win

FIGURE 10-11: PRIVATE AND SHARED WINDOWS CGI MAPPINGS FOR A VIRTUAL SERVER

7. If you plan to use *only* shared CGI programs, map each CGI URL path to the shared CGI directories. For example, map */webs/cgi-win/* to *C:\Website\cgi-win*. In this case, you do not have to add *shr-* to the URL.

8. Press Apply when you are finished.

9. Repeat steps five through eight for the standard and DOS CGI mappings for each virtual server. Note that for the standard interface, you must map the URLs */cgi-bin/, /cgi-shl/,* and */auth/*.

With the mapping complete, it is time to test your virtual servers.

TESTING THE VIRTUAL SERVERS

Now comes the moment of truth. If you have set up your virtual servers correctly and completely, the tests should be quick and painless. If not, the test results give you some hints about the source of the problem. We assume you already tested the connections and IP address/hostname resolution as described earlier in this chapter.

NOTE

Before testing your virtual servers, make sure you have created all the virtual server's working, document, and CGI directories. We recommend testing before adding any other documents to the virtual servers' webs.

WITH A BROWSER

Use a browser that displays full error message text (such as Spyglass Mosaic 2.1) for these tests, which tell you if the server names and IP addresses are correct and if the mapping for each server is correct. Follow these steps to complete the first test:

1. Create a subdirectory in each virtual server's document directory called *test*. Put nothing in the directory. For example, *C:\webs\webdocs\test*.

2. Ask your browser to fetch the URL for each *test* directory, without the trailing slash (/). For example, *http://webs/test*. You should see the trailing slash appear at the end of the URL and an empty directory listing of */test/*. If not, the server name for the identity is wrong.

   To fix this problem, make sure you have the correct server name and then fix it on the Identities page of Server Admin. Select the appropriate IP address from the pulldown list, enter the correct server name, and press Update. Close Server Admin and try this test again.

3. Ask your browser to fetch a non-existent URL for each virtual server. For example, *http://webs/bad* (a directory that does not exist). WebSite will return an error message showing the URL *and* the physical path for the URL. Check the pathname against the one you assigned to the server. If the path appears to be correct, go to step 4. If the path is not correct, fix the mapping assignments on the Mapping page of Server Admin. Note that an error message is the correct response to this test—you are looking for the correct URL to physical location mapping in the error message.

4. Repeat step 3 for each type of CGI, both shared and private. For example, for the URL *http://webs/cgi-win*. WebSite will return an error and a pathname as in step 3. Check the pathname to make sure it is correct. If not, fix the mapping. Also, make sure the proper directories exist if you are using private CGI programs. When the pathnames are correct, continue testing with WebView.

WITH WEBVIEW

The final test is to start WebView. If the mapping is correct and document root directories exist for each virtual server, WebView will start as usual and display a window for each virtual server. If the mapping is incomplete or the document root directories do not exist, WebView will display an error message and not start.

When WebView starts successfully and displays a window for each virtual server, switch to the File Name view to verify that the servers are mapped to the correct locations. If the server name or the mapping is incorrect, the WebView tree will not display as expected.

MODIFYING OR DELETING A VIRTUAL SERVER

Occasionally you may need to change a virtual server's identity or mappings. You may also need to remove one or more of the virtual servers. To do so, use the Identity page or the Mapping page of Server Admin. Follow the instructions under "Manual Setup" for making changes. Complete the above tests whenever you make a change.

If you change a URL prefix, make sure you change the document and CGI mappings as well. If you delete a virtual server, make sure you delete the mappings. Stray mappings in WebSite can cause unexpected results to users of your web.

REVERTING TO A SINGLE SERVER

To revert your WebSite server to a single identity, you must remove all identities and document and CGI mappings for the virtual servers. Doing so will not remove any documents associated with the virtual servers.

To revert WebSite to a single server, follow these steps:

1. On the Identity page of Server Admin, check off the Multiple Identities box. WebSite queries your action. When you press Yes, WebSite removes all server names and URL prefixes for the virtual servers from the Registry—*you cannot undo this action*. WebSite returns to a single identity server, using the server name you supplied during installation.

2. On the Mapping page, remove all document and CGI mappings for the virtual servers. Unused mappings can cause problems in the future.

3. Test the single server as described in Chapter 3, *Installing WebSite*.

ADDING ACCESS CONTROL TO VIRTUAL SERVERS

Assigning access control to virtual servers follows the same steps discussed in Chapter 12, *Controlling Access to Your Web*. This section is included here only so you can understand the principles of applying access control to virtual servers.

WebSite allows you to apply access control *to a specific URL path* by user/password authentication or IP address/hostname filtering. That principle remains the same whether you have a single server or multiple virtual servers. Each server has its own set of URL paths starting with the document root (for example, / for a single server, or */webs/* for a virtual server). You can restrict access to any or all parts of a virtual server's URL hierarchy, just as you would for a single server.

Restricting access to a virtual server's web by IP address or hostname is identical to restricting access to a single server. The server allows or denies access to the virtual server's web (or part of the web) based on the URL requested and the filtering restrictions defined for that URL.

The real issue in applying access control to virtual servers is user authentication. How do you keep different users and groups separate for each server? What if two of your virtual servers wanted to allow (or deny) Bob access to a part of the web, but there are two different Bobs? How do you keep from having a huge user database including all users for all the servers?

The answer to these questions is built into WebSite's user authentication scheme. In addition to users and groups, you can set up realms, which are simply collections of users and groups. You create a different realm for each virtual server (for example, one realm called *Webs* and another realm called *Food*). You then add users and groups for each server to the specific realm.

When you apply access control, you select a URL path for a virtual server *and* the realm for that server. All the users and groups appropriate for that virtual server are available and none of the users and groups for other virtual servers are; they are available only in the realm for their own virtual server. Thus, you can have a Bob in two realms but WebSite treats them as different Bobs with different passwords and can never have access to the other's information.

Using the principles discussed here, turn to Chapter 12, *Controlling Access to Your Web*, and follow the specific instructions for setting up users, groups, and realms and applying access control.

USING WEBSITE TOOLS WITH VIRTUAL SERVERS

The remainder of this chapter is dedicated to using the WebSite tools in a virtual server environment. For the most part, the tools function as they do in a single server environment; please refer to the appropriate chapters in this book for more detailed information on using the tools. Here we point out differences in the tools' behavior and give you some hints for working with them successfully in a virtual server world.

WEBVIEW

When running virtual servers, the most obvious difference in WebView is that each server's web is displayed in a separate window when you start the program.

The windows cascade and you can select the server with which you want to work. You can close the other windows, minimize them, or tile them for easy comparisons. Please see the section in Chapter 4, *Managing Your Web Using WebView*, on working with multiple windows.

If you prefer to see only one virtual server when WebView starts up, you can change the WebView preferences to do so. To make this change, follow these steps:

1. Select Preferences from the File menu. On the General page, you'll notice that the Home preferences are different from those of a single server installation. By default, "Display all virtual servers" is checked.

2. To have WebView start with only one virtual server's web displayed, click on the URL button and type the URL for that server in the URL field. Figure 10-12 shows an example. Make sure that you include the full URL, including the protocol (*http://*).

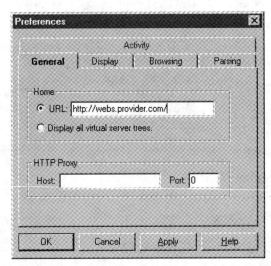

FIGURE 10-12: WEBVIEW HOME PAGE PREFERENCES FOR VIRTUAL SERVERS

3. Press Apply if you want to change other preferences. Press OK when you are finished. The change does not take effect until the next time you start WebView.

QuickStats also works differently when you are running virtual servers. When you ask QuickStats to give you a summary of the activity on a virtual server's web, it first asks you which virtual server to use. Then it displays the appropriate information.

WEBINDEX AND WEBFIND

When using virtual servers, the only difference you will see in WebIndex is in the listing of URL directories (excluded or included). Since WebSite no longer has a single document root, WebIndex does not list the URL for /. Instead, WebIndex lists the document roots for each of your virtual servers. You create and maintain indexes just as in a single server environment.

WebFind also works the same in a single or multiple server environment. However, since WebFind is a CGI program, you must make sure that the CGI mappings are correct for each server. (Yes, we've said this before.) If you used the wizard to set up your virtual servers, the mapping should be correct.

For example, if you plan for any of your virtual servers to have private CGI programs and you want to make WebFind one of those private programs, you must copy *webfind.exe* to the appropriate CGI directory for each server. The program *webfind.exe* is located in the directory *\WebSite\cgi-shl*. Copy it to the same CGI directory for each virtual server.

On the other hand, if you plan to share WebFind among servers (and have other private CGI programs), make sure you use the shared version of the URL to locate the program, for example *http://webs/shr-cgi-bin/webfind.exe*.

If you plan to share all CGI programs, make sure you've mapped the CGI URLs for each server to the shared CGI directories as described in the manual setup instructions above.

CGI PROGRAMS

If you have read this chapter, you already know what belongs in this section: *make sure the CGI mapping is correct!* Please see the instructions earlier in this chapter that deal with CGI mapping.

As you develop webs for your virtual servers, keep the following two guidelines in mind:

- Put CGI programs in the proper locations for either private or shared use
- Use the appropriate URL in hyperlink references (HREFs) for shared or private CGI programs; for shared programs, include *shr-* in URL path (for example, */shr-cgi-win/program.exe*).

CHAPTER ELEVEN

AUTOMATIC DIRECTORY LISTINGS

The discussion about mapping in Chapter 9, *Mapping*, hinted at automatic directory listings. This chapter fills in the details. The server can automatically create directory listings (also called indexes) any time a browser requests a URL for a directory that does not contain a home page or an index file. When the server builds an automatic directory list, it shows the files in the URL directory and makes each file available as a hypertext link. The user can click on the link and download the file.

But why read a description when you can look at a real-life situation? Take a break from this introduction and crank up your WebSite server. Launch a browser and enter the URL for the WebSite server self-test (*http://localhost/wsdocs/*). In the self-test, scroll down to the section on Directory Navigation. Click on the "Look Here First" link. What you see is an automatic directory listing with default features enabled. Now look at that same directory in the Explorer or File Manager (*WebSite\wsdocs\32demo\demotree*). You're looking at the source of the automatic directory list.

The directory listing can be very simple—files shown as a bulleted list of hypertext links—or it can be extended with headers, footers, icons, and file descriptions. You can exclude certain types of files from either simple or extended listings. In extended listings, you can also use icons as links, show content types, use descriptions from the <TITLE> tag in HTML files, or display the lists in HTML 3 table format.

WebSite's automatic directory listing is fully featured to let you create directory lists that are highly functional, flexible, and good looking. Although you set up automatic directory listings for your entire web, it is implemented on a per directory basis, allowing you to maintain traditional web pages as well as automatic directory lists on the same web.

This chapter describes the features of WebSite's automatic directory listing and gives instructions for using them. But first, let's take a look at why and how you might use automatic directory listing.

WHY USE AUTOMATIC DIRECTORY LISTINGS?

Once you see how automatic directory listing works, you will find lots of uses for it. But here are some ideas for starters.

SOME TIME-SAVING USES

- You have several directories of documents on your web, which you want to make available to users, but don't want to create an HTML home page for each directory. With automatic directory listing enabled, you can provide a list of each directory and a bit of additional information about the files.

- You have a library of documents that is constantly changing. Colleagues put up new files and take away existing files almost daily. Keeping a home page updated takes too much time, but the documents must be available to other users and the public. Automatic directory listing is the answer; the server creates a list when it receives a URL request for that location. Thus the directory listing is always current.

- You have a collection of documents that you want to make available, but a home page would add very little value to the listing. In fact, the home page would simply be a list with links. An automatic directory list saves you the effort of having to create and maintain such a home page.

NOTE

Because these automatic directory lists are part of your document web, you can apply IP address and hostname filtering restrictions and user authentication requirements to their URLs. See Chapter 12, *Controlling Access to Your Web*, for more information on setting access control.

USING WEBSITE AS AN FTP SERVER

The most common application of automatic directory listing is to use your WebSite server in place of an FTP server. FTP (which stands for File Transfer Protocol) is generally how files are uploaded to and downloaded from the Internet. FTP servers are essentially lists of files available for downloading. You can retrieve files from an FTP server either by using the FTP program or by using a Web browser and a URL with the *ftp* protocol instead of the *http* protocol.

Setting up and maintaining an FTP server requires both technical knowledge and time. If you want to provide FTP server-like capability, but don't want to set up an FTP server, using automatic directory listing for your WebSite server is the answer. You can provide a list or lists of documents for users to download using the *http* protocol and a web browser. WebSite also supports form-based uploading, supported by some browsers (for example, Netscape Navigator). Form-based uploading is described in the server self-test.

If you already have an FTP site but want to make those files available to Web users, you can simply map that site into your document map and publish the URL. Users can then reach your FTP site by using either FTP or the Web. See Chapter 9, *Mapping*, for instructions on adding locations to your document map.

INCLUDING INTERNET SHORTCUTS

If you are running under Windows 95, you can include Microsoft Internet Shortcut files in a directory. Internet shortcuts have the *.url* extension and include the URL for another location. When an Internet shortcut is shown in an automatic directory listing and a user clicks on it, the server sends the redirected URL to the browser, which then goes to the new location. The redirection is transparent to the user. Internet shortcut files are defined by the content type *wwwserver/redirection* and are shown in an automatic directory listing with the Microsoft Internet Shortcut icon. Internet shortcuts provide a quick way for users to get to another location on the Internet from your web.

NOTE

Automatic directory listing is optional. If you prefer not to have your web available for directory listing (and file downloading), disable all listing on the Dir Listing page of Server Admin. (See Figure 11-6.) The server sends an access denied error message, which is interpreted in various ways by different browsers. You can also disable automatic directory lists for specific URLs on the Access Control page of Server Admin. See Chapter 12, *Controlling Access to Your Web*, for more information.

SIMPLE VERSUS EXTENDED: A COMPARISON

As we noted in the introduction, the easiest way to understand automatic directory listing is to compare a simple directory list and an extended directory list with each other and against a standard directory listing (*à la* File Manager or Explorer). If you didn't have a chance to check out the server self-test, this section presents the pictures for you. Figure 11-1 shows the Explorer directory listing for the WebSite Server Self-Test directory, *\WebSite\wsdocs\32demo\demotree*.

The directory has seven files and one subdirectory. Four of the files begin with special characters, # or ~. Keep an eye on those. Figure 11-2 shows a simple directory list for the same location, using the URL *http://localhost/wsdocs/32demo/*

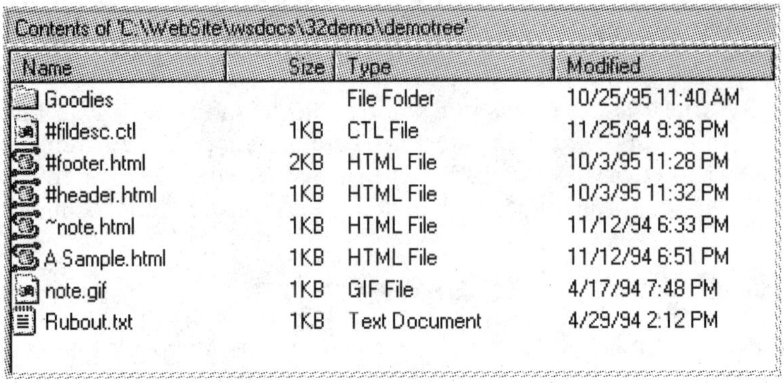

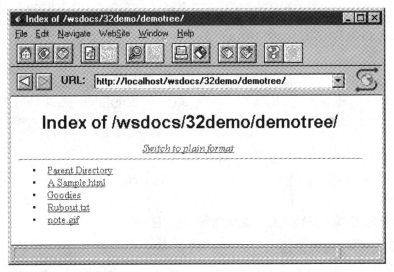

FIGURE 11-1: EXPLORER DIRECTORY LISTING

demotree/. (You probably didn't see this version when you checked out the server self-test.)

FIGURE 11-2: SIMPLE AUTOMATIC DIRECTORY LISTING

In the simple listing, the server provides the title (with the URL path) and creates a bulleted list of hyperlinked file and subdirectory names. The server also adds the footer with the *mailto* URL.

Did you notice that the files beginning with # or ~ aren't shown? They are excluded, based on the patterns set in Server Admin (discussed in the section "Excluding Files," later in this chapter). The server also adds a hyperlink for the parent directory. Note that when the parent directory is the parent of the document root (for example, *C:\WebSite*), the list shows the link but it doesn't go anywhere—users are restricted to the document web.

The simple list is functional, but it doesn't give much information to the user and looks, well, functional. Figure 11-3 is the same URL but with extended listing and some additional options turned on. This figure shows the default values.

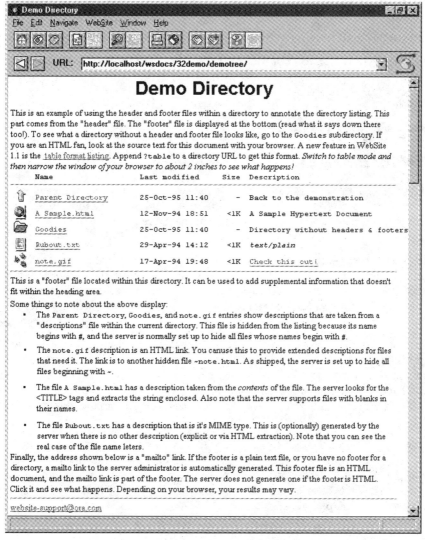

FIGURE 11-3: EXTENDED AUTOMATIC DIRECTORY LISTING

The text (and graphics) above the listing are from the *#header.html* file. The text below the listing is from the *#footer.html* file. In the listing itself, the bullets are replaced with icons, according to the file's content type. The filenames are links. The listing includes the date last modified and size of each file (handy information when you want to download a file). The final column in the listing is a file description, which can be text, a hyperlink, or a content type.

Two additional options that are not part of the default setting are using icons as links (in addition to filenames), and displaying the list as HTML 3 tables. Figure 11-4 shows the demo directory with these two options enabled. Note that not all browsers support tables.

With that overview, let's look at the mechanics of creating automatic directory listings. First, however, we have to discuss how the server knows whether to return a directory's home page (its index file) or an automatic directory list.

DEFAULT INDEX FILE NAME (HOME PAGE)

When you installed WebSite, the first test was to see if your server was running by asking your browser for the URL *http://localhost/*. If everything was working properly, the server returned the default home page. Yet, looking at that URL again, you notice it doesn't include a filename.

As you know, URLs can contain paths and filenames for specific documents (such as home pages) or not. If they don't, WebSite completes the request either by displaying a default home page or an automatic directory listing. How does the WebSite server know when to create a directory listing and when to return an existing document?

The mystery is solved when you look at the Dir Listing page of Server Admin (Figure 11-5) and especially the Special Documents section. The name that appears in the Index edit box is used by the server as the default home page name (or index filename) for every directory in the web. If the server doesn't find a file by that name in the directory, it generates an automatic directory listing instead.

The WebSite default home page or index filename is *index.** (generally for *index.html* or *index.htm*). You may have changed it during installation. If so, that name appears on this field. Once your web is installed, you can change the name to fit your web. Let's say you want to use *home.html*. To make that change, follow these three steps:

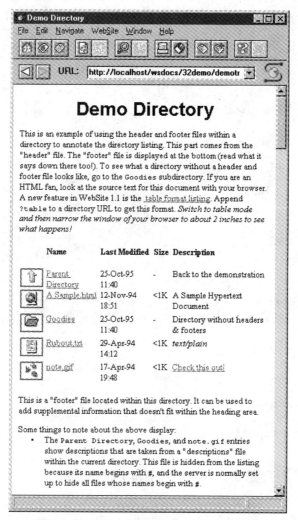

FIGURE 11-4: AUTOMATIC DIRECTORY LISTING WITH ALL OPTIONS

1. Launch Server Admin and click on the Dir Listing tab.

2. Highlight the current entry in the Default edit box of the Special Documents section and type in the new filename, *home.html*. You can also use a meta-character, such as *home.**, in this field.

3. Press OK to update the server.

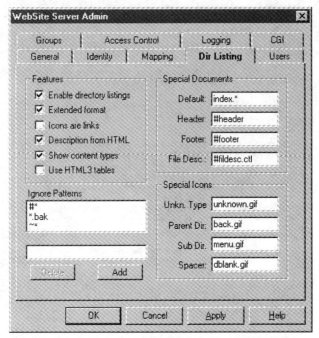

FIGURE 11-5: DEFAULT DIR LISTING PAGE

NOTE

If you make no entry in the Default edit box, WebSite will always create a directory listing unless you have disabled directory listings (for the entire web or for a specific URL) or a user includes a specific file in the URL.

SIMPLE DIRECTORY LISTINGS

WebSite's simple directory listing creates a document with a generic head and a bulleted list of all but excluded files, as shown in Figure 11-2.

ENABLING SIMPLE LISTING

The WebSite default is extended directory listing; to implement the simple version, you must remove extended features from the Dir Listing page of Server Admin. To do so, follow these steps:

1. Launch Server Admin and click on the Dir Listing tab.

2. In the Features section, unselect all features *except* Enable directory listings. The extended options and filenames are dimmed. (See Figure 11-6.)

3. Press OK to update the server.

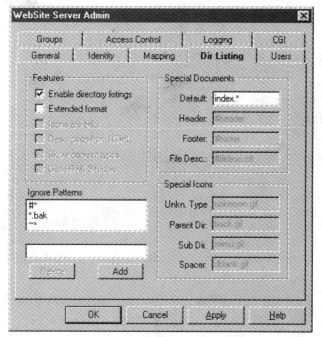

FIGURE 11-6: DIR LISTING PAGE SET FOR SIMPLE LISTINGS

EXCLUDING FILES

In both simple and extended directory listings, you can exclude certain files from the list. You may have backup files that are redundant or batch files that are not necessary to show. In extended directory listings, you probably don't want to show the files used for header, footer, and descriptive information. In short, the purpose of excluding files is to *include* only those that are really valuable to someone looking at a list on your web.

Figure 11-7 shows the Ignore Patterns section of the Dir Listing page with the default patterns. The patterns to be ignored can be full or partial filenames and can include standard metacharacters such as * and ?.

Files that begin with # are used by the default header, footer, and description files. Files that have the *.bak* extension are typically backup copies of other files and files with the extension *.ctr* are counter files for server-side includes. The ~

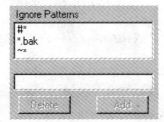

FIGURE 11-7: IGNORE PATTERNS SECTION OF DIR LISTINGS PAGE

excluded pattern is a convention used in WebSite for additional description files such as *~note.html* in the server self-test. You may have other conventions for naming files, or you may want to adopt the default conventions for naming files in the future.

NOTE

When you decide to exclude files from a directory listing, remember that files matching that pattern will be excluded from *all* directory lists. For example, you may not want to show GIF files in one directory, but you do in another. If you excluded the pattern **.gif*, no GIF files will be included in any automatic directory listing. The better solution is to name files you don't want to show with a unique pattern, such as prefixing the name with ~.

Sometimes you may want to exclude all files of a certain type from directory lists. Let's say you don't want to have any executable files available on your web (remember that listed files are automatically hypertext links). The easiest way to accomplish that is to add the file extensions for any executable files to the Ignore Patterns section. For example, let's say that the only executables in your document web end in *.exe* or *.bat*. To add these patterns to the Dir Listing page, follow these steps:

1. Launch Server Admin and click on the Dir Listing page.

2. Place the cursor in the edit box of the Ignore Patterns section and type in the pattern **.exe*.

3. Press Add. The new pattern is added to the Ignore Patterns list.

4. Repeat steps 2 and 3 for the pattern **.bat*.

5. Press Close to update the server. As on any other Server Admin page, the changes are not in effect until the server is updated.

To delete a pattern from the list, click on the pattern or type it into the edit box and press Delete.

EXTENDED DIRECTORY LISTING

Extended automatic directory listing is the WebSite default. Extended listing gives you greater control over what users see and how much information they receive when they request a directory on your web. Specifically, extended directory listing lets you

- Exclude certain types of files from the listing (as described above)
- Add headers and footers to the listing
- Add descriptions for all or some files in the listing
- Use descriptive icons rather than bullets to identify specific file types in the listing

This section describes these features and shows you how to apply them. We assume that you are familiar with the Directory Icon mapping in Server Admin and that you have either accepted the default mapping or changed it. (See Chapter 9, *Mapping*, for details.)

For extended directory listing, you must select *at least* the first two items in the Features area of the Dir Listing page: Enable directory listings and Extended format (Figure 11-8). Note that the remaining four features are available only when extended format is enabled. Those features are covered in the last section of this chapter.

ADDING HEADERS AND FOOTERS

To provide general information about a directory listing, you can have the server include headers and/or footers. The header appears before the file listing while the footer appears at the end of the file listing. (See Figure 11-3.) Typically, the header and footer files describe the listing, provide further instructions, and have links (if the files are HTML) to related material.

Header and footer files may be either HTML files or text files. You'll notice in the Special Documents section of the Dir Listing page (Figure 11-8) that the header and footer files are entered without extensions (*#header, #footer*). The server first looks for the filename plus *.html or .htm*, then for the filename plus *.txt*. By not including extensions on the default filename and having the server search for either type of file, you can maintain both types of header and footer files (HTML and plain text) on the same server.

An HTML header or footer file can contain any HTML coding, hypertext links, graphics, and so forth. A text file has no codes and the contents are displayed exactly as typed. When a text file is used, the server generates the necessary HTML code and puts the directory's URL path in <H1> . . . </H1> tags. The text is formatted using the <PRE> . . . </PRE> (preformatted) tags.

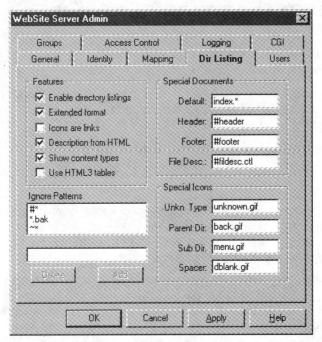

FIGURE 11-8: DIR LISTING PAGE WITH EXTENDED FORMAT ENABLED

HTML TAGGING RULES FOR HEADER AND FOOTER FILES

If you use HTML files for headers and footers, you must follow certain rules when tagging them. The server will not be able to use the files correctly if you do not follow these rules.

For the header, the server assumes you want total control of the appearance and adds nothing. Therefore, it expects that you will

- Include the proper starting tags: <HTML>, <HEAD>, </HEAD>, and <BODY> tags
- Include a title within <TITLE> . . . </TITLE> tags
- Include an appropriate <H1> . . . </H1> heading for the page
- Not include the closing </BODY> and </HTML> tags in the header file.

Example 11-1 shows the HTML coding for the server self-test *#header.html* file.

EXAMPLE 11-1: HTML HEADER FILE

```
HEAD><TITLE>Demo Directory</TITLE></HEAD>
<BODY BGCOLOR="#FFFFFF">
<center><H1>Demo Directory</H1></center>
This is an example of using the header and footer files within a
            directory to
annotate the directory listing. This part comes from the "header"
            file. The
"footer" file is displayed at the bottom. (Read what it says down
            there too!)
To see what a directory without a header and footer file looks like,
            go to the
<code>Goodies</code> subdirectory. If you are an HTML fan, look at
            the source
text for this document with your browser. A new feature in WebSite
            1.1 is the
<a href="./?table">table format listing</a>. Append <code>?table</
            code> to a
directory URL to get this format. <i>Switch to table mode and then
            narrow the
window of your browser to about 2 inches to see what happens!</i>.
```

The footer file is just a continuation of an HTML file that picks up where the automatic directory listing ends. Do not use the <HTML> or <BODY> start tags. The server adds all closing tags to the end of your footer file. For that reason, the server requires that you *not* include </BODY> or </HTML> closing tags either.

You may want to add a *mailto* URL to the footer so users can contact the person responsible for the directory. Since you can do this on a per directory basis (that is, in the footer file for each directory), the person can be different for each directory.

NOTE

WebSite automatically adds a *mailto* link with the server administrator's email address to any directory listing that does not have a footer file. If you don't want a footer *or* a *mailto* URL, create an empty footer file.

CHANGING THE DEFAULT FILENAMES

The WebSite default filenames for header and footer files are *#header* and *#footer*. (The extension can be either *.html, .htm* or *.txt.*) With extended formatting enabled, the server looks for these files in the directory to be listed (that is, when no home page file is found). If the files exist, the server reads them into the directory listing document. Note that these files must reside *in* the directory.

You can change the default header and footer filenames on the Dir Listing page. Let's say you already have header and footer files in most of your directories, and they are called *~head.html* and *~foot.html*. The ~ at the beginning of the filename follows the convention for hidden filenames. To make these the new default header and footer values, follow these steps:

1. Launch Server Admin and click on the Dir Listing page.

2. Highlight the current entry in the Header edit box of the Special Documents section and type in the new filename, *~head*. (Do *not* include the extension since the server supplies it.)

3. Highlight the current entry in the Footer edit box of the Special Documents section and type in the new filename, *~foot*. Figure 11-9 shows the changed names.

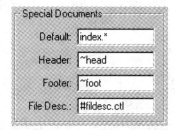

FIGURE 11-9: NEW HEADER AND FOOTER FILENAMES

4. Press Close to update the server.

NOTE

You can make multiple changes on this page by pressing Apply to save the changes. However, the server is not updated until you exit Server Admin by pressing Close.

ADDING FILE DESCRIPTIONS

Extended directory listing allows you to include a brief description for each file in the directory. These annotations may be simple text or a hypertext link to a file with a longer description. Annotations are kept in a standard file in each directory.

The default name of the file is kept in the Special Documents section of the Dir Listing page. (See Figure 11-9.) The default file, *#fildesc.ctl,* is an excluded file, like the header and footer files. To change the default filename, follow the same procedure as for changing header and footer default filenames.

Regardless of what you call the description file, the contents must follow a specific format, pairing an annotation with a file. The description file for the

WebSite server self-test directory used in Figures 11-1 to 11-3 is shown in Example 11-2.

EXAMPLE 11-2: DESCRIPTION FILE

```
Demo file descriptions

RubOut.txt is not included, so you can see the server's feature
of displaying the MIME type for the file, per the server's map.
Note that comments here begin with space or tab, so we can
describe files beginning with anything.
```

```
..|Back to the demonstration
Goodies|Directory without headers &amp; footers
note.gif|<A HREF="~note.html">Check this out!</A>
```

The first few lines are only comments, indicated by the beginning spaces or tab. The last three lines show the required format for annotations:

[filename] | [comment or hypertext link]

Each entry can be only one line and not all files need to be included in this file. Filenames should appear as they do in the directory listing. You'll notice that the first filename is .., which is the relative path for the parent directory. The | separates the filename from the description. The description can be a text comment or a link. Note the use of HTML codes for special characters such as ampersand (&). The server reads this file as an HTML file.

If you include long descriptions, you will probably want to have directory listings displayed in HTML 3 table format. This option displays long descriptions as multiple lines that fit within the current size of the browser window, rather than as a single long line requiring the user to scroll or enlarge the browser window. See the section later in this chapter, "Using HTML 3 Tables to Format Directory Listings."

The three descriptions in Example 11-2 are included in the automatic directory listing shown in Figure 11-10.

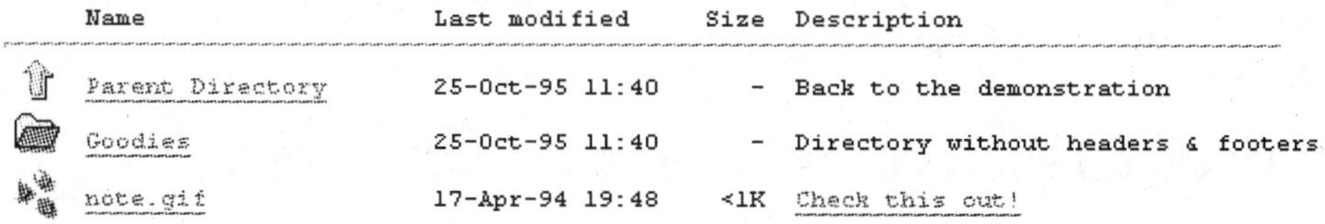

Name	Last modified	Size	Description
Parent Directory	25-Oct-95 11:40	-	Back to the demonstration
Goodies	25-Oct-95 11:40	-	Directory without headers & footers
note.gif	17-Apr-94 19:48	<1K	Check this out!

FIGURE 11-10: DESCRIPTIONS IN DIRECTORY LISTING

USING ICONS IN A DIRECTORY LISTING

Extended directory list formatting uses icons rather than bullets in the file listing. Which icon the server uses for a file depends on the file type. Icons for files are determined by content type and are assigned on the Mapping page of Server Admin. Mapping directory icons to content types is discussed in Chapter 9, *Mapping*.

Four special icons are defined in the Special Icons section of the Dir Listing page. The icon, its filename, and its use are given in Table 11-1. The icons used in automatic directory listings are called by the server from the */icons/* URL directory of WebSite. Any new icons you add must be in this directory.

TABLE 11-1: WEBSITE SPECIAL DIRECTORY ICONS

Icon	Filename	Description
	Unknown	Files whose type isn't defined
	Parent Directory	Directory above the current directory
	Sub Directory	Directory within the current directory
	Spacer	Placeholder used in headers

To change the special icons, follow these steps:

1. Launch Server Admin and click on the Dir Listing page.

2. Highlight the current entry in any of the icon edit boxes of the Special Icons section and type in the new icon filename.

3. Press Close to update the server.

4. Make sure the new icon file is in the *\WebSite\icons* directory.

NOTE

To change the icons used for content types, see the section on Directory Icon Mapping in Chapter 9, *Mapping*.

MORE DIRECTORY LISTING OPTIONS

Four additional options further enhance extended directory listing:

- Icons used as links
- HTML <TITLE> tags used as file descriptions
- Content types used as file descriptions

- HTML 3 table format used to display directory listings

You set these options through the checkboxes in the Features section of the Dir Listing page. (See Figure 11-11.) To turn them on or off, simply click on the checkbox.

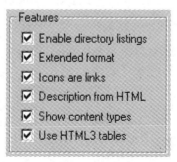

FIGURE 11-11: DIRECTORY LISTING FEATURES

USING ICONS AS LINKS

If you select this option, the server makes the icon in the directory listing (as well as the filename) a hypertext link. A user can click on either the icon or the filename to download the file. The icons used for links are borderless.

USING HTML TITLES AS DESCRIPTIONS

If you select this option, the server reads the first 250 bytes of every HTML file to find the contents of the <TITLE> . . . </TITLE> tag. This value is then used as the file description if no annotation exists in the default description file. Using HTML titles as descriptions saves time in creating and maintaining the description file.

The server requires that the title tags be in uppercase and that the complete title *and* start and end title tags be within the first 250 bytes of the file. Note too that annotations in the description file always takes precedence over HTML titles. Figure 11-12 shows an extended directory listing with an HTML title used as a file description (*sample.html*).

USING CONTENT TYPES AS DESCRIPTIONS

If you select this option, the server displays the file's content type as the description if no annotation exists in the description file. The content type is determined by the file extension and how it is mapped in Server Admin. (See Chapter 9, *Mapping*.) Annotations in the description file and HTML titles take precedence over content types in directory listing.

Figure 11-12 shows an extended directory listing with a content type used as a file description (*rubout.txt*).

Name	Last modified	Size	Description
A Sample.html	12-Nov-94 18:51	<1K	A Sample Hypertext Document
Rubout.txt	29-Apr-94 14:12	<1K	*text/plain*

FIGURE 11-12: CONTENT TYPE AND HTML TITLE USED AS DESCRIPTIONS

NOTE

The server replaces some of the *wwwserver* content types with more friendly descriptions. For wwwserver/redirection (*.url* files), the server shows "Internet Shortcut." For the wwwserver CGI content types, the server shows "[*Type*] CGI Program."

USING HTML 3 TABLES TO FORMAT DIRECTORY LISTINGS

If you select this option, the server formats the directory listing as an HTML 3 table. This nicer looking format has the advantage of fitting all the information in a directory listing into the current browser window size. For example, if a file has a long description, it is displayed as a multi-line block of text rather than a single long line. If the user resizes the browser window, the block of text resizes as well to fit in the new window. Figure 11-13 shows a directory listing in HTML 3 format in a very narrow browser window.

Not all browsers support HTML 3 tables. Recognizing this, WebSite makes it easy to switch between the table and non-table formats for automatic directory listings, overriding the Server Admin setting:

- To switch from a non-table (or plain) format to a table format, simply add *?table* to the URL for the directory. For example, to display the server self-test demo directory as a table, the URL would be *http://localhost/wsdocs/demo/demotree/?table*.

- To switch from a table format to a plain format, simply add *?plain* to the URL for the directory. For example, to display the server self-test demo directory not as a table, the URL would be *http://localhost/wsdocs/demo/demotree/?plain*.

Once you select a format by appending *?table* or *?plain* to a URL, WebSite remembers and formats the parent directory and subdirectories in the new format.

To provide the other type of listing to users, include an HREF in the header file to switch from the default format. For example, to allow users to see the listing in a table format include an HREF something like this one in the header:

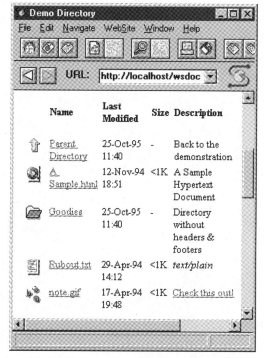

FIGURE 11-13: DIRECTORY LISTING IN HTML 3 FORMAT

```
<a href="/?table"> table format listing</a>
```

To allow users to see the listing in a plain format include an HREF something like this one in the header:

```
<a href="./?plain"> plain format listing</a>
```

Users can always press the Back button to return to the previous format.

NOTE

If you don't include a header file, the server automatically inserts an HREF for switching between formats at the head of the directory listing.

CHAPTER TWELVE

CONTROLLING ACCESS
TO YOUR WEB

Applying access restrictions to all or part of your web is an important tool in the server administrator's toolbag. You may have sensitive information that only a few people should see. Or you may be constructing a new section of your web and don't want anyone to stumble into it until you are finished. Or you may want to keep anyone from an Internet address other than your company's from gaining access to your web.

WebSite's combination of user authentication and access control restrictions enables you to set up these various security scenarios and more. For any portion of your web, you can restrict access by requiring a username and password. Or you can restrict access by the IP address or domain name making the request. You can also combine username and password authentication with IP address filtering for more flexible access control restrictions, a new feature of WebSite 1.1. If you are running virtual servers, you can set up independent access control schemes for each identity.

Another new feature of WebSite 1.1 includes disabling automatic directory listings on a URL basis, which allows you to protect sensitive areas of your web from unauthorized viewing. WebSite 1.1 also includes a utility (*wsauth*) for importing users and groups from a flat file database, managing that database from the command line, and allowing changes via the browser such as users changing their own passwords.

WebSite complies with the HTTP standard of Basic Authentication and makes setting up, applying, and managing access control easy through a graphical user interface. If your web requires transaction-level security (for example, to encrypt credit card numbers), you should upgrade to WebSite Professional. WebSite Pro includes support for both Secure HTTP (S-HTTP) and Secure Sockets Layer (SSL) protocols. These protocols provide full encryption and transaction-level security. See WebSite Central for more information on upgrading to WebSite Pro.

This chapter begins with an overview of the basic concepts of user authentication and access control. It next shows you how to set up access control using Server Admin. A tutorial walks you through some typical cases of applying access control. The chapter ends with coverage of the *wsauth* utility.

OVERVIEW OF ACCESS CONTROL

Access to your web is controlled either by authenticating users or by restricting certain classes of connections through IP address or hostname filtering. Unlike most Web servers, WebSite applies access control to URLs rather than physical paths. Access control can be applied either to the whole Web (the URL *http:// your.host.name/*) or to a specific URL path in the Web. A URL path maps to a directory and any files or subdirectories beneath it. Thus, when you restrict a URL path, you are protecting an entire directory, not a single file. Applying restrictions to URL paths rather than physical locations provides great flexibility in mapping, document locations, and setting up virtual servers.

BASIC RULES

There are two rules to remember when applying access control. These rules govern how the server handles access control along a URL path.

- A restriction on a URL path restricts that directory and all subdirectories unless another restriction exists below it in the path (that is, at a URL that is a subdirectory of the current URL). When restrictions are applied, the server refers to them as "control points."

- The "deepest" access control point determines the access restrictions at a particular level. In other words, when the server receives a request from a browser it starts at the level of the request and works up levels until it finds a control point. The server applies the restrictions at that point and stops; it does not look at restrictions above that point.

Keep these two principles in mind as you apply access control restrictions to URLs in your web.

USER AUTHENTICATION

When you control access by user authentication, users must prove to the server that they are allowed to view a certain part of the web. The server must know who the user is and that the username and password are valid for that URL path.

HOW IT WORKS

Briefly, here's how user authentication works. When someone requests a restricted URL, the server sends an error message to the browser indicating that authentication is required before it can return the document. The browser responds to that message by presenting an authentication dialog to the user. When the user enters a name and password, the browser resubmits the same request with the accompanying authentication data. If the user is authenticated, the server returns the document. Otherwise, the process starts over with the server sending the error message. There is no limit on the number of times a user may attempt to authenticate himself to the server.

Once a user is authenticated, the browser remembers the authentication information and supplies it on all subsequent requests. If that user is allowed access to the new URL, the server automatically returns the document and does not again query the user. However, if that user is *not* allowed access to a restricted area, the server sends the authentication required error message again.

USERS, GROUPS, AND REALMS

We've talked about user authentication only at the user and password level. However, dealing with individual users is not always practical for applying access control. The people who defined the Web standard for Basic Authentication recognized that and implemented the concepts of *realms* and *groups*.

You're probably familiar with the concept of groups; a *group* is simply a collection of users with a common property. Two standard groups included in WebSite are Users and Administrators. In fact, all users added to WebSite are automatically members of the Users group and may not be removed from the group. You can also create groups that make sense for your web, such as a group of people all working on the same project or in the same department. *WebSite users and groups are completely separate from users and groups set up under Windows NT or Windows 95.*

A Web *realm* is a collection of specific users and groups. A realm lets you segregate users and groups when applying access controls to portions of your web. In fact, when you add users and groups to WebSite, you must place them in a specific realm. WebSite is shipped with a default realm, *Web Server*, and a realm used for the server self-test, *Examples*. Members of the Examples realm have access to certain URLs in the server self-test that *no* members of the realm Web Server can reach. Take a few minutes and explore the access control section of the server self-test (see Appendix A).

Since a picture is worth a thousand words, Figure 12-1 illustrates the relationship between users, groups, and realms.

Once you have established a realm of users and/or groups (either the default realm or one you create), you can attach the realm to any URL path in your web. Attaching a realm does not automatically apply access control. You must now select from the realm users and/or groups who are authorized to have access to the URL. Figure 12-2 illustrates several user authentication scenarios.

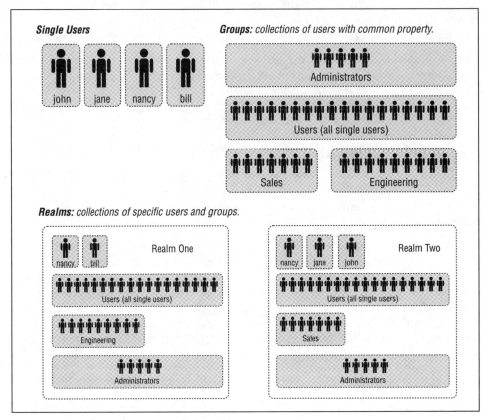

FIGURE 12-1: USERS, GROUPS, AND REALMS FOR USER AUTHENTICATION

NOTE

Realms are the key to applying access control to virtual servers. For each virtual server you set up one or more realm and add users and groups. You then apply the realm(s) to the URLs for the virtual servers. See the section later in this chapter, "Adding Access Control to Virtual Servers" and Chapter 10, *Virtual Servers and WebSite*.

IP ADDRESS FILTERING AND HOSTNAME FILTERING

IP address filtering and hostname filtering—generically called class restrictions—control access to the server by preventing certain Internet nodes from connecting to the server. For each request from a browser, the server can either deny or allow access based on the Internet node (identified by IP address or hostname) of the requester.

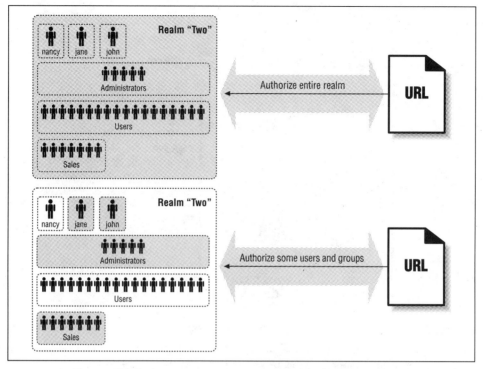

FIGURE 12-2: APPLYING USER AUTHENTICATION TO URL PATHS

When a browser requests a URL from the WebSite server, the server first looks at the IP address or hostname of the request and the URL. The server then checks to see what IP address or hostname restrictions apply for that URL. The restriction may allow or deny access to the URL, and the server responds accordingly by returning the document or sending an "access not allowed" message.

IP address and hostname filtering are helpful for quickly limiting access without creating groups and adding usernames. Figure 12-3 illustrates two class restriction scenarios.

In WebSite, setting up class restrictions requires selecting a URL path to be restricted, identifying the IP address or hostname, and then specifying whether you are allowing or denying access to that address.

TWO WAYS TO COMBINE USER AUTHENTICATION AND CLASS RESTRICTIONS

User authentication and class restrictions work together to provide access control for your web. By default, the server takes a logical approach to determining

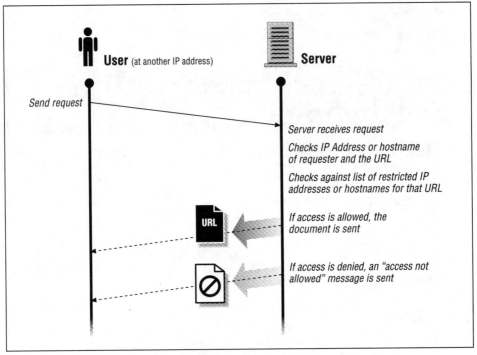

User (at another IP address)   **Server**

Send request

Server receives request

Checks IP Address or hostname
of requester and the URL

Checks against list of restricted IP
addresses or hostnames for that URL

URL

If access is allowed, the
document is sent

If access is denied, an "access not
allowed" message is sent

FIGURE 12-3: APPLYING IP ADDRESS FILTERING TO URL PATHS

access control points. It first checks the class restrictions setting and determines whether or not to accept the connection. If the class restriction test is met, then the server looks to see whether or not the URL path requires user authentication. If yes, the server sends an error message to the browser, causing it to present a user authentication form to the requester. The server checks the browser's response against the authorized list and either returns the requested document or the same error message. Note that if the class restriction wasn't met, the server stops looking for control points and denies access.

You can also combine username and password authentication with IP address or hostname filtering to have the server meet *either* access control condition. The benefit of combining access control requirements as an *OR* rather than an *AND* becomes apparent with a simple example.

Let's say there's a part of your web that your whole company or several departments, but only a few people from outside the company, need to see. You can tell the server to allow anyone from your company access by the IP address they are using. You can also tell the server to allow the outside users access, because you have set up have valid usernames and passwords for them. The server looks at both conditions and allows access if either one is met. If the server did not have this capability, you would have to add access control for each user (both within and outside the company).

TIP

Using the OR combination of restrictions is handy for colleagues who travel or work off-site and use different IP addresses to reach your web. If they need to reach areas restricted by IP address filtering, you can add user authentication to the restricted URLs and place the travelers and off-site workers in an allowed group.

DISABLING AUTOMATIC DIRECTORY LISTINGS

Chapter 11, *Automatic Directory Listings*, covered automatic directory listings in detail. If you have directory listing enabled, the server generates a list of files in any directory that does not contain an index (or home) page and returns that listing to the browser. The list shows all allowed files in the directory as links. By clicking on a link, the user can download the file.

To prevent the server from generating and displaying a list of files, you can disable directory listing on a URL basis. You select the URL and tell the server not to display a listing. A user can still obtain a document from the restricted area by using the full URL, *including the filename*, for the document. However, the user won't be able to view the contents of the directory. When directory listing is disabled, the server sends a message "Directory browsing not allowed" to the user requesting the directory's URL.

Disabling directory listings prevents users from viewing lists of sensitive documents or programs on your web. In addition, users can download only documents for which they have the complete URL, including filename. Since they must have the exact filename of the document, you can control what they can and cannot obtain.

CONTROLLING ACCESS THROUGH SERVER ADMIN

Perhaps the easiest way to understand access control is to see how you set it up in WebSite. This section covers the Server Admin pages used for defining realms, users, and groups, and attaching them to specific URL paths. It also describes combining user authentication and class restrictions as well as disabling automatic directory listings.

In Server Admin, access control is set using three different pages: Users, Groups, and Access Control.

MANAGING USERS AND PASSWORDS

Launch Server Admin and click on the Users tab (Figure 12-4). The Users page is for managing users and their passwords; it has three sections:

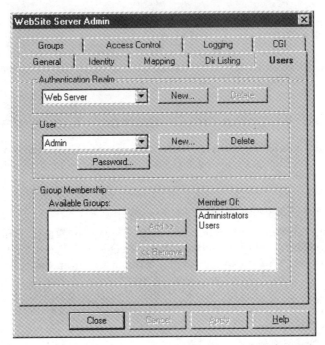

FIGURE 12-4: SERVER ADMIN USERS PAGE

Authentication Realm

You can select an existing realm to use (such as Web Server), create a new realm, or delete an existing realm. Your web can have one or multiple realms. If your WebSite installation has only a single server, we recommend you maintain one realm until your web demands more. If you are running multiple virtual servers, you may want to set up separate realms for each virtual server. When you create a new realm, it has no users. The realm you select here is the one affected by any users you add or change.

User

You can select an existing user in the realm, change a user's password, add a new user and password, or delete a user. The default Web Server realm has an Admin user; part of the installation process was to add this user to the Administrators and Users group. (If you didn't do so then, you should now). Figure 12-4 shows the Admin user.)

Group Membership

You can view and change the group membership status for the selected user. Every realm has an Administrators and a Users group. All users in a realm are part of the Users group and cannot be deleted from that group, unless, of course, you delete the user altogether.

The specific procedures for working with this page are covered in the tutorial. Note that the changes do not take effect until you close Server Admin.

TIP

If you plan to add users to a realm and put them in new groups, we suggest you create the groups *first* and then add the users. That way you can place the users in the new group as you add them and not have to add them one at a time later. WebSite does not allow you to add multiple users to a group at one time.

MANAGING GROUPS

To see the Groups page, click on the Groups tab (Figure 12-5). The Groups page is used for managing groups and group membership; it has three sections:

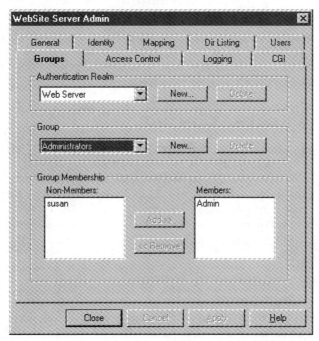

FIGURE 12-5: SERVER ADMIN GROUPS PAGE

Authentication Realm

You can select an existing realm to use (such as Web Server), create a new realm, or delete an existing realm. Your web can have one realm or multiple realms. The realm you select here is the one affected by any groups you add or change.

Group

You can select an existing group in the realm, add a new group, or delete a group. Every realm automatically has an Administrators and a Users group, which have no members when first created. All users in a realm are part of the Users group and cannot be removed.

Group Membership

You can view and change the selected group's membership list. In the above example, the Administrators group includes the user Admin but not the user Susan. We can add Susan to the group or remove Admin from the group. If we had selected the Users group, all users in the realm would be listed in the Members box and none could be removed.

The specific procedures for working with this page are covered in the tutorial. Note that the changes do not take effect until you close Server Admin.

WARNING

WebSite users and groups are completely separate from users and groups established for your operating system and/or network. WebSite users and groups are for restricting access to your web and have no connection with the system at large. If you want to restrict access to your web, *you must add users and groups to the WebSite server.*

MANAGING ACCESS CONTROL

To see the Access Control page, click on the Access Control tab. On this page you manage access control on URLs by user authentication and/or IP address/hostname filtering. You also use this page to disable automatic directory listings and determine how the server will process access control restrictions per URL. Figures 12-6 and 12-7 show two examples of applying restrictions, by user authentication and class restrictions, respectively. As you use this page to set access control, remember that restrictions are placed on URLs, and *not* on physical directory paths.

The Access Control page has several sections:

URL Path or Special Function

You can select, add, or delete a URL path or special function. A URL path is the directory portion of a full URL. The URL path cannot specify a file, only a directory. For that reason, a URL path includes all files and/or subdirectories

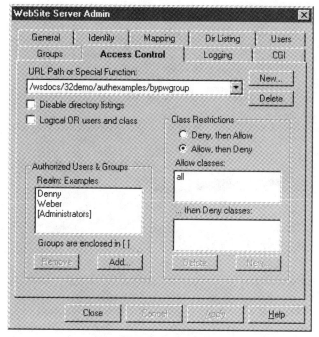

FIGURE 12-6: ACCESS CONTROL PAGE SHOWING USER AUTHENTICATION

under that directory. You can put access control on URLs for document or CGI program directories.

You can select an existing URL path from the pulldown list to view or change the access control. You can also add new URL paths to be protected. Note that when you do so, all files and subdirectories off that path will have the same protection. You can also delete a URL path from the list; however, deleting the URL path only deletes the access restrictions, not the actual URL from the Web. Figure 12-6 shows the URL path */wsdocs/32demo/authexamples/bypwgroup* while Figure 12-7 shows the URL path */wsdocs/32demo/authexamples/bydomain.*

A *special function* is a URL that starts with a ~ (tilde) character and is handled in a specific way by the server. Some special function URLs only retrieve data, such as *~stats* or *~imagemap*. Other special function URLs cause the server to perform an administrative task, such as *~cycle-acc* or *~cycle-err* to cycle the access and error logs. All of the special function URLs in WebSite are on the Access Control list, although only those that cause the server to do something are protected.

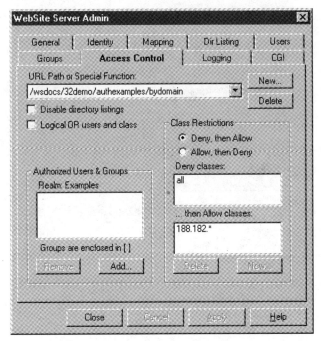

FIGURE 12-7: ACCESS CONTROL PAGE SHOWING CLASS RESTRICTIONS

NOTE

If you delete access control for a special function, that function is *completely disabled* for the server. No one, not even the administrator, can activate it. You can reenable the special function by adding it back into the access control list.

When you add a URL path or special function, you attach a realm to it. The groups and users in that realm are the only ones for which you can add user authentication to the URL path or special function. By default, any new URL path or special function you add is in the Web Server realm; you can select a different realm but only one realm per path.

Disable Directory Listings

This checkbox disables automatic directory listings for the selected URL. Users will be able to view or download documents in that URL directory hierarchy only with the specific filename. You can also add user authentication and class restrictions to a URL with disabled directory listings.

Logical OR Users and Class

This checkbox tells the server how to evaluate access control. When the box is not checked, the server uses the default method, first looking for class restrictions and then for user authentication (if the class restriction is met). If the box is checked, the server evaluates both class restrictions and user authentication. If either condition is met, the server returns the requested URL.

Authorized Users & Groups

You can view or change the users and/or groups authorized for the selected URL path or special function. The realm for this URL is displayed above the list. If no users or groups are shown in this box, then the URL has no user authentication restrictions. In the example in Figure 12-6, only the users Denny and Weber and the group Administrators have access to the URL path. You use the Add and Remove buttons to change the contents of the authorized list.

Class Restrictions

Figure 12-7 shows access control applied only by class restrictions (IP address/ hostname filtering). In this section of the Access Control page, you specify which connections to the Web are allowed and which are denied. First decide the logic the server should follow in testing connections. Should it first deny and then allow or first allow and then deny? In the example in Figure 12-7, the server will first deny *all* classes of connections and then allow connections from nodes that start with IP addresses *199.182*. In Figure 12-6, the server first allowed *all* and didn't deny any classes. If you want to deny access from a specific node, you first allow *all* and then deny the specific node.

Class restrictions accept three kinds of entries: all, a full or partial IP address, or a full or partial domain name. You can use metacharacters (* and ?) to match all or part of either IP addresses or domain names. If you use domain names, you must turn on DNS reverse lookup on the Logging page. The server then looks up the name for the IP address of each requesting node. We recommend that you don't use domain names or DNS reverse lookup because the extra DNS traffic and waiting time may adversely affect server performance.

The specific procedures for working with this page are covered in the tutorial. Note that the changes do not take effect until you close Server Admin.

RESTRICTING ACCESS TO YOUR WEB: A TUTORIAL

Enough theory and overview. Let's actually restrict access to a portion of your web so that you can see the steps involved. The tutorial includes two situations, reasons for restricting access, a plan for implementing it, and instructions for doing so.

THE BACKGROUND

You are the WebSite administrator for a small company. You have a web that you use for general advertising as well as providing customer support and product information to your clients on the Web. You really haven't had to worry about access control. However, two new developments are changing the picture.

SITUATION ONE: NEW PRODUCT IN BETA TEST

The first new development is that your product support group is about to launch a fantastic new product. They plan to create a new area on the existing web to use for promoting this product and for providing customer support. They want to develop this new area in private and test it with a few key beta customers. Of course, the CEO and VP of Marketing want to view the web during construction. When the product is released, the new product web will also be ready for the public.

SITUATION TWO: CUSTOM PRODUCT FOR MAJOR CLIENT

The second development is that your sales team has just completed a huge deal with a large client for a custom-designed product. Part of the deal is to provide dedicated product information and technical support to employees at the client's corporate office. After looking at various alternatives, the two companies have decided that providing this information over the World Wide Web makes the most sense, but only if you can control who may see it. Of course, the product support team at your company has to have access to this web as well.

THE PLAN

Before you knew about access control, you might have run to your boss and asked for two more dedicated machines, networking stuff, and two new copies of WebSite. But now you know that you can accomplish the above tasks with your existing WebSite server and carefully planned access control.

The first step is to collect some information about each case. Putting this in a chart makes it easier to plan and implement the restrictions. Figure 12-8 and Figure 12-9 show the result of your information gathering.

THE IMPLEMENTATION

Planning and gathering information are the hard parts. Implementing the access control is the easy part. WebSite's graphical user interface makes setting restrictions logical and intuitive. In the following sections, we'll walk through the procedures for each situation.

Summary			
Reason for Access Control: New product web under construction			
URL Path for Special Function to be Restricted: /newproducts/super-gizmo/			
Realm: Web Server			
User Authentication			
Groups/Users to Include	New?	Additional Users not in Groups	New?
Product Development/	No	tom (CEO)	No
cathy, richard, ron, sandy	No	cynthia (VP Marketing)	No
SG Beta/	Yes		
msmith, bjones, jfrost, kbooth	Yes		
Class Restrictions			
IP Address or Domain Name		Allow	Deny
all (default)		Yes	No

FIGURE 12-8: PLANNING CHART FOR SITUATION ONE

Summary			
Reason for Access Control: Custom product for big client			
URL Path for Special Function to be Restricted: /custom/big-client/			
Realm: Big Client			
User Authentication			
Groups/Users to Include	New?	Additional Users not in Groups	New?
Custom Support	No	tom (CEO)	No
mj, linda, robert, simon	No	cynthia (VP Marketing)	No
		jay (VP Product Development)	No
Class Restrictions			
IP Address or Domain Name		Allow	Deny
all (default)		No	Yes
Big Client IP Address (Partial) 123.234.100 *		Yes	No
		Yes	No

FIGURE 12-9: PLANNING CHART FOR SITUATION TWO

SITUATION ONE: USER AUTHENTICATION

From the information in Figure 12-8, you can see that the access control is based on user authentication. We'll assume that the Product Development group and the CEO and VP of Marketing are already in the Web Server realm. To finish the process and fully implement the restrictions, you have to do the following:

1. Add a group called *SG Beta*.

2. Add the users *msmith, bjones, jfrost,* and *kbooth* to the new group.

3. Attach the two groups (*Product Development* and *SG Beta*) and the two additional users (*tom* and *cynthia*) to the URL path */newproducts/super-gizmo*

Let's look at these major steps in more detail.

STEP ONE: ADD A NEW GROUP. Figure 12-10 shows the completed Groups page. To add the group *SG Beta,* follow these steps:

1. Launch Server Admin and select the Groups page.

2. Select Web Server as the authentication realm.

3. Press the New button in the Group section. Type the new group name in the dialog that appears and press OK. The new group now exists with no members.

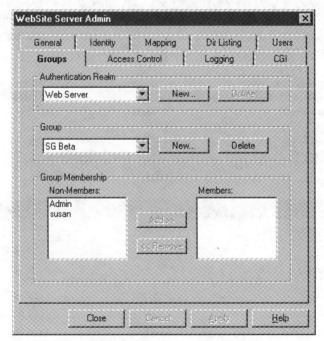

FIGURE 12-10: ADDING A NEW GROUP

STEP TWO: ADD NEW USERS. Figure 12-11 shows the completed Users page. To add the users *msmith*, *bjones*, *jfrost*, and *kbooth* to the new group *SG Beta*, follow these steps:

1. Select the Users page of Server Admin.

2. Select Web Server as the authentication realm.

3. Press the New button in the User section. A dialog box appears. Type in the first user name and the password (you must repeat the password to verify you typed it correctly) and press OK. The new user exists as a member of the group Users.

4. Highlight the group *SG Beta* in the Group Membership Available Groups box. Press the Add>> button or double-click on the group name. The new user is now a member of the group *SG Beta*.

5. Repeat steps 3 and 4 for each user.

6. To verify that the users you added are members of the group *SG Beta*, go to the Groups page and select the group. The Members list should include the users you just added.

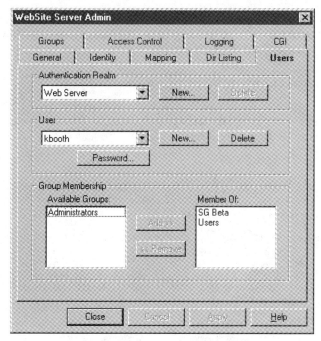

FIGURE 12-11: ADDING NEW USERS

STEP THREE: ATTACH USERS AND GROUPS TO URL PATH. Figure 12-12 shows the completed Access Control page. To attach the groups *Product Development* and

SG Beta and the users *tom* and *cynthia* to the URL path */newprod/super-gizmo,* follow these steps:

1. Select the Access Control page of Server Admin.

2. Press New for the URL Path field; a dialog box appears.

3. Type in the new URL path and select the realm Web Server. Press OK.

4. In the Authorized Users and Groups section, press Add. A list of available users and groups appears.

5. Highlight one of the users or groups to be added to the list of authorized users and press OK. The name appears in the Authorized Users & Groups box.

6. Repeat steps 4 and 5 for each user and group to be added. (You can add only one at a time.)

7. Verify that the class restrictions are set to allow all connections.

8. Press Close to update the server. When you hear the computer beep, the new access controls are in place.

NOTE

Until you press Close on any Server Admin page, the server is not updated and the changes are not in effect.

SITUATION TWO: CLASS RESTRICTIONS

From the information in Figure 12-9, you can see that the access control for this situation is based on a combination of user authentication and class restrictions. The major steps for implementing the restrictions are as follows:

1. Create a realm called *Big Client.*

2. Add a group called *Custom Support.*

3. Add the users *mj, linda, robert,* and *simon* to the new group. Add the users *tom, cynthia,* and *jay* to the new realm.

4. Attach the new group (*Custom Support*) and the three additional users (*tom, cynthia,* and *jay*) to the URL path */custom/big-client.*

5. Apply class restrictions to first deny all connections and then allow connections from IP address 123.234.100* to the URL path */custom/big-client.* The asterisk is a wildcard, meaning any IP address starting with 123.234.100 is allowed access.

6. Tell the server to look at both types of access control and allow access to users who meet either condition.

Let's look at these major steps in more detail.

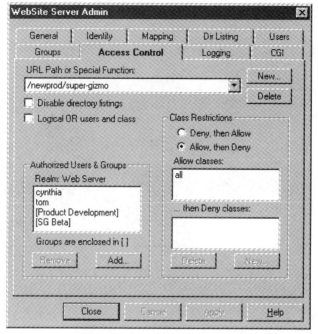

FIGURE 12-12: ATTACHING USERS AND GROUPS TO A URL PATH

STEP ONE: CREATE A NEW REALM. Figure 12-13 shows the completed Groups page for steps 1 and 2. To create the realm *Big Client*, follow these steps:

1. Launch Server Admin and select the Groups page. (If you're only adding new users and not a new group, complete this step from the Users page.)

2. Press New in the Authentication Realm section. A dialog box appears.

3. Type in the name of the new realm and press OK. The new name appears in the Authentication Realm field.

STEP TWO: ADD A NEW GROUP. The completed Groups dialog is shown in Figure 12-13. To add the group *Custom Support,* follow these steps:

1. On the Groups dialog, press the New button in the Group section. A dialog box appears.

2. Type in the new group name and press OK. The new group now exists with no members.

STEP THREE: ADD NEW USERS. Figure 12-14 shows the completed Users page. To add the users *mj, linda, robert,* and *simon* to the new group and the users *tom, cynthia,* and *jay* to the realm, follow these steps:

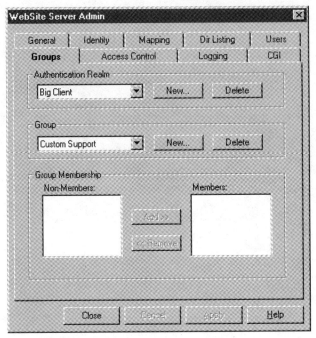

FIGURE 12-13: ADDING A NEW REALM AND GROUP

1. Select the Users page of Server Admin.

2. Select *Big Client* as the authentication realm.

3. Press the New button in the User section. A dialog box appears.

4. Type in the first username and the password (you must repeat the password to verify you typed it correctly) and press OK. The new user exists as a member of the group Users.

5. Highlight the group *Custom Support* in the Group Membership-Available Groups box. Press the Add>> button or double-click on the group name. The new user is now a member of the group *Custom Support*.

6. Repeat steps 3 through 5 for each user in the *Custom Support* group.

7. Repeat step 4 for each of the additional three users.

STEP FOUR: ATTACH USERS AND GROUPS TO URL PATH AND SELECT ACCESS CONTROL EVALUATION METHOD. Figure 12-15 shows the completed Access Control page (with user authentication and class restrictions in place). To finish setting access control, follow these steps:

1. Select the Access Control page of Server Admin.

2. Press New for the URL Path field; a dialog box appears.

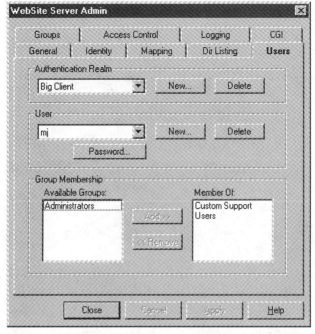

FIGURE 12-14: ADDING NEW USERS TO A NEW REALM AND NEW GROUP

3. Type in the new URL path and select the realm *Big Client*. Press OK.

4. Check the Logical OR users and class box.

5. In the Authorized Users and Groups section, press Add. A list of available users and groups appears.

6. Highlight one of the users or groups to be added to the list of authorized users and press OK. The name appears in the Authorized Users & Groups box.

7. Repeat steps 5 and 6 for each user and group to be added (you can add only one at a time).

8. In the Class Restrictions section, select the option Deny, then Allow.

9. Select the Deny classes box and press New. A dialog box appears.

10. Type all and press OK. The word *all* appears in the Deny classes box. (If any other entries are in this box, highlight them and press Delete.)

11. Select the Allow classes box and press New. A dialog box appears.

12. Type in the Big Client's IP address and press OK. The new address appears in the Allow classes box. (If any other entries are in this box, highlight them and press Delete.)

13. Press Close to update the server.

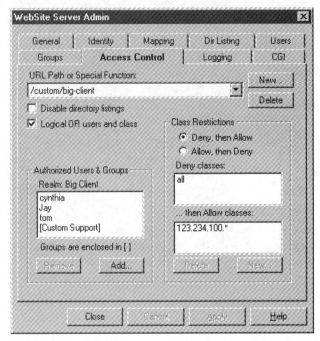

FIGURE 12-15: ATTACHING USER AUTHENTICATION AND CLASS RESTRICTIONS

ADDING ACCESS CONTROL TO VIRTUAL SERVERS

The principles of applying access control to specific URL paths by user/password authentication or IP address/hostname filtering remains the same when you are running multiple virtual servers under one copy of WebSite. Each virtual server has its own set of URL paths starting with the URL prefix (for example, */webs/*). You can restrict access to any or all parts of a virtual server's URL hierarchy, just as you would for a single server. Since WebSite applies access control by URL and not physical path, applying restrictions to virtual servers is quite simple.

Restricting access to a virtual server's web by IP address or hostname is identical to restricting access to a single server. The server allows or denies access to the virtual server's web (or part of the web) based on the URL requested and the filtering restrictions defined for that URL.

The real issue in applying access control to virtual servers is user authentication. How do you keep different users and groups separate for each server? What if two of your virtual servers wanted to allow (or deny) Bob access to a part of the Web, but they are two different Bobs? How do you keep from having a huge user database including all users for all the virtual servers?

The answer to these questions is to use realms, which are simply collections of users and groups. You create a different realm for each virtual server (for example, one realm called Webs and another realm called Food). You then add users and groups for each server to the specific realm.

When you apply access control, you select a URL path for a virtual server (remembering to include the URL prefix for the virtual server) and the realm for that server. All the users and groups appropriate for that virtual server are available and none of the users and groups for other virtual servers are; they are available only in the realm for their own virtual server. Thus, you can have a Bob in two realms but WebSite treats them as different Bobs with different passwords who can never have access to the other's information.

MANAGING USERS AND GROUPS WITH WSAUTH

In general you will want to use Server Admin to handle all aspects of access control for your web. However, some situations lend themselves to using the WebSite User/Group Utility, *wsauth,* to manage users and groups. You can use *wsauth* interactively from the command line, in batch mode as a script, or as a CGI program in a browser.

In essence, *wsauth* gives you access to the user data WebSite uses for access control security, data stored in the WebSite Registry. You can add and delete users, change their passwords, and move users in and out of groups. (To add and delete groups and realms, you must use Server Admin.) *wsauth* is a tool, which you can use to build custom solutions to manage users and groups. In fact, *wsauth* was developed and added to WebSite in response to the frequent requests of users for an easy way to:

- Make mass additions of users from external flat files
- Allow visitors to your web to self-register through a browser
- Allow users of your web to change their passwords through a browser

You can accomplish the first two tasks by using the capability provided by *wsauth* to build your own custom solutions taking into account the security policies of your environment. How you can use *wsauth* for these applications is described at the end of this section. Allowing users to change their passwords is easy with the CGI mode of *wsauth.*

This section first describes the commands that are part of the *wsauth* utility. Next it describes how to use the utility in each mode. Finally it describes some special uses of *wsauth*.

WSAUTH COMMANDS

The WebSite User/Group utility includes 10 commands as described below. Note that arguments to commands are shown in italic, optional arguments are in braces, and alternative arguments are separated by vertical bars. The next three sections show you how to use the commands in the various modes.

SetVerbose *on | off | yes | no | true | false*
> Used in interactive mode only, turns on (on, yes, true) or off (off, no, false) verbose reporting after *wsauth* executes commands.

Help
> Available in interactive mode only, displays a short command summary.

Exit
> Used in interactive mode only, quits *wsauth* and returns to the Command (MS-DOS) Prompt.

SetRealm *realm*
> Used in interactive and batch modes only, sets the realm to be used for subsequent commands that need a realm (such as NewUser and DelUser) but do not explicitly require it with the command. You must set a realm either with this command or with individual commands.

NewUser *user password {realm}*
> Used in all modes, adds a new user with the given password to the realm included with the command or specified by the SetRealm command. Every user added with this command is automatically placed in the Users group.

DelUser *user {realm}*
> Used in all modes, deletes a user from the realm included with the command or specified by the SetRealm command. This command deletes the user from all groups and from all access control entries.

ChangePass *user password {realm}*
> Used in all modes, changes the password for the specified user. The old password is not needed.

SetGroup *group*
> Used in interactive and batch modes only, sets the group to be used for subsequent commands that need a group (such as JoinGroup) but do not explicitly require it with the command. You can change the group set with this command by including a new group name with a subsequent command.

JoinGroup *user {group} {realm}*

Used in all modes, adds the user to the current group and realm. The group and realm may have been set with the SetRealm and SetGroup commands or may be included with this command. If you set group or realm with this command, it applies to each subsequent command. Note that you cannot add users to the Administrators group with this command; you must use Server Admin.

LeaveGroup *user {group} {realm}*

Used in all modes, removes the user from the current group and realm. The group and realm may have been set with the SetRealm and SetGroup commands or may be included with this command. If you set group or realm with this command, it applies to each subsequent command. Note that you cannot remove users from the Users group.

USING WSAUTH IN CGI MODE

As you can see from the commands listed in the preceding section, *wsauth* is a powerful tool for managing your server's users and groups. As a CGI program, *wsauth* presents a series of forms to the browser and accepts information by the POST method. *wsauth* then updates the WebSite Registry directly. This capability must be protected from unauthorized use. To that end, WebSite is shipped with (*/auth*) that is restricted to members of the Administrator's group.

NOTE

If you have multiple realms on your web, see the section below, "Using *wsauth* with Multiple Realms," for setup instructions. If you are running multiple virtual servers you have or will have multiple realms.

Before using *wsauth* as a CGI program, make sure the following security measures are in place (note that your drive specification and WebSite root directory name may differ):

- *wsauth.exe* is in the directory *C:\WebSite\cgi-shl-prot* (Use the File Manager or Explorer to confirm.)

- The URL */auth/* is mapped to *C:\WebSite\cgi-shl-prot* (Use the Mapping page, Standard CGI mappings, or Server Admin to confirm.)

- Access control for */auth/* does not allow for Logical OR users and class.

- The URL */auth/* is restricted to members of the Administrators group. (Use the Access Control page of Server Admin to confirm.) Note that you must change this restriction if you plan to allow users to change their own passwords. See the section on Non-Administrator Usage later in this section.

- You are a member of the Administrators group or have the Admin users password (Use the Users page of Server Admin.)

WARNING

If any of these security measures are missing, fix them immediately. Failure to do so leaves your server vulnerable to security breaches.

Finally, test that the URL is secure. Launch a fresh copy of your browser and request the URL *http://your.host.here/auth/wsauth.exe* with a browser. The browser should display an authentication dialog box, in which you enter your name and password as a member of the Administrators group. If the server returns a warning page, the URL is properly secured and can be used.

As a member of the administrator's group, you can use any of *wsauth*'s commands that are available in CGI mode. Non-members of the administrator's group may use only the ChangePassword command. These types of usage are described in the following sections.

ADMINISTRATOR USAGE

As an administrator, you can use the NewUser, DelUser, ChangePass, JoinGroup, and LeaveGroup commands in CGI mode. (The other commands are available only in batch or interactive mode.) Each command has a built-in HTML form for performing the desired function. To use *wsauth* in CGI mode, simply enter the wsauth URL and add one of the commands as an extra path element. For example,

```
http://your.host.here/auth/wsauth.exe/NewUser
```

causes the server to display the form shown in Figure 12-16. To add a new user, enter the name and password in the form and press the New User button. The server's Registry is automatically updated. Note that the password is not hidden when you type it in the form.

The other commands work the same way; simply add the command as the final element in the *wsauth* URL and complete the resulting form.

NON-ADMINISTRATOR USAGE

You can allow users who are not members of the Administrators group to use *wsauth* to change their passwords. However, you must first add these users to the server and allow them access to the */auth/* URL. This safety measure prevents unauthorized users from using *wsauth*. The advanced features of *wsauth* are still limited to members of the Administrators group.

To add the change password feature to your web, place an HREF to *wsauth* anywhere in your web. The HREF might look something like this:

```
<a href="auth/wsauth.exe/ChangePass">Change your password</a>
```

When the user clicks on this link, the server first makes sure he is authenticated. If not, the browser displays an authentication dialog and asks for the user's name

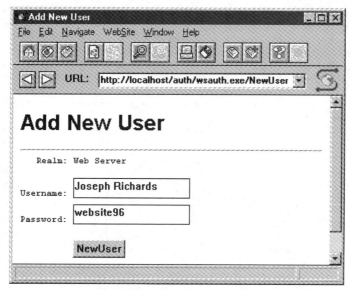

FIGURE 12-16: NEW USER FORM FOR WSAUTH

and current password. Once the user is authenticated, the server sends the Change Password form with the user's name entered to the browser (Figure 12-17). The user types in a new password and presses the Change Password button. Note that the user's password is not hidden.

The next time the user is required to authenticate himself, he will use the new password.

CREATING CUSTOM FORMS

Although *wsauth* comes with an HTML form for each command used in the CGI mode, you can create your own forms. Use the built-in forms as a guide. (The View Source feature of your browser shows the form tagging and text.) Make sure you use the Post method and the same names for the fields as used in the built-in forms. And remember to test your forms before letting others use them.

USING WSAUTH WITH MULTIPLE REALMS

By default the URL for *wsauth, /auth/,* is protected in the Web Server realm. If you have other authentication realms, you must provide access to *wsauth* through each realm. In CGI mode, *wsauth* picks up the realm from the user's authentication information and performs its operations on the appropriate realm. (In the other modes, you manually specify the realm.)

FIGURE 12-17: CHANGE PASSWORD FORM FOR WSAUTH

To provide access to *wsauth* through the other realms, you must add a protected URL for each realm. Each new URL must point to the same copy of *wsauth*. To do so, open Server Admin and click on the Mapping tab. In the Standard CGI mapping, add a unique URL path for each of your realms mapped to the same physical directory where *wsauth* is located. For example, if you have three realms, you could map them as follows:

```
/auth1/ C:\WebSite\cgi-shl-prot\
/auth2/ C:\WebSite\cgi-shl-prot\
/auth3/ C:\WebSite\cgi-shl-prot\
```

Now switch to the Access Control tab and add protection to the URL paths you just created, assigning a different URL to each of your realms. Add the group Administrators to each URL and update the server.

NOTE

If you are running virtual servers, you should follow this procedure for setting up the */auth/* URL for each realm for each server. Remember to use the URL prefix for */auth/*.

USING WSAUTH IN BATCH MODE

The batch mode for *wsauth* reads commands from a file (a script) and processes them. You can place any of the commands listed in the "*wsauth* Commands" section above in a script file and tell *wsauth* to use the script as input. If user, group, or realm names have spaces, enclose whole name in quotation marks. The *wsauth* executable is located in the *\WebSite\support* directory.

A SAMPLE SCRIPT

A typical script might look like the following:

```
SetRealm Sales
NewUser Jones bowser
NewUser "Floyd Smith" crocker
ChangePass Susan sunshine
ChangePass JeffR bleek
DelUser BadBoy
DelUser Mitnick
JoinGroup "Charles Smith" "Friends and Family"
```

Note that each entry is on a separate line. Note, too, that the script begins with the SetRealm command. You must identify a realm at the beginning of a script, either with the SetRealm command or one of the other commands that accepts realm as an option.

COMMAND LINE

The command line options for using *wsauth* in batch mode are as follows:

```
wsauth -vhs {-i script} {-o log} {-r remsys}
```

where,

```
-v          Verbose output
-h          Usage information
-s          Safe mode for scripts
-i script   Script file to use as input
-o log      File to receive output of a script execution
-r remsys   NetBIOS name of remote system (for example, \\CUSTSYS)
```

SAFE MODE OPTION

The safe mode causes *wsauth* to make two passes through the script. On the first pass, it checks to make sure each command is valid before making any changes to the Registry. For example, *wsauth* will fail if you try to add a user that already exists or you try to add a user to the Administrators group or delete a user from the Users group. A common failure occurs because the realm is not identified.

If *wsauth* completes the first pass with no errors, it executes each command on the second pass. With the verbose option set (*-v*), you can see the results. To save the results for later, use the *-o* option and the name of a log file. We recommend you use the safe mode to avoid manual cleanup if the script contains errors. The safe mode is especially useful when testing scripts generated from other facilities (databases, address books, and so forth).

Although the safe mode may save you manual cleanup, it has a limitation that requires some planning ahead. The limitation is actually caused by the Windows NT and Windows 95 Registry's lack of the concept of "transactions" where multiple operations can be tried without actually modifying the Registry. Instead, the safe mode option must run all commands against the current state of the Registry, checking to see if they can be completed successfully. If the script includes a command that is dependent on a previous command in the script, the safe mode pass fails. For example, these lines from the same script file will fail the safe mode test:

```
SetRealm Sales
NewUser Jones Foo
JoinGroup Jones MyGroup
```

Since Jones is not a user in the current version of the Registry, the JoinGroup command will fail. You can avoid failed passes by creating separate script files and running them sequentially.

USING WSAUTH INTERACTIVELY

Interactive mode is handy for making quick updates to the server's user and group data. To use *wsauth* interactively, open a Command or MS-DOS Prompt window and type *wsauth*. The program displays a startup banner and a command prompt (#). You can use any of the *wsauth* commands at this prompt.

To return to the Command or MS-DOS Prompt window, type *exit*.

SOME SPECIAL CASES FOR USING WSAUTH

The situations described in this section are special cases for using *wsauth*.

ENABLING SELF-REGISTRATION

You can use *wsauth* as a tool for building a self-registration system. Since policies regarding self-registration differ widely between sites, we leave it up to you to build the forms and CGI form-handlers to implement your specific application.

In general, you use *wsauth* to add users to your WebSite configuration under the control of your CGI program(s). *wsauth* does not run as a CGI program itself, but rather your CGI program executes it as a shell utility. You create a CGI program that first generates a script file containing the commands needed to register the user and then invokes *wsauth*. Make sure you use the -*i* and -*o* options to tell *wsauth* to read the generated script and log the results.

We recommend that you use *wsauth* with 32-bit CGI programs (for example, ones created with Visual Basic 4) because of problems in synchronizing exits of external programs with 16-bit CGI programs (those created with Visual Basic 3, for example). The 32-bit programs avoid this problem by using the **WaitOnSingleEvent()** function to synchronize.

ADDING USERS FROM A FLAT FILE DATABASE

If you made it this far, you know how to set this up. You simply create a flat file in the format of a *wsauth* script (see the example earlier in this section) and execute *wsauth* in batch mode. You are responsible for generating the flat file in the correct format from your database, address book, or other source. Make sure each entry is on a single line, is preceded by the proper command, and that entries with spaces are enclosed in quotation marks. Don't forget to set the realm at the beginning of the script. We recommend you run scripts created from other applications in safe mode, as described earlier in this section.

CHAPTER THIRTEEN

LOGGING

Collecting information about WebSite is the job of the WebSite logs. You can use this information to analyze traffic, performance, problems, and configuration changes. The logs are an important source of information for managing your web, providing statistics for users, debugging programs, and diagnosing problems.

WebSite has three main logs: the access log, the error log, and the server log. The access log records each request to the server and the server's response in one of three formats: Common (older NCSA/CERN), Combined NCSA/CERN, and Windows Log format. The error log records access errors, such as failed user authentication. The server log records each time the server is restarted or its configuration updated. The access log can record information in three different formats, providing you with a variety of useful information. In addition, you can set a variety of tracing options to have the server log collect more or less detailed information. The tracing information is used primarily for troubleshooting and debugging.

You are already familiar with summary reports from the access log available in WebView. QuickStats pulls information from the access log to give you a summary of all requests for your web and how they were handled, for the last seven days. If you are running virtual servers, QuickStats includes only the data for the virtual server you specify. WebView can also create domain and log reports for any node on a web. To generate these reports, WebView pulls information from the access log. For more information on these features, see Chapter 4, *Managing Your Web Using WebView.*

The WebSite logs contain a wealth of detailed information. If you need more detailed information than the WebView analysis reports contain, use a log analyzing program. A variety of log analyzers are freely available on the Internet. Check out WebSite Central for some recommended programs.

If you are running WebSite under Windows NT, two other system utilities provide tracking data for WebSite. The Monitor Server icon in the WebSite program group launches the Windows NT Performance Monitor and shows the current activity on the server. The Windows NT Event Viewer collects additional information, including start messages, stop messages, changes to the server's configuration, warnings, and errors.

This chapter first discusses how you set up and work with logging in WebSite. Next it covers the three logs and the tracing options available for the server log. Finally, the chapter ends with a brief look at the other tools available for monitoring and evaluating the server.

SETTING UP LOGGING IN SERVER ADMIN

The Logging page in Server Admin shows the paths of the three WebSite log files and the format for the access log. It also includes the options that affect logging: reverse DNS lookup and tracing options for the server log. Figure 13-1 shows the default Logging page.

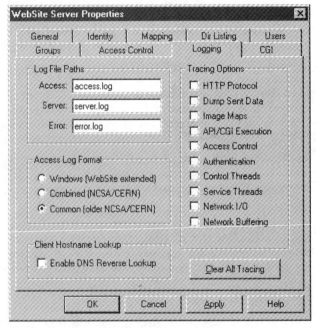

FIGURE 13-1: DEFAULT LOGGING PAGE OF SERVER ADMIN

CHANGING LOG NAMES AND LOCATIONS

The first section on the Logging page shows the current locations of the standard WebSite log files. During installation, WebSite installs the logs in the directory *\WebSite\logs* and names them *access.log, server.log,* and *error.log.* You can change the names and/or locations at any time. For example, you may want to identify the logs with a specific WebSite server name so as not to confuse them with logs for other applications. You may also want to store your logs in a different location, such as on another computer on the network.

NOTE

If the server cannot maintain logs, it shuts down. That means, if you locate the logging directory on a remote computer, make sure that it will be available whenever the server is running. If you have moved the logs to a remote computer and have trouble with the server, try changing the logging directory back to the local system.

Suppose you want to add WS to each log's name. To do so, type the following in each field: *WSaccess.log*, *WSserver.log*, and *WSerror.log*.

On the other hand, let's say you keep all your logs on another computer on your network called *starfire* in the directory *C:\network\logs*. The C: drive of this computer is shared to the network and uses the share name *cdrive*. To change the WebSite logging directory and identify each log as belonging to the WebSite server by changing its name, follow these steps:

1. Launch Server Admin.

2. Highlight the entry in the Access edit box and type in the new path and access log name, *\\starfire\cdrive\network\logs\WSaccess.log*.

3. Highlight the entry in the Server edit box and type in the new path and server log name, *\\starfire\cdrive\network\logs\WSserver.log*.

4. Highlight the entry in the Error edit box and type in the new path and error log name, *\\starfire\cdrive\network\logs\WSerror.log*.

5. Press OK to update the server and close Server Admin. The server is now using the new logs.

When you change the log locations, the server creates new logs in the new locations. That means the current logs do not move to the new location. If you wish to keep appending to the current logs, you must move them to the new location before restarting the server.

NOTE

If you are running virtual servers and set up separate logs for recording access requests, the names for those logs do not appear on the Logging page. To change those names, you must use the Identity page of Server Admin.

SELECTING AN ACCESS LOG FORMAT

WebSite supports three formats for the access log. The different formats allow you to collect different information in different ways for various uses. The three formats are as follows:

- The Windows (WebSite Extended) format collects server access data in a format that can be easily imported into most Microsoft Windows Office productivity packages, such as Access and Excel. The entries are tab delimited and require no additional parsing using Visual Basic or perl. If you plan to use your log data in a Windows application, we recommend this format. On the other hand, Windows format creates larger log files and uses more disk space.

- The Combined NCSA/CERN format collects server access data in a more standard web log format with fields delimited by quotation marks. This format includes two extra fields to identify the URL from which the browser made the current request (Referer), and to identify the browser type (User_Agent).

- The default format is the Common or older NCSA/CERN format. This is the standard format used by most web servers and has been used in previous versions of WebSite.

These three formats are described in more detail in the "Access Log" section of this chapter. Before selecting a logging format, we recommend that you determine how you plan to use logging data, and with what applications. If you are running virtual servers, the same access log format is used for each server.

ENABLING CLIENT HOSTNAME LOOKUP

Incoming requests always include the incoming IP address of the browser. WebSite records the address in the access log and uses it to verify access against class restrictions. By enabling DNS reverse lookup, WebSite looks up the hostname for a system's IP address and records it in the log instead of the IP address.

If you enable DNS reverse lookup, the server must perform an extra step for each request. Instead of accepting an incoming IP address, the server sends a request to a DNS name server and waits for the response before continuing. The server then puts the domain name (rather than the IP address) in the access log and also uses the name for checking class restrictions.

Although using domain names for class restrictions and having domain names listed in log files can make a server administrator's job easier, it can cause performance problems, especially with older versions of Windows NT (prior to Service Pack 4 for NT 3.51, which appears to have fixed a TCP/IP bug). Each browser request generates a request to the name server, thus slowing the transaction time. Unless you have a compelling reason to enable client hostname lookup, we recommend that you don't.

The WebSite default for looking up client hostnames is off. To turn it on, simply click on the Enable DNS Reverse Lookup checkbox on the Logging page and press OK to update the server.

CHANGING TRACING OPTIONS

WebSite has 11 different tracing options that provide detailed data about the server's activity in the server log. You can select one or more of these options by clicking on the appropriate checkbox(es) as shown in Figure 13-2.

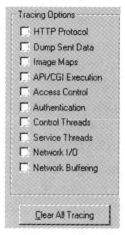

FIGURE 13-2: LOGGING TRACING OPTIONS IN SERVER ADMIN

The server log section of this chapter explains how and why you use these options. In general, these are used most often for troubleshooting and debugging. The first six are useful to the server administrator, while the last five are used mainly by technical support.

To remove tracing options, click on any checked boxes or press the Clear All Tracing button. Changes in tracing options do not take effect until you close Server Admin.

WORKING WITH THE LOGS

The purpose of having logs is to provide you with useful, timely information. WebSite allows you to pull information from the logs either as a snapshot or as a detailed history. The snapshot comes from features built into WebView—Quick-Stats and the activity reports. The history comes from seeing the complete logs in their raw form, which is ASCII text. You can read the log data in any text editor or use a log analyzer to create useful reports. This section covers how to work with the complete logs. The WebView reports and QuickStats are covered in Chapter 4, *Managing Your Web Using WebView*.

When the WebSite server is running, the logs are active and are being constantly updated. You cannot view an active log and see updates being made; you would have to stop the server and then view the closed logs. However, this solution may not be practical or possible. To allow you to see the contents of the "old" log while the server writes to a new one, WebSite includes log cycling capability for the access and error logs. You should view the server log only when the server is stopped. Working with the raw log data includes two steps: cycling the logs and viewing the logs.

CYCLING THE LOGS

When the server cycles the logs, the old log is given a new extension, *.001 . . . .030*. Each time the server cycles either log, the newest one is assigned the extension *.001*, and the older ones are moved up one number. If your server is busy, the access log file will grow quickly, so we recommend cycling at least that log regularly, perhaps once a day or at least once a week.

The WebSite server gives you two ways to cycle the access and error logs:

- The special URLs */~cycle-acc, /~cycle-err,* and */~cycle-both* to cycle the access log, the error log, and both logs, respectively
- The Logcycle utility program to cycle the logs from the command line

How to use these methods is described in the following section. If you set up separate logs for virtual servers, these methods cycle *all* logs, not just the main access log. Note that the logs cycle only when the server is idle.

NOTE

Since the server log grows so slowly, you must cycle it manually. To do so, stop the server, rename *server.log* to *server.xxx* (where *xxx* is a meaningful extension such as a number), and restart the server. A new server log will be started as well.

USING THE SPECIAL URLS

The special URLs are demonstrated in the server self-test, under the Server Administration section. Because these URLs *do* something, they must be issued with the POST method (according to the HTTP specification). Forms can issue POSTs and they can have buttons, so you may want to create an HTML form for cycling the logs with a simple button press. To make it easy, you can copy the source from the server self-test to make your own cycle form.

NOTE

By default, these special URLs are protected by user authentication access control. Only members of the Administrators group in the WebServer realm can use these special URLs. See Chapter 12, *Controlling Access to Your Web*, for more details on user authentication.

Building forms is covered in Chapter 5, *HTML Tutorial and Quick Reference*, so here we just show the code and the final results. These three segments of code produce the buttons shown in Figure 13-3.

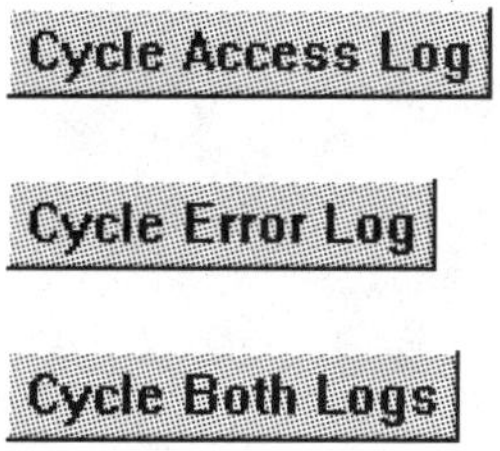

Cycle Access Log

Cycle Error Log

Cycle Both Logs

FIGURE 13-3: LOG CYCLING BUTTONS

```
<FORM METHOD="POST" ACTION="/~cycle-acc ">
<INPUT TYPE="SUBMIT" VALUE="Cycle Access Log">
</FORM>
<P>
<FORM METHOD="POST" ACTION="/~cycle-err">
<INPUT TYPE="SUBMIT" VALUE="Cycle Error Log">
</FORM>
<P>
<FORM METHOD="POST" ACTION="/~cycle-both">
<INPUT TYPE="SUBMIT" VALUE="Cycle Both Logs">
</FORM>
```

When you request the HTML document with this code and press one of the cycling buttons, the user authentication dialog pops up. Once you provide proper credentials as a member of the Administrators group, the server executes the function (cycles the logs) but returns a 204 No Response code (variously translated by different browsers). If the log(s) cycled successfully, you will see the old log(s) in the logs directory with the numeric extension.

USING THE LOGCYCLE UTILITY

The Logcycle utility program causes the server to cycle the access and error logs in the same manner as the special URLs. Logcycle is a command-line program that sends a message to the server while it is running, to cycle the logs. The cycle logs are given numeric extensions, and all access and error logs for the server are cycled.

The Logcycle command is as follows:

```
logcycle -[ae]
```

The *–a* option causes the server to cycle the access log, and the *–e* option causes the server to cycle the error log. You can combine the two options, *–ae*, to cycle both logs. With no options, the server cycles only the access log.

You can run Logcycle from the Command Prompt or from the Run command line. You can also create a program item for Logcycle and place it in the WebSite program group or program folder. The utility is located in the *WebSite\support* directory. For Logcycle to work, the server *must be running but idle*.

VIEWING THE LOGS

The WebSite logs are ASCII files. You can view them using any text editor or word processor. Viewing the logs this way shows you the "raw" log contents. To help in interpreting and using this data, we recommend that you use a log analyzer program. Check WebSite Central for some suggested analyzers.

THE ACCESS LOG

The access log records every attempt by the server to retrieve a URL and reports whether or not it was successful. This information helps you determine which portions of your web are most popular, where those requests are coming from, how often the request is successful (or not), and which users attempted access to restricted URL paths. The main access log and any separate logs you create for virtual servers have the same format—whichever format you chose on the Logging page of Server Admin (see Figure 13-1). This section describes the three formats of the access control log.

COMMON (OLDER NCSA/CERN) FORMAT

The default format for access logging in WebSite is the older NCSA/CERN format, generally called the common format. Example 13-1 shows a few lines from an access log using the common format.

EXAMPLE 13-1: ACCESS LOG SAMPLE, COMMON (OLDER NCSA/CERN) FORMAT

```
127.0.0.1 localhost - [25/Sep/1995:14:36:12 -0500] "GET / HTTP/1.0"
        200 1224
127.0.0.1 localhost - [25/Sep/1995:14:36:12 -0500] "GET /wsdocs/
        images/website-sm.gif HTTP/1.0" 304 162
127.0.0.1 localhost - [25/Sep/1995:14:36:23 -0500] "GET /wsdocs/
        32demo/ HTTP/1.0" 200 26864
127.0.0.1 localhost - [25/Sep/1995:14:36:24 -0500] "GET /wsdocs/
        images/rfinger.gif HTTP/1.0" 200 194
127.0.0.1 localhost - [25/Sep/1995:14:36:24 -0500] "GET /wsdocs/
        images/question.gif HTTP/1.0" 200 229
127.0.0.1 localhost - [25/Sep/1995:14:36:25 -0500] "GET /wsdocs/
        32demo/images/file-imap.gif HTTP/1.0" 200 486
```

EXAMPLE 13-1: ACCESS LOG SAMPLE, COMMON (OLDER NCSA/CERN) FORMAT

```
127.0.0.1 localhost - [25/Sep/1995:14:36:25 -0500] "GET /wsdocs/
        images/note.gif HTTP/1.0" 200 275
127.0.0.1 localhost - [25/Sep/1995:14:36:26 -0500] "GET /wsdocs/
        32demo/images/imapdemo.gif HTTP/1.0" 200 5382
192.100.58.94 sapphire.west.ora.com - [25/Sep/1995:14:13:06 -0500]
        "GET / HTTP/1.0" 401 288
192.100.58.94 sapphire.west.ora.com Reviewer [25/Sep/1995:14:13:16 -
        0500] "GET /ch06.zip HTTP/1.0" 200 87491
198.112.209.140 localhost [10/Oct/1995:12:09:53 -0400] "POST /~cycle-
        acc HTTP/1.0" 401 310
198.112.209.140 localhost Admin [10/Oct/1995:12:10:21 -0400] "POST /
        ~cycle-acc HTTP/1.0" 204 157
```

The first set of lines shows the URLs fetched in response to the request for the WebSite server self-test's URL, *http://localhost/wsdocs/32demo*. Each HREF in the document is a URL, which adds an entry into the access log. The next set shows a request from another IP address. The URL requested required user authentication. The final set shows a request for the *~cycle-acc* URL, which used the POST method and also required user authentication.

The access log follows the common log format as defined by the NCSA and CERN. Let's use the last two sets of lines in Example 13-1 to illustrate this format. The first line is the initial URL request, to which the server responds with the user authentication form. The second line includes the username and positive server response. Table 13-1 details the fields in these two entries.

TABLE 13-1: ACCESS LOG FIELDS, COMMON NCSA/CERN FORMAT

Field Description	Examples
IP Address or Client Hostname (if enabled)	192.100.58.94 198.112.209.140
Domain Identity for the Request (formerly unused; see Note below)	sapphire.west.ora.com, localhost
Authenticated User Name (if required; the user authentication request generates another URL)	Reviewer, Admin (name entered in form)
Date and Time of Request (in Greenwich Mean Time Format, GMT)	[25/Sep/1995:14:13:06 -0500] [10/Oct/1995:12:09:53 -0400]
Complete HTTP Request (method, full URL path, protocol version)	"GET / HTTP/1.0", "POST /~cycle-acc HTTP/1.0"

TABLE 13-1: ACCESS LOG FIELDS, COMMON NCSA/CERN FORMAT (CONTINUED)

Field Description	Examples
HTTP Response Code (you can find a list at WebSite Central or at *http://www.w3.org/pub/ WWW/Protocols/HTTP1.0/draft-ietf-http- spec.html*)	401 (authentication required), 204 (no response)
Number of bytes transferred (actual data, not including the header)	288 (bytes), 157 (bytes)

NOTE

The second field of the access log shows the identity (either domain name or IP address) of the server for which the request is intended. This feature is especially useful if you are running virtual servers. Using the contents of this field, data for each virtual server can be pulled from the access log for analysis. Note that some log analyzers assume that the content of this field is always – (a dash) and may not function properly. Formerly, this field was designated for the RFC931 username, a now unused field.

COMBINED (NCSA/CERN) FORMAT

The combined format uses the common format and adds two fields, Referer and User_Agent. Example 13-2 shows two lines from a log using the combined format.

EXAMPLE 13-2: ACCESS LOG SAMPLE, COMBINED (NCSA/CERN) FORMAT

```
127.0.0.1 localhost - [12/Apr/1996:16:42:49 -0800] "GET /wsdocs/
        32demo/demotree/goodies HTTP/1.0" 302 0 "http://localhost/
        wsdocs/32demo/demotree/" "Spyglass_Mosaic/2.10 Win32
        WebSite/1"
198.112.209.115 localhost - [12/Apr/1996:16:42:49 -0800] "GET /
        wsdocs/32demo/demotree/goodies/ HTTP/1.0" 200 811 ""
        "Spyglass_Mosaic/2.10 Win32 WebSite/1"
```

These lines show the two fields added to the end of each entry. In the first request, the user had come to the current location from the URL *http://localhost/ wsdocs/32demo/demotree* and was using the special edition of the Spyglass Mosaic browser for WebSite. The second request shows the Referer field as empty, meaning that the user stayed on the same page.

The Referer and User_Agent field are useful for tracking the movement on your web, how users found it, and also what browsers they are using. If you know that most of your users are using a browser that supports specific capabilities (such as

Netscape Frames), you might want to add that to your web. On the other hand, if most users are *not* using a browser that supports HTML enhancements, you should not use them.

WINDOWS LOG FORMAT

The Windows log format, extended for WebSite, collects logging data in a format useful for importing into Windows applications such as Excel and Access. The fields are delimited by tabs, and specific data (such as date and time) are stored in the way these applications expect. Example 13-3 shows a line from a Windows log format.

EXAMPLE 13-3: ACCESS FILE SAMPLE, WINDOWS LOG FORMAT

```
04/13/96 01:06:26 127.0.0.1 localhost WebServer sam GET /wsdocs/
        images/website-sm.gif http://localhost/wsdocs/32demo/
        Spyglass_Mosaic/2.10 Win32 WebSite/1 200 981 2178
```

Table 13-2 lists the fields included in the Windows log format and example of what each field might contain.

TABLE 13-2: ACCESS LOG FIELDS, WINDOWS LOG FORMAT

Field Description	Example
Date and time at which the request was received. The format is per the local system's international locale setting, which allows importing to Windows programs without parsing or reformatting.	04/13/96 01:06:26
IP address of the remote browser. If reverse DNS lookup is on, the DNS hostname is in this field.	127.0.0.1
Server hostname on which the request was received. Most useful on multiple identity servers.	localhost
Authentication realm, if present in request. Note that an entry in this field does not mean the requested URL was access controlled.	WebServer
Authentication username, if present in request. Note that an entry in this field does not mean the requested URL was access controlled.	sam
HTTP method of the request	GET

TABLE 13-2: ACCESS LOG FIELDS, WINDOWS LOG FORMAT (CONTINUED)

Field Description	Example
Path portion of the requested URL. Does not contain any query or parameter information.	/wsdocs/images/website-sm.gif
Complete referring URL, if present in the request.	http://localhost/wsdocs/ 32demo/
Email address of the browser user. Currently no browsers generate this field due to privacy concerns.	N/A
Identity of the browser (software name and version)	Spyglass_Mosaic/2.10
HTTP Response Code (you can find a list at WebSite Central or at http://www.w3.org/pub/ WWW/Protocols/HTTP1.0/draft-ietf-http-spec.html)	200 (OK)
Number of bytes transferred (actual data, not including the header)	981
Time, in milliseconds, between the arrival of the request and the time it was logged, including the time to process, receive content data (such as from a form), transmit the response, close the TCP connection, and clean up. Due to buffering in the TCP/IP kernel, the time may be optimistic, since several thousand bytes of data can be buffered beyond the time the server closes the connection.	2178

THE ERROR LOG

The error log records errors that occur during URL requests. The error data help you pinpoint problems in the web such as missing files or bad URL paths. The error log also records incorrect access control requests.

Example 13-4 shows a segment of an error log. In general, error logs are small since they report only requests that have problems.

EXAMPLE 13-4: SAMPLE ERROR LOG

```
[08/Nov/1995:13:49:10 -0500] Access to D:/WebSite/htdocs/../wsdocs/
        32demo/temp.html failed for 127.0.0.1, reason: file does
        not exist, referer:
[08/Nov/1995:13:55:00 -0500] Access to D:/WebSite/htdocs/../wsdocs/
        32demo/AuthExamples/bydomain/demodoc.html failed for
        127.0.0.1, reason: access denied by server configuration,
        referer: http://localhost/wsdocs/32demo/#useracc
```

Each entry in the error log includes the date and time of the request (in GMT), the IP address or hostname, if appropriate, and the error message. The first line in this sample shows a request for a nonexistent file. The second line was generated when a user tried to access a URL restricted by IP address, and the requesting IP address was not allowed access. Note that this error message includes the referring URL, which will help you trace problems.

THE SERVER LOG

The server log is used primarily to accumulate tracing data from the server's activity through a variety of tracing options you can set. The tracing options are used primarily for troubleshooting and debugging. The server log also records fatal internal server errors, the time when the server is restarted, and the time when the server's configuration is changed.

When no tracing options are selected, the server log records the date and time when the server starts and when it is updated (via Server Admin):

```
=============================
Tue Oct 24 05:52:24 1995
Server startup: WebSite/1.1
=============================
=============================
Tue Oct 24 20:20:07 1995
Server Configuration Updated
=============================
```

The rest of this section looks at the tracing options.

TIPS FOR USING TRACING

Note the following tips when using tracing options:

Cycle the Server Log
  When tracing options are selected, the contents of the server log may expand
  to pages of data. Since the server log collects data cumulatively, you should
  occasionally cycle the log. Stop the server, rename *server.log* to *server.xxx*
  (where *xxx* is a meaningful extension such as a number), and restart the
  server. A new server log will be started as well. You can use the old log to
  analyze problems.

Focus on Errors for Tracing
  To make the tracing data more readable, run the tracing tests on the most
  limited portion of the suspected problem. Running tracing on documents with
  multiple HREFS or large numbers of inline images generates huge tracing files
  where requests for various parts of a document are interspersed (depending
  on the browser used). We recommend that you follow these guidelines:

  – Minimize the size and/or complexity of the HTML document being
    requested; for example, turn off inline images.

  – Reduce the number of simultaneous connections allowed by the browser
    to one.

  – Request an object (such as a GIF file) directly rather than an entire HTML
    document.

HTTP PROTOCOL TRACING

The HTTP Protocol tracing option records the incoming header data for each
request from a browser and the server's response to the request. Essentially it is
what the server sees when receiving and responding to a request. Example 13-5
shows a single request/response entry in the server log with HTTP Protocol
tracing on.

EXAMPLE 13-5: HTTP PROTOCOL TRACING SAMPLE

```
** REQUEST from 198.112.209.140 **
GET  /wsdocs/readme.html?HTTP/1.0
Accept: */*, q=0.300
Accept: audio/x-aiff
Accept: audio/basic
Accept: image/jpeg
Accept: image/gif
Accept: text/plain
Accept: text/html
User-Agent: Enhanced_Mosaic/2.1 Win32 Spyglass/1
Referer: http://sapphire/
```

EXAMPLE 13-5: HTTP PROTOCOL TRACING SAMPLE (CONTINUED)

```
Authorization: Basic c3VzYW46
node=D:/WEBSITE/wsdocs/readme.html: args=
-- REPLY --
>>send file D:/WEBSITE/wsdocs/readme.html args=
>> done <<
```

The first line of the tracing gives the complete HTTP request (method, URL, and protocol version). The next several lines contain the rest of the header information from the browser. At the end of the tracing, the server's reply is recorded. The server sends the file and reports that the activity is completed.

DUMP SENT DATA TRACING

The Dump Sent Data tracing is what the browser sees when the server responds to a request. The HTTP Protocol tracing and Dump Sent Data tracing work together to provide a detailed picture of the "conversation" between the client and the server. If you suspect a problem somewhere, turn on these two tracing options to convince yourself that the server is working properly and that the problem is elsewhere. The contents of these tracings will also be useful to technical support staff in diagnosing specific problems. Example 13-6 shows a small portion of the server log with Dump Sent Data tracing turned on.

EXAMPLE 13-6: DUMP SENT DATA SAMPLE

```
13:07:59 SEND ==> sock 180 [198.112.209.140] (209, 0x00D1)
-----|-----------------------------------|---------------
0000  48545450 2F312E30 20323030 204F4B0D  HTTP/1.0 200 OK.
0010  0A446174 653A2046 72696461 792C2031  .Date: Friday, 1
0020  302D4D61 722D3935 2031383A 30373A35  0-Nov-95 18:07:5
0030  3920474D 540D0A53 65727665 723A2057  9 GMT..Server: W
0040  65625369 74652F32 2E306232 64202866  ebSite/2.0b2d (f
0050  69656C64 20746573 74290D0A 4D494D45  ield test)..MIME
0060  2D766572 73696F6E 3A20312E 300D0A43  -version: 1.0..C
0070  6F6E7465 6E742D74 7970653A 20746578  ontent-type: tex
0080  742F6874 6D6C0D0A 4C617374 2D6D6F64  t/html..Last-mod
0090  69666965 643A2054 75657364 61792C20  ified: Tuesday,
00A0  32312D46 65622D39 35203033 3A30373A  21-Feb-95 03:07:
00B0  30342047 4D540D0A 436F6E74 656E742D  04 GMT..Content-
00C0  6C656E67 74683A20 31393035 370D0A0D  length: 19057...
00D0  0A                                   .


13:07:59 SEND ==> sock 180 [198.112.209.140] (8192, 0x2000)
-----|-----------------------------------|---------------
0000  3C544954 4C453E57 65622053 65727665  <TITLE>Web Serve
0010  72204465 6D6F6E73 74726174 696F6E3C  r Demonstration<
0020  2F544954 4C453E0D 0A3C4831 3E3C494D  /TITLE>..<H1><IM
0030  47205352 433D222E 2E2F696D 61676573  G SRC="../images
0040  2F776562 73697465 2E676966 223E2053  /website.gif"> S
```

EXAMPLE 13-6: DUMP SENT DATA SAMPLE (CONTINUED)

```
0050   65727665  72205365  6C662D54  6573743C     erver Self-Test<
0060   2F48313E  3C503E0D  0A3C4120  48524546     /H1><P>..<A HREF
0070   203D2022  2E2E2F52  6561644D  652E6874      = "../ReadMe.ht
0080   6D6C223E  52657475  726E2074  6F205765     ml">Return to We
0090   62536974  65205265  6164204D  653C2F41     bSite Read Me</A
00A0   3E3C503E  0D0A0D0A  3C48523E  0D0A3C48     ><P>....<HR>..<H
00B0   323E3C49  4D472053  52432020  3D20222E     2><IMG SRC  = ".
00C0   2E2F696D  61676573  2F726669  6E676572     ./images/rfinger
00D0   2E676966  223E2053  656C662D  54657374     .gif"> Self-Test
```

As you might guess from this example, turning on Dump Sent Data tracing generates huge server logs. One valuable use of the Dump Sent Data tracing is to collect browser error messages that some browsers throw away. If you suspect a problem between your server and browser, turn on Dump Sent Data tracing, recreate the problem, and view the logs.

IMAGE MAP TRACING

The Image Map tracing option records the information the server sends back when a client requests a location on a clickable image map. This tracing is useful for determining why an image map may not be working properly. Example 13-7 shows a portion of the server log with Image Map tracing turned on.

EXAMPLE 13-7: IMAGE MAP TRACING SAMPLE

```
==>IMAGEMAP Thread=BC, Map = 32demo
  GET/ISMAP: CoordStr = "162,48"
  Coordinates = [162,48]
Imagemap -> GET /wsdocs/32demo/rect.html, args
==>IMAGEMAP Thread=A2, Map = D:/WebSite/htdocs/../wsdocs/32demo/self-
          test.map
  GET/ISMAP: CoordStr = "126,35"
  Coordinates = [126,35]
Imagemap -> GET /wsdocs/32demo/ellipse-f.html, args
==>IMAGEMAP Thread=BC, Map = 32demo
  POST/IMAGE: CoordStr = "x=224&y=48"
  Coordinates = [224,48]
Imagemap -> GET /wsdocs/32demo/noshape.html, args
```

This sample shows three image map requests. Each request includes details about the image map, such as the method used (GET/ISMAP or POST/IMAGE) and the coordinate string (and its interpretation). The tracing also shows the server's response.

CGI TRACING

The CGI tracing option records the server's activity when a browser requests a URL containing a CGI program. CGI tracing is particularly useful for debugging your CGI programs, which is discussed in detail in Chapters 15 through 18. In Example 13-8 we show only a portion of the server log with CGI tracing on.

EXAMPLE 13-8: CGI TRACING SAMPLE

```
SpawnWait("D:\WebSite\cgi-win\cgitest.exe D:\WebSite\cgi-
         temp\23ws.ini"...)
  ...exited with status 0
Script output needs header parse.
Script returned local document path /wsdocs/32demo/cgitest.html
CGI -> GET /wsdocs/32demo/cgitest.html, args

SpawnWait("D:\WebSite\cgi-win\pizza.exe D:\WebSite\cgi-
         temp\25ws.ini"...)
  ...exited with status 0
Script output needs header parse.
Script: copy remainder of outfile to net

SpawnWait("D:\WebSite\cgi-win\pizza.exe D:\WebSite\cgi-
         temp\26ws.ini"...)
  ...exited with status 0
Script output needs header parse.
Script: copy remainder of outfile to net
```

When you enable CGI tracing, the server notifies the CGI program, which causes the CGI program to adjust its behavior—to start tracing into its own log, to display tracing, or any of several other options described in Chapter 16, *Developing Applications with Windows CGI*. Also, when you enable CGI tracing, the standard and DOS CGI interfaces start the shell with an open window instead of as an icon, which lets you see any malfunctions that generate output to the standard error (usually the screen). Finally, any temporary files generated as part of the CGI process are left in the \cgi-temp directory (rather than being deleted). These files allow you to inspect the CGI input and output data to help isolate problems.

ACCESS CONTROL TRACING

The Access Control tracing option records the server's actions in checking access control restrictions and then denying or allowing access to a specific URL path by the requester. Access Control tracing shows both the class restrictions (IP address or hostname) and user authentication requirements. This information is useful to ensure that Access Control restrictions are working properly. Example 13-9 shows a portion of the server log with access control tracing turned on.

EXAMPLE 13-9: ACCESS CONTROL TRACING SAMPLE

```
ACC-CHK: Path = "/wsdocs/32demo/index.html"
  => Found ACE for "/"
  Check access to / --
  type=Basic  realm=Web Server  order=allow,deny
  allow all?
     of course.
  Access is ALLOWED at this level.
ACCESS ALLOWED.
  [deleted data]
ACC-CHK: Path = "/wsdocs/32demo/AuthExamples/bygroup/demodoc.html"
  => Found ACE for "/"
  Check access to / --
  type=Basic  realm=Web Server  order=allow,deny
  allow all?
     of course.
  Access is ALLOWED at this level.
  => Found ACE for "/wsdocs/32demo/authexamples/bygroup/"
  Check access to /wsdocs/32demo/authexamples/bygroup/ --
  type=Basic  realm=Examples  order=allow,deny
  users/groups requirements appear at this level.
  allow all?
     of course.
  Access is ALLOWED at this level, look for users/groups here.
  Access permitted as member of group "Users"
ACCESS ALLOWED.
ACC-CHK: Path = "/wsdocs/32demo/AuthExamples/bydomain/demodoc.html"
  => Found ACE for "/"
  Check access to / --
  type=Basic  realm=Web Server  order=allow,deny
  allow all?
     of course.
  Access is ALLOWED at this level.
  => Found ACE for "/wsdocs/32demo/authexamples/bydomain/"
  Check access to /wsdocs/32demo/authexamples/bydomain/ --
  type=Basic  realm=Examples  order=deny,allow
  deny all?
     of course.
  allow 199.182?
     198.112.209.140 in 199.182?
  no.
  Access is ALLOWED at this level.
ACCESS DENIED.
```

The first set of lines in this sample shows an access control "conversation" in which there are no restrictions. The next record shows the conversation for a URL path that is restricted by group membership. Note that this tracing doesn't show the user's name and group name; that information is included in the authentication tracing record. The last record shows a URL that is restricted by IP address. Since the request was not coming from an allowed IP address, access to the URL was denied.

AUTHENTICATION TRACING

The Authentication Tracing option records all user authentication attempts. It shows which attempts were successful, which weren't, and why they weren't. Authentication tracing is useful for determining who has attempted to reach your server and what problems they had. It is also useful for testing user authentication restrictions on your web. Example 13-10 shows a portion of the server log with authentication tracing on.

EXAMPLE 13-10: AUTHENTICATION TRACING SAMPLE

```
=>198.112.209.140 AUTH_REQUIRED: [(null)], Basic realm="Examples"
  AUTHENTICATE: U=Dougherty P=balloon R=Examples
    Sent PW hashes to ypBap3YlXISGw - compare to ypBap3YlXISGw
  =>User Dougherty authenticated.
  =>198.112.209.140 AUTH_REQUIRED: [(null)], Basic realm="Examples"
  AUTHENTICATE: U=Weber P=Bob R=Examples
    Sent PW hashes to 2osRbIrSpZUIY - compare to 2ohHpDrJgg7T.
  =>198.112.209.140 AUTH_REQUIRED: [    user Weber: password
            mismatch], Basic realm="Examples"
  AUTHENTICATE: U=Weber P=Jay R=Examples
    Sent PW hashes to 2ohHpDrJgg7T. - compare to 2ohHpDrJgg7T.
  =>User Weber authenticated.
  =>198.112.209.140 AUTH_REQUIRED: [(null)], Basic realm="Examples"
  AUTHENTICATE: U=susan P= R=Examples
  =>198.112.209.140 AUTH_REQUIRED: [user susan not found], Basic
            realm="Examples"
```

Note that the records do not include the URL path for the authentication attempt. They do include the username, the password, and the realm. The record also shows the server's comparison of the sent password to the stored password (both encrypted) and then the results of the authentication. If a user isn't authenticated, it includes a reason. Note that the records do not include the URL path for the authentication attempt. To see a full picture of how the server handles access control restrictions, set tracing for both Access Control and Authentication.

TRACING OPTIONS USED BY TECHNICAL SUPPORT

The remaining tracing options are used only by technical support staff for diagnosing and treating problems you may encounter. When you call technical support, they may ask you to turn on one or more of the following tracing options:

- Control Threads
- Service Threads
- Network I/O
- Network Buffering
- SSL and S-HTTP

ADDITIONAL TOOLS

In addition to the logging capability of WebSite, other tools are available to provide more information about your server's performance and activity. These tools include:

- QuickStats, a feature in WebView (See Chapter 4)
- The special URLs ~*stats* and ~*zero-ctrs*
- Windows NT Performance Monitor
- Windows NT Event Viewer

THE SPECIAL URLS ~STATS AND ~ZERO-CTRS

In addition to the logs, the WebSite server keeps a set of internal statistics of server activity. You can see these statistics at any time by using the ~*stats* URL, a special URL of the WebSite server. When you request this URL with a browser (for example, *http://localhost/~stats*), the server responds with a summary of server activity. Figure 13-4 shows a statistics report for WebSite Central.

You can include the ~*stats* URL in any HTML document (for example, <A HREF="/ ~stats">statistics report</a>). If you want visitors to your web to see the server's statistics, include it on your home page. If you want to limit its use, apply access control to the URL path.

To reset the server's internal statistics counters, you use the special URL ~*zero-ctrs*. This URL causes the server to reset the counters to zero and record the time. The next time you request */~stats*, you will see the time recorded by ~*zero-ctrs*.

Since this URL does something to the server, it is protected for use by members of the Administrators group. And, like the ~*cycle* URLs, it must be issued with the POST method. You can create a form with a Zero Counters button that issues the URL with the POST method. The code for such a button might look like this:

```
<FORM METHOD="POST" ACTION="/~zero-ctrs">
<INPUT TYPE="SUBMIT" VALUE="Zero Statistics">
</FORM>
```

The Server Administration section of the server self-test shows the Zero Counters button with the Cycle Logs buttons. You may want to create a similar administrative form with all four buttons.

PERFORMANCE MONITOR

The Windows NT Performance Monitor provides several classes of information about the WebSite server that can be displayed graphically by the performance monitor. The Monitor Server program item included with WebSite for Windows

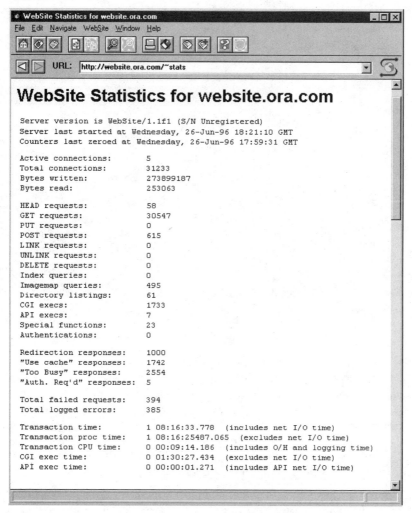

FIGURE 13-4: STATISTICS FROM WEBSITE CENTRAL

NT launches the Performance Monitor with some of these classes charted, as shown in Figure 13-5. You can use Monitor Server to check the activity on your server at any time. You can also add other counters from the object WebServer to track WebSite performance.

You can combine the WebSite classes of information with other monitored classes (CPU usage, memory usage, etc.) to provide a valuable tool for diagnosing performance bottlenecks and (possibly) network problems.

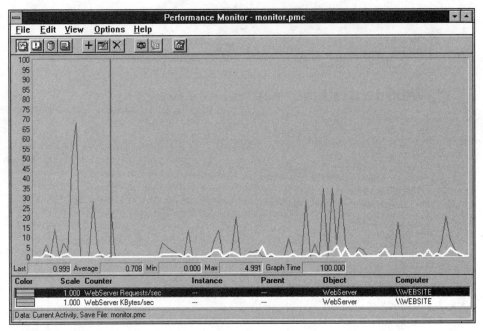

FIGURE 13-5: MONITOR SERVER

You can also set alerts to notify you of specific situations. For example, you may want to know when the thread count reaches 200 or 500 or higher (depending on your hardware and networking setup) in order to ease some of the connections on the server. You set alerts by selecting Alert from the View menu and then Add Alert from the Edit menu. On the Add Alert dialog, select the computer on which WebSite is running, the Object (Process), Instance (httpd32), and the Counter (Thread count). Set the number to trigger the alert, and the program (if any) that should run. The server's idle thread count is four.

The Windows NT Resource Kit documentation contains a wealth of useful tips on using the Performance Monitor to tune your system. The Performance Monitor is also available from the Windows NT Administrative Tools program group.

EVENT VIEWER

The Windows NT Event Viewer provides additional logging information about the WebSite server. When you encounter errors with the server (usually indicated by a problem with the browser retrieving a document), check the applications log of the Event Viewer. Detailed error reports accompany one-line warning entries in the viewer. Figure 13-6 shows a warning report from the Event Viewer. The Event Viewer is available from the Administrative Tools program group.

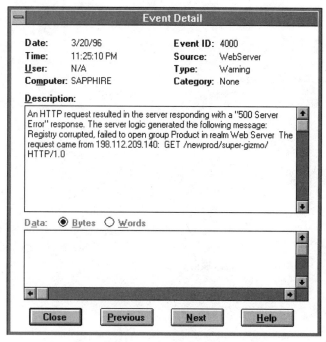

FIGURE 13-6: WINDOWS NT EVENT VIEWER

CHAPTER FOURTEEN

REMOTE ADMINISTRATION

Thus far we have shown you how to administer a *local* WebSite server, that is, a server running on the same computer as Server Admin. You can perform these same administration tasks on a WebSite server running on a different—a *remote*—computer. WebSite's tools WebView, WebIndex, and QuickStats also work remotely, allowing you to build, refine, and monitor a web on a remote system.

For example, your WebSite server may be installed on a dedicated system, located elsewhere in your building. You can administer it from the PC on your desktop. Or perhaps you are a consultant and installed WebSite at a client's site. You can tweak the server or help troubleshoot problems without making a trip to the client's offices. And you can use remote administration to manage your own server when you are on a business trip or working from home. (Or maybe even heading to the beach or the mountains for a few days!) Remote administration is also useful for technical support in diagnosing and troubleshooting problems.

WebSite can be running on another computer on your local network (for example, a Microsoft Windows Network) or on a computer connected to a wide area network (for example, the Internet). As long as you can reach the remote computer over a network, you can administer the server and maintain the web.

Making remote administration work requires some special WebSite setup and a good working knowledge of networking with your operating system. This chapter covers the setup procedures and how to use WebSite's tools remotely. This chapter only lightly touches on the networking issues, which are individual to each installation. For that reason, we highly recommend that you *do not attempt remote administration unless you have a good understanding of your operating system and network.*

HOW IT WORKS

In remote administration, the WebSite server runs on the remote computer, while the WebSite tools—for administration and document management—run on the local computer. Figure 14-1 illustrates a typical remote administration situation. *Computer R* is the remote computer, while *Computer L* is the local computer. The WebSite tools running on *Computer L* are reading and changing the information on *Computer R*. That information may be the server's configuration (stored in the remote computer's Registry) or the documents that make up the web. The network is the conduit between the two systems.

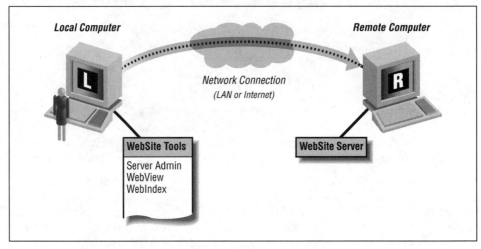

FIGURE 14-1: ADMINISTERING WEBSITE REMOTELY

In more technical terms, the local tools are launched with a switch to read the WebSite Registry and documents of a remote computer. Accomplishing these tasks means that all network connections and mappings (server's working directory, documents, and CGI programs) are correct.

NOTE

In this chapter we assume that the local computer is the one sitting on your desk. However, WebSite may be installed on a network server that you reach via a network pathname. If that is the case, substitute that name in all commands given. By the same token, you can launch the WebSite tools directly on the remote computer rather than on the local computer. Again, just use the network pathname instead of the local name for the tools. You must still complete the steps described in "Remote Administration Setup."

REMOTE ADMINISTRATION SETUP

For remote administration to work properly, some setup is required, mostly relating to the operating system and the network itself. For that reason, we strongly recommend that you be experienced with Windows Network account security, drive sharing, and Registry use before relying heavily on remote administration. Some topics discussed in the following sections are specific to the

Windows operating and networking environments and go beyond the scope of this book. If you have additional questions, consult your operating system's documentation or your system administrator. *O'Reilly technical support cannot assist you in solving operating or networking system-specific problems.*

As you work through the requirements given below, you may want to check them off. Most setup items are one-time-only and need not be repeated.

SOFTWARE REQUIREMENTS

Remote administration of WebSite requires the following software setup:

- The remote and the local computer must each have WebSite installed, or have access to a network-shared WebSite installation.
- The remote (server) computer can be running Windows NT and be administered from a local computer running Windows NT or Windows 95.
- The remote (server) computer can be running Windows 95 and be administered from a local computer running Windows 95, *if the remote system is on the same domain as a Windows NT server.* The Windows NT system is necessary to provide the user-level security needed to administer WebSite remotely.

NOTE

As of this writing, a local computer running Windows NT could not administer a remote (server) computer running Windows 95. This situation may change; check WebSite Central for the latest information on remote administration.

You may be concerned about violating the WebSite software license agreement by installing the software on more than one computer. The WebSite license permits you to run the server software as a *single* process at any given time. In addition, if you are doing remote administration as described in this chapter, you can run WebSite in up to *three* processes at any given time, including on separate computers. So, you can have the server running on one computer and the tools running on one or two other computers. If you have further questions, please consult the WebSite software license.

SETTING UP SECURITY

Security and permissions affect both the ability to administer WebSite remotely and the protection of your server. Make sure you have the correct security measures in place before attempting remote administration.

GENERAL REQUIREMENTS

Remote administration of WebSite requires the following account security and permissions setup:

- You must be logged in to your local computer as a user who has administrator privileges on the remote computer. The operating system uses your local login information to log you in automatically to the remote system. Thus, you need an account on both systems that uses the same name and password and that has administrator privileges.

- You must enable remote Registry administration on the remote computer. During remote administration, Server Admin on the local computer reads and updates the Registry on the remote computer. Under Windows NT, remote Registry administration is the default. Under Windows 95, you must install the Remote Registry service and select User-Level security (rather than Share-Level security). You must also Enable Remote Administration on the Password property sheet of your Control Panel settings.

TESTING SECURITY

Test the security setup by using the Registry editor on the local computer to connect to the remote computer. See your operating system documentation for instructions on connecting to a remote Registry. If you can read and change the remote Registry successfully, you can continue setting up your systems for remote administration over a local area network or a wide area network.

ALTERNATIVE SECURITY APPROACH UNDER WINDOWS NT

You can also administer WebSite running on a remote Windows NT system without administrator privileges. Windows NT lets you assign permissions to specific Registry keys, so that you can allow a user who is not an administrator to remotely administer WebSite. WebSite uses two sub-keys:

```
\HKEY_LOCAL_MACHINE\SOFTWARE\Denny\
\HKEY_LOCAL_MACHINE\SOFTWARE\EIT\
```

WARNING

Make sure you have made backup copies of these Registry keys before making any changes. See the instructions in Chapter 3, *Installing WebSite*. Mistakes in the Registry can be fatal to your system.

To change the permission on these keys and all sub-keys, follow these steps:

1. Launch the Windows NT Registry Editor (*regedt32.exe*).

2. Select one of the WebSite sub-keys (listed above).

3. From the Security menu, select Permissions.

4. Change the permissions for the key as appropriate for your installation. To change permissions on all sub-keys, check the Replace Permission on Existing Sub-Keys box. We assume that you are familiar with setting permissions under Windows NT.

5. Repeat steps 2 through 4 for the second WebSite key.

6. Exit the Registry editor.

SETTING UP FOR REMOTE ADMINISTRATION ON A LOCAL AREA NETWORK

Remote administration of WebSite requires the following setup on a local area network: the local and remote computers must have access to each other via a network connection. If you can connect (or mount) a remote share on your local system, then you should be ready to administer WebSite remotely.

A successful connection means you have access to the remote computer's Registry and can make configuration changes to the WebSite server via Server Admin. To manage the remote web's documents using the WebSite tools—WebView, WebIndex, and QuickStats—you must have access to the remote files. This topic is covered in the section "Setting Up to Manage Documents Remotely," later in this chapter.

SETTING UP FOR REMOTE ADMINISTRATION ON A WIDE AREA NETWORK (THE INTERNET)

When the remote and local systems are separated by a wide area network (most typically the Internet), you must complete additional setup steps. In essence, you must make the two systems believe that they are on the same Microsoft Windows-based network, even though they may be separated by miles and time zones.

GENERAL CONCEPT

You do this by convincing the networking components on the local system that the remote system is part of its own local network. The specific networking components are part of the NetBIOS services (commonly used for Windows file and print sharing), which can use TCP/IP as the transport. NetBIOS identifies the various systems available to it through adapter names. The NetBIOS adapter name is the same one used for each system's identity or computer name.

For the local computer to connect to the Registry of a remote computer, the remote computer must have a NetBIOS adapter name on the local computer. Since the remote computer is on a TCP/IP network (the Internet) and is running

Windows NT, it has its own NetBIOS adapter name. All you have to do on the local system is map the remote computer's NetBIOS adapter name to the remote system's IP address.

These mappings are contained in the *Lmhosts* file. On Windows NT, this file is usually located in *windows\system32\drivers\etc*; on Windows 95, it is located in *windows*. If the *Lmhosts* file does not exist, you should find a sample file, *Lmhosts.sam*, which you can copy and edit.

SPECIFIC STEPS

To create, test, and use this type of connection, follow these steps on the local computer:

1. Add an entry to the *Lmhosts* file to map the IP address of the remote system to a local NetBIOS adapter name. The name should be the remote computer's NetBIOS adapter name. Make sure that no other computer on your network uses the same name. The entry should be on one line, separated by at least one space; for example:

   ```
   198.123.45.67  MYWEBSRV
   ```

2. If you are running under Windows NT, make sure the use of *Lmhosts* is enabled. From the Control Panel, select Network, TCP/IP Configuration, and Advanced Settings. Enable the option to use *Lmhosts* if it is not currently enabled.

3. Update the NetBIOS adapter table by rebooting the system or by issuing the following command at a Command/MS-DOS Prompt:

   ```
   NBTSTAT -R
   ```

4. Test the setup by trying to run a command on a shared directory of the remote system. For example, if the remote system shares its C:\ directories as CDRIVE, type the following command at a Command/MS-DOS Prompt to list the contents of the remote drive:

   ```
   DIR \\MYWEBSRV\CDRIVE\*.*
   ```

   If you see a directory listing of the remote drive, you're all set to begin remote administration. If not, complete the following steps to solve the problem:

   – Recheck the *Lmhosts* file to make sure the remote system's IP address is correct.

   – Check the IP address by executing the *ping* command on the IP address; for example:

   ```
   ping 198.123.45.67
   ```

- If the *ping* response was negative (that is, no response), verify that the remote system is up and connected to the network and that the IP address is correct before proceeding.

If the *ping* response is positive (that is, the remote system responds), make sure the remote system's share is active. Execute the following command (using the appropriate NetBIOS adapter name) at the Command/MS-DOS Prompt to list all the available shares on the remote system (note that this command may take a while to run):

```
NET VIEW \\MYWEBSRV
```

When the Net View command completes, you should see a list of active shares (or an error message).

- If the share you used in step 4 is not listed, repeat the command with a share that is listed. If the share exists, you may have been denied access for security reasons. Remember that the security requirements for connecting to a remote system over the Internet are the same as those on a local network, as described earlier in this chapter.

A successful connection means you have access to the remote computer's Registry and can make configuration changes to the WebSite server via Server Admin. To manage the remote web's documents using the WebSite tools—WebView, WebIndex, and QuickStats—you must have access to the remote files. This topic is covered in the next section.

SETTING UP TO MANAGE DOCUMENTS REMOTELY

To use the WebSite tools to maintain documents in the remote web, you must have access to the remote files over the network, either a local area network or the Internet. That means you must network share the web directories and reflect the network filenames in the remote server's configuration.

We recommend that you use Universal Naming Convention (UNC) format for all network path and filenames. The UNC format for network pathnames includes the computer host name preceded by two backslashes (for example, *mycomputer*) and the volume name and/or directories, preceded by one backslash (for example, *mycomputer\volume\directory*).

NOTE

Problems encountered with remote administration are most likely networking or mapping related. We recommend that you first make sure remote Server Admin works successfully before changing the server's working directory or any document or CGI.

For example, you might do the following:

1. On the remote computer, share the WebSite working directory. This step establishes a network path for the remote web, for example, *\\server-host\WebSite or \\MYWEBSVR\WebSite.*

NOTE

If you used Remote Administration for WebView and the other WebSite tools with a previous version of WebSite, you should note that this procedure has changed. In earlier versions, you needed to use the UNC pathname for the server's *working directory*. However, doing so caused other problems in some situations. The new procedure requires that you change only the *document root* mapping to a UNC pathname. Other document and CGI mappings must be relative or be UNC pathnames.

2. On the remote computer, launch Server Admin and change the WebSite document root (/) on the Mapping page to be a UNC pathname, for example, *\\MYWEBSVR\WebSite\htdocs or \\serverhost\WebSite\htdocs.*

3. On the remote computer, check the other document and CGI mappings on the Mapping page of Server Admin. If these mappings use absolute pathnames (for example, *C:\WebSite\htdocs*), change them to relative pathnames (for example, *moredocs*) or to network pathnames (for example, *\\server-host\WebSite\moredocs*). Refer to Chapter 9, *Mapping*, for instructions.

4. If the remote web has documents in directories outside the WebSite working directory, you must share those directories as well on the remote computer.

5. If the remote web has CGI programs in directories outside the WebSite working directory, you must share those directories as well on the remote computer.

6. On the local computer, connect the shared directory as a network drive, using the path specified. You now have access to the server and to web documents and CGI programs on the remote computer.

Consult your network administrator if you have specific questions about sharing directories and drives.

USING SERVER ADMIN REMOTELY

Once you establish the remote connection, you can launch Server Admin to make changes on the remote computer. Server Admin looks and functions the same as it does on a local WebSite installation, because you are running the application locally; however, you are using and changing the configuration from the remote system's Registry. The only change necessary to use Server Admin remotely is in how you start it.

The easiest way to use Server Admin on a remote system is to create a new Program Item icon for it (under Windows NT) or to add it to the Program List (under Windows 95). Call the new item Remote Administration or something similar and set the command line to

```
C:\WebSite\admin\srvadmin.exe -r-
```

(Note that your drive specification and working directory name may differ.) In this command line, the final – stands for any system name, and it causes Server Admin to display a pop-up dialog box for selecting a specific remote server (Figure 14-2).

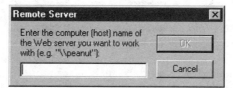

FIGURE 14-2: REMOTE SERVER SELECTOR DIALOG BOX

Note that the name you enter in this box is the remote computer's name as defined by the Microsoft Windows-based network, *not* the DNS name (for example, *serverhost* or *MYWEBSRV*). If you are administering a system over the Internet, the name you enter is the NetBIOS adapter name you defined for the remote system's IP address.

After you enter the name and press OK, Server Admin makes the connection and displays the Server Admin application with the values from the remote system. You can proceed with administration as you would on a local system.

NOTE

During remote administration, you cannot change the server's run mode, the port numbers used by the server for TCP/IP and SSL, the server's document root (/) mapping, or the server's working directory. Also, the Identities page is unavailable.

If you plan to administer the same remote server regularly, you may want to modify the remote Server Admin icon to include the remote computer's name in the program item's command line. For example, setting the command line to:

```
C:\WebSite\admin\srvadmin.exe -r serverhost
```

causes Server Admin to launch and connect immediately to the remote server *serverhost*.

Of course, you can always launch Server Admin for a remote system by executing the command (either with the – value or with a specific system name) from an MS-

DOS command prompt, or by using Run from the Program Manager or the Start Menu.

NOTE

If you encounter problems running Server Admin on a remote server, re-check the requirements sections of this chapter, and make sure that the remote connections are working properly and that you have the appropriate permissions on the remote system.

USING OTHER WEBSITE TOOLS REMOTELY

Like Server Admin, the WebSite tools WebView, WebIndex, and QuickStats work transparently, once the connection to the remote server's Registry is made. Unlike Server Admin, these tools require access to the WebSite directories and files on the remote system. Specifically, you must make sure that the remote server's document root and any document or CGI directories outside the document root are shared and that the permissions are correct. This requirement is described in "Setting Up to Manage Documents Remotely," earlier in this chapter.

This section describes how to launch each tool. Once the tool is running, you work with it as described earlier in this book. Please refer to the chapters about each application for instructions on using it. Note that if you use WebView remotely, Server Admin, WebIndex, QuickStats, HotDog, and Map This! are available from the toolbar.

NOTE

If you encounter problems running the WebSite tools on a remote server, recheck the requirements sections of this chapter, and make sure that the remote connections are working properly, that you have the appropriate permissions on the remote system, and that the mapping is complete and correct.

WEBVIEW

To launch WebView, create a program item as described in the previous section on Server Admin using the −r− option. For example, a program item with the command line

```
C:\WebSite\admin\webview.exe −r−
```

displays a dialog box in which you enter the remote computer's network (not DNS) name. You can also use the −r option and a specific system name if you plan to administer the same remote system (or systems) regularly. You can use the same commands to launch WebView from an MS-DOS command prompt or the Run command.

Once WebView launches, it displays the web for the remote system. Since it is reading the remote system's Registry, all preferences are those set on the remote system. From WebView you can invoke the wizards, WebIndex, QuickStats, the browser, Map This!, and HotDog. WebView looks for all of these programs except HotDog on the remote computer (in the directory *WebSite\admin*). If the programs are not installed on the remote computer or are older versions, you may encounter problems. For HotDog, WebView picks up the content type association from the local Registry and launches the program from the local computer.

WEBINDEX

You can use WebIndex on a remote web either through WebView or as an independent program, launched from the local system. To launch WebIndex, create a program item as described in the previous section on Server Admin using the *–r*–option. For example, a program item with the command line

```
C:\WebSite\admin\webindex.exe -r-
```

displays a dialog box in which you enter the remote computer's network (not DNS) name. You can also use the *–r* option and a specific system name if you plan to use WebIndex on the same remote system (or systems) regularly. You can use the same commands to launch WebIndex from an MS-DOS command prompt or the Run command.

Once WebIndex launches, it displays the URLs on the remote system. Since it is reading the remote system's Registry, all indexes listed and preferences set are those for the remote system. If not all the URLs you expected to see are displayed, you may not have mapped all the document URLs to UNC pathnames, or you may not have properly shared the directories or set permissions.

QUICKSTATS

You can use QuickStats on a remote web either through WebView or as an independent program, launched from the local system. To launch QuickStats, create a program item as described in the previous section on Server Admin using the *–r*–option. For example, a program item with the command line

```
C:\WebSite\admin\qstats.exe -r-
```

displays a dialog box in which you enter the remote computer's network (not DNS) name. You can also use the *–r* option and a specific system name if you plan to use QuickStats on the same remote system (or systems) regularly. You can use the same commands to launch QuickStats from an MS-DOS command prompt or the Run command.

Once QuickStats launches, it reads the access log and displays a report for activity on the remote system.

MAP THIS! AND HOTDOG

The image map editor, Map This!, and the HTML editor, HotDog, which are shipped with WebSite, both support UNC pathnames for working on remote files. Because they do not use the remote Registry or log files, they do not need to be launched in a special way. Just make sure you have access to the remote files through proper network sharing, permissions, and mapping. When you open or create a file on the remote system in either application, use the UNC pathname. You can also use these two programs through WebView.

SECTION 4

THE COMMON GATEWAY INTERFACE

The Common Gateway Interface, or CGI, is the part of the WebSite server that runs external programs. CGI programs are usually used for processing form input, but WebSite's CGI capability also allows you to write programs that interact with other applications on your system. WebSite supports three CGIs: Windows CGI, Standard CGI (such as programs written in perl), and DOS CGI. The Windows CGI is the most powerful, with full support for 32-bit programming languages such as Visual Basic 4.0, C++, and Delphi. Using the Windows CGI, you can create a Web interface to Windows-based applications such as relational databases or spreadsheets and make that data available to anyone on your local network or on the Internet. Chapter 15 provides a conceptual and practical overview to writing CGI programs. In Chapter 16 you will learn how to write CGI programs that tap Windows applications using Visual Basic, while Chapter 17 covers the same material for C++. Chapter 18 covers the Standard and DOS CGI, especially how to port existing programs to WebSite. The many examples in these chapters show you how to create useful and powerful programs for your Web.

CHAPTER FIFTEEN

INTRODUCTION TO THE COMMON GATEWAY INTERFACE

The most exciting development on the Web today is getting information from users and manipulating it via the Common Gateway Interface (CGI). WebSite's CGI features let you use external programs that you write (or get from others) to process HTML forms, generate documents, and do other processing in response to a request from the browser.

When you write a CGI program, you are essentially writing a special-purpose web server, using the general-purpose support provided by the "real" server. So it's important to understand how the web works, at least conceptually. This chapter provides that conceptual framework, along with general information on how the CGI interfaces work, a variety of programming techniques, and some operating system issues to consider. If you are familiar with HTTP and CGI, you may want to skip to Chapter 16, *Developing Applications with Windows CGI*, and refer to this chapter for bits of information you need.

CGI programs frequently use data from HTML forms to guide their processing. Forms are the feature of HTML that allow the user to fill in fields, or choose from a series of options. You might use a form to find out a user's email address or to have users choose from a list of options. On its own, HTML doesn't have any direct way of doing anything with this information. It just gathers your input and then passes it to the server, which in turn starts a CGI program, and the CGI program uses the form data.

How CGI Works

On one level, CGI processing follows a very simple model. The browser specifies a URL (and possibly some data) for a CGI program and sends the request to the server. The server starts the CGI program and tells it about the request. The CGI program does some things and generates a response, then exits. The server sends the CGI program's response back to the browser. From the browser user's perspective, the process is transparent. It looks the same as fetching a static document (except the URL might have a filename ending in .EXE or .PL). Figure 15-1 sketches out the CGI model.

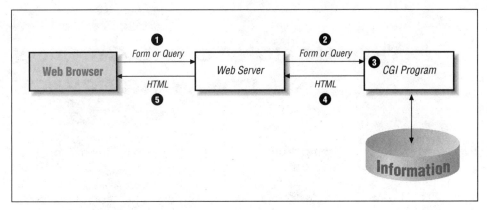

FIGURE 15-1: THE CGI MODEL

CGI PROCESSING STEPS

When WebSite determines that it needs to run a CGI program, it first identifies the program from the URL it receives from the browser. Next, it gathers up all of the information it has regarding the browser's request, including any form content, and packages it for the CGI program. Finally it starts the CGI program, then goes about servicing other requests until it sees that the CGI program has exited.

Once the CGI program is running, it retrieves the details of the request from the request package that the server created, including the form content if any. Then it performs its job, generates a response for the browser and packages it for the server to send back. Finally, the CGI program exits.

When the server sees that the CGI program has exited, it opens the response package and sends its contents back to the browser. Once all of the response has been sent to the browser, the server deletes the request and response packages.

Next, we'll look at WebSite's unique triple CGI interface. In contrast to virtually all other web servers (which support only one CGI interface), WebSite has three different CGI interfaces, each designed for a particular environment.

WEBSITE'S THREE CGI INTERFACES

CGI programs can be written in any language, as long as it can take input from the CGI interface of the Web server and send output back. On UNIX-based Web servers, CGI programs are generally written in UNIX scripting languages such as the UNIX shell, Perl, and TCL. Occasionally they are also written in C or C++.

You can transfer CGI programs written for UNIX to the WebSite server if you have the right tools and skills to port those programs to Windows. But the truly exciting part of WebSite in terms of CGI development is the ability to run native Windows programs (*.exe* files) as CGI programs.

WebSite's three CGI interfaces are:

Windows CGI

Windows CGI lets you run most Windows programs, and is by far the most powerful CGI interface supported by WebSite. We emphasize writing CGI programs using Visual Basic, but you can also run programs written in Delphi, Visual C++, or any other Windows programming environment you choose. You can write "console" style or native Windows style programs for Windows CGI. If you intend to develop your own CGI programs for WebSite, we encourage you to use Windows CGI. Windows CGI is discussed in detail in Chapter 16, *Developing Applications with Windows CGI*.

Standard CGI

Standard CGI provides support for 32-bit programs that use "standard I/O" facilities and shell environment variables. These include programs written in C and C++, scripting languages like Perl and TCL, and shells such as the 32-bit 4DOS (4NT), the Korn Shell clone that comes with the Windows NT Resource Kit's POSIX toolkit, and even the Windows NT CMD.EXE "DOS Command Prompt." You are likely to use the Standard CGI for porting CGI scripts from a UNIX-based server to WebSite. Users who are more comfortable in a UNIX environment may also want to write new programs using Standard CGI. Only 32-bit programs can use the Standard CGI interface. Standard CGI is discussed in detail in Chapter 18, *The Standard and DOS CGI Interfaces*.

DOS CGI

The DOS CGI allows you to run 16-bit programs that use a Standard CGI-like interface, and for using the DOS command interpreter COMAND.COM (which is also 16-bit, even on Windows 95). It is not possible for a 32-bit program (WebSite) to redirect a 16-bit program's standard I/O or pass environment variables to a 16-bit program. Therefore WebSite creates a fake Standard CGI environment using temporary "batch" files. The CGI program itself uses the same programming techniques as the "real" Standard CGI interface. Avoid using the DOS CGI interface for anything but 16-bit Standard CGI programs. The DOS CGI is discussed in Chapter 18.

CGI PROGRAMMING BASICS

People learn in different ways. Some of us prefer to jump right in and write some code and see what happens. Others like to read everything on a subject before they write their first "hello, world."

This chapter covers a number of useful techniques for CGI programming, regardless of the particular CGI interface used. However, we realize that many users, having read this far, may now be impatient to write a CGI application without dealing with details they may not fully comprehend yet. Therefore, we include some CGI programming basics you'll need to get started. The idea is that impatient readers can skip the rest of this chapter for the time being, and return when they begin to have questions.

WHAT YOU NEED TO KNOW ABOUT CGI

CGI is the server interface for executing external programs. To be effective, it has to be able to convey information to the program as given by the browser, and must have a mechanism for reading output generated by the program and then sending that output back to the browser. It also must pass a number of bits of information to the CGI program via *CGI variables*.

So at a minimum, to write a CGI program you need to know:

- How to read GET and POST data
- How to read CGI variables
- How to send output back to the browser

The detailed answers to these questions depend on which of WebSite's three CGI interfaces you use. There are, however, some things that all CGI programs have in common, regardless of which interface they use.

- The output you send from your CGI program must start with an HTTP header section, generally declaring a content type. The last line in the header *must* be a blank line. In most cases, you output HTML code, so the first lines you output should be:

```
Content-type: text/html

<HTML><HEAD><TITLE>Thanks for filling out the form ...</TITLE>
    ...
```

The text after the blank line can be any HTML code. We included a sample line to make it clear that there's a blank line after the content-type header, and to demonstrate that the rest of the output is in HTML form as indicated by the content type.

- The *name=value* pairs sent by the browser are sent in a special format, called *URL-encoded format*. Every CGI program must translate URL-encoded data before it can use that data effectively. The Windows CGI interface does this automatically for you. If you use the Standard CGI interface, you can either do it by hand or use one of the commonly available CGI libraries from WebSite Central.

- Before you can run any CGI program, you have to place the executable in an appropriate *execution directory*. In the Server Admin utility, under Mapping, you'll find that WebSite maps special execution directories. The initial CGI execution directories that were set when installing WebSite are *C:\WebSite\cgi-win*, *C:\WebSite\cgi-dos*, and *C:\WebSite\cgi-shl* (for Windows, DOS, and Standard CGI programs, respectively).

Given this information, some readers can get away with jumping to one of the subsequent chapters on the individual CGI interfaces to learn how to put it in practice. For example, users who are familiar with Visual Basic might skip to Chapter 16, *Developing Applications with Windows CGI*, and users who are more familiar with Perl might read Chapter 18, *The Standard and DOS CGI Interfaces*. The rest of this chapter covers CGI programming techniques that are common to all three of WebSite's CGI interfaces. If you do jump ahead, you may want to come back to this chapter after you have gained some experience. Some of the topics covered here are not covered elsewhere.

HTTP ESSENTIALS

It's important to understand how the browser and server work together if you are going to develop CGI programs. The Hypertext Transfer Protocol (HTTP) describes the rules that a browser and server use to cooperate. It's really quite simple in concept. You need to know a bit about HTTP because:

- Your CGI program is required to generate at least one HTTP header, `Content-type:` and you may want to use and generate others for special purposes. For example, the Netscape persistent-state "cookie" scheme uses HTTP user-defined headers to negotiate state information across multiple transactions.

- The URL you receive from the browser may contain a query string or other arguments, extra path information needed to handle the request, and/or parameters such as byte-range specifications.

- The request may contain HTTP headers whose contents are needed to interpret the request properly. You may also need to supply special HTTP headers with your response.

- You may want to take advantage of two recent additions to HTTP: keep-alive and byte-ranging.

HOW HTTP WORKS

You probably already know that HTTP is a "transaction" style protocol. The browser (the client) sends a request to the server. The server obeys the request if it can and sends a response back to the client. The server then completely forgets about the transaction. The browser may or may not forget about it.

The rest of this section describes the essentials of HTTP and URLs to the level of detail you need to write CGI programs. The descriptions are informal and simplified. Consult the current Internet Drafts or RFCs for HTTP and URLs if you want a complete rigorous description. URLs for these documents are available from WebSite Central.

HTTP REQUEST TYPES

There are only two commonly used types of request, GET and POST. A GET request asks the server to "get" a piece of information, typically a document, and return it to the client. A POST request moves the information in the opposite direction, from the client to the server. POST is almost exclusively used to send HTML form contents to the server.

Most servers cannot handle POST data internally. Normally, POST requests are handled by CGI programs. A POST request may also return any kind of data, of any size. So you can look at a POST request as a GET that carries data from the client. One rule that is hard and fast: *A GET request must never change anything*. Don't write a CGI program that makes changes to a database in response to a GET request. Of course, the server's logfile will change as a result of a GET request, but that doesn't count.

FORM SUBMISSION

A user enters input into each field in the form. When the form is submitted, the data entered into each of those fields are transferred to the server, which then passes them to the program via CGI. These data are sent in the format *name=value*, where *name* is a name given to a field using the NAME= attribute and *value* is the value entered in that field. For example, if the user enters "Fabio" in a field prompting for his first name, the browser may send along the string *first_name=Fabio*.

If the form is written to use METHOD=GET, the form data is appended to the URL as an argument string (see the section on URLs below). If the form contains many fields, or fields that can contain long strings of text, the complete URL can become very large. If the CGI program is 16-bit, the large URL could be truncated by the 16-bit environment.

Using METHOD=POST, the *name=value* pairs are sent as the *body* of the request instead of being appended to the URL. WebSite is very efficient at reading the request body from the browser. It is necessarily less efficient at reading the header part of the request (which includes the URL). So using POST is more efficient.

An important rule in HTTP is that a GET request must not change anything. Consider this scenario: you design a form and a companion CGI program to check tools in and out of the tool crib. Let's say you use METHOD=GET in the form. When the form is submitted, the URL might look like:

```
/cgi-win/tools.exe?evt=checkout&tool=2301&who=Bob&when=Oct10
```

Tool #2301 has been checked out by Bob on October 10.

Browsers always issue GET requests when the user asks for a URL or clicks a hypertext link. So it would be possible for a user to type this URL into the browser and submit it, causing the data in the tools database to be changed without using a form. This may not seem so bad, but a mischievous webmaster might embed this URL into a link, making it invisible to an unsuspecting user. If the link text was innocuous looking, the unsuspecting user could make changes to the tools database without knowing it. *The Web's model depends on the users' belief that clicking a hypertext link is always "safe."* That's why browsers will only issue a POST in response to a form submission.

NOTE

Always use the POST method with forms that change something or cause any irreversible action (most do). POST is safer and more efficient; GET should never be used to change anything.

THE STRUCTURE OF A URL

A complete URL consists of six parts, in the order listed:

1. The *protocol*, for example http:// or ftp://

2. The *hostname*, for example warp.bozonics.com. A dotted-quad IP address is also legal here, for example 123.234.213.1

3. The *port*, for example :4921. May be omitted if the port is 80, the default for HTTP.

4. The *path*, for example /sales/reports/FY94.html.

5. *Parameters*, for example ;bytes=0-100,300-500. A relatively new URL part, not required.

6. *Argument String*, for example ?name=Bob&age=25. Typically used as input to CGI programs.

Of the six URL parts, only the last three are seen by a server. The client uses the first two (or three if the port is present) to choose a protocol and establish a connection with the server. It then sends only the path, parameters, and query to the server. The path is required. Parameters are new to the Web; they are currently used only to request parts of a document by byte offset and length (called *byte-ranging*). Parameters are optional, as are arguments. Arguments are often used to specify a query, but they can be used for anything. URL arguments are analogous to command-line arguments for other programs. A complete URL with all parts is shown below:

```
http://x.y.com:8765/sales/FY94.html;bytes=0-100?name=Bob
```

URL ARGUMENTS AND CGI

As described in the preceding section, a URL can contain an *argument string*. URL arguments are the last part of a URL, and are always preceded by a question mark. For example:

```
http://a.b.com/cgi-win/search.exe?name=Bob
```

You can look at URL arguments as if they are "parameters" for your CGI program. The Standard CGI interface actually puts the URL arguments on the command line used to launch the CGI program. Windows CGI puts the URL arguments in a CGI variable.

EXTRA PATH INFORMATION AND CGI

The path part of a CGI URL can contain *two* paths. For example:

```
http://a.b.com/cgi-win/images.exe/images/night.index?21
```

If you look closely at this URL, you will notice that the path to the CGI program is only part of the complete path. The remainder of the path (`/images/night.index`) is not needed to run the CGI program. WebSite will detect this "extra path" and pass it to the CGI program. It will also use its document mapping facilities to translate the extra path and pass the corresponding physical path to the CGI program. Both of these items are passed via CGI variables.

The example URL might be used with a generic "image fetcher" CGI program. The extra path could specify an "index" file that contains a list of images indexed numerically. The URL argument (21) might be the index of the image to fetch.

THE HTTP HEADER

Headers are the most misunderstood part of HTTP. Yet understanding the role of headers is essential for CGI programmers.

Take a look at any internet email message. It consists of two parts, the header and the body. The header consists of several lines that *describe* the body of the message and perhaps the way the message was handled as it was routed to you. The header and body are separated by a blank line. For more information on header syntax, consult RFC-822.

An HTTP message (either a request or a response) is structured the same way. The first line is special, but the rest of the lines up to the first blank line are headers just like in a mail message. The header *describes* the request and its content, if any, or the response and its content.

WARNING

All HTTP header lines, including the blank header/body separator *must* be terminated by a CR-LF pair. This is the Windows line termination convention. If you open a file in binary mode, however, you must explicitly write CR-LF pairs to terminate all header lines.

THE REQUEST

Here is an example of a simple HTTP request:

```
GET /sales/FY95.html HTTP/1.0
Accept: image/gif, image/jpeg, */*
User-Agent: Mozilla/2.0N (Windows; I; 32Bit)
                    mandatory blank line
```

The first line describes the type of request (or *method*), in this case GET, the URL, and finally the protocol version that the client uses. The second line describes the types of documents that the client can accept. The third line is an "extra" header, not strictly part of HTTP. It gives the name and version of the client software.

THE RESPONSE

Here is an example of a simple HTTP response:

```
HTTP/1.0 200 OK
Date: Thursday, 02-Nov-95 08:44:52 GMT
Server: WebSite/1.1
Last-Modified: Wednesday, 01-Nov-95 02:04:33 GMT
Content-Type: text/html
Content-length: 8151
                    mandatory blank line
<HTML><HEAD>
<TITLE>...
```

The first line contains the protocol version the server uses, plus a *status code* and a *reason phrase*. The server informs the browser how things went via the status code and reason phrase. The next line contains the date and time the server handled the request. Next is a header line describing the server software and version. The next line indicates the date and time when the requested document was last modified. The last two lines describe the type of data and the number of bytes in the requested document. This is followed by exactly one blank line, then the document data.

EXTRA HEADERS

The set of headers defined by HTTP are described in the HTTP/1.0 specification, currently an Internet Draft. HTTP/1.0 permits additional headers to be included in requests and responses. These "extra headers" can be used for anything that a cooperating client and server (or CGI program) want. The protocol engine simply ignores them. For example, many browsers include a User-Agent: header, which describes the name and version of the browser software. User-Agent: is not currently part of HTTP (it may soon be). A CGI program can identify the browser that sent a request by retrieving the value of the User-Agent: extra header.

Another example of the use of extra headers is the Netscape "persistent-state cookie" protocol. The server or CGI program includes a special extra header in its response. The browser remembers the value and sends it back with each subsequent request. This makes it possible for a server or CGI program to keep track of the state of something across multiple transactions. An example of this is a "shopping basket" application, where a user picks products from various pages, then goes to an ordering page to get the total and submit the order. The server or CGI program needs to keep track of which items the user has selected by matching up the cookie in a request with in-progress shoppers. All of WebSite's CGI interfaces pass extra headers to the CGI program and permit CGI programs to pass extra headers back to the client.

CGI AND RESPONSE HEADERS

All three of WebSite's CGI interfaces process HTTP header information from a CGI program identically. Normally, a CGI program needs to supply only a minimal set of HTTP headers in its response. WebSite adds the status code and reason phrase, and the rest of the headers before sending the response to the client.

A CGI program may, however, supply a complete HTTP response. The server looks at the data returned from the CGI program and if it sees HTTP/1.0 as the first eight characters of the first line, it assumes that the CGI program wants to return a complete response. In this case, the server skips its normal header processing. Note that HTTP/1.0 is the first part of the first line of an HTTP response.

This feature, called *transparent return* is described in detail later in this chapter in the section "CGI Programming Techniques."

RECENT ADDITIONS TO HTTP

Soon after HTTP 1.0 came into general use, it became clear that it had a couple of weaknesses. The need to create a separate TCP connection for each request added unnecessary overhead to the protocol. Also, there needed to be some way to restart an interrupted transfer without resending the data that had been successfully transferred. The latter problem was recognized as a special case of a more general problem, the need to transfer one or more parts of a document.

These two recent additions to HTTP are backward-compatible. They are activated only if the browser and server negotiate their use. They are both potentially useful to CGI programs. The details of these HTTP protocol enhancements are contained in Internet Draft documents available on WebSite Central. WebSite supports both of them.

THE KEEP-ALIVE OPTION

HTTP has been enhanced with an option that permits TCP connections to be reused. This is transparent to most CGI programs. If you return the usual partial HTTP response, the server will automatically handle keep-alive for you. However, if your CGI program returns a complete HTTP response, and the Keep-Alive variable is TRUE, you can still keep the connection alive. Include the `Connection:` `Keep-Alive` and `Content-length:` headers in your HTTP response. The content length must be exact. Details on using keep-alive are given later in this chapter.

NOTE

WebSite's CGI interfaces normally use file spooling for CGI output. Therefore, WebSite can always determine the content length of CGI output when doing its default header processing. In this case, WebSite transparently handles keep-alive for your CGI programs.

THE BYTE-RANGE OPTION

Another recent HTTP enhancement allows a request to specify one or more *parts* of a document. The browser request one of more *byte-ranges* from the target document, and the server returns the pieces as a multipart response. Ordinarily, this is not combined with a CGI program. It is possible, however, to use byte-ranges with CGI. If a CGI request contains a byte-range specification, the ranges are passed through the CGI interface as part of the extra path. Details on using byte-ranging are given in the following section.

MULTIPART CONTENT

As mentioned in the preceding section, byte-range support sends the requested range(s) as a "multipart" response. The Netscape server-push feature also requires returning a multipart response, and other applications are certain to appear in the future. The format follows that of the MIME specification with a small variation: multipart body parts usually contain HTTP header fields that are significant to the meaning of that part.

For a multipart response, the HTTP header is the same except for the `Content-type:` header line, which declares that the body actually consists of one or more parts, and specifies a delimiter line that separates the parts. For example, a server push application uses the following format:

```
...
Content-type: multipart/mixed;boundary=ThisRandomString
            blank line
--ThisRandomString
Content-type: text/plain
            blank line
Data for the first object.
            blank line
--ThisRandomString
Content-type: text/plain
            blank line
Data for the second and last object.
            blank line
--ThisRandomString-- trailing double-dash
```

The exact format of each part depends on the application. Other header lines may be required or at least present in each part. Note that the boundary must be preceded by a CRLF, and followed by a double CRLF. The boundary string may be anything, but it must be chosen so that it cannot occur within the data for any part.

INPUT AND OUTPUT SPOOLING

WebSite's CGI interfaces use temporary files ("spooling") for exchanging data with CGI programs. The server creates these files in a directory specified on the General page of the server's property sheet. There are several reasons the designers chose to use this technique:

- If a CGI program were to do I/O directly to the client socket, it would require the CGI programmer to be familiar with Windows Sockets programming techniques. In particular, doing efficient I/O to sockets requires specialized knowledge. WebSite has highly optimized functions for line-wise and bulk network I/O to and from files.

- If a CGI program encounters a runtime error, the spooled output can be rewound and replaced with a properly formatted HTTP error message. If the CGI program is directly connected to the socket, an error can cause garbage (or nothing at all) to be transmitted to the browser.

- The input (e.g., form content) can be memory-mapped, providing the opportunity for extremely efficient processing.

- 16-bit programs cannot inherit operating system handles (e.g., sockets) from the 32-bit WebSite server program.

- Most Windows programs, including those built with Visual Basic or Delphi, cannot use operating system "standard" handles without special programming techniques.

For a CGI program that does any "real work," the additional overhead introduced by the input and output spooling is minimal. And the spooled interface allows many more Windows applications to handle CGI tasks. It is possible to write a CGI program in WordBasic or Visual Basic for Applications in Excel.

CGI Programming Techniques

The rest of this chapter presents a number of CGI programming techniques that you can use. The explanations are purposely "high level" as they apply to any programming language and to any of WebSite's three CGI interfaces.

Returning an HTML Document

Most CGI programs, regardless what other things they do, finish by returning an HTML document. The document might contain links to images and other documents that were also generated (or updated) by the CGI program.

To return an HTML document, simply start the CGI output with a Content-type header, followed by a blank line. For example:

```
Content-type: text/html
        required blank line
<HTML><HEAD>...
```

WebSite will supply the rest of the HTTP response including a 200 OK status code and reason phrase, and other required HTTP headers including Content-length: as required for the keep-alive option.

Returning an Image or Other Content Type

Suppose you place the following in an HTML document:

```
<IMG SRC="/cgi-win/genimage.exe">
```

This will work as expected if the CGI program returns an image that the browser can display. To return a GIF image, the CGI program generates the following:

```
Content-type: image/gif
        required blank line
Gif89aA>kQ_[#neO image data starts here
```

Remember that all HTTP header lines must end in a CR-LF pair. Therefore the Content-type header must end in a CR-LF and be followed by exactly one more CR-LF (the blank line). WebSite will supply the rest of the HTTP response including a `200 OK` status code and reason phrase, and other required HTTP headers including `Content-length:` as required for the keep-alive option.

RETURNING A REDIRECTION RESPONSE

Suppose your CGI program wants to send the browser to some document that already exists in your web (or the Web on another system). You can do this by returning a redirection response. WebSite's built-in header processing recognizes the `Location:` and `URI:` headers. If the value of the `Location:` header is a complete URL (including the `http://host.name.here`), the server ignores everything else and generates a `302 Moved Temporarily` HTTP response. When the browser receives this, it will automatically fetch the given URL.

REDIRECTION OPTIMIZATION

WebSite has a feature called *redirection optimization* that attempts to avoid sending a redirection needlessly. If the `Location:` header contains a *server-local* URL (one without the `http://host.name.here`), it knows that the document resides within the local server's web. In this case, the server simply returns the document itself.

One note of caution: if a document returned via redirection optimization contains relative links, those links will be invalid. The browser thinks the document it fetched is the CGI program that generated the `Location:` header. Therefore, its current URL will be that of the CGI program. Relative links within the returned document will be combined with the URL of the CGI program to make them absolute, resulting in an incorrect URL.

NOTE

If a document contains relative links, do not use redirection optimization to return the document from a CGI program. Instead, put the complete URL for the document into the `Location:` header so that the browser will directly fetch the document.

RETURNING A COMPLETE HTTP RESPONSE

There may be times when you want to return a response with a status other than `200 OK` and control the contents of the HTTP headers. This is an advanced technique, as you are completely responsible for the validity of the HTTP response, including all headers. The following sections describe a couple of examples.

RETURNING AN ERROR MESSAGE

When a CGI program encounters an unexpected error, it should recover and return a useful error message to the browser. WebSite's spooled CGI interfaces make this easy. Simply *rewind the output file* to get rid of any junk that the failed program may have generated, and replace it with a complete HTTP error message. The proper status code and reason phrase to use is `500 Server Error` despite the fact that the server itself did not have the error.

Most browsers display the contents of error messages. It is a good idea to include an HTML "document" describing the error to the best of your ability. For example:

```
HTTP/1.0 500 Server Error
X-CGI-Program: e:\WebSite\cgi-win\badprog.exe
        required blank line
<HTML><HEAD><TITLE>CGI Program Failure</TITLE></HEAD>
<BODY BGCOLOR="#FFFFFF">
<CENTER><H1><CODE>badprog.exe</CODE> Failed</H1>
The CGI program <CODE>badprog.exe</CODE> encountered an error.
<P>Message: Divide by zero exception at EIP=0x00421000
<P>Please write down what you were doing at the time this error
occurred and contact the
<A HREF="mailto:webmaster@acme.com">server administrator</A>.
```

There are several things to note about the error message:

- The second header is a user-defined header specifying the physical pathname of the failed CGI program. It is not necessary.

- An error message from the programming environment or operating system is included so the CGI program author can better identify the problem.

- A `mailto:` link is included so the user can easily send email to the server administrator alerting him of the problem. You could also include a `mailto:` link to yourself, the CGI program author.

WebSite's Visual Basic CGI framework uses this technique to send error messages in the event the program encounters a trappable error.

CGI-BASED USER AUTHENTICATION

Suppose you have an application that needs to validate users against its own database rather than using WebSite's built-in user authentication and access control. You can do this by returning a `401 Not Authorized` response and using the username and password that will accompany the next request. The `401 Not Authorized` response causes the browser to display its username/password dialog. If the user fills in the dialog and clicks OK, the browser will resubmit the same request again, this time including the supplied username and password. The username and password are available as CGI variables.

NOTE

Your CGI program's name must start with a dollar sign ($) in order for it to receive the password via CGI.

Write your program so it *always* tests the username and password. Then if the test fails (missing or incorrect data), return a `401 Not Authorized`. For example:

```
HTTP/1.0 401 Not Authorized
WWW-Authenticate: basic realm="ABC Sales Data"
     required blank line
```

The `realm=` parameter can be anything you want. It is displayed in the browser's username/password dialog. It should at least be something descriptive. You can get really fancy by implementing multiple username/password databases and assigning a realm name to each. Then when the request comes in after the user fills in the username/password dialog, you can tell which of your databases to use for authentication by looking at the realm name. It is available as a CGI variable. WebSite includes a sample program that demonstrates this technique.

NOTE

Check out the section on Netscape persistent-state cookies later in this chapter. It describes a powerful tool that you can use in combination with CGI-based user authentication.

USING SERVER-PUSH

The Netscape Navigator browser has a feature called *server-push* that permits a server to send multiple "documents" with a single request. Typically, this is used to create animation effects by sending a sequence of images at timed intervals. The server (actually a CGI program) controls the time interval between each successive image.

This is one instance where WebSite's spooled CGI interface gets in the way. Normally, a CGI program's output is written to a temporary file that the server sends to the browser after the CGI program exits. For server-push, the CGI program needs to control the timing of the response data and the spooled interface prevents this control.

WebSite's Standard CGI interface (only) supports server-push applications. To enable this feature, the CGI program's name must begin with an exclamation point (mnemonic: *now*). When WebSite sees a standard CGI program whose name begins with an exclamation point, it bypasses its output spooling and connects the live socket to the browser via the CGI program's Win32 standard output handle. This permits the CGI program to write directly to the browser's network connection. WebSite includes a sample server-push application written in C.

USING PERSISTENT-STATE "COOKIES"

One of the most perplexing issues facing CGI programmers is "state." Sometimes there is a need to keep track of a particular user as he moves through the various web pages that make up an application. The classic example is the "shopping basket" application where the CGI program must keep track of items purchased by the user across multiple HTTP transactions.

The Netscape Navigator browser supports an HTTP extension that Netscape calls "cookies." When the CGI program identifies a new user, it can add an "extra header" containing an identifier for that user to its response. After that, all requests from the browser will include this identifier as an extra header in the request. The CGI program can use this request extra header to identify the user on subsequent requests.

Actually, the cookie contains more than a simple user identifier. It also contains a URL range, a domain name, and a time limit for which the cookie is valid. The validity time can be hours or even days. The cookie is stored persistently by the browser so it will be available even if the browser is restarted. The validity tests for cookie use are described in the Netscape cookie specification. Refer to the current cookie specification, which is available online at Netscape's web site.

GIVING A COOKIE TO THE USER

To give a cookie to a user, the CGI program adds an extra header to its HTTP response. For example:

```
...
Set-Cookie: NAME="AbzDio9"; path="/shop"; domain="acme.com";
  expires="Wednesday, 01-Nov-95 00:00:00 GMT"
```

The example sets a cookie that is valid only for a server in the `acme.com` domain, and only for URL paths starting with `/shop`, and only until midnight GMT on November 1, 1995.

READING A COOKIE

If the browser's validity tests are passed, it will send the cookie as an extra header in its request, for example:

```
Cookie: NAME=AbzDio9; NAME=...
```

where all valid cookies known to the browser will be sent. The CGI program can access this as an extra header in the request.

CHAPTER SIXTEEN

DEVELOPING APPLICATIONS WITH WINDOWS CGI

If you intend to write CGI programs for WebSite, we strongly encourage you to work with the Windows CGI interface. Using Windows CGI, you can write programs in Microsoft Visual Basic and Visual C++, Borland Delphi, or any other Windows development environment you choose. Be careful of graphically intensive development packages such as PowerBuilder, though. They are designed primarily for user interface building, and applications developed using such tools can be far larger and more memory intensive than necessary.

On the most basic level, you can use Windows CGI for programs that write data to local files, collect data from the file system, etc. However, the true power of using Windows native development tools is that you can hook into other Windows and mainframe data sources such as databases or spreadsheets using ODBC, OLE and OLE Automation. You can share your latest financial calculations with your immediate workgroup, or share your database of movie trivia with the entire world.

To run Windows CGI programs no special tools are needed. All you need is an executable *.exe* file that understands the Windows CGI interface installed on the machine running the WebSite server. However, to develop and compile your own Windows CGI programs, you need a development package for Windows.

Although much of the information in this chapter can apply to developing programs in any development environment, the examples in this chapter use Visual Basic 4.0 (32-bit). Also, this chapter presents a plain "procedural" approach to development so that the concepts are broadly applicable.

NOTE

If you choose to use Visual Basic, we strongly recommend that you upgrade to the 32-bit version of Visual Basic 4.0. Visual Basic 3.0 produces 16-bit programs, which start more slowly, cannot support long filenames, and have no access to the Win32 native system services of Windows NT and Windows 95.

Visual Basic 4.0 is sold in Standard, Professional, and Enterprise editions. Although we recommend the Professional edition, the Standard edition is sufficient for most CGI development. You will need the Professional edition if you intend to write CGI applications involving databases and ODBC. You will need the Enterprise Edition if you plan to use Remote OLE Automation to manipulate objects across the network.

This chapter does not attempt to teach you how to program in Visual Basic. You should still be able to follow the chapter without much experience in Visual Basic programming. However, if you need to learn how to program in the Visual Basic development environment, refer to the documentation distributed with VB, or a third-party book on programming in Visual Basic.

TIP

Many WebSite users highly recommend writing Windows CGI programs using Borland's Delphi programming environment. Delphi is an Object Pascal-based development environment that uses the Borland Database Engine to support Paradox, dBase, and Interbase file formats, plus ODBC connections to Access, Oracle, Sybase, and Informix. Reuse of code, class hierarchies, and good object relationships make Delphi an easy-to-use, efficient way to create CGI programs. You can learn more about writing CGI programs with Delphi in the Developers Corner at WebSite Central, where you'll find examples, explanations, and links to other sites providing Delphi components and expertise. We also highly recommend you check out the WebHub tools for Delphi, from HREF Tools Corporation (*http://www.href.com*). Built on and for WebSite, WebHub gives you the necessary framework and components to quickly write Windows CGI programs in Delphi.

WORKING WITH WINDOWS APPLICATIONS

You can use Windows CGI to do the same things everyone else can do in Perl or TCL. But that's like buying a Range Rover to go grocery shopping. The part of Windows CGI that you'll find irresistible is the ability to tap into other programs to run spreadsheet calculations, perform database queries, or get the most recent schedule on a project, and make that information visible to your web clients. You can also use forms to capture updates to spreadsheets and databases.

Visual Basic is designed to work with the Microsoft Office and Microsoft Back Office suites of programs and servers to combine databases, spreadsheets, documents, and project coordination into a single application. You can also work with other relational databases using the ODBC support of Visual Basic, or link to any program with OLE automation support. The result is that if there's data on your computer, there's probably a way to access and manipulate it via Visual Basic, and thus incorporate it into your web.

The following are a few scenarios that should give you a taste of what you can do with a Windows-based CGI program.

SCENARIO: A BRIDAL REGISTRY ON THE WEB

Department stores and specialized housewares stores often have bridal registries whereby the bride and groom identify several things in the store that they like, and friends and family can buy things off the list. The attractive thing about buying something from a Registry is that you know it's something the newlyweds chose for themselves, and that the store tracks whether or not someone already bought it, so you ensure that the happy couple doesn't end up with a dozen juicers.

Currently, you have to go down to the store and ask a clerk to print out the Registry list. But why not put a Registry on the Web? Here's how it would work:

- You have one database table with a record for each item in the store's inventory. For each item in the store, the database lists the item number with the corresponding description, distribution code, unit cost, and unit price.

- You have a second table with information about the bride and groom and the item numbers of each fondue set, asparagus plate, or ice bucket they want. In addition, we list how many of each item the couple wants (e.g., 12 place settings) and the number they already have (initially zero).

- You need to create a relationship between the item numbers in the first table and the item numbers in the second table.

The Registry CGI program can be initiated from the store's home page—e.g., *http://www.bloomies.com/* would have a hyperlink to the */cgi-win/bridal.exe* program. From there, you see a form asking for either the bride's name or the groom's name similar to that in Figure 16-1.

FIGURE 16-1: SELECTING A REGISTRY RECORD

The program runs a query to return all matches in the database under the name given and presents that in a selection box similar to that shown in Figure 16-2.

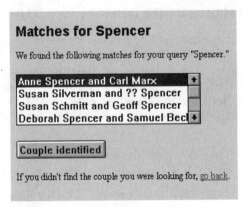

FIGURE 16-2: SELECTING A COUPLE

Finally the program does the work. It locates the couple's entry in the Registry table and also performs a query to get complete descriptions of each of the items in their Registry from the item table. It might also get the URL of the online catalog entry for the item, either from the item table or from another table entirely. The user may see something similar to Figure 16-3.

Registry for Deborah Spencer and Samuel Becket

Wedding date: June 3 1995

```
Asterisk (*) indicates that request is already filled
```

	ITEM	DESCRIPTION	UNIT PR	WANTS	HAS	
	DRA453	WINE GOBLETS BLK THR	$5.50	8	4	Catalog entry
*	DRA454	CHAMPAGNE FLUTE BLK TH	$5.50	8	8	Catalog entry
	IRX289	ICE BUCKET SWED CRYSTA	$55.00	1	0	Catalog entry
*	THW756	JUICER CHAMPION RED	$179.00	1	1	Catalog entry

FIGURE 16-3: THE REGISTRY DISPLAY

To see more about an item you're interested in, select the "Catalog entry" hyperlink to get to its page in the online catalog. You might also then order the item online and even arrange to have it shipped directly to the couple.

SCENARIO: SHARING SPREADSHEETS

Companies often send out monthly reports listing the latest sales figures: how many units were sold, how many were returned, current inventory, net profit, etc. These are the sort of reports that no one reads right away, but just files for when they do need it, for example, when the distributor calls to find out whether the company needs to replenish its supply of Tuffy Tooth Action Dolls. Rather than sending out the written reports every month to become lost under stacks of other reports, sales figures could be kept online, accessible via the Web.

The program should be put in a protected area—for example, it might be placed into a new CGI executable directory (as described in Chapters 9 and 15) that has access control enforced (as described in Chapter 11, *Automatic Directory Listings*). Each user would then have to supply a username and password before he or she could run the CGI program. The program could then use OLE automation to run a spreadsheet macro to pull out the latest sales information and return it to the user.

If the information is truly sensitive, it would be best if these transactions could be done on a local area network so that possible Internet snoops wouldn't be able to read the data regardless of access control.

SCENARIO: A REAL ESTATE NETWORK

Real estate agents often subscribe to some sort of multiple listing service. The service takes listings from each agency and sends out updated reports of all the properties on the market every week to every subscribed real estate agent in the region. The real estate agent then distributes the listings to each of their clients. All this information is already kept in a relational database, so why not put it on the Web where it can be accessed by everyone?

The way it might work is that the home page of the multiple listing service lists the different towns it services (e.g., Cambridge, Arlington, Somerville, etc.). Once you select a town, it returns with a form asking you to supply certain information about the house you want to buy, with a clickable image map at the end of the form.

The form may ask you:

- What kind of home you want (single-family, two-family, condominium, etc.)
- What price range you're interested in. It might do this using a SELECT box with MULTIPLE specified
- How many bedrooms you require (minimum)
- How much square footage you require (minimum)

You might then submit the form by clicking on a map of the city. The map can be included as an <INPUT> tag with TYPE=IMAGE. When you click on a neighborhood, the form is submitted to a CGI program that determines where in the image you clicked and finds the properties in that neighborhood that meet your requirements. The top of the form that the user sees over the Web might look like Figure 16-4.

When the form is submitted, the CGI program executes a query definition asking for a list of properties meeting this description. The program then returns the

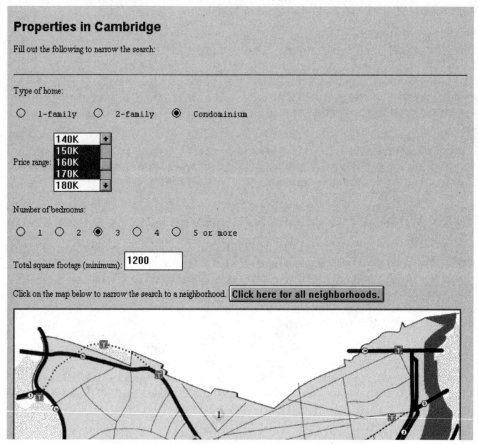

FIGURE 16-4: CHOOSING A PROPERTY

complete listing of properties, perhaps including hyperlinks to photographs of the properties. Figure 16-5 shows some sample output.

You might also show thumbnails of the properties directly on this output page, or include complete descriptions ("This charming 3-bedroom condominium is located in an elegant Victorian that's close to everything...").

HOW WINDOWS CGI WORKS

Before we dive into developing a CGI program that uses Windows CGI, let's take a look at how the interface works. When the server decides that it needs to run a CGI program, it first identifies the program from the URL it received from the browser. Next, it gathers up all of the information it has regarding the browser's

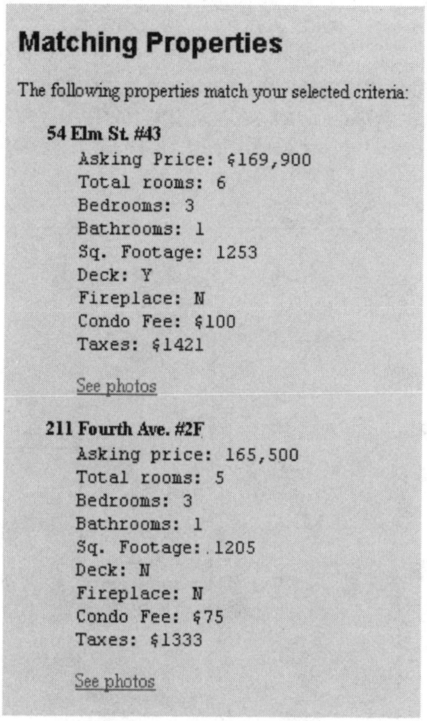

Matching Properties

The following properties match your selected criteria:

54 Elm St. #43

```
    Asking Price: $169,900
    Total rooms: 6
    Bedrooms: 3
    Bathrooms: 1
    Sq. Footage: 1253
    Deck: Y
    Fireplace: N
    Condo Fee: $100
    Taxes: $1421
```

See photos

211 Fourth Ave. #2F

```
    Asking price: 165,500
    Total rooms: 5
    Bedrooms: 3
    Bathrooms: 1
    Sq. Footage: 1205
    Deck: N
    Fireplace: N
    Condo Fee: $75
    Taxes: $1333
```

See photos

FIGURE 16-5: DISPLAY OF MATCHING PROPERTIES

request, including form content, and packages it for the CGI program. Finally it starts the CGI program, then goes about servicing other requests until it sees that the CGI program has exited.

NOTE

The CGI URL target does not need to be an executable. If the URL target is a document, and you have "associated" that type of document with the executable, the server will launch the associated executable.

Once the CGI program is running, it retrieves the details of the request from the request package that the server created, including the form content, if any. Then it performs its job, generates a response for the browser and packages it for the server to send back. Finally, the CGI program exits.

When the server sees that the CGI program has exited, it opens the response package and sends its contents back to the browser. Once all of the response has been sent to the browser, the server deletes the request and response packages.

The Windows CGI interface differs from the more common Standard CGI interface only in the way the request and response packaging is done. Windows CGI is designed to operate harmoniously in both the 16-bit and 32-bit Windows environments, and to permit the (32-bit) WebSite server to launch 16-bit CGI programs and exchange packages with them. Also, the Windows CGI interface provides decoded form data to the CGI program, a feature not present in any other known CGI interface.

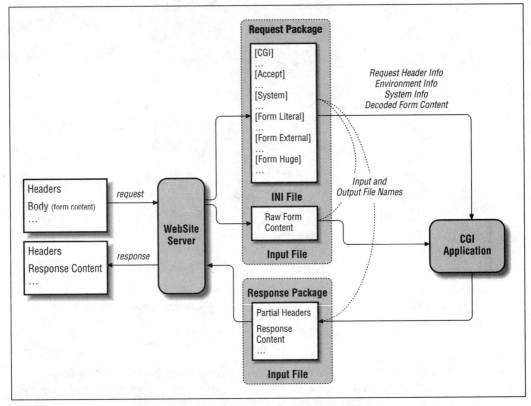

FIGURE 16-6: WINDOWS CGI PROCESSING FLOW

Figure 16-6 shows the processing flow for a Windows CGI program. The server splits the request into headers and content (if any), and spools the raw content into the (temporary) input file. The headers are converted into named variables within the server. The header variables are combined with other server variables and written into the (temporary) INI file. In addition, if there is form content, the server decodes it and creates named variables for each form field, adding them to the INI file. Finally, the server creates an output spool (temporary) filename and includes the names of the input and output spool files in the INI file.

The INI file contains everything the CGI program needs to process the request and package the response. Once the server has created the request package (the INI file and the input file), it launches the CGI program.

The CGI program must first retrieve the variables it needs from the INI file, including the decoded form data, if any. How does the CGI program know where to find the INI file? The server includes the full directory and filename on the CGI program command line. How does the CGI program extract data from the INI file? Fortunately, there is an efficient Windows system call, `GetPrivatePro-fileString()` that does this. Once the INI file has been located and its contents extracted, the CGI program can perform its task.

Once it has performed the task, the CGI program next constructs a response to send back to the browser. Ordinarily, this is an HTML document, but it can be anything, like plain text, or even an image. Later in this chapter, we'll create a CGI program that returns a random image. To construct the response, the CGI program creates an output spool file using the name that the server assigned and passed in the INI file. Then it writes its response data to the output file and closes it. At this point the CGI program exits; its work is done.

When the server detects that the CGI program has exited, it retrieves the response data from the output file. It knows where to look for the output file because it generated the output filename itself and passed it to the CGI program to use. The output file consists of two parts: headers and content. The header and content parts are separated by a blank line. The content can be any type of data, as indicated by the (required) `Content-type:` header.

The CGI program has two choices for header handling. The most common choice is for the CGI program to specify a minimal set of headers. In this case, the server constructs a complete HTTP-compliant response, including the header(s) supplied by the CGI program, and sends the completed headers and the response data to the browser. The other choice is for the CGI program to generate the complete HTTP response itself, in which case the server simply transmits the contents of the output file verbatim to the browser.

At this point the CGI transaction cycle is complete.

THE WINDOWS CGI FRAMEWORK FOR VISUAL BASIC

There is a fair bit of work for the CGI program to do before it gets to its actual task. WebSite comes with a "framework" module for Visual Basic that takes care of most of the interface work. If you are using another development package, you may decide to create a framework of your own. Before you do this, however, check WebSite Central. Someone may have already created a framework for your development package. For example, one of our customers has created a set of

Borland Delphi components that encapsulate the Windows CGI interface. There is a link to this Delphi framework on WebSite Central.

WebSite ships with two versions of the Visual Basic framework. CGI.BAS is for Visual Basic Version 3 and CGI32.BAS is for Visual Basic Version 4. We strongly recommend that you use the 32-bit Visual Basic Version 4. The rest of this chapter uses Visual Basic Version 4.

The framework module:

- Defines the `Main()` routine for your CGI program
- Defines variables for use by your program
- Defines a number of functions to simplify CGI programming and error handling
- Establishes a global exception handler to catch runtime errors and produce a useful error message to the browser

THE MAIN() ROUTINE

Projects you create for CGI programs that use the framework should be set to start in Sub Main (rather than in a form). When the CGI program starts, it enters at `Main()` in the framework. The framework extracts all of the variables, special request headers and form content (if any) and stores them in global variables. It also establishes a global exception handler (On Error) so that runtime errors in your CGI program are trapped, preventing the CGI program from exiting without producing a response.

Once the CGI environment has been set up, the framework calls a routine called `CGI_Main()` that you must write. This is where your code starts. *Always return from CGI_Main(). Never do an abort or exit within a CGI program using the framework.*

If the CGI executable is double-clicked, it will not have the correct information on its command line (no INI file). If this happens, the `Main()` routine calls a routine `Inter_Main()`, which you must also write. For most applications, simply display a message box telling the user that this is a CGI program, then exit.

CGI VARIABLES

The framework reads the CGI variables from the INI file and stores them into global variables in the Visual Basic environment. Each global variable is named in a way that makes it easy to identify its corresponding Windows CGI variable. For more information on the Windows CGI variables as they appear in the INI file, see the Windows CGI 1.2 Specification. It is shipped with WebSite in HTML format, and is available via a link on the Server self-test page. Table 16-1 shows the Visual Basic global CGI variables that are defined by the framework.

TABLE 16-1: GLOBAL CGI VARIABLES FOR VISUAL BASIC

Variable name	Description	Data type
Information About the Server		
CGI_ServerSoftware	The name and version of the server software (e.g., WebSite/1.1)	String
CGI_ServerAdmin	The email address of the server's administrator	String
CGI_Version	The CGI version to which this server complies (e.g., CGI/1.2)	String
CGI_GMTOffset	The number of seconds from GMT	Variant
Information About the Browser or User		
CGI_RequestProtocol	The name and revision of the information protocol (e.g., HTTP/1.0)	String
CGI_Referer	The URL that referred to the CGI script	String
CGI_From	The email address of the user (rarely supplied by the browser)	String
CGI_RemoteHost	The hostname of the remote host running the browser	String
CGI_RemoteAddr	The IP address of the remote host running the browser	String
CGI_AcceptTypes	The CGI accept types	Tuple
CGI_NumAcceptTypes	The number of CGI accept types	Integer
Executable, Logical, and Physical Paths		
CGI_ExecutablePath	The path of the CGI program being executed	String
CGI_LogicalPath	The logical path or extra path information	String
CGI_PhysicalPath	The physical path (i.e., translated version of the logical path)	String
Information About the Request		
CGI_RequestMethod	The method with which the request was made (GET, POST, or HEAD)	String
CGI_ServerPort	The port number associated with the request	Integer

TABLE 16-1: GLOBAL CGI VARIABLES FOR VISUAL BASIC (CONTINUED)

Variable name	Description	Data type
CGI_ServerName	The server hostname for this request (varies in multi-homed configuration)	String
CGI_QueryString	The encoded portion of the URL after the ?, containing GET data or query string (if any)	String
CGI_ContentFile	The full pathname of the file containing any attached data (i.e., POST data)	String
CGI_ContentType	The MIME content type of requests with attached data (i.e., POST data)	String
CGI_ContentLength	The length of the attached data (content file) in bytes	Long
CGI_FormTuples	The name=value pairs supplied in form data, if any	Tuple
CGI_NumFormTuples	The number of name=value pairs	Integer
CGI_HugeTuples	Large name=value pairs	HugeTuple
CGI_NumHugeTuples	The number of huge tuples	Integer

Security

CGI_AuthUser	The name of the authorized user	String
CGI_AuthPass	The password of the authorized user (only if enabled)	String
CGI_AuthType	The authorization method	String
CGI_AuthRealm	The realm of the authorized user	String

Miscellaneous

CGI_ExtraHeaders	The "extra" headers supplied by the browser	Tuple
CGI_NumExtraHeaders	The number of extra headers	Integer
CGI_OutputFile	The full pathname of the file in which the server expects the CGI program's response	String
CGI_DebugMode	CGI Tracing flag from server	Integer

UTILITY FUNCTIONS

The CGI32.BAS framework module contains a number of utility functions designed to handle common CGI programming tasks. One of these is a global exception handler that is used to catch trappable errors in your CGI program and return a properly formatted HTTP error message back to the browser. Table 16-2 shows the utility routines provided by the framework.

TABLE 16-2: UTILITY ROUTINES

Routine names	Descriptions	Returns
Information About the Server		
ErrorHandler()	Global exception handler	n/a
FieldPresent()	Test for the presence of a named form field	T/F
GetSmallField()	Retrieve the contents of a named form field.	String
PlusToSpace()	Remove "+" delimiters from a string, converting to spaces	n/a
Send()	Write a string into the output spool file	n/a
SendNoOp()	Send a complete response causing the browser to do nothing, staying on its current page	n/a
Unescape()	Remove URL-escaping from a string, return modified string.	String
WebDate()	Return a Web-compliant date/time string (GMT)	String

The next few sections describe the most commonly used utility functions. The others are documented in the framework source module (CGI32.BAS) and their use is shown in supplied examples.

GETSMALLFIELD() FOR NAME=VALUE PAIRS

As described in Chapter 5, *HTML Tutorial and Quick Reference*, HTML forms supply their data in *name=value* pairs defined. These values are passed to the CGI program either as part of the URL (for GET data) or as the body section of the request (for POST data). *The server and framework process only POST data.* We strongly recommend that you use POST for all of your forms.

The framework grabs each *name=value* pair and places it in a user-defined structure called a Tuple. For retrieving values from these Tuples, the framework defines the GetSmallField() function. For example, if the user's email address is passed in the variable named *email*, you can place that value in the *sEmail* variable with the following code:

```
Dim sEmail As String
...
sEmail = GetSmallField("email")
```

If the named field does not exist, GetSmallField() generates a runtime error.

FieldPresent() for Testing Checkboxes

Normally, you would want your program to generate an error if you inadvertently tried to get a field's contents using a misspelled field name. Otherwise you might think that the field was simply empty. Checkboxes in forms are an exception. If a checkbox is checked, its *name=value* pair appears in the form data. If it is not checked, however, it does not appear in the form data at all. Using `GetSmall-Field()` to retrieve a checkbox's value will cause a runtime error whenever the checkbox is not checked. Use `FieldPresent()` to test for the existence of the checkbox field. It will return True if the checkbox is checked, and False if it is not.

Send() for Response Output

The framework module opens the response output spool file for writing, and defines a routine called `Send()` for sending response data to the server (and ultimately the browser). For example, to write the obligatory "Content-type: text/html" line and the blank line separating the headers and response content:

```
Send ("Content-type: text/html")
Send ("")
```

Of course, you can also embed expressions into the Send statement. For example:

```
Send ("Your IP address is " & CGI_RemoteAddr )
```

Error Handling

If a runtime error occurs, the program should return a descriptive error message to the browser. The framework includes an `ErrorHandler()` function that returns an error message, including the Visual Basic error text describing the runtime error, to the browser. The error handler is armed by an OnError statement in the framework's `Main()` function. This will catch any runtime errors, returning the error messages to the browser. You can also enable a local error handler so you could do some cleanup tasks if an error occurs, then pass the error to the global error handler.

Debugging Techniques

It can be difficult to test a CGI program in its "live" environment. Typically, it will fail, causing the output file to be empty or corrupted. In this case the server will return a "500 Server Error" message to the browser, indicating that "something" failed. If you use the Visual Basic framework, the 500 Server Error message is generated within the framework and includes the Visual Basic error message. Still, this is not much help when the program is in its early stages of development.

USING THE DEVELOPMENT ENVIRONMENT

What is needed is a way to test the program in its development environment where it can be single-stepped, and where variable values can at least be inspected. Fortunately, Windows CGI makes this much easier than the Standard CGI interface. All that is needed is an INI file and perhaps one or more Form External files. Create an INI file that looks like one that would result from a typical form you might use. Here is an example:

```
[System]
Input File=d:\vb4\cgi\formbasher\test.inp
Output File=d:\vb4\cgi\formbasher\test.out

[CGI]
Server Admin=foo@bar.com
Server Software=WebSite/1.1

[Form Literal]
Name=John Q. Public
Address=123 Main Street.
Address2=Suite 1000
City=Anywhere
State=ZZ
Country=USA

[Form External]
Comments= d:\vb4\cgi\formbasher\test.001
```

Look at this carefully. It has input and output file specifications pointing to the home directory for the development tree of the application. The input file is not used, as the INI file has all of the (fake) decoded form data in it. Two CGI variables that are needed by the CGI program are present, as are several Form Literal items and one Form External item. The latter points to another file, which you must create. You can put anything in it you want, such as the Gettysburg Address. Create this INI file in the development directory and call it TEST.INI.

Next, set up your development environment so that the fake INI file is placed on the command line of the CGI program when it is run under test. For Visual Basic, open the Options property sheet (Tools menu), select the Advanced tab, and enter the full pathname of the INI file into the Command Line Arguments field, as shown in Figure 16-7.

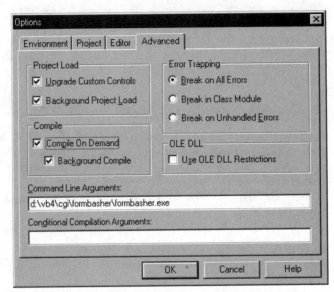

FIGURE 16-7: SETTING COMMAND LINE ARGUMENTS IN VISUAL BASIC

This tells Visual Basic to start the program with the INI file on its command line, simulating the action of the Windows CGI interface. Now compile and test the program. Step into it and follow it through. Correct any compiler errors or exceptions. Once the program runs to completion, look in the output file (which it should have created) and see that it contains the correct output.

LIVE TESTING

Once you have your program running in the development environment with the fake input it's time to do some live testing. Build an executable and move it into the *cgi-win* directory. Create a form for your program if it uses one, and test the form using the *cgitest32.exe* utility supplied with WebSite. Access *http://localhost/ cgi-win/cgitest.exe* for instructions on its use.

USING WEBSITE'S CGI TRACING

Next, enable WebSite's CGI tracing option, one of the tracing options on the Logging tab of the server's property sheet. This does two things. First, it preserves the INI, input, form data and output files in the CGI temporary directory. This makes it easy to see the inputs your program receives and the output it produces. Plus, you can move a set of these files back into your development environment and use them for testing as described in the previous section.

The other thing CGI tracing does is change the value of the Debug Mode CGI variable from *no* to *yes*. Your program can read this variable and do things that can help you debug it. For example, you can include Debug.Print statements in a Visual Basic program that execute only if the Debug Mode variable is set. The program can use pop-up message boxes as sentinels at various points or it can trace into the document that it returns to the browser.

A CGI "Hello, World" Example

No programming tutorial is complete without the obligatory "Hello, World" example. In this section we cover the detailed steps needed to create a minimal Windows CGI program using Visual Basic 4.0 and the CGI32.BAS framework supplied with WebSite.

Creating the Project

The first step to the development of Visual Basic applications for WebSite is to create a Visual Basic project and include the CGI32.BAS framework module, distributed in the \website\cgi-src\ directory. It is useful to create a subdirectory under \cgi-src\ (e.g., \cgi-src\HelloWorld\) for your project file. Create the project file in the subdirectory

Removing unneeded forms, custom controls and references

When creating a new project, Visual Basic automatically includes a form *.FRM* file and several custom control *.OCX* files, and has references to a number of OLE-type libraries that you normally will not use for CGI. Before you start, remove the blank *.FRM* and each of the *.OCX* files from the project by repeatedly selecting Remove File from the File menu. Then select Custom Controls... in the Tools menu, and uncheck all items in the Available Controls list. Once you have done this, you can remove references to most OLE-type libraries by selecting References... in the Tools menu. Uncheck everything you can. A few items will alert an error if you try to uncheck them. They are the ones you need.

Once you have removed all the built-in Windows interface components, add the framework module to the project by selecting Add File from the File menu. The Project window should resemble Figure 16-8.

CGI_Main() and Inter_Main()

After you have added the framework module to your project, create a new module by selecting Module from the Insert menu. Then select Save File As... in the file menu and give your new module a filename, say, HELLO32.BAS. Be sure to save it in the subdirectory you created for your project. In your new module,

FIGURE 16-8: THE INCLUDED CGI32.BAS FILE

don't define your own `Main()` sub procedure, but write your CGI program in two portions: `CGI_Main()` and `Inter_Main()`.

`CGI_Main()` is the CGI portion of your program, the part of the program where all of the CGI work is done. In this chapter, we concentrate primarily on the `CGI_Main()` portion of a Windows CGI program.

`Inter_Main()` is the portion of the program to be used from the Windows interface. You may want to supply a Windows interface to your program so you can configure your CGI program from Windows, monitor its usage, or just provide a pretty splash screen.

You must define both `CGI_Main()` and `InterMain()` functions in your code, or the Visual Basic program won't compile.

After adding the new module, create a new procedure `CGI_MAIN()` as shown:

```
Sub CGI_Main ()
   Send ("Content-type: text/html")
   Send ("")
   Send ("<HTML><HEAD><TITLE>Hello!</TITLE></HEAD>")
   Send ("<BODY><H1>Hello!</H1>")
   Send ("Hello from Visual Basic!")
   Send ("<P>It is now " & Now)
   Send ("</BODY></HTML>")
End Sub
```

All this does is use the `Send()` function described previously to send output back to the server (and thus to the browser). The first thing the script does is print out the content type as text/html, and the required blank line afterwards. Then it prints out a title, major heading, and some simple paragraph text, including the current date and time in Visual Basic's format.

Figure 16-9 illustrates what the procedure should look like when you are finished.

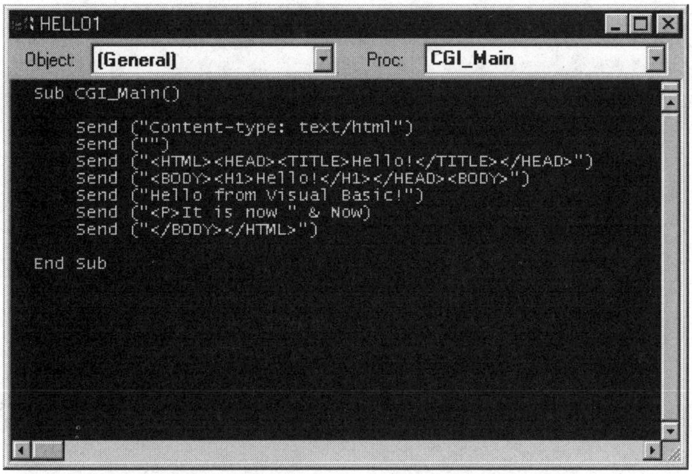

FIGURE 16-9: THE CGI_MAIN() PROCEDURE

Next create another procedure `Inter_Main()`:

```
Sub Inter_Main ()
  ' Say it's a cgi prog and exit.
  MsgBox "This is a CGI Program."
End Sub
```

The `Inter_Main()` just calls the MsgBox statement to tell users that it's a CGI program. Although the `Inter_Main()` must be included in the program, it does not have to be much more elaborate than this.

CREATE THE .EXE FILE

When the two procedures `CGI_Main()` and `Inter_Main()` are defined, you can create the executable by selecting Make EXE File... from the File menu. Assuming that there are no syntax errors, you are prompted for the filename and directory for the new *.EXE* file. Save the file in the *website**cgi-win* directory, under the name *hello32.exe*, as shown in Figure 16-10.

If you want, you can click Options in this dialog and assign a version number, an application name, and an icon for the executable. You can also enter version information, which gets added as a version resource, to the executable. For this simple example, none of this is needed. The new executable program is created once you press the OK button.

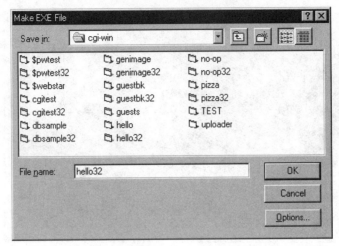

FIGURE 16-10: SAVING YOUR .EXE FILE

TESTING YOUR NEW CGI PROGRAM

To test the script, just point your Web browser to the URL of the executable program. Since you placed the executable in the *cgi-win* subdirectory of your WebSite distribution (e.g., *\website\cgi-win*), then the URL is just *http://localhost/ cgi-win/hello32.exe*. Figure 16-11 shows the *hello32.exe* program when called from a browser.

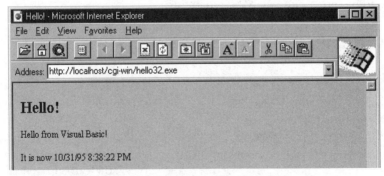

FIGURE 16-11: BROWSING "HELLO, WORLD"

CALLING THE CGI PROGRAM FROM WINDOWS

If you execute the CGI program from Windows, you get a small message box telling you that it is a CGI program. For example, if you run the command from the File Manager or from the DOS command shell, you should see the window shown in Figure 16-12.

SAVING THE PROJECT

To save your Visual Basic program, select Save Project from the File menu. You save both your program module file (with a *.BAS* suffix) and your Project file (with a *.VBP* suffix).

THE SAMPLE GUEST BOOK PROGRAM

Now for a slightly more elaborate (and possibly even useful) example. WebSite is distributed with the source code and executables for a guest book CGI program. You can test this program by using the URL *http://localhost/cgi-win/guestbk32.exe*. Your browser should display the form shown in Figure 16-13.

This program is written using Visual Basic. To look at the source code, open the project *guestbk32.vbp* in the *\website\cgi-src* directory. You'll see two modules, *CGI32.BAS* and *GUESTBK32.BAS* You're already familiar with *CGI32.BAS*, so select the *GUESTBK.BAS* module and open it (either by double-clicking or pressing the View Code button).

The Guest Book program contains five defined procedures. In addition to CGI_Main() and Inter_Main(), it includes the following functions:

ReturnForm()
> Return the form for the guest book (as shown in Figure 16-13).

EnterGuest()
> Record the guest in the guestbook and send back a confirmation to the browser.

FindExtraHeader()
> Get data from the extra header (in this case, the name of the browser).

Let's take a look at the overall structure of the program and what each of these functions do, looking at sections of code when relevant.

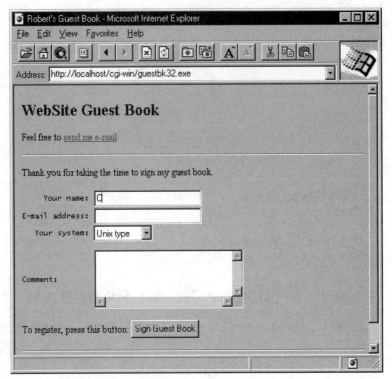

FIGURE 16-13: BROWSING THE GUEST BOOK

RETURNING THE FORM

The first thing the Guest Book program does is check for the request method and return a form. It assumes that if it is called with POST data, then it was obviously called from a form and should process that data. If not, it assumes that it was not called from a form, and returns one.

The `ReturnForm()` function simply uses a series of calls to the `Send()` function and writes a form for the browser. The first two `Send()` calls write the minimal HTTP header information, declaring the content type of the form document (HTML) for the browser.

```
Sub ReturnForm ()
  '
  ' First create the header info. This will be an HTML document
  '
  Send "Content-type: text/html"
  Send ""               ' Header-document separator
```

`ReturnForm()` then sends a title, first-level heading, and a welcome notice.

```
'
' Now send the sign-in form document
'
Send ("<HTML><HEAD><TITLE>WebSite Guest Book</TITLE></HEAD>")
Send ("<BODY><H1>WebSite Guest Book</H1>")
Send ("Feel free to <A HREF=""mailto:" & CGI_ServerAdmin & _
    """>send me email</A>")
Send ("<HR>")
Send ("Thank you for taking the time to sign my guest book.")
```

Note that the **CGI_ServerAdmin** variable is used within a **Send()** function to display the email address of the administrator. Readers who are new to Visual Basic might also note the ampersands (&) used to combine multiple constants and variables, and the doublequotes to represent a single quote in output. **Send()** statements can sometimes become a little overcrowded with doublequotes, but if you follow them carefully they should make sense. Also note the use of the "_" line continuation character, making it possible to break up a single statement into easier to read multiple lines.

The form itself comes next. We aren't going to show all of it, but notice that the <FORM> tag uses the ACTION keyword to refer to itself. This same CGI program serves the form *and* processes submission from that form. Using the **CGI_ExecutablePath** variable is safer than hard-coding the program's URL. What if you move the CGI program to a different place and its URL changes? Will you remember to edit the program's source code and change that hard-coded URL? Probably not. **CGI_ExecutablePath** always contains the real URL for the current CGI program. Also note that METHOD specifies POST.

```
Send ("<FORM ACTION=""" & CGI_ExecutablePath & _
    """ METHOD=""POST"">")
Send ("<PRE>")
Send ("   Your name: <INPUT SIZE=25 NAME=""name"">")
Send ("Email address: <INPUT SIZE=25 NAME=""email"">")
```

Another way of writing the <FORM> line might have been to remove the ACTION attribute altogether, since the form will then default to the current URL automatically.

The form text is written "preformatted," so that the text input boxes line up. You could also embed the form's labels and live fields in a borderless HTML 3 table. This way, the labels could be in a more pleasing proportional typeface, and the fields would still line up. The NAME attributes place the user's name in the *name* variable, the user's email address in the *email* variable, and so on.

ENTERING THE GUEST

When the program receives a POST request, the `EnterGuest()` routine processes the form data. It's worthwhile to take a look at this routine since it displays some techniques you may want to use in writing your own CGI programs.

The first thing done in `EnterGuest()` is to declare local variables. Then it uses `GetSmallField()` to get values for the user's name, email address, system type, and comment (using the variable names previously specified in the form printed by the `ReturnForm()` function).

```
Sub EnterGuest ()
  Dim iLockTries As Integer
  Dim sDate As String
  Dim sName As String
  Dim sEmail As String
  Dim sSystem As String
  Dim sComments As String
  Dim sBrowser As String
  Dim sFirstName As String
  Dim fn As Integer


  '
  ' First, get the form data.
  '
  sName = GetSmallField("name")
  sEmail = GetSmallField("email")
  sSystem = GetSmallField("system")
  sComments = GetSmallField("comments")
```

Next, the program searches for the name of the browser. Not all browsers supply this information, but if they do, they give it in a User-Agent header and send it as an "extra" header. The program uses the `FindExtraHeader()` routine to look for "User-Agent" as an extra header.

```
  sBrowser = FindExtraHeader("User-Agent")
  If sBrowser = "" Then sBrowser = "unknown"
```

`FindExtraHeader()` is defined elsewhere in the program. It steps through the `CGI_ExtraHeaders` structured array searching for the specified header.

```
Function FindExtraHeader (key As String)
  Dim i As Integer

  For i = 0 To (CGI_NumExtraHeaders Ñ 1)
    If CGI_ExtraHeaders(i).key = key Then
      FindExtraHeader = Trim$(CGI_ExtraHeaders(i).value)
      Exit Function      ' ** DONE **
    End If
  Next i
```

```
'
' Not present, return empty string
'
    FindExtraHeader = ""
End Function
```

Once all of the data is gathered, the program opens the guest book file to record it. The guest book file *name* is defined as a global constant in the "declarations" portion of the code module.

```
Const BOOK_FILE = "guestbk.csv"
```

Next, you need to create/open the guest book file in the same directory as our CGI program (*cgi-win*\\). Construct the complete pathname for the guest book file from the App object's Path property, add a backslash, and the guest book file-name.

```
Open App.Path + "\" + BOOK_FILE For Append _
    Lock Read Write As #fn
```

Since more than one person might be running the program at the same time, you need to make sure that two users aren't writing to the file at the same time. Lock the file upon opening it. If it can't be opened (i.e., if it's already locked), the program waits a second (using the Win32 native `Sleep()` function that is defined in the "declarations" section) and tries again, quitting after 10 attempts. We won't reproduce this portion of the code in this chapter, since it doesn't have much to do with CGI processing; if you're interested, just look at the source online. The only part that's worth looking at is the line that writes the file:

```
sDate = Now        ' Catch date/time
Write #fn, sDate, sName, sEmail, sSystem, sBrowser, _
    sComments, CGI_RemoteAddr
```

The current time is taken from the Now statement, and then the date, username, email address, system type, browser name, comments, and the remote IP address are placed in the guest book file. By using the Write statement, this information is supplied as a comma-separated list.

Assuming all goes well, the `EnterGuest()` routine sends back a note to the user thanking them for signing in, and showing them what data they have registered. It uses the `Trim()` function to pull out the user's first name. As always, it starts by printing out a "Content-type" line and blank line immediately afterwards.

```
sFirstName = Trim$(Left$(sName, InStr(sName, " ")))
If sFirstName <> "" Then sFirstName = sFirstName & ", "
Send ("Content-type: text/html")
Send ("")
Send ("<HTML><HEAD><TITLE>Thank you!</TITLE></HEAD>")
Send ("<BODY><H1>" & sFirstName & _
    "Thanks for Signing In</H1>")
Send ("<A HREF=""/"">Return to home page</A>")
```

```
Send ("<HR>")
Send ("You are registered as follows:<PRE>")
Send ("Date:     " & sDate)
Send ("Name:     " & sName)
  ...
```

What if something doesn't go well? Although this program is, of course, flawless in conception and design, it's still a good idea to protect against errors. The Guest Book program protects against the possibility of the guest book file not being opened properly. If it fails to open after 10 attempts, the program returns a message describing the error, as shown below:

```
Send ("HTTP/1.0 500 Server Error")
Send ("Server: " & CGI_ServerSoftware)
Send ("Content-type: text/html")
Send ("")
Send ("<HTML><HEAD>")
Send ("<TITLE>Error in " + CGI_ExecutablePath + _
   "</TITLE>")
Send ("<H1>Error in " + CGI_ExecutablePath + "</H1>")
Send ("</HEAD><BODY>")
Send ("An error has occurred in " + CGI_ExecutablePath + _
   ".<P>")
Send ("<PRE>Failed to open the guestbook file " & _
   BOOK_FILE)
Send ("It appears hopelessly locked.</PRE>")
  ....
```

The special code **HTTP/1.0 500 Server Error** is recognized by browsers as meaning an error occurred. Not all browsers do the right thing with this; some browsers will throw away this text and all the user sees is an "internal server error." However, those users with browsers that do relay this message will have an opportunity to alert the WebSite administrator of the problem. In this case, since the server sees "HTTP/1.0" at the beginning of the first line of the response, it assumes that the CGI program produced a complete HTTP response and adds nothing of its own.

A DATABASE CGI EXAMPLE

As we sketched out earlier in this chapter, you can use Windows CGI to give your databases a Web interface. In this example, we demonstrate how to work with relational databases in Visual Basic. We do not teach you how to use a relational database or how to write queries in SQL language; we just show you how you might work with such a database from your CGI program. The techniques to pay attention to are:

• Using HTML forms as a front-end to a relational database

- Basic relational data access, addition, removal and updating using Visual Basic Professional 3.0 or Visual Basic Professional 4.0

- Data normalization and forming many-to-many relations by using a linking table

- Using Access "queries" to keep complex SQL statements in the database as precompiled, stored procedures

- Using Access's referential integrity features to simplify removal of objects that are referred to by other objects

- Exception handling techniques that send useful error messages back to the browser instead of letting the CGI program fail silently

NOTE

Microsoft Access 2.0 and Access 95 have Jet database engines that are incompatible with Visual Basic 3.0. While there is a compatibility patch for Visual Basic 3.0 and Access 2.0, we strongly recommend that you use Visual Basic 4.0 Professional or Enterprise Edition for all database work. The example below uses the proper syntax for the Data Access Objects in Visual Basic 4.0. The older Visual Basic 3.0 syntax is obsolete and requires a special runtime library in Visual Basic 4.0.

THE DATABASE STRUCTURE

In working with databases, we strongly recommend that you set up your database before you start working on the CGI program that manipulates it. If you take the time to set up your database structure properly, you are less likely to run into problems later on, requiring you to retrofit the CGI program to a poorly designed structure. For that reason, we'll start by taking a look at the database itself.

In this scenario, we have a small technical college that keeps information about its classes and students in three database tables. The first table lists each class offered by the college. The three fields for each class record list the class name, the instructor, and a class ID. Figure 16-14 displays the ClassName field of the table.

The primary key, ClassID, is a unique integer: each class is assigned its own unique ID. The ClassName field has a maximum size of 50 (as shown), is required, and must be unique. The Instructor field is also required but does not have to be unique (since one instructor might teach several different courses).

The second table lists students enrolled at the college. The three fields list the student's name, the student's ID, and her major. Similar to the Classes table, each student has a unique name and ID, but the student's major doesn't have to be unique. Since this table is very similar to the Classes table, we won't show a figure of it.

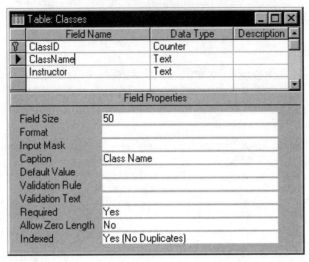

FIGURE 16-14: THE CLASSNAME FIELD OF THE CLASSES TABLE

Now we have a problem. More than one student can take a class and a class can have more than one student in it. How should we relate the two? Normally relations are one-to-many. But here we have a many-to-many relationship. The trick is to use a *linking table*, each row of which contains a student-class pair, relating a student to a class. So the third table contains class IDs and student IDs, as shown in Figure 16-15. It represents which students are enrolled in which classes.

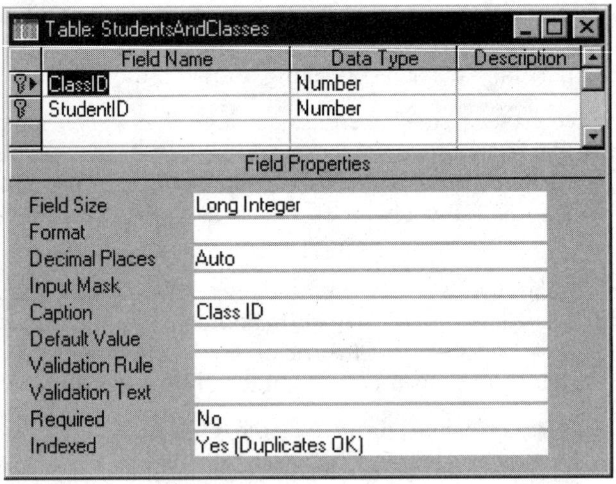

FIGURE 16-15: ASSIGNING CLASSES TO STUDENTS

The primary key in this table is actually a composite primary key, created from the concatenation of the ClassID and StudentID fields. Although neither the ClassID nor StudentID fields need to be unique, the combination of the two must be unique; that is, you can't enroll a student into the same class twice.

What if we want to delete a student (or a class)? Simply deleting the student from the Students table isn't enough. We also must delete all references to that student from the StudentsAndClasses table. Otherwise, the latter table will have references to students that don't exist. The referential integrity of the database would be destroyed. We could write procedures to take care of this, of course, but Access has a better (and *much* faster) way.

By declaring the relationships between the tables globally, you tell Access which fields in which tables relate to each other and how. For our database, the StudentAndClasses table has a many-to-one relationship to both the Students and the Classes table. These relationships are shown in Figure 16-16.

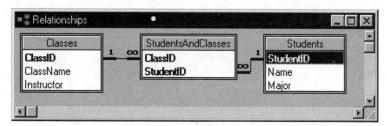

FIGURE 16-16: RELATIONSHIPS BETWEEN THE THREE TABLES

Since each item in the StudentsAndClasses table is a primary key in another table, the relationships are defined to enforce referential integrity. They are also set to cascade deletions and updates to the StudentAndClasses table. Also, note that both ClassID and StudentID are unique in the tables in which they are the primary keys, but they do not have to be unique in the StudentsAndClasses table (thus the one-to-many representation of their links).

In order to have Access enforce referential integrity automatically, you must enable this feature yourself. Double-click on the relation line between the Classes and StudentsAndClasses table. The dialog shown in Figure 16-17 appears.

The important items for our application are the Enforce Referential Integrity and Cascade Delete Related Records checkboxes. By enabling these options, Access will automatically remove all references to a deleted Student from the Student-AndClasses table. This is much easier and much faster than writing a procedure to step through the StudentsAndClasses table looking for records that match the student being deleted. See how it pays to learn the features of your tools?

As you can see, this example database is really bare-bones, just to have a relational database in place that we can use for our example. A real school, of course,

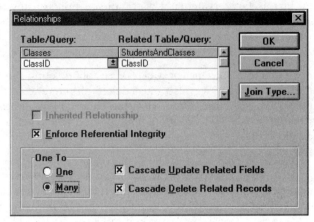

FIGURE 16-17: ENABLING AUTOMATIC REFERENTIAL INTEGRITY

would keep much more information in their records. However, you should notice a few things about the structure of the database:

- The database handles issues like unique fields and referential integrity. This saves the CGI programmer from having to bend over backwards to enforce uniqueness or worry about cascading updates. It is also much faster, a very important consideration for interactive CGI programs.

- The assignment of classes to students is done in a separate table, rather than just including classes as another field in the student's record. If you did the latter, how many classes would you provide for in a student's record? How much wasted space for unused class entries would you want to live with? How would you produce a listing of students in a given class? Consider what would happen if a class was renamed? Or if a class was deleted? What if you wanted to store the instructor's name, classroom, and schedule with the class info? Would you want a repeat of all of this in the record of every student that takes this class? Learn how to normalize your data. And forget any old dBase habits you may have.

DEFINING QUERIES

The next thing you must learn in order to be successful is *avoid using SQL statements in your code.* Use Access' query objects to hold your SQL statements. Sending SQL to the database engine at run-time forces it to translate the SQL statement, analyze the data structures, generate an execution plan, and finally perform the operation indicated by the SQL statement. Storing the SQL statement in the database at design time lets the database engine do all but the last step at that time, eliminating all of that overhead from run-time execution.

If you hard-code SQL statements in your program, then decide later to change the data layout in the database, you will have to go back through all of your code to find and update the affected SQL statements. But if the SQL statements are stored as queries in the database, you can alter the data structures and the queries together, with no need to change your program's code at all.

You are probably thinking "But I have SQL statements that change all the time!" Well, sort of. Almost all SQL statements that "change" vary only in their parameters. Let's say we want to produce a list of classes for a student:

```
SELECT DISTINCTROW Classes.ClassName
FROM Students
   INNER JOIN (Classes
     INNER JOIN StudentsAndClasses
   ON Classes.ClassID = StudentsAndClasses.ClassID)
  ON Students.StudentID = StudentsAndClasses.StudentID
 WHERE ((Students.Name="Clint Eastwood"));
```

Each time this fairly complex SQL statement is used, only the student's name changes. What if there were a way to store this SQL statement as a query object and "plug in" the student's name, then run the query? There is. Access supports *parameter queries* for just this reason. As we'll see shortly, the variable part(s) of a SQL statement can be represented by parameter variables. Just before executing the query, we'll plug in values for the parameters.

NOTE

Learn the features of the database you plan to use. Carefully normalize your data. Make use of referential integrity protection features. Avoid putting SQL statements into your code. Use parameter queries and cursors wherever possible. Failure to do so will result in a sluggish and difficult to maintain application.

Now that all of the tables and relationships are defined, the next step in preparing a database for a CGI front-end is to create query definitions. In this example, we create the following queries:

ClassesForStudent

Display the student's course load, i.e., the classes that the student is currently enrolled for. Takes a parameter of **pName** to identify the student.

DeleteClass

Delete a class from the list of classes. Takes a parameter of **pClass** to identify the class to delete. Referential integrity ensures that all references to the class in the StudentsAndClasses table are also deleted.

DismissStudent

Expel a student. Takes a parameter of **pName** to identify the student to remove from enrollment. Referential integrity ensures that all references to the student in the StudentsAndClasses table are also deleted

DropClass

Drop a class from a student's course load. Takes two parameters: `pName` to identify the student, and `pClass` to identify the class.

StudentsInClass

Display the current enrollment for a class. Takes a parameter of `pClass` to identify the class.

TakeClass

Add a class to a student's course load. Takes two parameters: `pName` to identify the student, and `pClass` to identify the class.

We aren't going to examine all of these in detail. Let's just take a look at the ClassesForStudent query. The query window in Access' query-by-example grid appears as shown in Figure 16-18.

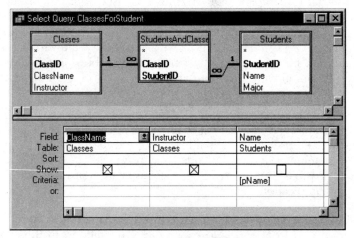

FIGURE 16-18: THE TAKECLASS QUERY

In SQL language, the query appears as follows:

```
PARAMETERS pName Text;
SELECT DISTINCTROW Classes.ClassName, Classes.Instructor
FROM Students
  INNER JOIN (Classes
    INNER JOIN StudentsAndClasses
    ON Classes.ClassID = StudentsAndClasses.ClassID)
  ON Students.StudentID = StudentsAndClasses.StudentID
WHERE ((Students.Name=[pName]));
```

Take the time to examine the other queries using Access. This example uses most of the various query types supported by Access. Each has its own characteristics, and you should be familiar with them all.

THE CGI FRONT-END PROGRAM

Believe it or not, the hard part is now done. The hard part was setting up the database correctly and defining the queries properly. Once those work, the CGI program is just a matter of putting it all together.

The design of the program is to have one program do all the work. The single program:

- Produces the forms allowing the user to enter in a name and major, or to specify the name of a class to add to a student's course load
- Processes each form using the query definitions described previously
- Lists the possible functions (such as creating a new class, adding a class to a student's course load, etc.)

Altogether, there are 11 possible uses for the program:

- Add a class to the college course list
- Remove a class from the college course list
- Display classes in the college course list
- Add a student to the enrollment
- Remove a student from the enrollment
- Display all students currently enrolled in the college
- Add a class to a student's course load
- Remove a class from a student's course load
- Display all classes a student is currently enrolled in
- Display all students currently enrolled in a class
- Display the listing of the functions listed above

The program juggles these responsibilities by using the logical path, or extra path information, as a selector. When called with no logical path (e.g., /cgi-win/ dbsample32.exe), it displays a listing of all its possible functions. When called with a valid selector such as ADD (i.e., URL /cgi-win/ dbsample32.exe/ADD), the program adds a class to the course list. The 10 selectors below are accepted using the GET method:

STUDENTS
    List all students currently enrolled

CLASSES
> List all classes currently in the course list

FRM_ENROLL
> Serve a form for enrolling a student

FRM_DISMISS
> Serve a form for expelling a student.

FRM_ADD
> Serve a form for adding a class to the course list

FRM_DEL
> Serve a form for deleting a class from the course list

FRM_CL4ST
> Serve a form for displaying the classes for a student

FRM_ST4CL
> Serve a form for displaying the students in a class

FRM_TAKE
> Serve a form for enrolling a student into a class

FRM_DROP
> Serve a form for dropping a student from a class

The selectors starting with FRM_ serve forms, which in turn call one of the following eight selectors using the POST method:

ENROLL
> Enroll a student in the college

DISMISS
> Dismiss a student from the college

ADD
> Add a class to the catalog

DEL
> Delete a class from the catalog

CL4ST
> Display all classes in a student's course load

ST4CL
> Display all students enrolled in a class

TAKE
> Add a class to a student's course load

DROP
> Drop a student from a class

To accomplish this, the CGI program contains the following five routines:

```
CGI_Main()
```
The main part of the CGI program

```
DoGet()
```
Print out the selection menu, class or student list, or serve the appropriate form, depending on the selector (i.e., what's in the logical path)

```
DoPost()
```
Return the requested information, depending on the selector (i.e., what's in the logical path), and the contents of the form

```
OptionList()
```
Return a selection box allowing the user to select a user or class

```
Inter_Main()
```
The interactive portion of the program (to tell anyone running it from Windows that it's just a CGI program)

The program contains the following declarations:

```
Option Explicit
Dim sSelector As String
Dim db As Database
Dim qd As QueryDef
Dim ds As Recordset
```

Option Explicit specifies that all variables must be explicitly declared. Usually, an undeclared variable assumes the Variant data type. The advantage of Option Explicit is that it guarantees that any typos will prevent compilation of the program, rather than going unnoticed until a run-time error occurs.

The variable **sSelector** defines the selector when running an instance of the program, i.e., the contents of the logical path. **db** is defined as type Database, **qd** is defined as QueryDef, and **ds** is defined as Recordset. These last three are all Data Access Objects, special types for working with databases in Visual Basic.

The **CGI_Main()** for this program reads as follows:

```
Sub CGI_Main ()
  sSelector = UCase$(Mid$(CGI_LogicalPath, 2))' Remove leading "/"
  Set db = DBEngine(0).Workspaces(0).OpenDatabase_
      (App.Path & "\dbsample.mdb")
  Send ("Content-type: text/html")
  Send ("X-CGI-prog: Access Demo V1.0")
  Send ("")
  Select Case UCase$(CGI_RequestMethod)
    Case "GET":
      DoGet
    Case "POST":
      DoPost
    Case Else:
      Send ("<H2>Cannot do """ & CGI_RequestMethod & _
```

```
         """ method</H2>")
  End Select
  db.Close
End Sub
```

The first thing the `CGI_Main()` does is remove the initial / from the logical path using the `Mid()` function, and place it in the `sSelector` variable. It also converts the selector to uppercase as an easy way of making sure that the selectors can be case-insensitive.

Next, the program creates the Database object `db` using the `OpenDatabase()` method on the current database engine and workspace.

The program sends header information next. The content type of text/html is sent, along with an extra header that we made up. Since the CGI will pass on any headers that we feel like supplying, we throw in a comment saying that this is an example CGI program. The header ends as all headers must, with a blank line.

The request method is now examined. If sent with the GET method, the `DoGet()` routine is called next. If sent with the POST method, `DoPost()` is called. If anything else (e.g., the HEAD method), the program just says "no way" and quits, ensuring that the program doesn't do any extra work for a request method that won't appreciate its efforts.

Finally, the program destroys the Database object.

The program is designed so that when called with the GET method, it can:

- Return a form as appropriate
- Process a simple information request (i.e., a list of all classes or all students)
- Return a list of everything the program can do

The `DoGet()` routine takes care of this. `DoGet()` starts out by defining a string called LinkStart, as follows:

```
Sub DoGet ()
  Dim LinkStart As String

  LinkStart = "<A HREF=""" & CGI_ExecutablePath
```

LinkStart is a string containing the beginning of an anchor to be appended as needed. The anchor starts with the URL of the current program (`CGI_ExecutablePath`). Now the program tests the value of the selector (if any) and behaves accordingly.

If given no selector, the program lists everything the program can do, using `LinkStart()` to create a hyperlink for each item. The user sees a listing of each possible action the program can take as hyperlinks back to the program with the appropriate selector. When the user clicks on the anchor, the program is called once again with the anchor. Note that since it isn't called from a form, it will be called with the GET method and come right back to the `DoGet()` routine.

```
Select Case sSelector
  Case ""           ' No "selector", list choices
    Send ("<H2>Choices:</H2>")
    Send (LinkStart & "/students"">List of students</A><BR>")
    Send (LinkStart & "/frm_Enroll"">Enroll a student</A><BR>")
    Send (LinkStart & "/frm_Dismiss"">Dismiss a student</A><P>")

    Send (LinkStart & "/classes"">List of classes</A><BR>")
    Send (LinkStart & "/frm_Add"">Add a class</A><BR>")
    Send (LinkStart & "/frm_Del"">Delete a class</A><P>")

    Send (LinkStart & "/frm_cl4st"">Classes for student</A><BR>")
    Send (LinkStart & "/frm_st4cl"">Students in class</A><BR>")
    Send (LinkStart & "/frm_Take"">Take a class</A><BR>")
    Send (LinkStart & "/frm_Drop"">Drop a class</A><BR>")
```

The `DoGet()` routine then just goes through the selectors. For example, when the user selects "List of students," the Logical Path selector is set to STUDENTS (since it is made uppercase in the `CGI_Main()`), and the following code is executed:

```
Case "STUDENTS"      ' List all students
  Send ("<H2>Students:</H2>")
  Set ds = db!Students.OpenRecordset(dbOpenTable)
  Do Until ds.EOF
    Send (ds("Name") & " (" & ds("Major") & ")<BR>")
    ds.MoveNext
  Loop
  ds.Close
```

Since the program doesn't need any additional information, it can just display the names of all enrolled students. It uses the `OpenRecordset` method to grab a listing of all students and their majors into the `ds` Recordset object, and then loops through and prints each name and major until EOF. Finally it closes the Recordset.

When the user selects "Enroll a student," the selector becomes FRM_ENROLL, and the following code is executed:

```
Case "FRM_ENROLL":     ' Send Enroll Student form
  Send ("<H2>Enroll a Student</H2>")
  Send ("<FORM METHOD=""POST"" ACTION=""" & CGI_ExecutablePath
      & "/enroll"">")
  Send ("Name: <INPUT TYPE=TEXT NAME=""Name""><BR>")
  Send ("Major: <INPUT TYPE=TEXT NAME=""Major"">")
  Send ("<P><INPUT TYPE=SUBMIT VALUE=""Enroll"">")
  Send ("</FORM>")
```

The program just sends a form allowing the user to enter a name and major. Notice that the <FORM> tag specifies the POST method and sets the ACTION to the current URL (`CGI_ExecutablePath`) appended by the "/enroll" selector. This selector is used later in the `DoPost()` routine.

The rest of `DoGet()` continues in this vein. It appears as follows:

```
Case "FRM_DISMISS":    ' Send Dismiss Student form
  Send ("<H2>Dismiss a Student</H2>")
  Send ("<FORM METHOD=""POST"" ACTION=""" & CGI_ExecutablePath
      & "/dismiss"">")
  OptionList "Student", "Students", "Name"
  Send ("<P><INPUT TYPE=SUBMIT VALUE=""Dismiss"">")
  Send ("</FORM>")
Case "CLASSES"         ' List all classes
  Send ("<H2>Classes:</H2>")
  Set ds = db!Classes.OpenRecordset(dbOpenTable)
  Do Until ds.EOF
    Send (ds("ClassName") & " (" & ds("Instructor") & ")<BR>")
    ds.MoveNext
  Loop
  ds.Close

Case "FRM_ADD":        ' Send Add Class form
  Send ("<H2>Add a Class</H2>")
  Send ("<FORM METHOD=""POST"" ACTION=""" & CGI_ExecutablePath
      & "/add"">")
  Send ("Class Name: <INPUT TYPE=TEXT NAME=""ClassName""><P>")
  Send ("Instructor: <INPUT TYPE=TEXT NAME=""Instructor"">")
  Send ("<P><INPUT TYPE=SUBMIT VALUE=""Add Class"">")
  Send ("</FORM>")

Case "FRM_DEL":        ' Send Delete Class form
  Send ("<H2>Delete a Class</H2>")
  Send ("<FORM METHOD=""POST"" ACTION=""" & CGI_ExecutablePath
      & "/del"">")
  OptionList "Class", "Classes", "ClassName"
  Send ("<P><INPUT TYPE=SUBMIT VALUE=""Delete Class"">")
  Send ("</FORM>")

Case "FRM_CL4ST":      ' Send Classes for Student form
  Send ("<FORM METHOD=""POST"" ACTION=""" & CGI_ExecutablePath
      & "/cl4st"">")
  OptionList "Student", "Students", "Name"
  Send ("<P><INPUT TYPE=SUBMIT VALUE=""List Classes"">")
  Send ("</FORM>")

Case "FRM_ST4CL"       ' Send Students in Class form
```

```
        Send ("<FORM METHOD=""POST"" ACTION=""" & CGI_ExecutablePath
            & "/st4cl"">")
        OptionList "Class", "Classes", "ClassName"
        Send ("<P><INPUT TYPE=SUBMIT VALUE=""List Students"">")
        Send ("</FORM>")

    Case "FRM_TAKE":        ' Take a class
        Send ("<FORM METHOD=""POST"" ACTION=""" & CGI_ExecutablePath
            & "/take"">")
        OptionList "Student", "Students", "Name"
        Send ("<P>")
        OptionList "Class", "Classes", "ClassName"
        Send ("<P><INPUT TYPE=SUBMIT VALUE=""Take Class"">")
        Send ("</FORM>")

    Case "FRM_DROP":        ' Drop a class
        Send ("<FORM METHOD=""POST"" ACTION=""" & CGI_ExecutablePath
            & "/drop"">")
        OptionList "Student", "Students", "Name"
        Send ("<P>")
        OptionList "Class", "Classes", "ClassName"
        Send ("<P><INPUT TYPE=SUBMIT VALUE=""Drop Class"">")
        Send ("</FORM>")

    Case Else:
        Send ("<H2>Bad GET selector """ & sSelector & """</H2>")

    End Select

End Sub
```

You'll notice that for some of the selectors, a routine called `OptionList()` is called. `OptionList()` prints a selection list for the user, listing either all the classes or all the users who are enrolled. An example of a situation in which it is used is when asking to enroll in a class. A selection list is displayed allowing you to choose the class to enroll in from the complete list of classes. `OptionList()` is defined locally as:

```
Sub OptionList (FieldName As String, Tbl As String, Col As String)

    Send ("Select " & FieldName & ": <SELECT NAME=""" & FieldName &
            """>")
    Set ds = db.OpenRecordset(Tbl, dbOpenDynaset)
    Do Until ds.EOF
        Send ("<OPTION>" & ds(Col))
        ds.MoveNext
    Loop
    ds.Close
    Send ("</SELECT>")
```

End Sub

`OptionList()` takes a field name, a table name, and the column in the table to list. The field name is the name to associate with the selected value; it is used in the NAME attribute of SELECT. The table name is either Classes or Students, and the column is the field to be returned in the selection list. The `OptionList()` routine creates a Recordset object, prints a selection list by starting with a <SELECT> tag, prints an <OPTION> tag for each of the field values, closes the Recordset, and ends the selection list with the </SELECT> tag.

When the user submits one of the forms created in the `DoGet()` routine, the request method is specified as POST and the selector is set to identify the user's intent. `DoPost()` processes the forms as needed. It also does some rudimentary error handling.

`DoPost()` starts out by defining two string variables. It also enables the `OnPost-Error` error handler, defined at the end of the routine.

```
Sub DoPost ()
   Dim buf As String
   Dim buf2 As String


   On Error GoTo OnPostError     ' We need to handle errors here
```

Next, the selector is examined, and the program processes the forms as appropriate. For example, when the selector is ENROLL, the program creates a new record:

```
Select Case sSelector
   Case "ENROLL":   ' Enroll a student
      buf = GetSmallField("Name")
      Set ds = db!Students.OpenRecordset(dbOpenTable)
      ds.AddNew
      ds("Name") = buf
      ds("Major") = GetSmallField("Major")
      ds.Update
      ds.Close           ' ** THIS IS EASY TO FORGET! **
      Send ("<H2>" & buf & " enrolled successfully</H2>")
```

The user's name is placed in the `buf` variable to avoid calling `GetSmall-Field()` twice (since it is used both in the database entry and in the response to the user). The dynaset is opened for the Students table and the `AddNew` method is called to initiate the new record. `GetSmallField()` is called again to get the user's major. Finally the dynaset is updated and closed, and the response is sent to the user.

When the selector is DISMISS, the program needs to call one of the query definitions shown previously. It calls the `DismissStudent` querydef, setting the pName parameter to the student's name as retrieved from GetSmallField(). It then executes the querydef and closes it, sending a message to the user that the transaction was successful.

```
Case "DISMISS":    ' Dismiss a student
  buf = GetSmallField("Student")
  Set qd = db.QueryDefs!DismissStudent
  qd.Parameters!pName = buf
  qd.Execute
  qd.Close
  Send ("<H2>" & buf & " dismissed successfully</H2>")
```

The remainder of the selectors are processed in this manner, as shown below.

```
Case "ADD":
  buf = GetSmallField("ClassName")
  Set ds = db!Classes.OpenRecordset(dbOpenDynaset)
  ds.AddNew
  ds("ClassName") = buf
  ds("Instructor") = GetSmallField("Instructor")
  ds.Update
  ds.Close
  Send ("<H2>" & buf & " added successfully</H2>")

Case "DEL":
  buf = GetSmallField("Class")
  Set qd = db.QueryDefs!DeleteClass
  qd!pClass = buf
  qd.Execute
  qd.Close
  Send ("<H2>" & buf & " deleted successfully</H2>")

Case "CL4ST":
  buf = GetSmallField("Student")
  Send ("<H2>Classes for " & buf & ":</H2>")
  Set qd = db.QueryDefs!ClassesForStudent
  qd!pName = buf
  Set ds = qd.CreateDynaset()
  Do Until ds.EOF
    Send (ds("ClassName") & " (" & ds("Instructor") & ")<BR>")
    ds.MoveNext
  Loop
  ds.Close
  qd.Close

Case "ST4CL"
  buf = GetSmallField("Class")
  Send ("<H2>Students in " & buf & ":</H2>")
  Set qd = db.QueryDefs!StudentsInClass
  qd!pClass = buf
```

```
        Set ds = qd.CreateDynaset()
        Do Until ds.EOF
          Send (ds("Name") & " (" & ds("Major") & ")<BR>")
          ds.MoveNext
        Loop
        ds.Close
        qd.Close

      Case "TAKE":
        buf = GetSmallField("Student")
        buf2 = GetSmallField("Class")
        Set qd = db.QueryDefs!TakeClass
        qd!pName = buf
        qd!pClass = buf2
        qd.Execute
        qd.Close
        Send ("<H2>" & buf & " is now taking " & buf2 & "</H2>")

      Case "DROP":
        buf = GetSmallField("Student")
        buf2 = GetSmallField("Class")
        Set qd = db.QueryDefs!DropClass
        qd!pName = buf
        qd!pClass = buf2
        qd.Execute
        qd.Close
        Send ("<H2>" & buf & " has dropped " & buf2 & "</H2>")

      Case Else:
        Send ("<H2>Unknown POST selector """ & sSelector & """</H2>")

    End Select
```

When through, the program cleans up and quits if everything has gone well.

```
DoPostFinish:              ' Can come here via error,
                ' State of ds & qd unknown
  On Error Resume Next     ' Make sure ds and qd are closed
  ds.Close              ' else db.Close will fail and you lose
  qd.Close

  Exit Sub
```

However, if there was an error, the program should jump to the **OnPostError** label. If there was an error, a message is sent to the browser reporting a possible problem area. It tries to print out a guess of the sort of problem that might occur for each selector. "Internal error" messages are used for problems that shouldn't have happened—for example, if the class used by the ADD routine came from the selection box generated by `OptionList()`, there's absolutely no reason it should have failed except for a bug in the program.

```
' ==================
' Exception Handler
' ==================
'
OnPostError:

  If Err >= CGI_ERR_START Then Error Err ' Resignal if a CGI.BAS
        error

  Send ("<H2>There was a problem:</H2>")
  Send ("VB reports: <CODE>" & Error$ & " (error #" & Err & ")</
        CODE><H3>Best Guess:")

  Select Case sSelector
    Case "ENROLL":    ' Probably a duplicate name (enforced by
          database)
      Send ("Already enrolled")

    Case "DISMISS":   ' This is ugly, name came from dropbox
      Send ("Internal Error: Student is not enrolled")

    Case "ADD":
      Send ("Class already exists")

    Case "DEL":
      Send ("Internal error: Class does not exist")

    Case "CL4ST":
      Send ("Internal error: Could not create list of classes")

    Case "ST4CL"
      Send ("Internal error: Could not create list of students")

    Case "TAKE":
      Send ("Already taking this class")

    Case "DROP":
      Send ("Not in this class")

    Case Else:
      Send ("Internal error: Unknown selector in POST exception
            handler.")
  End Select

  Send ("</H3>")
```

```
    Resume DoPostFinish
```

End Sub

For example, if the user tries to add a class that already exists, the resulting message should resemble the one in Figure 16-19.

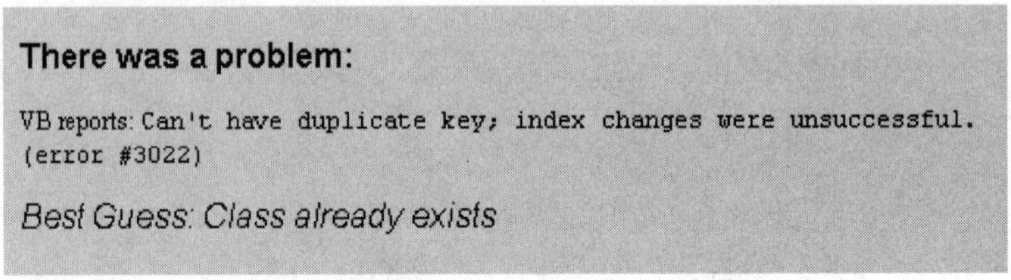

There was a problem:

VB reports: Can't have duplicate key; index changes were unsuccessful.
(error #3022)

Best Guess: Class already exists

FIGURE 16-19: ERROR HANDLER IN ACTION

We don't claim that this is the most elegant error handling. However, we think it's a good policy to always make an attempt to handle errors, even if you can't do it as thoroughly as you'd like.

CHAPTER SEVENTEEN

DEVELOPING WINDOWS CGI
APPLICATIONS WITH C++ AND MFC

In this chapter you will learn how to write an MSVC program that reads CGI data using the Windows CGI interface, and learn how to parse and process CGI input by writing a C++ class to handle all the work in a highly transparent way. This class will include member functions to access all the data supplied by the client browser and the Web server. You'll also learn how to generate a properly formatted HTML reply.

Although it is common for C and C++ developers to use the Standard CGI interface, you can also use the Windows CGI interface. Windows CGI offers a major advantage over Standard CGI. The server does all of the form decoding for you, using thoroughly tested and optimized code. As we'll see in this chapter, it is very easy to get the form data into MFC CStrings.

READING CGI DATA

CGI data consists of a set of server-generated variables containing potentially useful information, and if the request is the result of a form, the contents of the form's fields. There are two ways to receive data from a form, Get and Post. Since the Get method can't handle large amounts of data, and the server does not decode form data when using the Get method, we will only work with processing Post data. It is strongly recommended that you use the Post method in all of your forms.

When a form is filled out and returned, the server searches for and runs the proper CGI executable. The name of the CGI is included as part of the form. It will then set up the data in a standard format and call the executable with one command line parameter—the INI file that contains the environment and decoded form data (if any).

The INI file has many useful environment variables. The most important of these is the Output File pathname. Your Windows CGI program must write its output into a file that you create using the Output File pathname. The rest of the information in the INI file is split up into six sections.

- *CGI*. The CGI section contains information on protocol, request methods, and general information about the server. This includes things like product and protocol version numbers.

- *System*. This section contains information on time zones, debugging, and file names for input and output.

- *Form Literal*. The Form Literal section contains the decoded form data for fields that do not contain multiple lines, and that are less then 256 characters in length. Each variable is on its own line with the field name and the corresponding string value.

- *Form External*. This section is a list of files containing the data from certain form fields. The external files are used whenever the form field data occupies multiple lines, or exceeds 256 characters in length. This data is decoded, identical to the way it was entered into the form.

- *Accept*. This section lists the file formats that are viewable by the HTML client software.

- *Extra Headers*. This section contains information on extra HTTP headers supplied by the client software. Examples include User-Agent, which describes the type of browser used, and HTTP-Cookie, which is used to implement the Netscape persistent state "cookie" service.

There are many reasons you will want to look through this data and use it in the response that is returned to the client. You can use it to include a "Go back" button to return to the form in case of incorrect data. Another use is to include a contact line to send email to the website administrator. We will be going into more detail on this as we go over how to write HTML replies to CGI calls.

The input file contains the raw form data, and is formatted as a one-line string. Because of special formatting, it can take a little work to process the field data, so we will use the Windows CGI interface's server-decoding feature to make things easier. For reference, form data special encoded characters are:

- % followed by two characters is interpreted as a single character shown in hexadecimal notation

- + converts to a space character

- = separates variable names from their values

- & appended to variable values to separate the variable from the next variable name

For example, the string *text=Hi%20there&button=1* means a variable named "text" contains the value "Hi there", and a variable named "button" contains the value 1. There is no ampersand (&) at the end of the data.

GENERATING THE RESPONSE

When using Windows CGI, the response generated by your CGI program must be "spooled" into a file. The full pathname for this file is determined by the server and passed to the CGI program as one of the CGI variables as described in the previous section. You are responsible for creating the output file and writing your program's response data into it.

The response in the output file must be in two parts, separated by a blank line. The first part consists of HTTP header lines describing the data in the response, followed by a blank line. The rest of the output file consists of the actual data that you want to return to the client. Normally this is HTML, but it may also be an image, a sound, or anything else that the browser can accept. For example, it is perfectly legal to embed

```
<IMG SRC="/cgi-win/gengraph.exe">
```

in an HTML document. In this case, the *gengraph.exe* CGI program could return a GIF or JPEG image, resulting in a generated image in the middle of a normal HTML page.

CREATING THE CGI APPLICATION

Our sample CGI program will use the C++ language and the Microsoft Foundation Classes (MFC). MFC contains many classes that can be useful to CGI programmers. However it also contains a large number of classes and support for complex Windows GUI applications. For this reason, you should consider whether to use MFC for a given CGI application. If you link with the static library, even the smallest program is several hundred kilobytes in size, and if you link with the MFC DLLs, several large DLLs load with your program. Either way, your program's memory footprint (and the program startup time) may be much larger than it would be if you avoided using MFC.

This example, as with all C++ in this book will use Microsoft Visual C++ version 2.0 or newer. The code in this chapter was created using Microsoft Visual C++ version 2.2 under Windows NT. You can duplicate much of the functionality in other environments.

CREATING THE PROJECT WITH THE MFC APPWIZARD

The first step is to create a new MFC application with the MFC AppWizard. Be sure to create an EXE file and not a DLL. Let's name the project *CGIBase* since you can later take the base program and turn it into several different CGI programs. When you have filled in the first dialog of the AppWizard, select "Create" to go on to the next step.

This will be a dialog-based application. It won't use an interface when run from a CGI, so it will use the dialog interface to display a useful message to users who run it interactively. It is possible to create advanced applications that can use this standard Windows interface to access administration functions for database-enabled programs.

Since we have no need of a complicated user interface, turn off the About Box. For those who run the program directly in Windows instead of as a CGI, you can give it a name that helps inform them about the problem. Let's call it "World Wide Web CGI."

At the next step change it to statically include the MFC library to make the program self-contained. That way you can copy it without having to worry about copying any related files. Note that the project included in the WebSite kit uses linking with the MFC DLLs to reduce the disk space needed.

That's all of the customizations we'll make in the AppWizard, so go ahead and generate the code. The rest of the modifications will be done in the editor.

CREATING THE CGI CLASS

You could simply process the variables and data directly inside the `CCGIBase-App::InitInstance()` function, but that would bypass some of the most useful aspects of C++. By designing a simple C++ class to handle the CGI data, you can make the program much more flexible, and make it possible to implement complex CGI programs in minutes.

NOTE

The code presented here will be much easier to understand if you are at least somewhat familiar with the Windows CGI 1.2 Specification. This specification is included with the WebSite product, and is available via a link on the Server Self-Test page.

The new CGI class, called *CCGI* to conform to MFC, will exist in the files CGI.CPP and CGI.H. The header file defines the member functions and variables you will be using.

```
// cgi.h : CGI Class definition.
// Version 1.1
#include <afxtempl.h>
class CCGI
{
public:
    CCGI(char *szParam);
    ~CCGI();
    BOOL CalledAsCGI(void);
    CString GetCGIVar(const char *szName);
```

```
    CString GetSysVar(const char *szName);
    void EnumFormFieldNames(CStringArray& csaFields);
    CString GetFormField(const char *szName);
    CString GetFormField(CString csName);
    void WriteHTMLHeader(void);
    void WriteHTMLBody(CString strMsg);
    void WriteHTMLBody(char *szMsg);
    void WriteHTMLFooter(void);
protected:
    char m_szINI[MAX_PATH], m_szInput[MAX_PATH],
          m_szOutput[MAX_PATH];
    CFile fileOutput;
};
///////////////////////////////////////////////////////////////////
          ///////
```

Notice a few things about this header file. First, the include at the top is to make MSVC precompiled headers work properly. Without that include statement you may have problems getting things to compile. Also, the constructor is a bit unusual in that it requires a parameter. This parameter is the command-line argument string, which is easily accessible in the WinApp class. We will use that to find the pathname of the INI file, as you will see when we get to the constructor code.

Notice that the INI, input, and output filenames are protected, inaccessible by users of the class. There is no reason to expose these names. Instead we will expose several methods with which the class users can read CGI variables and form data, and write to the output file. This is proper object-oriented design.

Most of the header for the CGI.CPP file is MFC-based so you can have precompiled headers and friendly debugging. The only portion you will use directly is the inclusion of the CGI.H file.

```
#include "stdafx.h"
#include "cgi.h"

#ifdef _DEBUG
#undef THIS_FILE
static char BASED_CODE THIS_FILE[] = __FILE__;
#endif
```

THE CONSTRUCTOR AND DESTRUCTOR

The constructor first gets the INI filename from the program's command line, then reads the input and output filenames from the INI file. Then it opens the output file, hidden from class users and accessible only through some method calls we will write. Already you can see how the CCGI class will hide the gory details of the CGI interface, leaving you to concentrate on the specifics of the task at hand.

```
CCGI::CCGI(char *szParam)
{
    // Get INI filename, use it to get the input and output filenames
    sscanf(szParam,"%s", m_szINI);
    ::GetPrivateProfileString("System", "Input File", "", m_szInput,
                sizeof(m_szInput), m_szINI);
    ::GetPrivateProfileString("System", "Output File", "",
            m_szOutput,
                sizeof(m_szOutput), m_szINI);

    if(CalledAsCGI())
    {
        // Create output file
        fileOutput.Open(m_szOutput, CFile::modeCreate);
        fileOutput.Close();
        // Open output file in BINARY mode. Can be used for images,
            stc.
        fileOutput.Open(m_szOutput,
                (CFile::modeWrite |
                CFile::typeBinary |
                CFile::shareDenyWrite));
    }
}
```

The destructor needs only to close the file that was left open by the constructor. The output file was left open so we could write to it efficiently with member functions. There would be a lot of unnecessary overhead if the program had to open and close the file each time we wanted to write to it. The way the class is designed, we hide the implementation details. This makes it possible to rewrite the class later without changing the code that uses the CCGI class.

```
// The output file was left open by the constructor.
CCGI::~CCGI()
{
    // Close output file.
    fileOutput.Close();
}
```

TESTING IF THE PROGRAM WAS RUN VIA WINDOWS CGI

You can tell if the program was started via the Windows CGI interface if (1) it has at least one command-line parameter, (2) if that parameter is the pathname of a real INI file, and (3) if the INI file contains a [System] section with "Input File" and "Output File" named values. Prior to calling this member function, the constructor used the first command-line parameter to make calls to GetPrivatePro-fileString() to retrieve the input and output filenames. If all of this worked, there will be non-empty strings in all three filename member variables. It is unlikely that the tests done below would succeed unless the program was activated using the Windows CGI interface.

```
BOOL CCGI::CalledAsCGI()
{
    return((m_szINI[0] != '\0') &&
           (m_szInput[0] != '\0') &&
           (m_szOutput[0] != '\0'));
}
```

RETRIEVING SYSTEM AND CGI VARIABLES

Now we need to create some methods (member functions) with which class users can retrieve the values of CGI variables. As usual, the goal is to hide the implementation details and the details of the CGI interface. The distinction between the "system" variables and the CGI variables is significant enough to expose to class users, so we'll create separate methods for retrieving their values.

The two functions below return a CString containing the value of a variable, given its name. The implementation calls the Win32 GetPrivateProfileString() function, using our class-protected member variable containing the INI file pathname.

```
// Get the value of a "System" variable (from the [system] section)
CString CCGI::GetSysVar(const char *szName)
{
    char szBuf[4096];

    ::GetPrivateProfileString("System", szName, "",
                              szBuf, sizeof(szBuf), m_szINI);
    return(CString(szBuf));
}

// Get the value of a "CGI" variable (from the [CGI] section)
CString CCGI::GetCGIVar(const char *szName)
{
    char szBuf[4096];

    ::GetPrivateProfileString("CGI", szName, "",
                              szBuf, sizeof(szBuf), m_szINI);
    return(CString(szBuf));
}
```

The technique used for returning a CString from the function is somewhat inefficient, as it causes the construction of a CString in the return statement, and that CString is copied into the class user's CString when it is assigned in the class user's code. A less clear but more efficient way of doing this would be to pass the class user's CString target as a by-reference (CString&) parameter, and simply assigning the szBuf contents to it by reference.

ENUMERATING FORM FIELD NAMES

Fields in a form have names. When the form data is posted, both the field names and their data are sent to the CGI program from the browser. Looking ahead, we realize that it would be nice if we had an array of these field names that we could iterate over. The next function creates a CStringArray containing the names of all of the fields in the form (except fields containing data over 64KB in length). In this case, we do return the data via a by-reference parameter, filling in the class user's array object directly.

```
// Enumerate the form field names. Ignore the [Form Huge] ones.
// Put the names into the array passed by reference.
void CCGI::EnumFormFieldNames(CStringArray& csaFields)
{
    char szBuf[4096];     // Room for all field names
    char *cp;

    // First, do the [Form Literal] names
    ::GetPrivateProfileString("Form Literal", NULL, "",
                         szBuf, sizeof(szBuf)-1, m_szINI);
    cp = szBuf;
    while(*cp != '\0')
    {
        CString csName(cp);
        csaFields.Add(csName);
        cp += csName.GetLength() + 1;
    }

    // Then, do the [Form External] names
    ::GetPrivateProfileString("Form External", NULL, "",
                         szBuf, sizeof(szBuf)-1, m_szINI);
    cp = szBuf;
    while(*cp != '\0')
    {
        CString csName(cp);
        csaFields.Add(csName);
        cp += csName.GetLength() + 1;
    }
}
```

The first thing to note is the use of GetPrivateProfileString() with a NULL second parameter (the keyword). This returns a series of concatenated null-terminated strings, ending in a double null. Each of the strings is one of the keywords within the specified section of the INI file. The code iterates over these strings until the double null is reached, storing each field name into the class user's string array. This process is done for the [Form Literal] and [Form External] sections of the INI file. The result is an array containing all of the field names.

RETRIEVING FORM FIELD DATA

Clearly, any CGI program that processes forms must have a way to retrieve the data that was posted from the form. Normally, the form and the CGI program are a matched set; the CGI program knows the names of the fields in its companion form. Here, we create a member function that permits class users to retrieve the contents of a form field, given the field name. The implementation details are completely hidden. The class user has no idea that the interface uses two different schemes to pass data (Form Literal and Form External). The function retrieves the form data by using the GetPrivateProfileString() function to access the decoded form data in the INI file (or in the external data file in the case of Form External fields).

```
// Get the value of a form field, given the field name
// Uses Windows CGI server-based form decoding
CString CCGI::GetFormField(const char *szName)
{
    CString csDat;              // Make a CString to hold data
    LPTSTR cp;
    int l;
    char *szSentinel = "====";

    // First try for the common case, [Form Literal]
    cp = csDat.GetBufferSetLength(256);// Set to hold longest literal
    l = ::GetPrivateProfileString("Form Literal", szName, szSentinel,
                        cp, 255, m_szINI);
    csDat.ReleaseBuffer(l);// Release CString internal buffer
    if(csDat != szSentinel)// If got a real result
        return(csDat);          // We're finished

    // Not there, try [Form External]
    char szBuf[MAX_PATH];
    ::GetPrivateProfileString("Form External", szName, szSentinel,
                        szBuf, sizeof(szBuf), m_szINI);
    if(strcmp(szBuf, szSentinel) == 0)// If no luck here
        csDat.Empty();          // Return empty string
    else
    {
        CFile fd(szBuf, CFile::modeRead);// Open the field data file
        l = fd.GetLength();// Get data length for re-use
        cp = csDat.GetBufferSetLength(l);// Expand to hold data, get
            buf
        fd.Read(cp, l);         // Read the data
        fd.Close();             // Close the file
        csDat.ReleaseBuffer(l);// Release CString internal buffer
    }
    return(csDat);                      // Done
}
// Overloaded for CString field name
```

```
CString CCGI::GetFormField(CString& csName)
{
    return(GetFormField(LPCTSTR(csName)));
}
```

The function first tries to retrieve the field data as a Form Literal. If this fails, it tries to retrieve it as a Form External. In order to tell whether the GetPrivatePro-fileString() call for the Form Literal case succeeds or fails, a "sentinel" is used as the default to return if the named value does not exist. The pattern "====" is very unlikely to occur in real form data. If GetPrivateProfileString() returns the sentinel value, then there was no real value in that section by that name. Note also that we supplied a variation of the function that takes a CString field name instead of a null-terminated string.

RETURNING DATA TO THE CLIENT

In keeping with the "implementation hiding" principle, you should expose some methods for the class user to send data back to the browser. The class user will be shielded from the output spooling of Windows CGI. The following member function provides a way to send arbitrary data back to the client. This is a low level method, on which we'll next build some more specific methods. Two varia-tions are provided: one that takes a (by-reference) CString field name, and the other that takes a null-terminated string.

```
// Write the specified data as-is to the output.
void CCGI::WriteHTMLBody(CString& strMsg)
{
    fileOutput.Write(LPCTSTR(strMsg), strMsg.GetLength());
}

// Overloaded in case they want to send (char *) instead of CString.
void CCGI::WriteHTMLBody(char *szMsg)
{
    fileOutput.Write(szMsg, strlen(szMsg));
}
```

Recall that the *fileOutput* variable is protected, inaccessible to class users. The member function simply writes the contents of the class user's CString to the output file.

The next routine is merely a time saver. Since in most cases a CGI is returning HTML, we have some specialized routines for building an HTML response. This one writes out the minimal HTML header, a single Content-Type header speci-fying text/html as the content type of the data to follow. Then it writes out the blank line separating the HTML headers and the response body. Finally, it writes out the <HTML> tag that should start all HTML document bodies. You may want to make this fancier, writing out a more complete/strict HTML document preamble.

```
// Write out the HTTP header required for CGI replies.
// HTTP headers must be CRLF terminated. File is binary.
// Then write out the starting HTML tag.
void CCGI::WriteHTMLHeader(void)
{
    WriteHTMLBody("Content-type: text/
        html\015\012\015\012<HTML>\015\012");
}
```

Note the use of explicit carriage return ('\015') and linefeed ('\012') characters as line terminators. This is the safest way to ensure that line terminations are correct. In MFC, the CFile object always represents a file in "binary" mode. Trying to use text mode will cause an assert in a debug build, and will have no effect in retail builds. Also, you may want to return binary data such as an image or sound, so the CCGI class *should* open the output file in binary mode anyway.

The HTTP specification requires that header lines be CRLF-terminated. Within the body of an HTML document, most browsers will accept UNIX-style LF-only terminators. However, it has become the Internet custom to use CRLF for line termination, and the Windows text file format uses CRLF terminators, so it is a good idea to use CRLF.

Finally, here is another time saver. This one simply writes out the </HTML> tag that matches the one written by the previous member function. You may want to make this fancier, adding a horizontal rule, and perhaps a *mailto*: link to the server administrator.

```
// Write the close codes which match those in the header.
void CCGI::WriteHTMLFooter(void)
{
    WriteHTMLBody("</HTML>\n");
}
```

The CCGI class implementation is now complete, so you need to add it to our CGIBase application. Go to the Project menu and bring up the Files dialog. You only need to add the .CPP file. The .H file will be added when you update the dependencies.

USING THE NEW CLASS

Now you need to customize the CGIBASE.CPP file to take advantage of the new class. So far, this file is still as it was when the AppWizard created it for us. There are three main things you need to do to get the CGI skeleton ready to fill in.

PROVIDING ACCESS TO THE CCGI CLASS

First, include the CGI.H file so we have access to our new class. Without this, you will get errors when you try to create a CCGI object, and you won't be able to see the member functions. You also need to put in a prototype for a function you will add. With the new include and prototype (underlined), the top of the file looks like this:

```
// CGIBase.cpp : Defines the class behaviors for the application.
// Version 1.0

#include "stdafx.h"
#include "CGIBase.h"
#include "CGIBadlg.h"
#include "cgi.h"

#ifdef _DEBUG
#undef THIS_FILE
static char BASED_CODE THIS_FILE[] = __FILE__;
#endif

// Declare our only local function.
void ProcessCGI(CCGI *cgi);
```

INITINSTANCE()

Next you need to rewrite InitInstance(). You only want to run the original code, which brings up the dialog box if the program is run in a non-CGI mode. You will also create a new function ProcessCGI() in order to isolate the CGI code within its own routine. Most of the InitInstance() function is new. For now, we don't care what button the user presses when exiting the dialog.

Note that, for this application, "InitInstance" is a misnomer. The entire application runs within this function, and it returns FALSE, causing the application to exit (as if initialization had failed). This prevents the application from starting the elaborate MFC user interface machinery.

```
BOOL CCGIBaseApp::InitInstance()
{
    CCGI cgi(m_lpCmdLine);

    if(cgi.CalledAsCGI())
    {//==================
        ProcessCGI(&cgi); // Do all of the real work
    }//==================
    else // We were not called as a CGI.  Pop up dialog with
            instructions.
    {
        Enable3dControls();
        AfxEnableWin40Compatibility();// Undocumented, for new look

        CCGIBaseDlg dlg;       // Instantiate our Dialog
```

```
        m_pMainWnd = &dlg;// Make its window our app's main
        int nResponse = dlg.DoModal();// Run the dialog
        if (nResponse == IDOK)// Act on the response
        {
        }
        else if (nResponse == IDCANCEL)
        {
        } .
    }
    // Since the dialog has been closed, return FALSE so that we
            exit the
    //  application, rather than start the application's message
            pump.
    return FALSE;
}
```

PROCESSCGI()

This is the actual CGI "application," which is called from the InitInstance() function. It is not a member function, so you only need to include the CGI.H file in one place. First, we grab the values of a couple of the CGI variables. The available variables and their meanings are documented in the Windows CGI 1.2 Specification. Then we create an array of form field names, as we're going to iterate over the field names later in the program.

```
void ProcessCGI(CCGI *cgi)
{
    CString strWebmaster = cgi->GetCGIVar("Server Admin");
    CString strReferer = cgi->GetCGIVar("Referer");
```

Now we build a generic empty reply. The first pass will include only the generic header and footer designed in the CCGI class.

```
    cgi->WriteHTMLHeader();// Start the response
    cgi->WriteHTML("Hello World!");// Send something recognizable
    cgi->WriteHTMLFooter();// Finish the response
}
```

FINAL TIDBITS

At this point you will need to go into the resource editor and put something useful in the dialog box. This dialog box will appear when the program is run interactively instead of as a CGI. Some good text to use would be "This program will only do something useful when run by a World Wide Web server as a CGI program." You can also delete the Cancel button for this example. It can be added back in if you later make use of the dialog as a second user interface.

And there it is. A functional, but severely limited, CGI program. You've learned how to process CGI data by writing a C++ class that puts the data into an easily handled format. You also know how to send a reply back to the sender, letting them know the form was received.

TESTING THE PROGRAM

It can be difficult to test a CGI program in its "live" environment. Typically, it will fail, causing the output file to be empty or corrupted. In this case the server will return a "500 Server Error" message to the browser, indicating that something failed. What we need to do is test the CGI program from within the Visual C++ development environment. Fortunately, this is easy to do. All we need is an INI file and perhaps one or more Form External files. Create an INI file that looks like one that would result from a typical form you might use. Here is an example:

```
[System]
Input File=e:\website\cgi-src\cppsample\test.inp
Output File=e:\website\cgi-src\cppsample\test.out

[CGI]
Server Admin=foo@bar.com
Referer=http://localhost/cgi-win/cgibase.exe

[Form Literal]
Name=John Q. Public
Address=123 Main Street.
Address2=Suite 1000
City=Anywhere
State=ZZ
Country=USA

[Form External]
Comments=e:\website\cgi-src\cppsample\test.001
```

Look at this carefully. It has input and output file specifications pointing to the home directory for the development tree of the application. The input file is not used, as the INI file has all of the (fake) decoded form data in it. Two CGI variables that we'll use later are present, as are several Form Literal items and one Form External item. The latter points to another file that you must create. You can put anything in it you want, such as the Gettysburg Address. Create this INI file in the development directory and call it TEST.INI.

Next, open the Project Settings property sheet in Visual C++, select the Debug tab, and enter the full pathname of the INI file into the Program Arguments field, for example

```
e:\website\cgi-src\cppsample\test.ini
```

This tells Visual C++ to start the program with the INI file on its command line, simulating the action of the Windows CGI interface. Now compile and test the program. Step into it and follow it through. Correct any compiler errors, asserts or exceptions. Once the program runs to completion, look in the output file (which it should have created) and see that it looks like this:

```
Content-type: text/html

<HTML>
Hello World!
</HTML>
```

ADDING FUNCTIONALITY

Now you're ready to build some real functionality into the CGI program. You'll create some content to send back to the user so they can tell that their CGI form was received. Remove the line of code that sends the "Hello World!" `declare int i;` at the beginning, and add the code as seen in the following sections.

BEGINNING THE HTML REPLY

To make the returned HTML document look normal, you should give it a title. This title will, in most browsers, appear in the title bar of the browser window. You also need to create a body. All of the fun tricks and tips in this chapter will appear within the body of the returned HTML document.

```
// Set the title bar text.
cgi->WriteHTMLBody(
        "<HEAD><TITLE>Title goes here</TITLE></HEAD>\015\012n");
// Start body here.
cgi->WriteHTMLBody("<BODY>\015\012");
cgi->WriteHTMLBody("<H3>This is a reply.</H3>\015\012");
```

Now we'll fetch the values of a couple of CGI variables that we'll use later.

```
CString strWebmaster = cgi->GetCGIVar("Server Admin");
CString strReferer = cgi->GetCGIVar("Referer");
```

Recall that we included a method in CCGI to enumerate the field names into a CStringArray. We'll use this in a couple of places, so we'll get those field names.

```
// Get an array of the form field names & the number of fields.
CStringArray csaFields;
cgi->EnumFormFieldNames(csaFields);// Get the field name array
int nFields = csaFields.GetSize();
```

ECHOING FORM FIELD CONTENTS

The next thing you will set up is very useful for debugging CGI programs. The program will return a copy of the data that was sent in via the form. By defining

DEBUG_FIELDS you can turn on the code to include a list of fields and their values in the HTML response. Here's the first place we use the field name array.

```
#define DEBUG_FIELDS
#ifdef DEBUG_FIELDS
    for(i = 0; i < nFields; i++)// Write out the field names
    {
        CString strOut = csaFields[i] + " = " +
                cgi->GetFormField(csaFields[i]) + "<BR>\015\012";
        cgi->WriteHTMLBody(strOut);
    }
#endif
```

RETURNING THE LOCAL DATE AND TIME

It may also be useful at some time to send back the local time and date. These two sections can be removed from the code easily by removing the #define lines. The time and date are formatted based on the current system preferences.

```
#define SHOW_TIME
#ifdef SHOW_TIME
    char szTime[80];
    GetTimeFormat(0,0,NULL,NULL,szTime,80);
    cgi->WriteHTMLBody("<P>The time is ");
    cgi->WriteHTMLBody(szTime);
    cgi->WriteHTMLBody(".</P>\n");
#endif
```

```
#define SHOW_DATE
#ifdef SHOW_DATE
    char szDate[80];
    GetDateFormat(0,0,NULL,NULL,szDate,80);
    cgi->WriteHTMLBody("<P>The date is ");
    cgi->WriteHTMLBody(szDate);
    cgi->WriteHTMLBody(".</P>\n");
#endif
```

LINKING TO THE PREVIOUS PAGE

Most pages give you a button or hypertext link to get you back where you came from. The Referer: header is generated by most browsers when the request came from a hypertext link. In this case, Referer contains the URL of the document containing the link. Recall that we created the strReferer object earlier.

```
    // Give them a link to where they came from.
    if(!strReferer.IsEmpty())
    {
        cgi->WriteHTMLBody("<P>Go <A HREF=\"");
        cgi->WriteHTMLBody(strReferer);
```

```
        cgi->WriteHTMLBody("\">Back</A> where you came from.</P>\n");
}
```

ADDING A MAILTO: LINK

It is also a good idea to put some contact information on the page. Recall that we fetched the Server Admin CGI variable earlier. Now we'll use this to put a *mailto:* link into the CGI response.

```
// Tell them who to contact.
if(!strWebmaster.IsEmpty())
{
    cgi->WriteHTMLBody("<P>Please email comments to ");
    cgi->WriteHTMLBody("<A HREF=\"mailto:");
    cgi->WriteHTMLBody(strWebmaster);
    cgi->WriteHTMLBody("\">");
    cgi->WriteHTMLBody(strWebmaster);
    cgi->WriteHTMLBody("</A>.</P>\n");
}
```

Finally we come to the closing call that we entered for the Hello World! Test. Leave it there.

```
// Done with the body.
cgi->WriteHTMLBody("</BODY>\n");
```

LOGGING POSTS TO A FILE

Next is a slightly more complicated bit of data processing. This block of code allows you to write the data to a tab delimited file. This format is ideal if you are importing the data into a database program. This format also lets you bypass the complexity of creating an ODBC program. The down side is that you must import the data into your database by hand on a regular basis.

If your database structure follows your CGI form very closely, then importing the data can be clean and simple. If there is not a close match, then you may be able to import parts of the data automatically, based on the features of your database program. Some database programs allow for complex processing of imported data.

First, select a filename for our data. There are many reasons to choose a file name where the base is the same as the executable, followed by a standard TXT extension. This allows you to consistently find the data file because it will always be in the same directory as the executable file. And, if you want to have more than one data file, you can simply copy and rename the executable, and it will store the data in separate files under multiple distinct names.

```
#define TAB_DELIM
#ifdef TAB_DELIM
    // Write to a tab delimited data file.
    // Force it to have a .txt extension.
```

```
CString strData = AfxGetApp()->m_pszHelpFilePath;
strData.SetAt(strData.GetLength()-1,'t');
strData.SetAt(strData.GetLength()-2,'x');
strData.SetAt(strData.GetLength()-3,'t');
```

MFC's CFile object does not have a mode to conditionally create a file or open an existing one without truncating the existing file to 0-length. So we need to first test for the file's existence and if it does not exist, create it. Otherwise we simply open the existing file. Finally, we seek to the end of the file so we can append the new data.

```
CFile fileOut;
CFileStatus statusFileOut;
// We always want read/write and deny write sharing
UINT uiOpenMode = CFile::shareDenyWrite | CFile::modeReadWrite;
if(!fileOut.GetStatus(strData, statusFileOut))// File exists?
    uiOpenMode |= CFile::modeCreate;// No, add Create mode
fileOut.Open(strData, uiOpenMode);// Open or create the file
fileOut.SeekToEnd();      // Seek for appending
```

The next step is to actually write the data. The loop is similar to the one used to echo form values back to the user, but it writes the variable data to the open text file instead. You want to put a tab after all fields but the last one, and end the line with CRLF. When all the data has been written, close the file.

```
for(i = 0; i < nFields; i++)// Write out the fields
{
    CString csField = cgi->GetFormField(csaFields[i]);
    fileOut.Write((LPCTSTR)csField,csField.GetLength());
    if(i < (nFields - 1)) // Don't delimit last field
        fileOut.Write("\t", 1);
}
fileOut.Write("\015\012", 2);// CRLF-Terminate
fileOut.Close();                 // Close the file
#endif
```

Now you can go back and remove some of the #define statements to customize the sample application to your needs. This structure allows you to create several different test programs by changing just a few lines of code.

ERROR HANDLING

One of the worst habits to develop is adding error handling to a program after it is written and tested. The result can be a total mess of nested if statements and sneaky logic paths. For illustration purposes, we have done exactly that, and now we are faced with adding error handling after the fact. When you write your CGI programs, be sure to include error handling in your thought and design process from the beginning.

In this section, we cover the basics of MFC's structured exception handling, and add an error handler to our CCGI class. MFC uses C++ structured exceptions throughout. As an MFC programmer, it is essential that you follow this architecture. For example, the CFile::Open() method returns an exception object, and errors within CFile::Write() will generate exceptions if there are problems. Unless you handle these exceptions carefully, your CGI program can simply abort without producing output, or worse, leaving garbage in the output spool file.

NOTE

The MFC documentation (Visual C++ Volume 2, *Programming with MFC and Win32*) presents structured exception handling in a confusing way. Ignore *all* information about "MFC Exceptions" and concentrate only on the "ANSI C++ Exceptions," which use MFC CException (and children) objects. These use the native *try, catch*, and *throw* statements of the C++ language. ANSI C++ structured exceptions can use any object as the exception object. Within MFC, which is a framework built on top of C++, the convention is to use objects derived from CException for structured exception objects.

PREVENTING A "500 SERVER ERROR"

If the CGI program fails without producing an output file, WebSite will return a 500 Server Error response, indicating that the CGI program produced no output. If the output file contains garbage, a missing HTTP header section, or an incomplete document, the poor browser user will be left without a clue, and so will you when the user asks for help.

Since MFC generates exceptions under a variety of error conditions, you can do the same. Include an exception handler that returns something useful when there is a serious error. Furthermore, there is no reason you can't generate exceptions yourself, catching them with the same handler you use to catch low-level and MFC exceptions.

Our exception handler will be used to return a properly formatted HTML document to the browser when any sort of exception is thrown within the CGI-specific part of the program. If an exception occurs while constructing the CCGI object, or in the handling of interactive starts, we'll be satisfied with the program just exiting after the default exception catcher runs.

ADDING AN EXCEPTION HANDLER
TO THE CCGI CLASS

The first thing we need to do is add a new method to CCGI that can be used to "handle" the exception. For illustration purposes, we'll return a generic HTML error message to the browser. You could write a more elaborate exception handler that looks at the type of exception thrown and return a more specific error. For this reason, we'll design the method interface so it takes the thrown exception object as a parameter. Then the changes to make error messages more specific can be made in the handler method's implementation in CCGI without impacting the actual CGI code.

Suppose an exception occurs while writing to the output file? If the exception handler attempts to write the error message to the output file, it could cause a recursive exception. We need to provide for that, and let the program silently exit.

Add the following to CCGI.H (underlined) in the public declaration section:

```
...
void WriteHTMLBody(char *szMsg);
void WriteHTMLFooter(void);
void HandleException(CException* e);
```

Our exception handler will use a canned response from a string resource. Using the Visual C++ resource editor, add a string resource whose identifier is IDD_ERROR_MESSAGE:

```
HTTP/1.0 500 Server Error
Content-type: text/html

<HTML>
<HEAD><TITLE>CGI Program Failed</TITLE></HEAD>
<BODY><H1>CGI Program Failed</H1>
This CGI program encountered a fatal internal error.
</BODY></HTML>
```

The listing above shows where the line breaks should occur in the string resource. If you reedit the resource, they will show as \n, yet they are actually CRLF sequences in the resource. Use Ctrl-Enter to put line breaks into the string resource.

NOTE

Notice that the above response starts with HTTP/1.0 rather than just the content type. If WebSite sees this at the beginning of a CGI response, it bypasses its HTTP header generation and uses only the headers in the response. This feature allows a CGI program to generate any kind of HTTP response, rather than being limited to the 200 OK response that WebSite normally builds for CGI output. We wanted to send back an HTTP 500 Server Error response, so we constructed the HTTP response ourselves.

Next we need to add an #include to CGI.CPP so the string resource identifier is known:

```
...
#include "cgi.h"
#include "resource.h"
```

Add the exception handler member function to CCGI.CPP:

```
// Exception Handler
void CCGI::HandleException(CException* e)
{
    try                     // Protect against recursive exceptions
    {
        CString csMsg;

        fileOutput.SetLength(0);// Prevent unwanted garbage
        csMsg.LoadString(IDS_ERROR_MESSAGE);
        fileOutput.Write(LPCTSTR(csMsg), csMsg.GetLength());
    }
    catch(CException* re)
    {
        re->Delete();// Junk this exception, we tried!
    }
}
```

Within the exception handler itself, the *try/catch* block stops recursive exceptions from causing infinite looping. The code within the *try* block is safe, but you may want to add additional features that could generate exceptions.

Also note that the output file is reset back to 0-length before writing out the response data. This prevents unwanted partial output from preceding the error message in the spool file. Do not use CFile::SeekBegin() to reset the file. It does not truncate the file and leaves garbage after the error message.

ADDING THE EXCEPTION CATCHER

Now we need to add the exception catcher to our CGIBASE.CPP code. Add the following around the call to ProcessCGI():

```
    try                         // Guard for exceptions
    {
        ProcessCGI(&cgi);// Do all of the real work
    }
    catch(CException* e)
    {
        cgi.HandleException(e);// Handle the exception
        e->Delete();            // Delete it
    }
```

It is important to delete the exception after processing it. This ensures proper termination of the program.

If, for any reason, an exception occurs within the CGI processing of the program, it will be caught and a CGI-specific error response will be sent back to the browser. Of course, you can customize the exception handler `CCGI::HandleEx-ception()` to your specific needs.

SUMMARY

The CCGI class that was created lets you hide many of the details of the CGI interface. You can now completely ignore the parsing of data and can quickly get to whatever environment variables you need. The class and base program allow you to concentrate on the actual work of getting data from the user and getting the HTML replies back to the client without getting bogged down in the low level details.

Now that the base program is complete, it is very simple to create complex CGI programs with much less effort. Instead of writing out the tab delimited data, you could create and send graphics, do interactive games, or any other World Wide Web code you can think up.

CHAPTER EIGHTEEN

THE STANDARD AND DOS CGI INTERFACES

Most WebSite users will choose to write their applications using Windows CGI and Visual Basic, as described in Chapter 16, *Developing Applications with Windows CGI*. However, some users who are not familiar with programming under Windows may prefer to write CGI programs in another environment.

WebSite includes CGI interfaces for UNIX-based programs and also DOS-based programs. The UNIX-based CGI interface is called the "Standard" CGI, since most CGI programming up to now has been done in the UNIX environment. You may be interested in using the Standard CGI if:

- You want to take advantage of the collections of CGI scripts available over the Internet.

- You are moving an existing Web from a UNIX system to WebSite, and you want to be able to port your scripts painlessly.

- You want to develop robust CGI programs without investing in Visual Basic.

Under the Standard CGI, you can configure your machine to run programs written in Perl or in the Korn shell, or actually any UNIX programming language as long as you can make it run on Windows. For example, if you installed a TCL interpreter that runs on your Windows machine, you would be able to run TCL-based CGI programs as well.

This chapter concentrates on using Perl to develop CGI programs in the Standard CGI. Although you can also run programs written in the Bourne or Korn shell, there isn't much you can do with it without a full suite of UNIX utilities to back it up. Perl, on the other hand, is a full-featured scripting language that is operating system-independent.

For the convenience of lifelong DOS users, WebSite includes a CGI interface to the DOS command shell. The DOS CGI can be used to run both DOS *.bat* scripts and Windows NT *.cmd* scripts. However, CGI development in the DOS shell has very limited potential, since there are no built-in utilities for manipulating CGI data.

PREPARING TO USE THE STANDARD CGI

Both Perl and the Korn shell are interpreted languages. In simple terms, this means that the source code is not compiled into an executable, which can be run independently from the compiler (as in a "real" programming language like C or Visual Basic). Instead, the code is directly executed at runtime using an installed copy of Perl or the Korn shell as the interpreter.

In order to run Korn shell or Perl CGI programs, therefore, you must have Korn shell and Perl interpreters installed on your system. These packages are not included with WebSite, but you can retrieve them as follows:

- Both Windows NT and Windows 95 users can use an updated version of Perl, available on WebSite Central. Windows NT users can also use the older version of NT Perl available on many sites throughout the Internet.

- Windows NT users can find a version of the UNIX Korn shell in the POSIX compatibility component of Microsoft's Windows NT Resource Kit.

Once you have installed these utilities, you need to:

- Make sure that they are in your system path. Use the System utility (from the Control Panel) to add these programs to your system path, if the installation procedure didn't already do this for you.

- Make sure that you have properly associated the program's extensions to the executables, using the File Manager (File Associate New):

- Associate the *.pl* extension to the Perl executable (e.g., *\ntperl\perl.exe*).

- Associate the *.sh* extension to the Korn Shell (*sh*) executable (e.g., *\reskit\posix\sh.exe*).

- You must ensure that your Perl and Korn shell scripts are named with the appropriate extensions (*.pl* for Perl scripts and *.sh* for Korn Shell scripts).

If you want to use another UNIX-based interpreter (like TCL) that has been ported to Windows, you must follow the same procedure in order for the Standard CGI to be able to use it.

GETTING DATA IN THE STANDARD CGI

For any CGI program, you need to know how to get name=value pairs, how to send output back to the server, and how to read CGI variables.

- CGI variables are given as environment variables. You can read these environment variables as you would for a script running on a UNIX system. For example, in Perl, you can get the browser's IP address from the %ENV associative array—for example, $ENV{REMOTE_ADDR}. In the Korn shell, you can access the same variable with the syntax $REMOTE_ADDR.

- GET data is given in the QUERY_STRING environment variable, in URL-encoded format. It must be decoded manually.

- POST data is given in standard input. Since it is also URL-encoded, it is simply one long line of standard input, which must be decoded manually.

- CGI output (to be sent to the server and presumably transferred to the browser) can be printed to standard output.

In other words, you can write the scripts just as you would on UNIX.

NCSA EXTRA HEADER FORMAT

Some variables passed to CGI programs are not strictly CGI variables, but are extra headers sent by the browser. The most common example of a variable that is sent as an extra header is USER_AGENT. Since the CGI passes these variables as environment variables, you can treat them in your scripts the same way you treat real CGI variables, with one caveat: the actual names of the variables depend on whether NCSA Extra Header Format is checked in the CGI page of the Server Admin utility.

The reason for this format is that the NCSA server passes these variables with an HTTP_ prefix—for example, HTTP_USER_AGENT. You may prefer this format if you are porting Perl scripts from an NCSA-based Web server.

The following are some environment variables you can access in both the Standard and DOS CGI. See Chapter 15, *Introduction to the Common Gateway Interface*, for more information on using these variables.

Server Information

SERVER_SOFTWARE	The name and version of the server software
SERVER_NAME	The server's hostname
SERVER_PORT	The port number the server runs on
SERVER_ADMIN	The email address of the server's administrator
GATEWAY_INTERFACE	The CGI version to which this server complies
GMT_OFFSET	The number of hours from GMT

Information About the Browser or User

USER_AGENT	The browser the client is using to send the request
REMOTE_HOST	The hostname making the request
REMOTE_ADDR	The IP address of the remote host making the request
HTTP_REFERER	The referring document

HTTP_FROM	The email address of the user
SERVER_PROTOCOL	The protocol name and revision that the request came in with
HTTP_ACCEPT	The file list of the MIME types and the content types the client will accept

Executable, Logical, and Physical Paths

PATH_INFO	The extra path information, also known as the logical path
PATH_TRANSLATED	The translated PATH_INFO, also known as the physical path
SCRIPT_NAME	The path to the script being executed, also known as the executable path

GET and POST Data

REQUEST_METHOD	The request method, i.e., GET, HEAD, or POST
QUERY_STRING	The GET data (the part of the URL after the ?)
OUTPUT_FILE	The file containing POST data (unnecessary since it can be taken from *stdin*)
CONTENT_TYPE	The content type of POST data
CONTENT_LENGTH	The size of the content file

Security

AUTH_NAME	The authenticated realm
AUTH_USER	The authenticated user
AUTH_TYPE	The authentication method used to validate the user (if any)

Output

CONTENT_FILE	The file to write data into

Debugging Mode

DEBUG_MODE	True when CGI debugging is turned on

To see a full listing of the environment variables set by your Perl script, just print them individually from the %ENV array, with the names and values separated by tabs. For example:

```perl
print "Content-type: text/html\n\n";
print "<PRE>";
foreach (keys(%ENV)) {
    print "<BR>";
    print ("$_\t$ENV{$_}");
}
```

```
print "</PRE>";
```

In the Korn shell, you can use the set command without any arguments to see all defined environment variables.

```
echo print "Content-type: text/html"
echo ""
echo <PRE>
set
echo </PRE>
```

PERL-BASED CGI

Since Perl is the language you are most likely to use in the Standard or DOS CGI, we'll concentrate on writing Perl-based CGI programs. Note that we don't attempt to teach Perl to new users; for that, we recommend *Learning Perl* by Randal L. Schwartz, or *Programming perl* by Larry Wall and Randal L. Schwartz (both published by O'Reilly & Associates). Instead, we concentrate on the procedure for developing Perl programs for CGI processing.

THE CGI-LIB LIBRARY

If you're going to be doing any rigorous Perl CGI programming, we recommend that you either build your own library of routines to parse URL-encoded data, or that you download a library for that purpose from the Web. WebSite Central includes a CGI library that we recommend. It includes the following routines:

MethGet
> Returns 1 if REQUEST_METHOD is "GET", 0 otherwise.

ReadParse
> Decodes GET or POST data and reads the *name=value* pairs into an associative array %in, a standard array @in, and a single variable $in.

PrintHeader
> Prints the "Content-type: text/html" header.

PrintVariables
> Prints all *name=value* pairs, nicely formatted in "glossary" form.

PrintVariablesShort
> Prints all *name=value* pairs, separated by line breaks.

We'll show examples of using some of these routines below.

Your Perl distribution is installed with a *lib* subdirectory. After downloading the CGI library, place it in the *lib* directory, and then you can include it in your Perl programs using the require routine:

```
# Call in CGI library.
require("cgi-lib.pl");
```

If you write your own routines that you want to include in all your CGI programs, just add them to the *cgi-lib.pl* file.

A SIMPLE BUG REPORT PROGRAM

If you write programs, then you're going to write bugs. Although you'll catch many of them yourself, you might also want to allow other users of your Web to report bugs. Of course, they can always do that by sending you email, but then there's no easy way for users to know if their bug has already been reported.

The *bugreport.pl* sample program lets you submit a bug report that is saved in a file called *bugs.txt*. You can then include in your documents two hyperlinks: one to the bug report program, and another to the *bugs.txt* file so they can see what bugs are already known. The document might read:

```
<A HREF="bugs.txt">There are known bugs.</A>  Since there are also
undoubtedly unknown bugs, you can
<A HREF="/cgi-shl/bugreport.pl">
submit a bug report or suggestion by clicking here.</A>
```

NOTE

This example shouldn't be taken as a model for programming in Perl. It is simply meant to illustrate CGI program development in Perl. We have deliberately tried to keep the code uncomplicated, so you can follow the CGI-specific procedures without being distracted by more rigorous but less lucid Perl techniques.

THE PROGRAM STRUCTURE

The *bugreport.pl* program follows a standard model for CGI programs: return a form if it's GET data, and process the form if it's POST. The "main" section of the program appears below:

```
#
# Script for getting bug reports.
#

# Call in CGI library.
require("cgi-lib.pl");

if ( &MethGet ) {
    # Under GET, return form.
    &ReturnForm;
} else {
    # Under POST, full speed ahead.
```

```
        &WriteReport;
}
```

The first thing we do is read in the CGI library. Next, we use the `MethGet` routine to test for GET or POST data. If `MethGet` returns 1, then the program was called with the GET method, and you should return a form. Otherwise, the program calls the `WriteReport` function, defined later in the program.

Many CGI programs are written this way so that if a form actually sends data to the CGI program using the GET method, it is ignored completely, and the program just returns a form again. Note, however, that you could also write the program to process GET data as well as POST. The "ReturnForm" portion of the code above could have read:

```
if ( &MethGet ) {
    # Under GET, look for data in QUERY_STRING.  If there is some,
    # process it.  If none, return form.
    if ( "$ENV{QUERY_STRING}" ) {
        &WriteReport;
    } else {
        &ReturnForm;
    }
} else {
    ...
```

Instead of immediately returning the form, the script checks if the QUERY_STRING environment variable is empty. If not, the script processes it; if so, it returns the form.

RETURNING THE FORM

The `ReturnForm` routine sends the form to the server. It reads:

```
sub ReturnForm {
    # Return the form
    print &PrintHeader;
    print "<TITLE>Bug report.</TITLE>\n";
    print "<BODY>\n";
    print "<H1>Enter a bug report.</H1>\n";
    print "<HR>\n";
    print "<FORM METHOD=\"POST\">\n";
    print "<PRE>\n";
    print "    Your name: <INPUT TYPE=TEXT SIZE=25
        NAME=username>\n";
    print "Email address: <INPUT TYPE=TEXT SIZE=25 NAME=email>\n";
    print "<P>\n";
    print "Severity of bug (1=not serious, 5=very serious): \n";
    print "    1 <INPUT TYPE=RADIO NAME=\"severity\" VALUE=1
        CHECKED>";
    print "    2 <INPUT TYPE=RADIO NAME=\"severity\" VALUE=2>";
```

```
    print "   3 <INPUT TYPE=RADIO NAME=\"severity\" VALUE=3>";
    print "   4 <INPUT TYPE=RADIO NAME=\"severity\" VALUE=4>";
    print "   5 <INPUT TYPE=RADIO NAME=\"severity\" VALUE=5>\n";
    print "<P>\n";
    print "Please describe the bug:\n";
    print "<BR>\n";
    print "<TEXTAREA ROWS=5 COLS=50 NAME=bugtext></TEXTAREA>";
    print "<P>\n";
    print "<INPUT TYPE=SUBMIT VALUE=\"Submit bug report\">";
    print "   <INPUT TYPE=RESET VALUE=Clear>\n";
    print "</PRE>\n";
    print "</BODY>\n";
}
```

The first line of the routine prints the header using the PrintHeader routine. This is equivalent to:

```
    print "Content-type: text/html\n\n";
```

NOTE

Although the \n\n in Perl works for generating two linefeeds (ending the Content-type line and inserting an additional blank line), the current HTTP specification requires both a carriage return and a linefeed to end each line in the header. Under Perl, this would read \r\n\r\n instead.

When used without an explicit file handle, the `print` routine defaults to sending text to standard output. The rest of the form should be recognizable HTML, sent via the `print` routine. Since Perl uses double-quotes as delimiters, any quotes that you want to print have to be escaped with a backslash. The form is a simple one, asking for the user's name, email address, the severity of the bug on a scale of 1 to 5, and a description of the bug. The user might see the form shown in Figure 18-1.

If you ever want to see the HTML code that created this form, use the View Source feature of your browser. View Source will display the HTML code generated by the CGI program for creating this form.

WRITING THE REPORT

Once the form is submitted, we want to store that information into the *bugs.txt* file and then send a thank you note to the user. The `WriteReport` routine takes care of this. The `WriteReport` routine should be easy to follow since it doesn't try to do anything fancy.

```
sub WriteReport {
    # Open the report file.
    open (REPORT, ">>/bugs.txt")
        || die ("Couldn't write to bug file.\n");
```

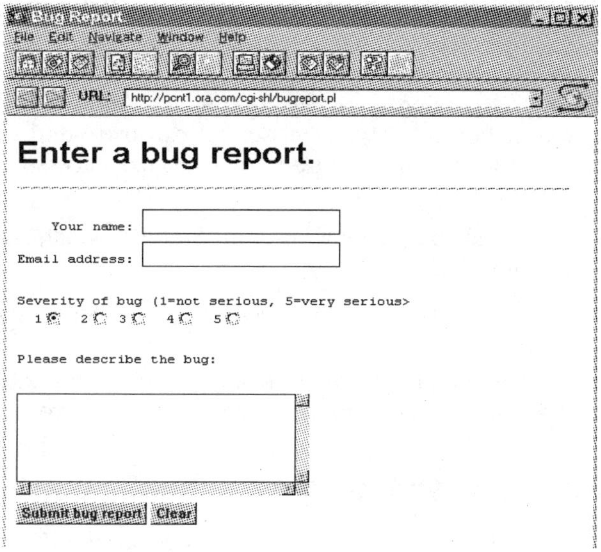

FIGURE 18-1: THE BUG REPORT FORM

```
    &ReadParse;
    print REPORT "Bug severity: $in{severity}\n";
    print REPORT "$in{bugtext}\n";
    print REPORT "\t(Submitted by $in{username}, $in{email})\n\n";
    close REPORT;

    print "Content-type: text/html\n\n";
    print "<TITLE>Bug submitted.</TITLE>\n";
    print "<H1>Bug submitted.</H1>\n";
    print "Thanks for submitting your bug report.\n";
}
```

We open the bug report file for appending using the file handle REPORT. If the file doesn't open, we use the die routine to print an error. This error can be found in the script's output file (i.e., the corresponding *.out* file in *\temp* if CGI debugging is enabled.)

Next, we parse out the data using the ReadParse routine. Now we can just print the data to the report file—the severity of the bug, the bug description, and the username and email address of the person who reported it.

Finally, we send a simple thank you back to the user.

This should give you an idea of how a CGI program in Perl works with form data. If you want to actually use this program, however, we recommend making the following improvements to `WriteReport` (which we don't go into since they don't teach anything new about CGI):

- You should use a file-locking mechanism to protect the program against more than one bug report coming in at the same time. Windows NT users with the updated version of Perl from Website Central can use Windows NT mutexes; we encourage you to use this feature to synchronize access to files and other objects within Perl scripts.

- You might write the bug report file in HTML format, rather than just appending it to a text file.

- You can get the time and date and store that information in the bug report file.

- The program should handle runtime errors so the appropriate status code is generated and the user is sent a message describing the error.

DEBUGGING PERL PROGRAMS

When you have a Perl syntax error, there are two ways of finding the error message:

- Turn on debugging and look for the *.out* file in *\temp*, as described in Chapter 16, *Developing Applications with Windows CGI*.

- Run the program directly on the command line. For example, from the DOS command shell:

```
C:\website\cgi-shl>perl bugreport.pl
syntax error in file C:\WEBSITE\cgi-shl\bugreport.pl at line 18..
```

For non-syntax errors, running from the command line isn't perfect since you don't have all the environment variables and *name=value* pairs assigned. However, you can get form input from *.inp* log files. Just turn on debugging, fill out the form, and then, after submitting the form, use the *.inp* file as input to the file:

```
C:\website\cgi-shl>type \temp\ws4ad343.inp | perl bugreport.pl
```

This works because the CGI script takes its POST input from standard input.

SHELL-BASED CGI PROGRAMS

In addition to Perl, you can use the Standard CGI to write programs in the UNIX Korn shell. The Korn shell is a superset of the Bourne shell, which before Perl was the most common scripting language used on UNIX systems.

The Korn shell, however is not as self-reliant as Perl; the Korn shell does not have any built-in utilities that can be used for parsing out *name=value* pairs. Most Korn shell programs depend on UNIX programs like *sed*, *awk*, and *cut*, which aren't distributed with the NT Resource Kit.

So your use of the Korn shell is liable to be limited. The following example program prints out a selected set of CGI variables back to the browser, for testing purposes:

```
echo Content-type: text/plain
echo
echo "CGI/1.2 (POSIX shell, args.sh) report:"
echo
echo $# "args:"
echo $1 $2 $3 $4 $5 $6 $7 $8
echo
echo environment variables:
echo REQUEST_METHOD:      $REQUEST_METHOD
echo SCRIPT_NAME:         $SCRIPT_NAME
echo QUERY_STRING:        $QUERY_STRING
echo PATH_INFO:           $PATH_INFO
echo PATH_TRANSLATED:     $PATH_TRANSLATED
if $REQUEST_METHOD = "POST" then
    echo CONTENT_TYPE:       $CONTENT_TYPE
    echo CONTENT_FILE:       $CONTENT_FILE
    echo CONTENT_LENGTH:     $CONTENT_LENGTH
    echo
    echo ---- begin content ----
    cat
    echo
    echo ----- end content -----
    echo
fi
echo -- end of report --
```

The script uses *text/plain* as its content type, since fancy formatting isn't needed here. It then uses a series of *echo* commands to send data to standard output.

CASE SENSITIVITY

The Korn shell is case-sensitive. So when calling Korn shell programs, be sure that the URL matches the name of the script exactly. For example, the script shown above is installed as *ARGS.SH*, so it must be called with the URL */cgi-shl/ ARGS.SH*. If you use the URL */cgi-shl/args.sh* (for example), the shell will complain that it can't find the file. The error message that you'll find in the *.out* file is:

```
//C/WEBSITE/cgi-shl/args.sh: cannot open.
```

DOS-BASED CGI PROGRAMS

Like the Korn shell, the DOS shell is not rigorous enough to handle a non-trivial CGI program. However, some users may still find some use for it. Here are some particulars on using the DOS CGI:

- You can read POST data from the content file.
- In DOS .bat scripts, you can write data to the pathname contained in the `%OUTPUT_FILE%` environment variable.
- In Windows NT *.cmd* scripts, you can write data to standard output.
- You can read CGI variables as environment variables.

You can access each of these environment variables as you would any other environment variable. For example:

```
echo The request method is %REQUEST_METHOD%
```

To see a full listing of the environment variables set in your DOS script, use the *set* command.

A SAMPLE .CMD CGI SCRIPT

WebSite is distributed with a sample .cmd batch file that just reports the name of our browser software, *browser.cmd*. That script reads:

```
echo Content-type: text/html
echo.
echo ^<title^>Browser Software^</title^>
echo ^<h1^>Browser Software^</h1^>
echo Your browser reports its name as ^<code^> %User-Agent%^</
        code^>^<P^>
echo ^<a href=^"/wsdocs/32demo/index.html#doscgi^"^>Return to self-
        test^</a^>
```

The script declares a content type and then prints out HTML code declaring the name of the browser. Note that the angle brackets used for HTML coding need to be escaped with carets (^). All the text is sent to standard output.

A SAMPLE .BAT CGI SCRIPT

WebSite also contains a sample *.bat* batch file that reports the name of the browser software, called *browser.bat*. That script reads:

```
set of=%OUTPUT_FILE%
echo Content-type: text/plain >%of%
echo. >>%of%
```

```
echo The old DOS command interpreter cannot echo angle brackets, so
          >>%of%
echo you cannot make scripts that generate HTML. >>%of%
echo. >>%of%
echo Your browser reports its name as %User-Agent% >>%of%
echo. >> %of%
echo If the name is blank, your browser doesn't send the User-
          Agent:  >> %of%
echo header, or you have the NCSA extra-header compatibility
          switch  >> %of%
echo turned on.  >> %of%
```

Note that we cannot use HTML code in *.bat* files, since the angle brackets are reserved and cannot be escaped. Therefore, the output must be sent in the *text/plain* format. Also, we can't send output directly to standard output, so it must be redirected to the output file stored in the %OUTPUT_FILE% environment variable.

APPENDIXES

The four appendixes included in this book provide more detailed information about WebSite. You will find this material useful as you administer WebSite and need more detailed information on specific aspects of the server. You may also be asked by technical support to use some of the appendix procedures to diagnose and solve server problems. Appendix A gives you a chart to fill in when completing the server self-test. Appendix B lists all the Registry keys used by WebSite with brief explanations. Appendix C gives you some troubleshooting tips to help you fix problems before calling technical support. Appendix D provides information on upgrading to other versions of the HotDog HTML Editor from Sausage Software.

WebSite Server Self-Test

The WebSite server self-test is an interactive journey through the server's capabilities—from basic functions to highly advanced features. The self-test also provides more information on CGI programming and server administration tasks, such as statistics and logging.

Because the self-test covers the server's functions, successfully completing the self-test means your server is configured and running properly. To track the server's responses, this appendix includes a form to be completed as you work through the self-test. On the form, record whether the server passes or fails each task. Make note of any error messages.

Some tasks may fail unless you have added external viewers, made changes to the server's setup through Server Admin, or have additional application tools installed. That's okay. The information you collect during the self-test will guide you through fine tuning the server and in providing information to technical support, should you have a problem with the server. Also, instructions are often included in the self-test for configuring the server properly.

We recommend that you rerun the server self-test whenever you make major changes in Server Admin. This ensures that the server is still configured and operating properly.

NOTE

For ease of use and reuse, we recommend that you photocopy the blank form before proceeding.

Server Self-Test Requirements

Before performing the server self-test, make sure:

- You are using a browser that supports forms, image maps, tables, and basic authentication (such as Spyglass Mosaic)
- You have enabled automatic loading of inline images
- Your browser is configured to accept and view GIF files, and basic sound files

- You have a GIF viewer and sound player installed and you have tested with your browser
- The WebSite server is running
- You are reading the server self-test document from the server (not as a local file)
- For the Windows CGI examples, you have at least the Visual Basic 4.0 runtime modules installed
- For the Access/VB integration sample, you have the Visual Basic Professional runtime modules (or Access 95 and VB standard) installed
- You have added yourself as a user in the Web Server realm, and added yourself to the Administrators group
- If you are running the self-test under Windows 95, you have added the line ComandEnvSize=8192 to the [NonWindowsApp] section of the *system.ini* file and rebooted the system. This change is required only for the DOS CGI examples.

RUNNING THE SERVER SELF-TEST

To start the WebSite server self-test, complete the following steps:

1. With your web browser, open the URL *http://localhost/wsdocs/32demo/*; or, in the Getting Started section of the WebSite Resources Welcome page, click on the link to *Server Self-Test and Demonstration*.

2. Work through the self-test and indicate the server's responses on the following form. Circle Pass or Fail for each item and write down any error messages or unexpected results. For ease of use and so you can use this form again, we recommend you photocopy the form first.

NOTE

Some tests require a browser with specific capabilities, such as Java support. These requirements are noted in the self-test. In general, a recent version of Netscape Navigator has the necessary capability.

Description	Results	Error Messages	Notes
Basic Document Retrieval			
Plain text document	Pass/Fail		
Hypertext document	Pass/Fail		
GIF image	Pass/Fail		
Audio clip	Pass/Fail		
Directory Tree Navigation			
Server creates automatic directory	Pass/Fail		
HTML-3 table format	Pass/Fail		
Directory browsing disabled	Pass/Fail		
Image Maps			
ISMAP link, internal	Pass/Fail		
ISMAP link, external	Pass/Fail		
Forms GET action	Pass/Fail		
Server-Side Includes			
SSI results page	Pass/Fail		
Automatic URL Fixup			
URL without trailing slash	Pass/Fail		
Java Applets			
Tumbling Duke	Pass/Fail		
Wire Frame	Pass/Fail		
WebSite Monitor	Pass/Fail		
Using CGI Programs			
Order entry application, VB 4	Pass/Fail		
Processing fill-in form	Pass/Fail		

Description	Results	Error Messages	Notes
Document based queries, NT	Pass/Fail		
Document based queries, Win 95	Pass/Fail		
Database integration, VB 4 and Access 95	Pass/Fail		
Server-push animation (NT only)	Pass/Fail		
Form-based file uploading	Pass/Fail		
WebSite's CGI Interfaces			
Windows CGI test	Pass/Fail		
Standard CGI test, Perl 5	Pass/Fail		
DOS CGI test, NT browser	Pass/Fail		
DOS CGI test, Win 95 browser	Pass/Fail		
DOS CGI test, NT data	Pass/Fail		
DOS CGI test, Win 95 data	Pass/Fail		
Security (Enhanced and Basic)			
One user with password	Pass/Fail		
Two users with passwords	Pass/Fail		
Group members	Pass/Fail		
Domain (IP address) allowed access	Pass/Fail		
Domain (IP address) denied access	Pass/Fail		
Statistics Report			
Local server statistics	Pass/Fail		
WebSite Central statistics	Pass/Fail		

Description	Results	Error Messages	Notes
Server Administration			
Zero statistics	Pass/Fail		
Cycle access log	Pass/Fail		
Cycle error log	Pass/Fail		
Cycle both logs	Pass/Fail		

WEBSITE REGISTRY KEYS

All configuration information for the WebSite server and tools is kept in the Windows NT or Windows 95 system Registry. This appendix describes each key and its value(s). Registry values are stored in either REG_SZ or REG_BINARY format. While many of the binary values are actually simple 32-bit longwords, the Windows 95 Registry editor handles only string and binary values, so the decision was made to store all binary information as REG_BINARY.

Under Windows NT, the Registry editor command is *regedt32*; under Windows 95, the command is *regedit*. For more information on using the Registry editor, see the operating system documentation.

All WebSite Registry information is kept in values in and under sub-keys of the root-keys:

```
HKEY_LOCAL_MACHINE\SOFTWARE\Denny
HKEY_LOCAL_MACHINE\SOFTWARE\EIT
```

SERVER ROOT KEY

All server-related Registry information is kept in values in and under sub-keys of the root key:

```
HKEY_LOCAL_MACHINE\SOFTWARE\Denny\WebServer\CurrentVersion
```

The values under the server's root key are as follows:

ConfigDone (REG_BINARY)
Records server reloads. Starts at 0 and is incremented whenever the server does a reload.

ExtErrDll (REG_SZ)
The filename of the error handler DLL for using the WSAPI error-handler extension. This may be a full pathname if the DLL is located somewhere other than in the directory where the server executable httpd32.exe is located.

ExtErrEntry (REG_SZ)
The name of the action entry point in your DLL for the WSAPI error-handler extension.

ExtPreDll (REG_SZ)

The filename of the pre-processor DLL for using the WSAPI pre-processor extension. This may be a full pathname if the DLL is located somewhere other than in the directory where the server executable httpd32.exe is located.

ExtPreEntry (REG_SZ)

The name of the action entry point in your DLL for the WSAPI pre-processor extension.

KeepAlive (REG_BINARY)

Value of the keep connection alive setting. KeepAlive is either on or off.

LoadLibrary (REG_SZ)

The full pathname of a dynamic library (DLL), which the server will load upon startup. The server keeps this DLL loaded until it exits. If there are no other references to the DLL at that time, the DLL will be unloaded.

MaxConnects (REG_BINARY)

Maximum number of connections allowed to the server at one time.

RecvTimeout (REG_BINARY)

Timeout seconds that the server will wait for a network receive to complete.

RevNumber (REG_BINARY)

The configuration revision number. When an administration tool makes changes to the server's configuration information, it should increment this number. The server monitors this number every five seconds, and if it increases, the server will reload its configuration from the Registry.

SendTimeout (REG_BINARY)

Timeout seconds that the server will wait for a network send to complete.

ServerAdmin (REG_SZ)

The email address of the server administrator. Used in the footer of internally generated HTML documents and as a CGI variable.

ServerName (REG_SZ)

The fully qualified domain name of the server's host machine. Used in "fixup" URLs and as a CGI variable.

ServerRoot (REG_SZ)

The file system path to the server root, normally where the server executable, the abort log, etc. are stored.

ServerSerial (REG_SZ)

The server's serial information, used to identify the software during installation.

ServiceMode (REG_BINARY)

The mode in which the server runs: 0 = desktop application, 1 = service with icon visible, 2 = service with icon hidden.

TCP Port (REG_SZ)
The TCP port number on which the server listens for incoming HTTP requests, normally 80. *There is a blank between TCP and Port in this name.*

TempDir (REG_SZ)
The location in which the server stores all of its temporary files. Mainly used by the Windows CGI interface.

\ACCESS\

This section of the Registry stores the access control lists by *method*. It is anticipated that additional methods will use different keys under the *\Access* key.

DefaultMethod (REG_SZ)
The method to be used by the server in the absence of specific method instructions. *Currently unused.*

\ACCESS\BASIC\

Access control for the "basic" method. Currently this is the only method supported.

DefaultRealm (REG_SZ)
The realm in which to apply access control in the absence of specific instructions. *Currently unused.*

\ACCESS\BASIC\<URL-PATH>\

Access control is applied using the URL before translating to physical space. Each protected URL path has its access control information contained under this key. The *URL-path* is the protected URL path.

Access Options (REG_BINARY)
Special options attached to the URL: 1 = OR class and users, 2 = unused, 4 = directory browsing disabled, 8 = unused.

Order (REG_BINARY)
The order in which the class restrictions are applied: 1 = allow then deny; 0 = deny then allow.

\ACCESS\BASIC\<URL-PATH>*ALLOW

The classes of clients that are allowed access to the protected URL.

Entry Format

Each class is listed under this key as a named value of the form

```
nnnn    <allowed class>
```

where *nnnn* is a four-digit numeric string with leading zeroes.

\ACCESS\BASIC\<URL-PATH>*DENY

The classes of clients that are denied access to the protected URL path.

Entry Format

Each class is listed under this key as a named value of the form

```
nnnn      <denied class>
```

where *nnnn* is a unique four-digit numeric string with leading zeroes.

\ACCESS\BASIC\<URL-PATH>\<REALM-NAME>\

The users and groups that are permitted access to the protected URL path. The realm name in the key determines from which realm the users and groups are taken.

Entry Format

Each user or group is listed under this key as a named value of the form

```
nnnn      user <user-name>
```

or

```
nnnn      group <group-name>
```

where *nnnn* is a unique four-digit numeric string with leading zeroes.

\AUTHENTICATION\

The server stores authentication information by *method*. Currently, only the "basic" method is supported. It is anticipated that additional authentication methods will store their information under additional sub-keys of *Authentication*\.

DefaultMethod (REG_SZ)
>   The name of the default authentication method. *Currently unused.*

ExtAuthDll (REG_SZ)
>   The full pathname of a dynamic library (DLL), which may be used to provide an alternative authentication system. If this string is non-blank, the server will load and call the named DLL to perform authentication instead of using its internal authentication mechanisms. Change this value to the filename of your authenticator DLL to use the WSAPI authenticator extension.

ExtAuthEntry (REG_SZ)
> The exported name of the authentication entry point in the external authentication DLL. Ignored if ExtAuthDll is blank. You must change this value to use the WSAPI authenticator extension.

\AUTHENTICATION\BASIC\

Authentication information for the "basic" realm.

DefaultRealm (REG_SZ)
> The default realm for authentication operations. *Currently unused.*

\AUTHENTICATION\BASIC\<REALM-NAME>\

The user and group lists for *realm-name.*

\AUTHENTICATION\BASIC\<REALM-NAME>\USERS\

The list of users belonging to this realm.

Entry Format

Each user is listed as a named value with the following format:

`<user-name>     <hashed-password>`

\AUTHENTICATION\BASIC\<REALM-NAME>\GROUPS\

Group membership lists are contained in sub-keys of this key.

\AUTHENTICATION\BASIC\<REALM-NAME>\GROUPS\<GROUP>

Contains a list of users belonging to *group.*

Entry Format

Each user belonging to *group* is listed as an empty named value, with the username as the name. The username must exist under the corresponding Users key.

\CGI\

The CGI interface configuration information.

NOTE

The "DOS" interface applies to the real DOS command interpreter—COMMAND.COM on Windows 95, and the CMD.EXE command interpreter on Windows NT.

ConsExecName (REG_SZ)

The pathname of the PIF file used to execute the DOS command interpreter. Server-root relative.

ConsExecOption (REG_SZ)

The command-line option added to execute the DOS command interpreter. Used to tell the command interpreter to exit when the command has been executed.

ConsExecOptionDebug (REG_SZ)

The command line option added to execute the DOS command interpreter if the server's "trace VDP" feature is enabled. Used to tell the command interpreter *not* to exit when the command has been executed.

ConsExecTemplate (REG_SZ)

Template used to construct the command line used to execute the VDP when using the DOS interface.

ConsInitTemplate (REG_SZ)

Template used to construct the command line that invokes the DOS command interpreter.

ConsQuietCmd (REG_SZ)

DOS command used to prevent the DOS command interpreter from echoing its commands to standard output.

NCSAExtraHeaders (REG_BINARY)

If non-zero, the server appends the string "HTTP_" to environment variable names used for "extra" HTTP headers when generating the CGI environment for the standard and DOS CGI interfaces. This action makes the environment variable names for HTTP extra headers compatible with those generated by the NCSA/1.3 UNIX web server. Used to provide compatibility for CGI scripts ported from the NCSA UNIX environment.

OldDosShell (REG_BINARY)

If non-zero, the server's DOS CGI interface assumes that the shell is incapable of having its standard in/out handles redirected and is incapable of receiving environment variables via the Win32 process creation service. This is the case on Windows 95, where the "shell" is really the old 16-bit COMMAND.COM program. This variable is normally set to 1 on Windows 95 and 0 on Windows NT.

ShellExecName (REG_SZ)

Executable pathname of the shell used for the standard CGI interface. If set to *, the server will use the file association for the URL target to determine the appropriate shell to start (e.g., *.pl* uses *perl.exe* or *.sh* uses *sh.exe*). Normally set to *.

ShellExecTemplate (REG_SZ)

Template used to invoke the POSIX shell.

WinExecTemplate (REG_SZ)

Template for constructing the command line used to execute the VDP when using the Windows interface.

\CGI\DLL\

Configuration information for using the WebSite API (WSAPI) generator extension. Up to 32 generators can be installed at one time. You must add these keys and values manually to use DLLs with the WSAPI generator extension.

\CGI\DLL\<GENERATOR-NAME>

The *generator name* is used in the URL path following the special path element *~wsapi* to call a specific generator (for example, *http://your.server.name/~wsapi/your_app*).

ExtCgiDll (REG_SZ)

The file name of the generator DLL. This may be a full pathname if the DLL is located somewhere other than in the directory where the server executable *httpd32.exe* is located.

ExtCgiEntry (REG_SZ)

The name of the action entry point to be called by WSAPI generator extension.

\ConsExeMap\

URL to physical mappings that specify a target to be executed using the DOS CGI interface.

Entry Format

Executable mapping table entries have the following form:

```
<URL fragment>      <absolute-path>|
                    <server-root-relative-path>
```

The physical portion can be either an absolute path (including a drive name) or a relative path. In the latter case, the path is relative to the *server root*.

\DirIndex\

This key contains the parameters used to control the server's directory indexing feature.

BlankIcon (REG_SZ)

Name of the spacer icon used to line up the heading on the extended format listing. Filename only, assumed to be located in IconDir.

DefaultIcon (REG_SZ)

Name of the icon used in the extended format listing if the file type is not listed in the type map. Filename only, assumed to be located in IconDir.

DescriptionName (REG_SZ)

Name of the file that contains description strings for the extended format listing. Filename only, the file must be located in the target directory.

DisplayContentType (REG_BINARY)

Flag that enables listing of the MIME content type in the extended format listing. Non-zero indicates TRUE.

EnableIndexing (REG_BINARY)

Flag that enables indexing globally. If FALSE, directory indexing is completely disabled for the server. Non-zero indicates TRUE.

ExtractHTML (REG_BINARY)

Flag that enables listing of the title for HTML documents in the extended format listing. Non-zero indicates TRUE.

FancyIndexing (REG_BINARY)

Flag that enables the extended and full-format listings. Non-zero indicates TRUE.

HeadingName (REG_SZ)

Name of the file that contains the header text (plain or HTML) for the extended format listing. Filename only, no extension, the file must be located in the target directory.

HTML3Tables (REG_BINARY)

Flag that sets default format of directory listings to HTML 3 table format. Non-zero indicates TRUE.

IconDir (REG_SZ)

Directory in which the type icon image files are located (server-root relative).

IconsAreLinks (REG_BINARY)

Flag that causes the type icons in the extended format listing to be hyperlinks to the corresponding file. Non-zero indicates TRUE.

IndexDoc (REG_SZ)

Name of the default document for a directory. Filename only, no extension, the file must be located in the target directory.

ParDirIcon (REG_SZ)

Name of the icon used in the extended format for the parent directory. Filename only, assumed to be located in IconDir.

ReadmeName (REG_SZ)

Name of the file that contains the footer text (plain or HTML) for the extended format listing. Filename only, no extension, the file must be located in the target directory. The name is historical; it should be FooterName.

SubDirIcon (REG_SZ)

Name of the icon used in the extended format for subdirectories. Filename only, assumed to be located in IconDir.

\DIRINDEX\ICONMAP\

Contains the mappings between a file's MIME content type and the icon to be displayed in an extended or full-format directory index listing.

Entry Format

Each entry in the icon map has the form:

```
<content-type>      <icon-name>
```

where *icon-name* is the filename of the icon image to use. Filename only, assumed to be located in IconDir.

\DIRINDEX\IGNORE\

Contains a list of filename "match patterns" that the server uses to eliminate filenames from a directory index.

Entry Format

Each entry in the ignore list has the form:

```
nnnn      <match-pattern>
```

where *nnnn* is a unique four-digit numeric string.

\DOCMAP\

Contains the mappings from URL space to physical space that the server uses for document objects.

Entry Format

The server *requires* just one mapping entry, the *root* entry, which has the form:

```
/      <absolute-path>|<server-root-relative-path>
```

This tells the server where to map the root of its URL space. The URL term is, of course, the root. The physical portion can be either an absolute path (including a drive name) or a relative path. In the latter case, the path is relative to the server's executable location, or the *server root*.

Syntax of Other Mapping Entries

All other document mappings have the form:

```
<URL fragment>    <absolute-path>|<doc-root-relative-path>
```

The physical portion can be either an absolute path (including a drive name) or a relative path. In the latter case, the path is relative to the *document root*, which is determined using the mapping described in the preceding section and *not* the server root.

\IMAGEMAPS\

All image maps are contained under this key, with the map name as the sub-key.

\IMAGEMAPS\<MAP-NAME>\

Image mapping information for *map-name*. The image map consists of a set of geometric shape descriptions and corresponding target URLs. The shape descriptions consist of a shape type name, a set of coordinates defining the extent of the shape, and a target URL in the following general format:

```
<shape-name>    <target-URL>      <defining coordinates>
```

\LOGS\

Configuration items that control the server's logging.

DNSRevLookup (REG_BINARY)
Boolean flag that controls whether the server performs DNS reverse lookups on client host IP addresses. Non-zero means TRUE.

ErrorLog (REG_SZ)
Pathname of the error log file. If relative, it is relative to the LogDir.

EventLogLevel (REG_BINARY)
Unused at present. Reserved for future use.

ExtLogDll (REG_SZ)
If non-blank, the pathname of a dynamic library (DLL) that the server will use for logging purposes. The call to this DLL is in addition to the server's normal logging functions. You must change this value to use the WSAPI logger extension.

ExtLogEntry (REG_SZ)
The name of the exported entry point for logging in the external logging DLL. Ignored if ExtLogDll is blank. You must change this value to use the WSAPI logger extension.

LogDir (REG_SZ)

Pathname of the directory in which the server's logfiles are placed if the names are relative.

LogKeepCycles (REG_BINARY)

The number of back issues of the server's logfile that are kept when cycling the log.

ServerLog (REG_SZ)

Pathname of the server log file. If relative, it is relative to the LogDir.

TraceFlags (REG_BINARY)

The 32-bit bitfield that specifies which server tracing feature is to be enabled. The values are listed below (1-bit means enabled; 4-byte means little-endian format).

```
DBG_MAIN          0x00000010L   Dispatcher thread
DBG_THREAD        0x00000020L   Service threads
DBG_SCRIPT        0x00000040L   Back end exec (CGI)
DBG_IMAGEMAP      0x00000080L   Image maps
DBG_TRACEHTTP     0x00001000L   HTTP protocol
DBG_TRACENETIO    0x00002000L   Network I/O
DBG_TRACENETBUF   0x00004000L   Network buffering
DBG_DUMPDATA      0x00040000L   Dump sent data
DBG_AUTH          0x00100000L   Authentication
DBG_ACCESS        0x00200000L   Access control
```

TransferLog (REG_SZ)

Pathname of the transfer log file. If relative, it is relative to the LogDir.

WinLogFormat (REG_BINARY)

The type of logging format to be used for the server's access log: Common, Combined, or Windows Log Format.

\MULTIHOME\

Contains information used when the server is to respond to requests arriving on multiple IP addresses (with different DNS names). If multihoming is in effect, the ServerName property is ignored. If no values appear under the keys listed below, multihoming is disabled.

\MULTIHOME\HOSTNAME\

Contains a list of hostnames by which the server is to be known when multi-homing is in effect. Each hostname is listed as a named value of the form

```
n.n.n.n    host-FQDN    (REG_SZ)
```

under this key, where *n.n.n.n* is the specific IP address and *host-FQDN* is the fully qualified domain name of the host as known on this IP address.

\MULTIHOME\TRANSFERLOG\

Contains a list of access logs into which the server is to record access requests when multihoming is in effect. Each transfer log is listed as a named value of the form

```
n.n.n.n     log-name     (REG_SZ)
```

under this key, where *n.n.n.n* is the specific IP address and *log-name* is the file-name to be used as the access log for this IP address. The filename can include a full path.

\MULTIHOME\URLPREFIX\

Contains a list of URL prefixes to be inserted by the server when multihoming is in effect. Each URL prefix is listed as a named value of the form

```
n.n.n.n     URL-prefix     (REG_SZ)
```

under this key, where *n.n.n.n* is the specific IP address and *URL-prefix* is the prefix to be added to all URLs given in requests that arrive on this IP address.

\POSTPROC\

Configuration information for using the WebSite API (WSAPI) post-processor. Up to 32 post-processors can be installed at one time, each associated with a particular MIME content type. You must add these keys and values manually to use DLLs for the WSAPI post-processor.

\POSTPROC\TYPE\<CONTENT-TYPE>

The *content-type* identifies documents for which the post-processor will be run. The content type must be defined as a MIME content type for the server. To define a global post-processor, add the content type */*.

ExtProcDll (REG_SZ)
> The file name of the post-processor DLL. This may be a full pathname if the DLL is located somewhere other than in the directory where the server executable *httpd32.exe* is located.

ExtProcEntry (REG_SZ)
> The name of the action entry point to be called by WSAPI.

\REDIRMAP\

Contains the redirection mappings.

Syntax

Redirection mapping table entries have the form:

```
<given-URL>     <redirected-URL>
```

Each URL must be complete, including the target object. URL fragments are not meaningful and are illegal.

\SHELLEXEMAP\

URL to physical mappings that specify a target to be executed using the POSIX CGI interface.

Syntax

Executable mapping table entries have the following form:

```
<URL fragment>     <absolute-path>|
                   <server-root-relative-path>
```

The physical portion can be either an absolute path (including a drive name) or a relative path. In the latter case, the path is relative to the server root.

\TYPEMAP\

The file extension to content type mappings.

Syntax

Each entry in the content type map has the following form:

```
<extension>     <MIME type>
```

\WINEXEMAP\

URL to physical mappings that specify a target to be executed using the Windows CGI interface.

Syntax

Executable mapping table entries have the following form:

```
<URL fragment>     <absolute-path>|
                   <server-root-relative-path>
```

The physical portion can be either an absolute path (including a drive name) or a relative path. In the latter case, the path is relative to the server root.

WEBFIND

The Registry data for WebFind are kept in the key

`\HKEY_LOCAL_MACHINE\SOFTWARE\EIT\WebFind\CurrentVersion`

There are no values or sub-keys for this key.

WEBINDEX

The Registry data for WebIndex are kept in the key

`\HKEY_LOCAL_MACHINE\SOFTWARE\EIT\WebIndex\CurrentVersion`

The values and sub-keys for this key are described below.

\INDEXEDDIRS\

Used to save the state of the WebIndex Create Index property page.

IndexName (REG_SZ)
Name of the index (default is index). All other data items correspond to the URLs displayed in the right listbox (i.e., the documents that were indexed).

\PREFERENCES\

Used to save the user preferences in the WebIndex Preferences page.

CheckSaveConf (REG_SZ)
Whether the check button for saving preferences into configuration files is checked or not. The default is not checked.

ConfFileName (REG_SZ)
Name of the file into which the preferences can be saved. The default is *<ServerRoot>\index\wiconf.txt*

CommonPercent (REG_SZ)
Any word that exists in this percentage of documents and in *CommonNumber* number of documents will be considered to be common and hence ignored when indexing. The default is 80.

CommonNumber (REG_SZ)
Any word that exists in this number of documents and *CommonPercent* percentage of documents will be considered as common and hence ignored when indexing. The default is 256.

IgnoreWords (REG_SZ)
Name of the file containing a list of words that must be considered as common and hence ignored when indexing. The default is SwishDefault.

IgnoreWordsBy (REG_SZ)

Whether the default list (0) or the file specified should be used (1). The default is 0.

IndexOnly (REG_SZ)

Only files with these types will be considered for indexing. The default types are *.html .htm .txt .gif .xbm .au .mov .mpg.*

NoContents (REG_SZ)

The contents of these types of files will not be indexed; only their filenames (without the extension) will be indexed. The default types are *.gif .xbm .au .mov .mpg .doc.*

WEBVIEW

The Registry data for WebView are kept in the key

`\HKEY_LOCAL_MACHINE\SOFTWARE\EIT\WebView\CurrentVersion`

The values and sub-keys for this key are described below.

ActivityReportNum (REG_BINARY)

Number of days to be included in the activity report. The default is 7.

BrowserCommand (REG_SZ)

Command line invocation syntax for the browser. The default is *<Server-Root>\emosaic\emosaic.exe.*

BrowserOpenIn (REG_SZ)

The way in which the document selected will be loaded into the browser. The legal values are: 1 = document will be loaded into the active window, 2 = a new window will be opened and the document will be loaded into it, 3 = a new instance of the browser will be created and the selected document will be loaded into its main window. The default is 1.

BrowserServiceName (REG_SZ)

The DDE service name supported by the browser; this will be used to invoke DDE topics in the browser. The default is Mosaic.

DisplayImg (REG_BINARY)

Whether or not inline images should be shown in the tree view. The default is 1.

DNSReverseLookup (REG_BINARY)

Whether or not WebView should look up domain names for the domain and log reports. The default is 1.

DomainReportLevels (REG_BINARY)

The number of levels in a fully qualified domain name (up to four) to be included in the domain report with **DNSReverseLookup** on. The default is 2.

HomePageURL (REG_SZ)
Start up page for WebView. If the value is "" then the single or multi-identity roots are used as start up pages. If HomePageURL is specified, then it is used as the start up homepage. The default is "".

HTMLParser (REG_BINARY)
Which parser WebView should use when running diagnostics on HTML files. The default is 0.

InBoundDir (REG_BINARY)
Whether or not the local server should be contacted for directory links. The default is 0.

InBoundVirtual (REG_BINARY)
Whether or not the local server should be contacted for virtual document links. The default is 0.

LogReportSort (REG_BINARY)
Whether the log report should sort by date or domain name.

OutBound (REG_BINARY)
Whether or not external links should be verified. The default is 1.

ProxyHost (REG_SZ)
Hostname for proxy support. The default is "".

ProxyPort (REG_BINARY)
Port number for proxy support. The default is 0.

ServerRoot (REG_SZ)
Server root directory. The default is <*ServerRoot*>.

\WIZARDS\

The key used by WebView wizards.

\WIZARDS\TEXT/HTML\

Key used by WebView wizards that generate text/html.

\WIZARDS\TEXT/HTML\FINDFORM\

Key used by FindForm wizard.

CommandLine (REG_SZ)
Command-line invocation syntax for the wizard; how the wizard will be invoked when selected. The command-line argument passed is the filename corresponding to the URL selected.

Description (REG_SZ)
Description of the wizard in the dialog that allows users to select the wizard.

\WIZARDS\TEXT/HTML\HOMEPAGE\

Key used by Home Page wizard.

CommandLine (REG_SZ)
Command-line invocation syntax for the wizard; how the wizard will be invoked when selected. The command-line argument passed is the filename corresponding to the URL selected.

Description (REG_SZ)
Description of the wizard in the dialog that allows users to select the wizard.

\WIZARDS\TEXT/HTML\UNDERCONSTRUCTION\

Key used by Under Construction wizard.

CommandLine (REG_SZ)
Command line invocation syntax for the wizard; how the wizard will be invoked when selected. The command line argument passed is the filename corresponding to the URL selected.

Description (REG_SZ)
Description of the wizard in the dialog that allows users to select the wizard.

\WIZARDS\TEXT/HTML\WHAT'SNEW\

Key used by What's New wizard.

CommandLine (REG_SZ)
Command line invocation syntax for the wizard; how the wizard will be invoked when selected. The command line argument passed is the filename corresponding to the URL selected.

Description (REG_SZ)
Description of the wizard in the dialog that allows users to select the wizard.

TROUBLESHOOTING TIPS

This WebSite troubleshooting appendix is divided into two main sections: a section of specific problems and solutions, and a section of guidelines for diagnosing and solving problems on your own. The problems and solutions have been collected from O'Reilly Technical Support and reflect questions users have had with previous versions of WebSite. The guidelines section describes the troubleshooting tools that come with WebSite (such as the various logs and tracing options), and suggests typical places to look for the causes of problems.

This appendix ends with information regarding other resources that can be used to help with WebSite, and for help on how to contact Technical Support. We highly recommend that you read this appendix and check the online resources before calling Technical Support.

NOTE

Many of the problems you may encounter while installing and starting your server are networking related. The specific problems can be myriad, from a mistyped IP address to a wrongly configured TCP/IP setup. These problems are beyond the scope of this book and should be addressed to your network administrator or your Internet service provider. If you suspect the problem is with your TCP/IP configuration, see the documentation for your operating and network systems.

PROBLEMS AND SOLUTIONS

The following specific problems have been encountered by WebSite users in earlier versions. The answers are from O'Reilly's Technical Support staff.

Problem

When using the NT command scheduler (AT or WinAT), *logcycle.exe* doesn't cycle the server logs.

Solution

Logcycle.exe is a desktop application. To successfully schedule log cycling, it must be able to communicate with AT and WebSite.

To ensure proper communication, set up the following services:

1. Scheduler service (must be running for AT to work)—allow service to interact with desktop (control panel, services, scheduler, startup button)

2. WebSite as a service—allow service to interact with desktop (control panel, services, webserver, startup button)

3. WebSite as a desktop application—no special requirements

4. AT—command line needs to have the argument /interactive

5. WinAT (GUI AT interface from resource kit)—interact with desktop checked

Note that any time you run WinAT and edit an entry, verify that /interactive is turned on. A bug in WinAT causes /interactive to be turned off when entries are edited.

Problem

When running WebSite as a service (under NT), the icon doesn't show.

Solution

To run as a service, WebSite must be run under a system account. Do not run WebSite as a service under a nonprivileged user account. Windows NT 3.51 security will not give an unprivileged process access to the desktop. The simplest solution is to run WebSite under the system account as it was installed.

Problem

How can I add more than five IP addresses to a Windows NT system? The Advanced Networking option of the Control Panel limits me to five IP addresses.

Solution

Having more than five IP addresses per Network Interface Card (NIC) is not supported by Microsoft. However, it is possible to add more IP addresses through the Registry.

WARNING

Mistakes with the Registry Editor (*regedit*) can be fatal to your system.

To add more IP addresses, follow these steps:

1. With the Registry editor, look under *HKEY_LOCAL_MACHINE\SYSTEM\ CurrentControlSet\Services* and locate the entry, or entries, for your Ethernet card. If you have more than one entry, you must determine which is the primary one. For example, a 3Com Etherlink III card probably has two keys, Elnk3 and Elnk31. Open each key and look in the Linkage sub-key to see which one points to the other. For the 3Com card, the Linkage sub-key Elnk3 points to Elnk31 as the primary key.

2. Open the primary key for your Ethernet card and locate the Tcpip key under the Parameters key. The hierarchical path should look something like this:

```
HKEY_LOCAL_MACHINE\SYSTEM\CurrentControlSet\Services\Elnk31\
    Parameters\Tcpip
```

3. Under the Tcpip key, locate the named value IPAddress. This value is of type *REG_MULTI_SZ* (multi-string). Each of the component strings represents one of the IP addresses on which the NIC will answer. If you have entered five IP addresses using the Control Panel, those five IP addresses are listed.

4. Double-click the IPAddress value, and the multi-string editor dialog appears showing all the IP addresses you have already assigned.

5. Add additional IP addresses by appending them to the list, each one on a separate line. We recommend that you have no more than 16 IP addresses total. If you add too many, TCP will not start.

NOTE

Don't forget to add an appropriate subnet mask for each entry.

6. Reboot the system. If TCP doesn't start, remove some of the addresses and try again.

You are now ready to set up multiple virtual servers (one for each IP address), using the Identity wizard on the Identity page of Server Admin.

Problem

I have a server that uses only CGI programs (no static documents), and I would like to allow users to self-register. How can I get the username and password information from the authentication dialog?

Solution

First rename your CGI program so the name starts with a $. This naming convention causes the server to pass the username and password through the CGI interface. The CGI-BAS that ships with WebSite (V1.7) includes the *CGI_AuthPass* and *CGI_AuthUser* variables.

To get the browser to display the username and password dialog (if the request doesn't contain a username), have your CGI program respond something like this:

```
Send "HTTP/1.0 401 Not Authorized" Send "WWW-Authenticate:
    Basic Realm=""My Cool App"""
```

This response causes the browser to display the username/password dialog. The user fills it in, presses OK, and the browser repeats the previous request with the username and password included. Your CGI application will get both username and password if you start its name with a $ in the variables *CGI_AuthUser* and *CGI_AuthPass*.

Note that this example is for CGI programs written in Visual Basic. If you aren't using Visual Basic, the process is still the same, except you need to know the key names for username and password that are used in the INI file. For more information on this, see the Windows CGI Specification that is shipped with WebSite (*\wsdocs\32demo\windows-cgi.html*).

If you are using the Standard or DOS CGI interfaces, the environment variable names are *AUTH_USER* and *AUTH_PASSWORD*.

Problem

My CGI execution is slow and my disk seems to be beaten to death.

Solution

Nothing will improve this situation better than adding more RAM. On Windows NT, 16 MB is not enough to run NT, WebSite, and do database CGI.

Note that the minimums for Windows NT (16 MB) and Windows 95 (12 MB) are *minimums*. If you have a heavy load and run complex CGI programs, or if you are running a mix of database CGI and local work on the same system, you should consider 64MB or 128MB. WebSite users universally attest to dramatically improved performance when they increase their RAM.

Problem

When I set up virtual servers, all my CGI programs stop working.

Solution

Make sure your CGI directories are properly mapped for each new server. Each virtual server must have a URL prefix. Add that prefix to the mapping for each CGI. For example:

/prefix/cgi-win/   C:\path\to\Win CGI directory

If you use the Identity wizard to set up your virtual servers, the document and CGI mapping is done automatically for you. See the Identity page in Server Admin and the instructions in Chapter 7, *Virtual Servers and WebSite Pro* in *WebSite Professional Basics*.

Problem

I have WebSite running under Windows 95 and I want to administer it remotely. Why am I having problems?

Solution

First, you cannot remotely administer the WebSite server running under Windows 95 from a computer running Windows NT. Administering the server from another Windows 95 system requires the following conditions:

- The remote computer (the one running WebSite) must be on a network (in the same domain) as a Windows NT system with a user list. The NT system enables user-level security for Windows 95 administration.

- Enable remote Registry administration on the remote Windows 95 computer by installing the Remote Registry service, and by selecting User-Level (rather than Share-Level) security.

Note also, in order to administer remotely, you must be logged into the local computer as a user who has administrator privileges on the remote computer (as defined by the user list on the NT system).

Problem

My CGI programs work okay except that images in the resulting documents are broken.

Solution

CGI programs create virtual documents, which have no location in file space. Thus, any relative URLs (for images or links) don't work because relative URLs are relative to the current document (see the next question for more on mapping). Note the following examples:

```
<img src="foo.gif">
```

This reference is bad because the URL path is completely relative. The server will not be able to locate this document.

```
<img src="/foo.gif">
```

This reference is better because the leading slash makes the URL path absolute to the document root of the server.

```
<img src="http://domain/foo.gif">
```

This is the best reference because the URL is complete, and it leaves no ambiguity for the image's location.

Problem

Some of my links work fine and others don't. I suspect my problem may be mapping. Can you give me some pointers?

Solution

First, read Chapter 9, *Mapping*, carefully and work through the examples. Apply the principles covered in that chapter to your own situation.

In a nutshell, here are some general principles on relative URLs that generally cause the most problems in creating document links in your HTML files:

Q: Relative URLs are relative to what?

A: To the current document.

Q: What is the current document?

A: The URL displayed by the browser when a document is loaded.

Q: Why is a URL with a leading slash different?

A: A leading slash denotes the current server's document root. Thus, the URL */index.html* equals *http://current_server/index.html*

Q: Are there any URL forms that I should avoid?

A: Yes, avoid URLs beginning in ../. These URLs can easily cause grief.

Problem

When I install WebSite under Windows 95 or try to run the server self-test under Windows 95, it fails.

Solution

You may have insufficient DOS environment space. Try adding the line `CommandEnvSize=8192` to the `[NonWindowsApp]` section of *system.ini*.

TROUBLESHOOTING GUIDELINES

The following guidelines will help you diagnose and solve problems you may encounter while using WebSite. Please work through these before calling technical support.

- Reboot the system to ensure that the effects of any unstable or faulty software are removed from memory.

- Make sure you have completed and used the WebSite Installation Requirements checklist (Chapter 2, *Before You Start*) during installation.

- Make sure you have tested the server according to the procedures outlined in Chapter 3, *Installing WebSite*.

- Run the WebSite server self-test (*http://localhost/wsdocs/32demo/*) to verify that your server is set up correctly. Then, complete specific examples in the server self-test for areas in which you are having problems. For example, if an image map you are creating won't work correctly, but the one in the server self-test does, compare the source code in the self-test with the code you created and find your error. (See Chapter 3.)

- Browse WebSite from the local computer and from a different computer. If browsing locally works, but remotely doesn't, you have a network problem. Contact your network administrator.

- Test your network connection with another tool or application, such as *ping* or *telnet*. For example, if you *ping localhost,* the true name it resolves to should be the same name used in Server Admin (Identity page) and in your TCP/IP configuration (computer name and host/domain name).

- Stop the server and check the error log. (See Chapter 13, *Logging*.)

- Stop the server and check the server log. (See Chapter 13.)

- Enable various tracing options for the server log, and recreate the problems you are having. Then stop the server and check the tracing data in the server log. (See Chapter 13.)

- Check the WebSite abort log (located in the WebSite directory) for fatal internal server errors. When the server won't start, the abort log may show you why.

- Check the Application Event Log (from the Windows NT Event Viewer) for information and warnings about problems with the application.

- Check the diagnostics information provided for HTML files in WebView for possible HTML tagging errors. (See Chapter 4, *Managing Your Web with WebView*.)

- Look closely at the error messages sent from the server to the browser. For example, in the "Not Found" return, the server reports both the URL and the physical file pathname for the URL target—information invaluable in diagnosing mapping problems. Not all browsers save error messages. If yours doesn't, we recommend that you try another browser or enable Dump Sent Data tracing, which shows what the server sent to the browser. (See Chapter 13.)

- Double-check your mapping. Make sure that CGI mappings do not conflict with document mappings. Remember that CGI directories cannot exist within document directories. (See Chapter 9.)

- Your web browser's View Source option often points out useful information— perhaps an HTML tag is missing or incomplete. (See Chapter 5, *HTML Tutorial and Quick Reference*.)

- If you are doing CGI work, enable CGI tracing in Logging *and* use the *DEBUG_MODE* CGI variable to enable debugging/tracing features of your CGI program. (See Chapter 16, *Developing Applications with Windows CGI*.)

OTHER RESOURCES

WebSite has several online resources for more information. WebSite Central, the web site maintained for WebSite users by the technical support staff at O'Reilly & Associates, provides product information, answers to frequently asked questions (FAQs), troubleshooting help, advice for particular implementations of WebSite, ideas for new uses of WebSite, sample HTML files, helpful utility programs, and opportunities to interact with other WebSite users.

You can tap the resources at WebSite Central with your browser, and find out how others have dealt with similar problems. In addition, the Frequently Asked Questions (FAQs) and Infrequently Asked Questions (IAQs) published on WebSite Central, may provide just the answer you need. You will also find pointers to other resources on the Web, such as specifications, helpful application tools, and resources for products bundled with WebSite.

CONTACTING TECHNICAL SUPPORT

If you've thoroughly tried all the other resources to solve your problem and you still need assistance, O'Reilly & Associates provides technical support for WebSite as listed below:

- On a per-incident basis. For per-incident tech support, call O'Reilly Technical Support at 707-829-0515 or 800-932-9302. Have your credit card ready.

- On an annual basis with a technical support contract. Contracts are available for a variety of needs and software package combinations. To learn more about annual support contracts, contact O'Reilly & Associates Customer Service at 800-998-9938 or send email to *website@ora.com.*

UPGRADING THE HOTDOG HTML EDITOR

WebSite includes a copy of the HotDog Standard HTML Editor, Version 2.53 from Sausage Software. This version of the HotDog software is a 16-bit program, designed to function better under MS-DOS and Windows 3.1 than under the 32-bit operating systems Windows 95 and Windows NT. As a 16-bit program, HotDog is limited to short filenames (the standard DOS 8.3 filename format, for example, *yourfile.txt*). When creating HTML files with HotDog, you should use the extension *.htm*, rather than *.html*. Web browsers are generally configured to recognize either file extension. In addition to being a 16-bit program, HotDog Standard also limits your HTML file size to 32 KB.

Solving these two problems is possible with various HotDog upgrades. As this book was going to print, the 32-bit version of HotDog Standard was in final testing. The 32-bit version supports long filenames and other Windows 95 conventions. As a WebSite user, you are entitled to a free upgrade to the 32-bit version of HotDog Standard. Contact Sausage Software directly at *http://www.sausage.com/* for more information. Make sure you obtain a fully-functional, non-time-limited copy of the software. Note that when you install the 32-bit version, it will create its own program group or Start menu folder rather than being added to the WebSite program group or Start menu folder.

You may also want to consider upgrading to the Professional edition of the HotDog editor. Available in both 16-bit and 32-bit versions, the Professional edition supports larger file sizes and long filenames (32-bit version only), and includes a spell checker, templates, a real-time output viewer, and many other useful features. The Professional version is available for purchase from Sausage Software (*http://www.sausage.com/*).

cycling log files, 318–320

D

daily accesses counter, 195
data, CGI (see CGI)
data, transferring from forms, 128
databases, accessing via web
documents, 371–372, 394–412
date/time strings
in includes, 197
returning from CGI programs, 428
DATE_LOCAL variable, 201
DATE_OMIT variable, 201
daycnt include directive, 200
<DD> (definition description) tags, 115, 144
debugging
CGI programs, 329, 382–385
Perl programs, 444
sample program for, 440–444
dedicated line, 25
default
content types, 231
directory index, 266–268
header and footer filenames, 273
home page, 266–268
HTML parser, 78
URLs for image maps, 180
definition lists, 114–116, 144
deleting
hotspots, 187
mapping values, 217
virtual web servers, 256
DelUser command (wsauth), 304
descriptions, file, 274, 277
designing web documents, 109–125
destructors, CGI class, 417
development environment, testing
programs in, 383
diagnostics, 77
dial-up shell accounts, 23
<DIR> (directory list) tags, 145
directories
adding paths to Server Admin, 226
execution, 354
icon mapping, 235–237
links of, 84
lists of, 145
web, 59–66, 94
working, 48

directory indexes, 261–279
adding file descriptions, 274
disabling, 263, 287
excluding files from, 269–270
formatting as HTML 3.0 table, 278
headers and footers in, 271–274
icons in, 276–277
Registry information for, 463–465
directory lists, 145
DISABLED attribute, 150
disabling directory indexes, 263, 287
displaying inline images, 84
<DL> (definition list) tags, 115, 144
DNS (Domain Name System), 26, 316
Reverse Lookup and domain reports, 80
document mapping, 218–226
document root, 220
DOCUMENT_NAME variable, 201
DOCUMENT_URL variable, 201
documents (see web documents)
domain names, 25, 80, 250
domain reports, 80, 88
DOS CGI, 353, 435–447
accessible environment variables, 437
Registry information for, 461–463
(see also CGI)
DOS-based CGI programs, 446
downloading files via hyperlinks, 120
<DT> (definition term) tags, 115, 144
Dump Sent Data tracing, 327

E

echo include directive, 201–202
editing
hotspots, 186–187
mapping values, 217
passwords (access control), 288
virtual web servers, 256
web documents, 67–68
editors
HotDog (see HotDog HTML editor)
HTML, 68
elliptical hotspots, 183–184
<EM> (emphasis) tags, 113, 147
email (electronic mail)
administrator's address, 25, 36, 48
footer files and, 273
links, 60
sending via mailto links, 120
encryption, 281

SOFTWARE

WebSite™ 1.1

By O'Reilly & Associates, Inc.
Documentation by Susan Peck & Stephen Arrants
2nd Edition January 1996
Four diskettes, 494-pg book, WebSite T-shirt
ISBN 1-56592-173-9; UPC 9-781565-921733
Upgrade offer from WebSite 1.0 available

Introducing the latest version of our award-winning WebSite™, a 32-bit multi-threaded World Wide Web server for Windows NT™ 3.5 and Windows®95. WebSite is the elegant and easy solution for anyone who wants to publish information on the Internet or on a corporate LAN. The WebSite server lets you maintain a set of Web documents, control access, index desktop directories, and use a CGI program to display data from applications such as Excel®, Access™, Visual Basic, and other programs. WebSite includes WebView™, a powerful Web management tool that provides a tree-like display of all documents and links on your server, logging statistics, and searching and indexing features. It also includes the new Spyglass Mosaic™ 2.1 Web browser and full online Help, as well as a WebSite book, which has won rave reviews from users and the press.

New version 1.1 features include the HotDog™ Standard HTML editor that supports text formatting, link building, tables, and forms; WebView printing, so you can print a view of your Web contents; a new graphical interface for creating virtual servers; enhanced search capabilities; server side includes (SSI), to combine static and programmed documents on the fly; and a Visual Basic 4 framework with sample applications, which significantly improves the speed and efficiency of working with spreadsheets, databases, and other programs. Order WebSite today to reach exactly the audience you want on the Web—within your own company or on the Internet.

WebSite Professional™

By O'Reilly & Associates, Inc.
Documentation by Susan Peck
1st Edition June 1996
Includes three books, ISBN 1-56592-174-7; UPC 9-781565-921740

In addition to all of the features contained in WebSite 1.1, WebSite Professional provides a complete Web server security solution that includes digital signatures and privacy for the exchange of payment information, personal identification, and intellectual property.

WebSite Professional Features:

- Supports the two major cryptographic security systems, Secure Sockets Layer (SSL) and Secure Hypertext Transfer Protocol (S-HTTP). SSL security applies to network connections; S-HTTP security applies to documents. WebSite Professional has an easy interface for S-HTTP administration through WebView.

- New WebSite Application Programming Interface (WSAPI) with enhanced logging, post processing, document generation, authentication, and other features.

- Cold Fusion™, a powerful database application development tool for easily incorporating database information into your Web documents. Cold Fusion lets you quickly develop applications to add customer feedback, online ordering event registration, interactive training, online technical, support and more to your site.

WebSite Professional is a must for sophisticated users who want to offer their audiences the best in Web server technology.

PolyForm™

By O'Reilly & Associates, Inc.
Documentation by John Robert Boynton
1st Edition May 1996
Two diskettes & a 146 page book, ISBN 1-56592-182-8

PolyForm™ is a forms tool that can help you make your Web pages interactive and fun for users. PolyForm works with WebSite or with any Web server that fully supports the Windows CGI interface. PolyForm enables you to create Web pages with forms, so you can generate and manage reliable marketing or product-related information. For example, with a PolyForm form, users can order products, request information, provide customer feedback, or answer surveys. Each form can be configured separately, so you can collect and store response data as well as recipient information. Information submitted on a form can be sent to specified email addresses and data can be sent back to the user who fills in the form. Order PolyForm now, and make your Web server an interactive experience that keeps users coming back!

Internet In A Box,™ Version 2.0
The Complete Internet Solution

By SPRY, Inc. (Product good only in U.S. and Canada)
2nd Edition July 1995
Two diskettes & a 528-page special version of
The Whole Internet Users Guide & Catalog *as documentation*
UPC 799364 012001

Now there are more ways to connect to the Internet—and you get to choose the most economical plan based on your dialing habits.

Internet In A Box is for PC users who want to connect to the Internet. Quite simply, it solves Internet access problems for individuals and small businesses without dedicated lines and/or UNIX machines. Internet In A Box provides instant connectivity, a multimedia Windows interface, and a full suite of applications. This product is so easy to use, you need to know only two things to get started: how to load software onto your PC and how to use a mouse.

Features of version 2.0 include:

• More connectivity options with the CompuServe Network and an improved interface with a variety of Internet hosts.

• Faster image downloading and drag and drop capabilities so that browsing the Internet has never been easier.

• MIME support, a spell-checker, and shopping safety with Secure HTTP.

WebBoard™
Web Conferencing System Software

By O'Reilly & Associates, Inc.
1st Edition February 1996
Three diskettes & a 98-page book, ISBN 1-56592-181-X

WebBoard™ is an advanced multi-threaded conferencing system that adds online conferencing capability to your Windows Web server. WebBoard runs with any Windows Web server that fully supports the Windows Common Gateway Interface (Win-CGI), including WebSite and others. With WebBoard, you can set up and maintain ongoing Web discussions about any number of subjects simultaneously; each subject is organized and maintained in its own area. You can control the level of access to any WebBoard conference on your site, so each discussion can be as public or as private as you like. WebBoard's intuitive, interactive nature can help attract users to your Web server, and keep them coming back.

Features:

• Runs with WebSite or any Web server that fully supports the Windows CGI interface.

• Like a newsgroup, each topic is organized and maintained in its own separate area.

• Users log in with a unique name and a password, and each transaction is verified to ensure a secure conferencing environment.

• Includes functions such as email, user listings, top-ten lists, caller logs, and bulletins.

Enhance your Web server today with WebBoard—
the full-featured, high-performance conferencing system.
(Requires Windows NT 3.51 or higher or Windows 95.)

PUBLICATIONS
(FROM O'REILLY & ASSOCIATES, INC.)

USING THE INTERNET

World Wide Web Journal: Volume 1, Issue 1

*A publication of O'Reilly & Associates and
the World Wide Web Consortium (W3C)
Winter 1995/96
748 pages, ISBN 1-56592-169-0; ISSN 1085-2301*

The mad rush to use the Web for commerce is on, and the standards process spearheaded by the World Wide Web Consortium (W3C) is more important than ever. The *World Wide Web Journal* provides timely, in-depth coverage of the W3C's technological developments, such as protocols for security, replication and caching, HTML and SGML, and content labeling. It also explores the broader issues of the Web with Web luminaries and articles on controversial legal issues such as censorship and intellectual property rights. Whether you follow Web developments for strategic planning, application programming, or Web page authoring and designing, you'll find the in-depth information you need here.

The *World Wide Web Journal* is published quarterly. This issue contains 57 refereed technical papers presented at the Fourth International World Wide Web Conference, held December 1995, in Boston, Massachusetts. It also includes the two best papers from regional conferences.

O'Reilly Online Publishing Report

*By Terry Allen
Annual subscription: 11 monthly issues, plus Annual Overview
ISSN 1087-4216*

The *O'Reilly Online Publishing Report*, a monthly newsletter, tracks the development and standardization of specifications for the technologies used to format, archive, search, and present documents online. These are the methods in practical use today by online publishers, their editors and document managers, and countless consultants who create new content, give new life to old content, move content from format to format, and present it to their online readers.

Terry Allen has been tracking the standards development for online publishing for years. Each month he'll update the shifting landscape of online publishing technology, assessing the impact of new developments and reporting on the latest news and emerging issues in HTML and SGML standards and digital libraries.

With the first issue, subscribers will receive a free copy of the *1995 Online Publishing Review*, a booklet providing background information on topics covered in the newsletter.

The Whole Internet User's Guide & Catalog

*By Ed Krol
2nd Edition April 1994
574 pages, ISBN 1-56592-063-5*

Still the best book on the Internet! This is the second edition of our comprehensive—and bestselling—introduction to the Internet, the international network that includes virtually every major computer site in the world. In addition to email, file transfer, remote login, and network news, this book pays special attention to some new tools for helping you find information. Useful to beginners and veterans alike, this book will help you explore what's possible on the Net. Also includes a pull-out quick-reference card. For UNIX, PCs, and the Macintosh.

"An ongoing classic." —*Rochester Business Journal*

"The Whole Internet User's Guide & Catalog is currently THE definitive user guide to the Internet, and it frankly has no rivals. A simple recommendation—if you are interested in the Internet, buy it."
—Jack Rickard, Editor, *Boardwatch Magazine*

The Whole Internet for Windows 95

*By Ed Krol & Paula Ferguson
1st Edition October 1995
650 pages, ISBN 1-56592-155-0*

The best book on the Internet...now updated for Windows 95! *The Whole Internet for Windows 95* is the most comprehensive introduction to the Internet available today. For Windows users who in the past have struggled to take full advantage of the Internet's powerful utilities, Windows 95's built-in Internet support is a cause for celebration. And when you get online with Windows 95, this new edition of *The Whole Internet* will guide you every step of the way.

This book shows you how to use Microsoft Internet Explorer (the World Wide Web multimedia browser) and Microsoft Exchange (an email program). It also covers Netscape Navigator, the most popular Web browser on the market, and shows you how to use Usenet readers, file transfer tools, and database searching software.

But it does much more. You'll also want to take advantage of alternative popular free software programs that are downloadable from the Net. This book shows you where to find them and how to use them to save you time and money.

Marketing on the Internet

By Linda Lamb, Tim O'Reilly, Dale Dougherty & Brian Erwin
1st Edition August 1996 (est.)
180 pages (est.), ISBN 1-56592-105-4, $19.95 (est.)

Marketing on the Internet tells you what you need to know to successfully use this new communication and sales channel to put product and sales information online, build relationships with customers, send targeted announcements, and answer product support questions. In short, how to use the Internet as part of your overall marketing mix. Written from a marketing—not technical—perspective, this guide gives marketing and sales people a model for thinking about what you can do online, in terms of activities already familiar to you.

Messages on the Internet can be either messages that you send out (such as email that the recipient pays to receive, directly or indirectly) or messages that come in to you (where you have invited customers and prospects to your information). There are different rules for each kind of communication, depending on who's footing the bill for the message and what people expect to see. When you're ready to make more of a commitment—in technical expertise and in time—you can create company information online that invites customers or prospects to come to you.

Every company has some valuable information to give away that will provide a motive for people to visit your online site. You'll succeed with this new channel if you start using the Internet as part of your overall marketing mix and build on your experience over time.

NetLearning

By Ferdi Serim & Melissa Koch
1st Edition June 1996
304 pages, ISBN 1-56592-201-8, $24.95

In this book, NetAngels—Internet users exploring the Internet's potential for education and educators who use the Internet in their classrooms—share stories to help teachers uncover the benefits and use this medium to its fullest potential in their own classrooms.

The stories take the reader through the use of tools from an educator's perspective and provide tips on how to effectively integrate the tools and resources into the classroom. They also serve as a guide for dealing with many of the instructional, curricular, professional development, administrative, and community issues that develop around the use of the Internet in schools. Educators must experience what it is to learn through project-based, technology-enhanced approaches in their own learning to support this kind of learning for their students.

This book is like a travel guide: It helps orient you to a new place and immerse yourself in a new culture. It offers advice on how to adapt, how to get what you want, and where to go to get help. The goal: to invite educators online with the reassurance there will be people there to greet them.

Bandits on the Information Superhighway

By Daniel J. Barrett
1st Edition February 1996
246 pages, ISBN 1-56592-156-9

Most people on the Internet behave honestly, but there are always some troublemakers. What risks might you encounter online? And what practical steps can you take to keep yourself safe and happy?

Bandits on the Information Superhighway provides a crash course in Internet "street smarts," revealing realistic risks that every user should know about. In addition, this book debunks the overhyped scare stories about Net pornography, computer crime, and dangers to children, perpetuated by the uninformed media. The Net really is a safe place, as long as you take a few simple precautions. *Bandits* provides that knowledge, covering online privacy, fake money-making schemes, deceptive advertising, electronic junk mail and "spamming," safe buying and selling, advice for parents, online romance do's and don'ts, pranks and hoaxes, users' rights, and much more.

Filled with first-person anecdotes, technical tips, and the advice of experts from diverse fields, *Bandits on the Information Superhighway* helps you identify and avoid risks online, so you can have a more productive and enjoyable time on the Internet.

PROVIDING WEB CONTENT

HTML: The Definitive Guide

By Chuck Musciano & Bill Kennedy
1st Edition April 1996
410 pages, ISBN 1-56592-175-5

HTML: The Definitive Guide is a complete guide to creating documents on the World Wide Web. To become a true master of HTML, you need to develop your own sytle. That means knowing not only what's appropriate, but what's effective. This book describes basic syntax and semantics and goes on to show you how to create beautiful, informative Web documents you'll be proud to display.

HTML: The Definitive Guide helps you become fluent in HTML, fully versed in the language's syntax, semantics, and elements of style. It covers the most up-to-date version of the HTML standard, plus all the common extensions, especially Netscape extensions. The authors cover each and every element of the currently accepted version of the language in detail, explaining how each element works and how it interacts with all the other elements. They've also included a style guide that helps you decide how to best use HTML to accomplish a variety of tasks, from simple online documentation to complex marketing and sales presentations.

CGI Programming on the World Wide Web

By Shishir Gundavaram
1st Edition March 1996
450 pages, ISBN 1-56592-168-2

The World Wide Web is more than a place to put up clever documents and pretty pictures. With a little study and practice, you can offer interactive queries and serve instant information from data-bases, worked up into colorful graphics. That is what the Common Gateway Interface (CGI) offers.

This book offers a comprehensive explanation of CGI and related techniques for people who hold on to the dream of providing their own information servers on the Web. Gundavaram starts at the beginning, explaining the value of CGI and how it works, then moves swiftly into the subtle details of programming. For most of the examples, the book uses the most common platform (UNIX) and the most popular language (Perl) used for CGI programming today. However, it also introduces the essentials of making CGI work with other platforms and languages.

Designing for the Web

By Jennifer Niederst with Edie Freedman
1st Edition April 1996
180 pages, ISBN 1-56592-165-8

Designing for the Web introduces you to the unique considerations of Web design and gives you the basics you need to hit the ground running. Although geared toward designers, this book covers infor-mation and techniques useful to anyone who wants to put graphics online. It explains how to work with HTML documents from a designer's point of view, outlines special problems with presenting information online, and walks through incorporating images into Web pages, with emphasis on resolution and improving efficiency.

You'll find a step-by-step tutorial on putting together a Web page from scratch, pointers on creating graphics that are optimized for the Web, tips on using background images and colors in Web pages, recommendations for reducing down-load times of images, and instructions for transparency and interlacing to Web graphics. This book also discusses the impact of different browsers and platforms on your design, explains how HTML tags are used for design, and offers guide-lines on navigational and orientation aids, as well as on con-ceptualizing your Web site as a whole.

Exploring Java

By Pat Niemeyer & Josh Peck
1st Edition May 1996
426 pages (est.), ISBN 1-56592-184-4

Exploring Java introduces the basics of Java, the hot new object-oriented programming language for networked applications. The ability to create animated World Wide Web pages has sparked the rush to Java. But what has also made this new language so important is that it's truly portable. The code runs on any machine that provides a Java interpreter, whether Windows 95, Windows NT, the Macintosh, or any flavor of UNIX.

With a practical, hands-on approach characteristic of O'Reilly's Nutshell Handbooks®, Exploring Java shows you how to write dynamic Web pages. But that's only the beginning. This book shows you how to quickly get up to speed writing Java applets (programs executed within Web browsers) and other applications, including networking programs, content and protocol handlers, and security managers. Exploring Java is the first book in a new Java documentation series from O'Reilly, that will keep pace with the rapid Java developments. Covers Java's latest Beta release.

Java in a Nutshell

By David Flanagan
1st Edition February 1996
460 pages, ISBN 1-56592-183-6

Java in a Nutshell is a complete quick-reference guide to Java, the hot new programming language from Sun Microsystems. This comprehensive volume contains descriptions of all of the classes in the Java 1.0 API, with a definitive listing of all methods and variables. It also contains an accelerated introduction to Java for C and C++ programmers who want to learn the language fast.

Java in a Nutshell introduces the Java programming language and contains many practical examples that show programmers how to write Java applications and applets. It is also an indispensable quick reference designed to wait faithfully by the side of every Java programmer's keyboard. It puts all the information Java programmers need right at their fingertips.

INTERNET ADMINISTRATION

Getting Connected:
The Internet at 56K and Up

By Kevin Dowd
1st Edition June 1996
424 pages, ISBN 1-56592-154-2

Everywhere you turn, the news is inescapable: The nation is hooking up to the Internet. Businesses publicizing their products; educators reaching out to rural communities; scientific researchers collaborating long-distance; consulting groups, church groups: Everybody's getting wired.

But getting your organization connected to the Internet is not as simple as requesting a telephone line. You have to learn about telecommunications technologies, the differences among networking hardware options, and internal networking issues. You need to figure out not only which Internet service provider is best for you, but which services you really need. You'll be faced with a series of technical decisions concerning network security, routing management, and email gateways. And, you'll want to know what's the best free software out there for rounding out your investment.

Getting Connected: The Internet at 56K and Up covers all of these issues and explains in detail everything you need to know to make informed decisions. And once you've set up your Internet connection, it helps you troubleshoot problems and introduces you to an array of Internet services, such as the World Wide Web. Tackles issues for PC, Macintosh, and UNIX platforms.

Networking Personal Computers with TCP/IP

By Craig Hunt
1st Edition July 1995
408 pages, ISBN 1-56592-123-2

This book offers practical information as well as detailed instructions for attaching PCs to a TCP/IP network and its UNIX servers. It discusses the challenges you'll face and offers general advice on how to deal with them, provides basic TCP/IP configuration information for some of the popular PC operating systems (Including Windows 95 and Windows NT), covers advanced configuration topics and configuration of specific applications such as email, and includes a chapter on NetWare, the most popular PC LAN system software.

Managing Internet Information Services

By Cricket Liu, Jerry Peek, Russ Jones, Bryan Buus & Adrian Nye
1st Edition December 1994
668 pages, ISBN 1-56592-062-7

This comprehensive guide describes in detail how to create services for the millions of Internet users. By setting up Internet servers for World Wide Web, Gopher, FTP, Finger, Telnet, WAIS (Wide Area Information Services), or email services, anyone with a suitable computer and Internet connection can become an "Internet Publisher."

Services on the Internet allow almost instant distribution and frequent updates of any kind of information. You can provide services to employees of your own company, or you can serve the world. Perhaps you'd like to create an Internet service equivalent to the telephone company's directory assistance. Or maybe you're the Species Survival Commission and you'd like your plans online; this book describes a prototype service the authors created to make SSC's endangered species Action Plans viewable worldwide. Whatever you have in mind, this book tells you how.

Creating a service can be a big job, involving more than one person. This book separates the setup and maintenance of server software from the data management, so that a team can divide responsibilities. Sections and chapters on data management, a role we call the Data Librarian, are marked with a special icon.

Stay in touch with O'REILLY™

Visit Our Award-Winning World Wide Web Site

http://www.ora.com

VOTED

"Top 100 Sites on the Web" —*PC Magazine*
"Top 5% Web sites" —*Point Communications*
"3-Star site" —*The McKinley Group*

*O*ur Web site contains a library of comprehensive product information (including book excerpts and tables of contents), downloadable software, background articles, interviews with technology leaders, links to relevant sites, book cover art, and more. File us in your Bookmarks or Hotlist!

Join Our Two Email Mailing Lists

LIST #1 NEW PRODUCT RELEASES: To receive automatic email with brief descriptions of all new O'Reilly products as they are released, send email to: **listproc@online.ora.com** and put the following information in the first line of your message (NOT in the *Subject:* field, which is ignored):
> **subscribe ora-news "Your Name" of "Your Organization"**
> (for example: **subscribe ora-news Kris Webber of Fine Enterprises**)

LIST #2 O'REILLY EVENTS: If you'd also like us to send information about trade show events, special promotions, and other O'Reilly events, send email to: **listproc@online.ora.com** and put the following information in the first line of your message (NOT in the *Subject:* field, which is ignored): **subscribe ora-events "Your Name" of "Your Organization"**

Visit Our Gopher Site

- Connect your Gopher to **gopher.ora.com**, or
- Point your Web browser to **gopher://gopher.ora.com/**, or
- telnet to **gopher.ora.com** (login: **gopher**)

Get Example Files from Our Books Via FTP

There are two ways to access an archive of example files from our books:

REGULAR FTP — ftp to: **ftp.ora.com** (login: **anonymous**—use your email address as the password) or point your Web browser to: **ftp://ftp.ora.com/**

FTPMAIL — Send an email message to: **ftpmail@online.ora.com** (write "help" in the message body)

Contact Us Via Email

order@ora.com — To place a book or software order online. Good for North American and international customers.

subscriptions@ora.com — To place an order for any of our newsletters or periodicals.

software@ora.com — For general questions and product information about our software.
- Check out O'Reilly Software Online at **http://software.ora.com** for software and technical support information.
- Registered O'Reilly software users send your questions to website-support@ora.com

books@ora.com — General questions about any of our books.

cs@ora.com — For answers to problems regarding your order or our product.

booktech@ora.com — For book content technical questions or corrections.

proposals@ora.com — To submit new book or software proposals to our editors and product managers.

international@ora.com — For information about our international distributors or translation queries
- For a list of our distributors outside of North America check out: http://www.ora.com/www/order/country.html

O'Reilly & Associates, Inc.

101 Morris Street, Sebastopol, CA 95472 USA
TEL 707-829-0515 or 800-998-9938 (6 A.M. to 5 P.M. PST)
FAX 707-829-0104

Listing of Titles from O'REILLY™

INTERNET

CGI Programming on the
  World Wide Web
Designing on the Web
Exploring Java
Getting Connected
HTML: The Definitive Guide
Java in a Nutshell
Online Publishing Report
Smileys
The USENET Handbook
The Whole Internet User's
  Guide & Catalog
The Whole Internet for
  Windows 95
World Wide Web Journal

SOFTWARE

Internet In A Box ™, Version 2.0
PolyForm™
WebBoard™
WebSite™1.1
WebSite Professional™

WHAT YOU NEED TO KNOW SERIES

Bandits on the Information
  Superhighway
Marketing on the Internet
  (Summer '96 est.)
When You Can't Find Your
  UNIX System Administrator
Using Email Effectively

HEALTH, CAREER & BUSINESS

Building a Successful
  Software Business
The Computer User's
  Survival Guide
Dictionary of PC Hardware and
  Data Communications Terms
The Future Does Not Compute
Love Your Job!

USING UNIX

BASICS

Learning GNU Emacs
Learning the bash Shell
Learning the Korn Shell
Learning the UNIX
  Operating System
Learning the vi Editor
MH & xmh: Email for Users
  & Programmers
PGP: Pretty Good Privacy
SCO UNIX in a Nutshell
UNIX in a Nutshell:
  System V Edition
Using and Managing UUCP
  (Fall'96 est.)
Using csh and tcsh

ADVANCED

Exploring Expect
The Frame Handbook
Learning Perl
Linux in a Nutshell
  (Summer '96 est.)
Making TeX Work
Programming Perl, 2nd Ed.
  (Summer '96 est.)
Running Linux
Running Linux
  Companion CD-ROM
sed & awk
UNIX Power Tools
  (with CD-ROM)

SYSTEM ADMINISTRATION

Building Internet Firewalls
Computer Crime:
  A Crimefighter's Handbook
Computer Security Basics
DNS and BIND
Essential System
  Administration
Linux Network
  Administrator's Guide
Managing Internet
  Information Services
Managing NFS and NIS
Managing UUCP and Usenet
Networking Personal
  Computers with TCP/IP
Practical UNIX & Internet
  Security
 sendmail
System Performance Tuning
TCP/IP Network Administration
termcap & terminfo

PROGRAMMING

Applying RCS and SCCS
C++: The Core Language
Checking C Programs with lint
DCE Security Programming
Distributing Applications Across
  DCE and Windows NT
Encyclopedia of Graphics File
  Formats, 2nd Ed.
Guide to Writing DCE
  Applications
High Performance Computing
Inside the Windows 95 Registry
  (Summer '96 est.)
lex & yacc
Managing Projects with make
Microsoft RPC
  Programming Guide
Multi-Platform Code
  Management
ORACLE Performance Tuning
ORACLE PL/SQL Programming
Porting UNIX Software
POSIX Programmer's Guide
POSIX.4: Programming for
  the Real World
Power Programming with RPC
Practical C Programming
Practical C++ Programming
Programming with curses
Programming with GNU
  Software (Summer '96 est.)
Pthread Programming
  (Fall '96 est.)
Software Portability with imake
Understanding DCE
Understanding Japanese
  Information Processing
UNIX Systems Programming
  for SVR4 (TBA)

BERKELEY 4.4 SOFTWARE DISTRIBUTION

4.4BSD System Manager's Manual
4.4BSD User's Reference Manual
4.4BSD User's Supplementary Docs.
4.4BSD Programmer's Reference Man.
4.4BSD Programmer's Supp. Docs.
4.4BSD-Lite CD Companion
4.4BSD-Lite CD Companion: Int. Ver.

X WINDOW SYSTEM

Volume 0: X Protocol
  Reference Manual
Volume 1: Xlib
  Programming Manual
Volume 2: Xlib Reference Man.
Volume 3: X Window System
  User's Guide
Volume 3M: X Window System
  User's Guide, Motif Ed.
Volume 4M: X Toolkit Intrinsics
  Programming Manual, Motif Ed.
Volume 5: X Toolkit Intrinsics
  Reference Manual
Volume 6A: Motif
  Programming Manual
Volume 6B: Motif Reference Man.
Volume 6C: Motif Tools
Volume 8: X Window System
  Administrator's Guide
X User Tools (with CD-ROM)
The X Window System
  in a Nutshell

TRAVEL

Travelers' Tales Brazil
  (Summer '96 est.)
Travelers' Tales France
Travelers' Tales Hong Kong
Travelers' Tales India
Travelers' Tales Mexico
Travelers' Tales San Francisco
Travelers' Tales Spain
Travelers' Tales Thailand
Travelers' Tales:
  A Woman's World

TO ORDER: **800-889-8969** (CREDIT CARD ORDERS ONLY); **order@ora.com**; http://www.ora.com

OUR PRODUCTS ARE AVAILABLE AT A BOOKSTORE OR SOFTWARE STORE NEAR YOU.